RUNNING A SCHOOL
2004/05:
LEGAL DUTIES AND
RESPONSIBILITIES

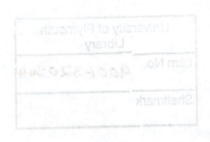

Richard Gold, MA (Cantab), LLB

Solicitor, Stone King

with

Nick Evans

Solicitor

and

Dena Coleman, PhD, MA, BSc

Headteacher, Bushey Meads School

J
JORDANS
2005

Published by
Jordan Publishing Limited
21 St Thomas Street
Bristol BS1 6JS

British Library Cataloguing-in-Publication Data
A catalogue record for this book is available from the British Library.

ISBN 0 85308 945 0

Typeset by Jordan Publishing Ltd
Printed in Great Britain by MPG Books Ltd, Bodmin, Cornwall

RUNNING A SCHOOL
2004/05:
LEGAL DUTIES AND
RESPONSIBILITIES

PREFACE TO THE FIRST EDITION

Education is one of the most highly regulated sectors of public life. Teachers and governors of State-maintained schools are in danger of being buried under mounds of barely comprehensible statutes and regulations which not only prevent them from working effectively, but also place them seriously at risk of legal challenge in the new age of the consumer. This often inhibits a robust course of action and is not healthy. This book is intended to help schools steer a course through the minefields of legislation, to identify areas of risk and to assist effective school government without an over-cautious approach.

This is, therefore, a law book, but one with a difference. Most law books have a distinctive style: they are written by and for lawyers and they expound rather than explain the law. Characteristically, they state the law and try to resolve its ambiguities by examining the words of the statute or regulation and the words of the judges. In doing so, they use the language of the Parliamentary draftsmen and the courts. This book, by contrast, written by a headteacher and a solicitor with day-to-day involvement as a school governor, is intended for senior school managers and governors, non-lawyers and non-specialists. We have deliberately excluded footnotes and references, and it is rare that we use the actual words of the law. Our aim is to *précis* and to illuminate, to tell readers in simple terms what the law is and, more importantly, how to apply it. We hope our readers will feel that they are being taken by the hand and guided through the topics that they find problematical.

Although written from the focus of the school, the book will also give parents a fuller understanding of what happens and why. By defining the responsibilities of the school, we are also demonstrating the rights of the parents and pupils. Many conflicts can be avoided if each side understands the other's perspective, and we believe that the book will be useful also to voluntary advice organisations who often need to understand and explain complex situations. We hope it may even be of use to hard-pressed LEA officers who are often placed in the same position.

RICHARD GOLD
STEPHEN SZEMERENYI
September 1996

PREFACE TO THE 2004/05 EDITION

This is the fifth edition of this work and the second where I have taken sole responsibility. I am deeply indebted to Dr Dena Coleman for her continuing guidance helping the book (hopefully) to reflect what actually happens in schools rather than what we lawyers think should be happening. I am also indebted to my former colleague, Nick Evans, who undertook a very large amount of the research needed to identify the changes since the last edition and who has contributed significantly to the revised text. However, as always, the responsibility is mine and mine alone.

Perhaps I have become inured to change but I do not sense the same complexity in the changes that have taken place, except, perhaps, in the new admissions process which is a radically new world promising (if it goes wrong) to redefine the meaning of chaos. It is a change of process rather than of the legal basis of admissions to schools but it greatly changes the nature of the game for secondary admissions in heavily over-subscribed areas. Despite the claims from government, it seems likely to increase rather than reduce parental stress levels. By contrast, many of the other reforms brought about by the Education Act 2002 have simplified the way things have done and, by taking many aspects out of primary legislation into regulations, have increased flexibility and the ability for government to change things that are not working without requiring Parliamentary time.

The courts have, naturally, been busy, in particular redefining exclusion law and the law relating to employee stress. Headteachers have been alarmed to discover that they are public authorities for the purposes of the Human Rights legislation and that there are circumstances in which damages can be awarded for breach of the human right not to be denied education but more often than not, the courts have handed down decisions that recognise the problems that schools face in a modern, litigious, society. That is not to say that parental pressure and the threat of litigation has diminished. The anecdotal evidence suggests that parents (and older students) are more active than ever in asserting rights, often without a great deal of legal justification but comfort can be taken that the courts will take a pragmatic and realistic view of school responsibilities. There may also be a reduction in cases that are litigated as a result of the severe restrictions now applying in relation to public funding, at least where the claim relates to personal injuries. This is two-edged: most schools would accept that compensation should be available where injury or loss has occurred through provable negligence and the non-availability of funding will lead to injustice.

Even so, there are large sections that are new or have required substantial revision. These include:

- New structures for governing bodies;
- National Curriculum changes and 14–19 consultation;
- Changes to the Inspection process;
- Disability discrimination and accessibility plans;
- Coordinated admissions schemes;
- New guidance and cases on discipline, drugs, anti-social behaviour, truancy and exclusions;
- The National Workload Agreement;
- Delegation of staff discipline and dismissal powers;
- Negligence including risk assessment and school visits;
- Complaints procedures;
- School Uniform including human rights and discrimination issues;
- Business activities; and
- Freedom of Information Act 2000 and disclosure of records.

The objective of this book remains as previously, to provide a single reference point for the myriad of legal issues or problems that can arise in the running of schools. It is a guide and a helping hand. Its aim is necessarily limited, to help busy headteachers, bursars, clerks, governors to find the right direction when faced with a problem rather than trying to present answers to every situation. As has been said in every edition, detailed expert advice should be sought where there is doubt. Repeating what was said in the previous edition, a book of this nature cannot provide answers, except in the simplest cases. What it does is to indicate where the problems lie and the direction in which a solution is found. Hopefully, by following the procedures and suggestions that are made, trouble will be avoided but the DIY approach has its dangers in law as in the home and part of the art of handling an unknown or unfamiliar issue is in judging when to call in the experts. Where education law is concerned, as often as not this should be sooner rather than later.

The book reflects the law as it was in July 2004 but some later developments have been incorporated.

Richard Gold
November 2004

CONTENTS

TABLE OF ABBREVIATIONS

ACCAC	the Qualifications, Curriculum and Assessment Authority for Wales
ACE	Advisory Centre for Education
ALI	Adult Learning Inspectorate
AST	advanced skills teacher
AT	attainment target
AVCE	Advanced Vocational Certificate of Education
AWPU	Age Weighted Pupil Unit
CAF	Charities Aid Foundation
CCTA	city college for the technology of arts
CEO	Chief Education Officer
CTC	city technology college
DFBO scheme	Design, Fund, Build and Operate scheme
DfES	Department for Education and Skills
DRC	Disability Rights Commission
EAZ	Education Action Zone
EDP	Education Development Plan
EWO	Education Welfare Officer
EWS	Education Welfare Service
European Convention on Human Rights	European Convention for the Protection of Human Rights and Fundamental Freedoms 1950
FE	further education
FSM	free school meals
GCE A level	General Certificate of Education Advanced Level
GCE AS level	General Certificate of Education Advanced Subsidiary level
GCSE	General Certificate of Secondary Education
GM schools	grant-maintained schools

GNVQ	General National Vocational Qualification
The Governor Regulations	Education (School Government) (England) Regulations 1999, and Education (School Government) (Wales) Regulations 1999
GRTP	graduate and registered teaching programme
HLTA	Higher Learning Teaching Assistants
HMCI	Her Majesty's Chief Inspectorate of Schools
HMI	Her Majesty's Inspectorate
ICT	information and communication technology
IEP	individual education plan
INSET	in-service training
ISR	individual school range
IT	information technology
LEA	local education authority
LMS	Local Management of Schools
LSC	Learning and Skills Council
NDS	New Deal for Schools
NI	National Insurance
NLS	National Literacy Strategy
NRA	National Record of Achievement
NVQ	National Vocational Qualification
OFSTED	Office for Standards in Education
PANDA report	performance and assessment report
PAYE	pay as you earn
PE	physical education
PFI	Private Financial Initiative
PICSI report	pre-inspection context and school indicator report
PPA	planning, preparation and assessment
PPP	Public Private Partnership
PRU	Pupil Referral Unit
PSC	public sector comparator
PSHE	personal, social and health education

PSP	Pastoral Support Programme
PTA	parent–teacher association
QCA	Qualifications and Curriculum Authority
RE	Religious Education
RgI	Registered Inspectorate
SACRE	standing advisory council on religious education
SCAA	Schools' Curriculum and Assessment Authority
SEN	special educational needs
SENCO	special educational needs co-ordinator
SENDIST	Special educational needs and disability tribunal
SIP	school improvement plan
SLT	Senior Leadership Team
SMT	Senior Management Team
STRB	School Teachers' Review Body
TA	teacher assessment
TPCD	Teachers' Pay and Conditions Document
TUPE	Transfer of Undertakings (Protection of Employment) Regulations 1981
VA school	voluntary-aided school
VAT	Value Added Tax
VC school	voluntary-controlled school
VFM	value for money
VGCSE	Vocational General Certification of Secondary Education
WOED	Welsh Office Education Department

Chapter 1

THE LEGAL STRUCTURE

Introduction – The structure of the law – The provision of education – Parents as consumers – Source material – Suggested reading

INTRODUCTION

This book deals with the law relating to schools (other than nursery schools and, except in relation to the curriculum and inspection, nursery classes in State primary schools) in England and Wales that are funded by the State. Generally, the law is stated as it applies in England. Since the establishment of the National Assembly, Wales has its own decision-making and regulatory provisions. These generally follow the pattern in England, but not necessarily so, and although some variants are noted no attempt has been made to list them. Those involved with schools in Wales should, therefore, be alert to the possibility of detailed differences. Privately funded schools, i.e. independent schools, are also outside the scope of this book. We also exclude Academies, which technically are independent schools albeit that they are fully funded by the State, although much of what we say will apply by analogy because of requirements imposed by the funding agreement. State-maintained schools face legislative prescription of a very high order, far greater than that which organisations of comparable size and complexity in the commercial world have to deal with, and we hope to help the reader to make some sense of it.

The law is written in language with which lawyers will be familiar (which is not to say that it does not cause difficulties even for the specialists) but it is not readily accessible to those who have to apply it. Our task is to summarise and *précis* the law so that its nature and extent become clear. We aim to raise awareness and to enable schools to function with an understanding of the law that will make it less necessary for them to consider its exact wording during their daily routine.

The book looks at each area of school life and attempts to explain the law's requirements: we hope this will ensure that schools do not subsequently need to explore the law further but we must issue a 'health warning' that summarising inevitably simplifies law which is often complex and has subtle distinctions. This book should help readers to identify problem areas and avoid running into disaster. It will not, however, provide solutions to complicated legal situations, and this book should not be treated as an alternative to taking good-quality professional advice when the need arises.

THE STRUCTURE OF THE LAW

The law relating to schools derives from two sources, legislation and case-law. Legislation itself divides into two categories: primary and secondary.

Primary Legislation

Primary legislation comprises the various Acts of Parliament which create the structure of the maintained education system.

The main legislative structure is now to be found in the Education Act 2002, the School Standards and Framework Act 1998 and the Education Act 1996. The 1996 Act was a consolidation of the previous statutes passed over the period from 1944 to 1994, starting with the epoch-making Education Act 1944. Commonly known as 'the Butler Act' after its prime mover, R.A. Butler, it created the post-war system of maintained schools and the responsibility of local education authorities for adequate provision to meet the needs of parents and children.

The sequence of Acts from 1980 to 1994 is now of historic interest only. The current structure of the State system and the management and funding of schools derives from the 2002 and 1998 Acts, while the 1996 Act remains in force for purposes (broadly) of the curriculum, inspection, special educational needs and a variety of administrative matters including, for example, the provisions for complaint to the Secretary of State.

Secondary Legislation

The characteristic of primary legislation in relation to schools is that it establishes concepts, principles and structures. By and large, it does not go into fine detail and there has been a perceptible move in the legislation over the years to place more and more power in the hands of the Secretary of State to stipulate how the detail is to be managed. This is done by providing in the primary legislation, i.e. the Act of Parliament, that the Secretary of State has power to make regulations (secondary legislation). Thus, to take examples at random, the detail of the National Curriculum (and its myriad changes over the years), the rules relating to how governing bodies conduct themselves, and the method of carrying out special educational needs assessments are all contained in regulations. Regulations take the form of statutory instruments, that is to say Orders which are created under the authority of an Act of Parliament but which are generally not discussed or voted upon in Parliament in the same way as for new primary legislation. Most secondary legislation relating to schools takes the form of a statutory instrument that has to be 'laid before' Parliament and which becomes effective (i.e. becomes law) if there is no vote against it. The inertia principle applies: there is no debate and no vote, and no parliamentary time is required. It is an effective way to deal with administrative detail, but the width of the powers that are vested in the Secretary of State to make Orders in this way is so great that its acceptability is dependent on the responsibility with which the power is exercised. It is technically possible for the Secretary of State to specify not just what is taught in the classroom, but also how and when it is taught. This has its clearest expression with the 2002 Act which is deliberately short on detail: the myriad regulations that have been made under its authority add the flesh to the bones of the primary legislation. In practical terms, this makes it easier for government to make changes to education law. A stated aim of the department in issuing this plethora of regulations is to simplify procedures and devolve powers to governing bodies. Whilst in the long term this may be true, schools have been bombarded by a great mass of new obligations, often with very short lead-in times. Ironically, the government has responded to concerns expressed to it about the volume of paperwork that schools receive from the department by monitoring it and requiring it only to be sent if considered absolutely necessary – it remains to be seen whether this trend of extensive use of regulation will now decrease. The use of electronic distribution has also reduced the quantity of paper produced by the department but the cynic says that this merely reduces the department's paper and printing bill at the expense of school budgets. Further concerns about electronic distribution arise from the difficulty of discovering what is new: the various department web-sites are inconsistent in the way they flag up new material and none are really good.

Departmental Guidance

Because of the complexity of both primary and secondary legislation
– the language of secondary legislation is often particularly
impenetrable and inaccessible – the Department for Education and
Skills (DfES) issues Guidance in the form of Departmental Guidance,
previously described as 'Circulars', which expression is still used for
those documents originally issued with that label. In this book, the
terms 'Circular' and 'Guidance' can be regarded as interchangeable.
The Guidance documents generally focus on a specific piece of
legislation and set out the Department's views on the meaning of
the legislation and how it should be implemented. Most of the
Guidance documents do this effectively, although at times they tend
to be written in similar style to the legislation. The problem is that,
despite attempts to differentiate, it can be difficult to disentangle
the interpretation from the advice on implementation. Much of the
text of the Guidance documents is written in somewhat prescriptive
terms, and the untrained (or, more to the point, busy) reader may
not readily appreciate the difference. This can be critical when, for
example, dealing with an exclusion; it is essential to follow the
procedure laid down by the legislation but there is scope for
discretion when considering whether to follow the Department's
Guidance on when, and when not, to exclude. This discretion must,
however, be used with caution. Increasingly, the legislation requires
that those involved 'have regard to' Departmental Guidance and the
courts have laid down that there need to be clear and cogent
reasons for not following it. The power to issue Guidance documents
widens ministerial power quite considerably. Guidance documents
are not laid before Parliament nor subject to any form of
parliamentary scrutiny.

This procedure can lead to very real tensions between executive and
judicial authority, particularly where a minister has overstepped the
limit of his or her power. This became a particularly live issue over
the debate that followed the amendments to Circular 10/99 by letter
from the Secretary of State in its application to exclusions. The
Secretary of State was under considerable political pressure to effect
change because of apparently perverse results and adverse publicity
in relation to a number of difficult cases, which led to a ministerial
amendment to the Guidance that was criticised very strongly by the
Court of Appeal. The court was saying that, Parliament having set
up an independent appeal panel to consider exclusions, it could be
objectionable for its discretion to be restricted by inappropriate
Guidance (issued to further policy issues) to which the panel had to

have regard: 'the independence which is given by the state with one hand is taken away with the other'.

That Court of Appeal case has provided assistance in defining what the requirement 'to have regard to' Departmental Guidance actually means. It emphasises that Guidance is simply that: it is not a direction, and certainly not rules. The central dilemma in using Guidance is that both to follow it slavishly or to ignore it completely is unlawful: the balance to be struck lies between these extremes. The court suggested that the safest way in which to approach Guidance is to treat it as a list of the factors to which headteachers, governing bodies, Local Education Authorities (LEAs) and appeal panels ought in general to have regard, without indicating any preferred outcome. The Guidance should not be treated as requiring a particular answer in a particular case – an independent judgment, taken within the context of the Guidance and depending upon the individual facts, must be made. The court acknowledged that this can be a very difficult balance to strike. Where a decision-maker opts not to follow Guidance, it is important to record that fact and to record the reasoning behind the decision. If the decision is questioned at a later stage, there is then a contemporary record to show that the Guidance was properly considered and that the decision not to follow it was not capricious.

Codes of Practice

Another development is the requirement by legislation for the Secretary of State to issue Codes of Practice on specified issues. The first was the Code of Practice relating to special educational needs in 1994, which was replaced by a revised Code in force from January 2002. The School Standards and Framework Act 1998 introduced two further Codes. One deals with the relationship between schools, LEAs and other bodies involved in the State school system. The second, which in fact is issued in two parts, concerns admissions which was itself reissued in February 2003. In a practical sense, the only difference between a Guidance or Circular and a Code of Practice is the label. There is, however, an important legal distinction in that the Secretary of State is obliged to consult on the contents of Codes of Practice and they have to be laid before Parliament in the same way as regulations.

Codes of Practice have been used in some quite sensitive ways. Some changes that are regarded in various quarters as controversial have been implemented perhaps because they are not subject to the same degree of scrutiny as, for instance, primary legislation. For example, the School Admissions Code of Practice seeks to prevent faith schools from interviewing prospective pupils, and the language it uses to do so is quite prescriptive. However, an admissions authority is simply required to 'have regard' to the Code of Practice and one can legitimately argue that provided it has done so, and is able to justify its decision for doing so, an admissions authority can depart from the Code of Practice for the reasons explored in the discussion of Departmental Guidance above.

The Code of Practice for Schools prepared by the Disability Rights Commission under the Disability Discrimination Act 1995 is now effective. It is well written and contains some very helpful practical examples of the application of the disability legislation to schools. However, its legal impact is slightly different from the other Codes of Practice mentioned above: it can be referred to in relevant proceedings and any adjudicating body must take into account any provision of it that it considers relevant to the issue it is deciding. In practical terms schools should be particularly cautious about deviating from the contents of the Code of Practice, and should consider taking specialist advice before doing so.

European Law

European law does not at present impinge to any great extent on specific school law, although the importation of the European Convention for the Protection of Human Rights and Fundamental Freedoms 1950 (European Convention) into English law is of significance in terms particularly of the relationship between school and pupil. It raises questions of the right to education, which may have particular relevance to the permanently excluded child, and the issue of appropriate punishment. There will also be issues relating to individual rights, affecting both parents and pupils, on which the European courts may at times be asked to rule, but the main impact of European law arises in the application of general law Directives, particularly in the areas of employment and health and safety. UK legislation is required to harmonise with EC law and, in case of conflict, EC law may prevail. All that schools can do on a day-to-day basis is to be aware of the European dimension and to keep an eye on reported developments.

Case-law – the Role of the Courts

Guidance documents and Circulars always state that they are not a definitive statement of the law and that only the courts can provide this. Case-law, which is the other element of law constraining schools, is at root the interpretation and exposition of the law applied to particular facts. The courts must interpret the meaning of the legislation and also rule on what the law is in circumstances (such as the application of the law of negligence) where there is no relevant legislation. If a court rules in a particular way on a particular piece of legislation, that is and remains the law unless and until the ruling is changed by a higher appeal court or by further legislation.

Rulings on the law relating to schools can arise in different contexts. There may, for example, be a need to interpret the law relating to governing body procedure when dealing with an unfair dismissal claim by an employee. The duty of a school to a pupil will be a prime issue in a claim for damages for a personal injury sustained by a pupil at school. The admission process will come under scrutiny if a parent seeks judicial review of a refusal by an appeal panel to allow an appeal against a refusal by a school to offer a place.

Judicial Review

The principles behind claims by individuals for compensation for a breach of the law are well understood and need not be elaborated on. Judicial review is, however, a different kind of legal process. It comprises a challenge to the lawfulness of a procedure, usually a decision by a body, for example a governing body, or by a person, for example the Secretary of State. The complainant will say that the law has not been correctly applied. This may be:

- procedural, i.e. the laid-down procedure has not been followed correctly and therefore the decision should not stand; or

- a substantive error of law, i.e. the procedure was correctly followed but the law was wrongly applied; or

- based on the unreasonableness of the decision. A challenge on this ground rarely succeeds because it is fundamental to the concept of judicial review that it is not an appeal process. This means that the court will not stand in the shoes of the party making the original decision and vary it simply because the court feels that a different decision should have been reached. It is the job of the body or person making the decision to assess the facts and weigh up the issues. The court will intervene only if it feels either that there was no evidence that could support the finding or that the decision was so unreasonable that no one considering the case properly could have come to the same conclusion.

The normal outcome of a successful application for judicial review is that the case is sent back to whoever had to make the decision with a direction to rehear it, following the correct procedure or applying the law correctly, as the case may be. It is a discretionary remedy so the court has to be satisfied that it is reasonable to make an order, and it is a remedy that is only available when the complainant has no private legal remedy. For example, an employee who is unfairly dismissed may not seek judicial review against his or her employer if a claim can be brought in an employment tribunal. There is a preliminary filtering process, in that leave of the court is required before judicial review proceedings can be started, and the complainant has to move very quickly in seeking that leave.

Schools should remember that they can be the target of applications for judicial review. This is just one reason for taking care to see that due form is followed wherever it is prescribed. Schools can, however, also bring proceedings against, for example, their LEA or the Secretary of State if the need arises: it is not a remedy restricted to the private individual.

THE PROVISION OF EDUCATION

The provision of State education was, under the Education Act 1944, the sole responsibility of the LEA. Government had an overall regulatory function but its opportunity to intervene was, generalising crudely, restricted to instances where the LEA acted unreasonably or outside its powers. Gradually, government has become more interventionist with increasing powers being given to the Secretary of State. It is noteworthy that this development has gone hand-in-hand with the devolution of powers to governing bodies and to parents in connection with the day-to-day functioning of schools. This process, started by the Conservative Government, has been continued and developed by the Labour administration to the point that the LEA function has radically changed. It is no longer a manager of schools. It has a strategic role in relation to the education needs of the area, working within considerable constraints arising from its obligations to consult and debate with the local community, and a dual function of service provider and target-setting and monitoring for individual schools. LEAs themselves are also now subject to targets, and to the inspection regime, and this is bound to produce a tension which may or may not be a creative one. We noted in previous editions the irony of increased centralisation coming from a Conservative administration wedded to doctrines of free markets and entrepreneurial skills and the new irony of a Labour Government stressing its concern that local decisions be taken locally while retaining and increasing powers to ensure that those decisions are kept within tightly controlled limits.

The Local Education Authority

For all the change, LEAs are still the predominant force in State school education in that they now determine the nature and extent of education provision throughout the country. The demise of the grant-maintained school left the LEA in control of the planning process and the development and expansion of Academies does at least proceed in consultation with LEAs and within the overall School Organisation Plan. The planning control must, however, be exercised in accordance with an Education Development Plan (EDP) which has to be approved by the Secretary of State. The LEA also controls the overall budget, although not how the bulk of it is spent, and its ability to make decisions on spending is, in common with all local government expenditure, subject to tight central government control. Its flexibility in funding issues is also constrained by the dependence on central government for the bulk of funds and by the regulatory guaranteed minimum funding levels and threats of capping of Council Tax increases.

With the advent of local management of schools, the delegation of spending power to the schools, the introduction of centralised inspection via the Office for Standards in Education (OFSTED) and the development of the National Curriculum, the LEA no longer has direct power over the classroom. Its role has changed to one of partnership within its overall strategic function in the provision of advisory and support services to schools and governing bodies. It has the tasks of monitoring school performance and of providing a limited range of key services for specific children, most notably the assessing and statementing of children with special educational needs and the provision of home–school transport. It has an obvious political role in influencing educational developments within the area.

The School Organisation Committee

The School Organisation Committee was created by the 1998 legislation to take the place of the Secretary of State's decision-making functions at local level. It is intended to be representative of the local community, with places guaranteed for the LEA, the Church of England and the Catholic Church. It deals with issues such as the provision of school places. It deals also with proposals for new schools and for significant alterations to existing ones. It does, though, lack teeth because its decisions have to be unanimous with each group represented on the Committee having a single vote and with an elaborate structure under which the groups decide how their collective vote is to be exercised. One can see why it would not be desirable for an unelected body to have the power to override minority views, but the requirement for unanimity means that in the absence of a consensus the decision will be made by the Adjudicator or by the Secretary of State. Possibly that prospect induces Committees to reach agreement, although it is difficult to tell. It seems more likely that in the main only proposals that have already secured acceptance through negotiation actually go forward to the formal voting stage.

The Adjudicator

As already mentioned, the Adjudicator has power to determine matters that are not resolved by the School Organisation Committee. He or she also has important functions in relation to admission policies and procedures. The Adjudicator is another product of the 1998 legislation, so that in most cases there will now be two layers between the LEA and central government. The Secretary of State does, however, have power to prescribe certain matters that the Adjudicator may not determine. One such, laid down by the Act, is the question of admission criteria that relate to a person's religion or religious denomination. Apart from being a sensitive issue, there is a clear need for consistency across the country and it is probably right that such a decision should be made centrally.

The Department for Education and Skills

The DfES has no direct role in the running of schools. It does, however, have a centrally important position in the setting of policy, the implementation of that policy through the introduction and drafting of both primary and secondary legislation, and a general regulatory function. It is the expression of central government and has the ability, either through legislation or through the exercise of powers that have already been conferred on the Secretary of State, to steer education in whatever direction the Government thinks fit.

The DfES also functions as a determiner of disputes arising out of the exercise of powers by LEAs and by schools. The Secretary of State has the power to determine on the reasonableness or lawfulness of action or proposed action and to give directions. The threat of referral can be a potent weapon in a dispute with an LEA or school, but anecdotal evidence suggests that intervention is quite rare. A refusal by the Secretary of State to intervene in a case that calls for intervention can be the subject of an application for judicial review, but cases concerning school admission and reluctance by teachers to teach a pupil reinstated after permanent exclusion show that the courts will be slow to overturn the Secretary of State's exercise of discretion.

The Commissioner for Local Administration

Otherwise known as the 'Local Government Ombudsman', the Commissioner for Local Administration plays a peripheral but important role in the education law structure. The Commissioner's prime function is to investigate local authority maladministration but there is also jurisdiction to investigate complaints of maladministration by LEAs, education appeal panels and governing bodies in relation to admissions issues. Although the functions of an LEA are open to review by the Commissioner, in certain circumstances the Commissioner will also consider dealing with a school where it has failed to respond to a parent's concerns about special educational needs. The Commissioner's functions are particularly relevant in relation to admission to and exclusion from schools, and the collective expertise and understanding of the process shown by the regional Ombudsmen is considerable. The weakness of this remedy for an aggrieved person is that the Ombudsman only has the power to make recommendations: the recommendations need not be acted upon.

PARENTS AS CONSUMERS

The thrust of the legislation since 1980 has been to reduce the power of the LEA and increase the power of schools and their governing bodies. At the same time, as in other areas of public life, elements of market forces have been introduced and these have set up a tension, often not creative, between the need to establish a country-wide co-ordinated education system and the wish to diversify and present a degree of choice. The resources that are available are finite and limited: in these circumstances, it is not possible to give everyone the same opportunities. Educational opportunity was, however, presented by the government of the day, for example in the Parents' Charter, as being available to all equally, and this gave rise to significant parental misconception, followed by bad feeling when the actuality did not meet the expectation. This manifests itself in a number of ways.

One cause for tension is admission decisions. The Code of Practice, and the legislation that underpins it, aims to produce locally co-ordinated admission arrangements that will reduce the chaotic situation that prevails in some parts of the country. Only time will show whether this, coupled with the drive to raise standards generally and, possibly, the eventual disappearance of selective schools, will create an environment in which parents are genuinely happy at the prospect of their child going to the neighbourhood school because that school is as good as any other.

Special educational needs (SEN) remains a prime area where there is a mismatch of expectation and achievement. The legislation, and the duties placed on LEAs, are not resource-limited. A child who is identified through due process as having particular special needs is entitled under the law to have those needs met. The LEA is not entitled to say that it has no budget or resources for this purpose. In practice, however, as all who work in this area know, LEAs do assess children with the resource implications in mind and, without saying so, will determine the child's need in relation to what the LEA is willing to allocate. If parents believe that the need is being underestimated they may become distressed at what they see as a failure to recognise what is required. This leads to confrontation where none should be necessary, and which would not arise if the system were such that it could recognise the limitation of funding and deal with statementing on the basis of prioritising the need. This would reduce the unfairness that arises at present, whereby those with the resources to battle, through the Special Educational Needs and Disability Tribunal and the courts if necessary, can suck resources away from more necessitous cases. It would, however, be a courageous (in 'Yes, Minister' terms) government which proposed a change of this kind and the Code of Practice did not bite this particular bullet.

Our last example is the conflict which arises over discipline, where schools have to balance the needs of the individual pupil against those of the school population at large. This, of course, is an age-old problem that has recently become more significant. First, the removal of the power to exclude a pupil for an indefinite period, coupled with a limit on the length of fixed-period exclusions, has led to schools having to exercise 'Hobson's choice' and permanently excluding pupils before suitable alternative arrangements have been put in place. This was eased by giving schools the power to exclude pupils for 45 school days continuously rather than, as previously, no more than 15 days in any school term, but it may still be an issue. Secondly, the formalising of the process of permanent exclusion (which in itself is entirely desirable) leaves schools at the mercy of appeal panels which may not have a clear view of the issues or which may have views that do not match either the school's or the parents' perception of what is appropriate. An appeal panel which returns a violent child to a school which feels it cannot cope creates a situation that cannot easily be managed, although cases of this sort may become more rare following the recent changes to the Guidance. Conversely, an appeal panel which appears always to 'rubber-stamp' the school's decision also brings the process into disrepute and, paradoxically, may not be good for the reputation of the school. This may become a more significant issue with changes to the composition of appeal panels that are generally perceived to favour schools. A decision of an appeal panel may depend on the forensic skills of those presenting the case: lawyers are (rightly) not welcome at such hearings but bad decisions may emerge for want of experience in case presentation. These conflicting pressures have led, on the one hand, to the Secretary of State diluting the original rigour of the Guidance on permanent exclusion to enable headteachers to take strong action even for first offences and, on the other, to court decisions that, if taken to extremes, would have a stifling effect on the power of the headteacher to conduct an effective investigation in a discipline matter. Indeed, the effect of one decision relating to standard of proof led to the Secretary of State promulgating a new regulation specifically to change the law, much to the understandable concern of those with the interests of parents and the excluded pupil to the fore.

All this arises from the attempt to persuade parents that they have rights as consumers while not, in truth, conferring very many tangible rights on them. Both schools and parents suffer as a result of this mismatch of expectation and actuality. One of the purposes of this book is to help all those involved to see, in non-legal terms, what the law says and does, and thereby to help each to understand the other's perspective, and to appreciate the limited scope within which decisions may be made.

SOURCE MATERIAL

Legislation

The major primary legislation comprises:

- Education Act 1996;

- School Inspection Act 1996;

- Education Act 1997;

- School Standards and Framework Act 1998;

- Learning and Skills Act 2000;

- Special Educational Needs and Disability Discrimination Act 1995;

- Education Act 2002.

The secondary legislation comprises a vast number of regulations dealing with the minutiae of school issues.

The text of both primary and secondary legislation can be accessed on the HMSO web-site at: www.hmso.gov.uk. There is a very good search engine and the 'What's New' section lists all legislation passed within the last 14 days. The statutory instruments part of this site is worth exploring just to see the vast quantity of regulation, in all aspects of life, coming out of Westminster.

Guidance and Related Material

Most information can be accessed via the Internet. Indeed, given the sheer volume of material available, this is often the only realistic medium. Storing documents on computer and using the search powers of word-processing is infinitely easier than filing masses of paper and using inadequate indexes. A word of warning, though. Internet sites have a habit of changing addresses, and few public bodies seem to be able to resist the temptation to 'continuously improve' what is on offer. The best way to access material is usually via a main site, such as the DfES site given below, and to follow links from there.

The starting point for specific education material is the DfES web-site at: www.dfes.gov.uk. Unfortunately, as this site has become more sophisticated, so it has become harder to use. In particular, the section that claims to contain the formal Guidance has not been kept up to date, and not all Guidance is to be found there. It does not help that not all published Guidance bears a DfES identification number. Furthermore, the main site search engine can be frustrating to use. One way to find material is via the 'A to Z of School Leadership' at: www.dfes.gov.uk/a-z. This can be searched either alphabetically or by categories. Each topic has a main text and, usually, links to the specific legislation, key documents and frequently asked questions. There is also a list of related topics with their own links. The site has, though, suffered from a lack of up-dating and often it is easier to locate documents through the use of a general search engine such as Google®·

The Teachernet site at: www.teachernet.gov.uk is specifically for teachers but also has a very comprehensive alphabetical list of other useful sites which ranges very widely and is not restricted to material that teachers might need. For example, the Advisory Centre for Education (which is largely parent-focused) appears on the list. That site, incidentally, at: www.ace-ed.org.uk, gives access to a wide range of material produced for parents. It is of very high quality and teachers and governors would also find it helpful, if only to understand the kind of advice that parents and students may be receiving.

Governors have their own dedicated DfES School Governor Centre at: www.governornet.co.uk which can be accessed also from the DfES home page. It includes a discussion board for which registration and a password are required.

There is a dedicated DfES site dealing with Public Private Partnerships (PPP) and Public Finance Initiative (PFI) at: http://www.dfes.gov.uk/ppppfi/index.cfm. This includes links to many useful organisations. Unfortunately, this site has not been developed or fully maintained and as a result, many parts of it are incomplete. It does not give direct access to Guidance documents. Information on critical issues regarding school PFI projects can be found on the 4ps (Public Private Partnership Programme) web-site at: www.4ps.co.uk.

Other Organisations

There are many organisations which have web-sites of interest to schools, and any list can only be a very selective one.

The Learning and Skills Council (LSC) will become increasingly relevant to schools in relation to post-16 education. Its web-site is at: www.lsc.gov.uk.

The OFSTED site, www.ofsted.gov.uk, has material on the inspection regime, and individual school inspection reports may be read.

Other sites of potential interest, selected very much at random given the huge range of possibilities, are:

- Association of Teachers and Lecturers at: www.askatl.org.uk
- BBC Learning at: www.bbc.co.uk/learning
- Commission for Racial Equality at: www.cre.gov.uk
- Equal Opportunities Commission at: www.eoc.org.uk
- The General Teaching Council for England at: www.gtce.org.uk
- Investors in People at: www.iip.co.uk
- Local Government Association at: www.lga.gov.uk
- National Association of Governors and Managers at: www.nagm.org.uk
- National Association of Headteachers at: www.naht.org.uk
- NASUWT at: www.teachersunion.org.uk
- National Audit Office at: www.nao.gov.uk
- National College for School Leadership at: www.ncslonline.gov.uk
- National Confederation of Parent Teacher Associations at: www.ncpta.org.uk
- National Grid for Learning at: www.ngfl.gov.uk
- National Union of Teachers at: www.teachers.org.uk
- Professional Association of Teachers at: www.pat.org.uk
- Qualifications and Curriculum Authority at: www.qca.org.uk
- The Religious Education (RE) Directory at: www.theredirectory.org.uk, which is designed as a 'first stop' reference point for those interested in religious education and which has links to a very wide range of faith organisations.
- Secondary Heads Association at: www.sha.org.uk
- The Society of Archivists at: www.archives.org.uk
- Teacher Training Agency at: www.canteach.gov.uk

- The *Times Educational Supplement* at: www.tes.co.uk

SUGGESTED READING

The Law of Education (Butterworths, loose-leaf), 3 vols (also available on CD-ROM).

The full text of all relevant statutes, regulations, DfES Circulars and Administrative Letters, together with commentary, cross-referencing and a summary of decided court cases.

Butterworths Education Law Manual (Butterworths, loose-leaf) (also available on CD-ROM).

A textbook exposition designed to be used with the law of education.

Oliver Hyams, *Law of Education*, 2nd edn (Jordans, 2004).

A heavyweight and expensive work but characteristically thorough and detailed.

Governor's Guide to the Law (DfES).

Published in various versions depending on the type of school. The format is similar in each case, giving an excellent, clearly written summary of the roles and responsibilities of the governing body, LEA and headteacher.

Headteacher's Guide to the Law and *Briefings for Headteachers and Governors* (Croner Publications).

These are detailed, practical guides with, in particular, useful precedent documents.

Chapter 2

SCHOOL GOVERNMENT

Types of schools – The constitution of the school – Election and appointment of governors – Collaboration and federation – Governors – Conduct of governors – Proceedings of governing bodies – Delegation of the functions of the governing body – Governing body meetings – Appeal functions – Policies – Removal, suspension and disqualification of governors – Declaration of interest and withdrawal from meetings – Personal liability of governors – Conflict inherent in the governors' role – Other school employees – Pupil involvement – Other observers – Significant change to the school – Suggested reading

TYPES OF SCHOOLS

Mainstream schools are either community schools, voluntary schools (with subcategories of voluntary-controlled (VC) schools and voluntary-aided (VA) schools) or foundation schools. The abolition of grant-maintained status has, in the main, led to those schools that were VA or VC schools reverting to their previous status and the others becoming foundation schools.

Community Schools

Community schools are wholly funded by the LEA. Staff working in them are employed by the LEA (although the duties and powers of the employer are delegated to the governing body), and the LEA has control over the premises during the school day.

Voluntary-aided Schools

VA schools are usually, but by no means universally, schools having a religious denominational foundation. Many are church schools. A number of VA schools have no denominational connection but have an independent foundation body in the form of a charity whose object is (or includes) the maintenance of the school. VA schools have greater autonomy than community schools. The premises, which are usually provided by the foundation body or trustees but which may in the case of former grant-maintained schools be held by the governing body, are under the control of the governing body, and the school is the employer – a distinction that has lost much of its significance with the advent of delegated funding and responsibility. There are significant other differences in the powers of the school, particularly in the way admissions of pupils is handled, which will be dealt with in detail in Chapter 6. The foundation body has the power to appoint a majority of the governing body and the school may stipulate that its teachers (including the headteacher) be members of a particular religious denomination or faith. The *quid pro quo* of this effective control of the governing body is that the governing body has responsibility for the maintenance of the structure of the school premises and will have to find at least 10 per cent of all capital costs.

Voluntary-controlled Schools

VC schools are mainly, but not exclusively, denominational schools and have a foundation body. The governing body has no responsibility for premises, but where the school has a religious character the governing body does have the right to appoint teachers of a particular religious denomination or faith for teaching religious education. The school cannot, however, specify that the headteacher should be of a particular denomination or faith. There is a minority of foundation governors and they have reserved rights in relation to the religious education syllabus.

Foundation Schools

As indicated, foundation schools were formerly grant-maintained schools and many of the characteristics of grant-maintained schools (GM schools) remain. Thus, the school is the employer and controls and has responsibility for the premises. It does not, however, have responsibility for capital costs which rests with the LEA. If the school has a religious character it has the same rights as a VC school in the appointment of staff for religious education. There are also significant differences in the composition of the governing body.

Other Publicly-Funded Schools

City Technology Colleges or Academies are technically independent schools funded by central government with contributions from sponsors. As indicated in Chapter 1, they are outside the scope of this book but their funding agreement with the DfES will require them to conform to similar practice to maintained schools in most key areas.

THE CONSTITUTION OF THE SCHOOL

All organisations have to have a constitution or set of rules to enable them to function in an orderly way. Also, the people who deal with an organisation need to know that they have legal remedies if the organisation breaches its agreements. If you sell goods to a school and do not get paid, who do you sue? Is it the headteacher, or the chair of governors, or the individual who happens to have placed the order? If you are an employee who has been wrongly dismissed, who do you make your claim against?

Incorporation

The governing body of a maintained school is a corporate body which means that the school, or more exactly the governing body, is a single and separate legal entity which can enter into contracts and sue and be sued in its own name. This means that individual governors do not have any personal responsibility for any contracts or obligations entered into by the school provided those contracts or obligations are within the powers of the governing body.

Extent of Governing Body Powers

An individual person has the ability to think and make decisions naturally: people have unlimited powers to act so long as they stay within the law. The reverse is true of an artificial person, e.g. a company, a charitable trust or an incorporated school. Because it has no natural powers, the law states that it can only do what it is authorised to do, either specifically or by necessary implication. Anything else is ultra vires. Schools therefore can only do things that are allowed under one of the following heads.

Legislation Applicable to All Schools

This includes statutory instruments, Ministerial Orders and regulations made under parliamentary authority, as well as Acts of Parliament themselves. It does not include Departmental Circulars or Guidance (which are only non-binding Guidance, despite the peremptory language often used) or Codes of Practice. However, where, as is increasingly common there is a specific requirement that the school 'has regard to' Ministerial guidance or to a Code of Practice it is a necessary assumption that the school has the legal power to implement such Guidance.

Powers Implied by Law

The law will imply any power that is necessary for the school to have to enable it to function. Note the word 'necessary'. The law will not imply a power simply because it is reasonable or makes good sense. For example, it may be sensible in certain circumstances for a school to depart from the formal admissions procedure but it is not allowed to do so; the procedure is a legal obligation and must be followed even if the result is unpalatable. The solution is to seek a change in the procedure by following the prescribed processes.

The Instrument of Government

This is the formal 'charter' of the school, defining its status and the composition of the governing body. In the case of schools with a religious character, the instrument will also contain an ethos statement. DfES has published Guidance dealing with the constitution of governing bodies under the new framework covered in detail below which includes model instruments of government, and examples (said to be non-exhaustive) of potential governing body composition that will comply with the rules. Separate Guidance has been issued for each category of school as follows:

- Community & Community Special – DfES/0323/2003
- Foundation & Foundation Special – DfES/0324/2003
- Maintained Nursery Schools – DfES/0329/2003
- Voluntary Aided – DfES/0325/2003
- Voluntary Controlled – DfES/0326/2003

The Instrument of Government is prepared in draft by the governing body and is submitted to the LEA for approval. A school that has foundation governors must first secure agreement to the draft from the foundation governors, any trustees of the school and the appropriate diocesan or religious authority. If the LEA is satisfied with the draft then it is finalised. If the LEA is not satisfied and further discussion fails to resolve matters then, in the case of a school with foundation governors, the Secretary of State will give directions and in other cases the LEA will, after indicating its concerns to the governing body and giving it a reasonable opportunity to reach agreement, make the Instrument in the form that it thinks fit.

The LEA will make the first instrument of government for maintained nursery schools.

The Instrument must cover a number of matters. They are:

- the name of the school;
- the category of the school, i.e. community, voluntary-aided etc;
- the name of the governing body;
- how the governing body is to be constituted specifying the categories and numbers of governors in each category;
- the term of office of a governor category if it is less than four years;
- if the school is a maintained special school, details of who is entitled to nominate an individual for appointment as a community governor;
- in the case of a school with foundation governors' details of who is entitled to appoint such governors and of any *ex officio* appointments;
- if the school has sponsor governors, details of who is entitled to nominate individuals for appointment;
- where the school is a foundation or VA school with a religious character, a description of the ethos of the school;
- the fact that there is a trust relating to the school, if that is the case;
- the date when the instrument of government takes effect.

The Instrument must comply with any trust deed relating to the school, although the statutory provisions will override anything to the contrary in the trust deed. The Secretary of State does, anyway, have power to modify trust deeds after due consultation.

The form of the Instrument is laid down by regulations. The Instrument may be reviewed by the LEA and the governing body at any time. Proposals for change broadly follow the procedure for making the Instrument initially. An up-to-date copy of the instrument of government must be provided to each member of the governing body, the headteacher, any trustees and the appropriate diocesan or religious authority.

The Composition of the Governing Body

Changes to the constitution and procedures of governing bodies were introduced in September 2003 as a part of the Government's stated aim to reduce the extent to which it regulates the way in which schools are run. Each governing body has been given the power to decide upon its own size and composition (provided it adheres to rules that vary according to the type of school concerned). All governing bodies must have chosen and adopted their own new constitution by 31 August 2006. Until then, schools will continue to operate under the old framework which was described in detail in the previous edition of this book and which is not repeated here. Governors appointed under the old regulations will retain office until the end of their current term, or 31 August 2006, whichever is the earlier. This means that until September 2006 there will be schools operating in a hybrid way with a governing body that reflects both old and new provisions. However, any governing body contemplating change during the interim period will need to be consistent with the new framework.

Governing Body Composition Under the New Regulations

Irrespective of the category of school, the governing body can choose its size but it must have between nine and 20 members (excluding sponsor governors or, in the case of VA schools, additional foundation governors). The instrument of government must specify the number of governors to be appointed from each category and the regulations specify the required balance between the different categories. The headteacher has the option whether or not to be a governor, but is brought (together with non-teaching staff) into the staff governor category. When calculating the number of staff governors required, the headteacher must be included even if the head concerned has resigned his or her governorship. In calculating governing-body composition, the number must be rounded up or down to the nearest whole number. The DfES Guidance referred to previously gives examples of different sized governing bodies for different types of schools.

Governor Categories

Depending on the nature of the school, the governing body must be composed of representatives from most of the following categories.

Parent Governors

Parent governors are usually parents or carers of pupils of the school, elected by the parents of the school. If there is a contest, there must be a ballot. In certain circumstances, and in particular if there are less candidates than there are vacancies, the governing body can appoint parent governors and it can in that case appoint from outside the body of parents of current pupils of the school. Parents who are paid to work at the school for more than 500 hours or who are elected members of the LEA are not entitled to become parent governors (although they are entitled to vote in the election).

Staff Governors

The staff governor category now includes the headteacher and the elected representatives of those who work at the school, including both teaching and non-teaching staff. At least one staff governor (in addition to the headteacher) must be a teacher at the school, unless none stands for election. If the governing body has three or more staff governors, at least one of them must be a non-teaching member of staff, unless none stands for election. The test of eligibility is whether or not the candidate is employed to work at the school: people employed by others, such as LEA staff or staff working for a PFI contractor, are eligible.

LEA Governors

The Local Education Authority appoints LEA governors. Individuals who are eligible to be elected as staff governors cannot be appointed as LEA governors.

Community Governors

This category replaces co-opted governors. Community governors are appointed by the governing body. They are defined in the regulations as individuals who either live or work in the community served by the school, or who are committed to the good government and success of the school. Pupils, individuals who are eligible to be elected as staff governors and elected members of the LEA cannot be appointed as community governors.

Special rules apply to community special or foundation special schools. If the school is a community or foundation special school established in a hospital, the LEA must designate a health trust as an appropriate body for the school; if the school is a community or foundation special school which is not established in a hospital, the LEA may have designated a voluntary organisation as an appropriate voluntary body for the school. The governing body must appoint individuals as community governors if they are nominated by an appropriate body or an appropriate voluntary body.

Foundation Governors

Foundation governors are appointed by the school's founding body, church or other organisation to the governing bodies of voluntary and foundation schools. If the school has a particular religious character, they must preserve and develop it; if there is a trust relating to the school, they must ensure that the school is conducted in accordance with it. If the school is a foundation school but has no foundation or equivalent body the foundation governors are replaced by partnership governors appointed by the governing body after a nominations process.

The school's instrument of government will specify who appoints foundation governors. At least one fifth of governors appointed as foundation governors of a voluntary aided school must be parents.

Partnership Governors

The governing body appoints partnership governors, following a nomination process from the parents or carers of registered pupils. Parents, registered pupils, individuals eligible to be a staff governor or elected members or employees of the LEA are ineligible for appointment as a partnership governor.

Sponsor Governors

The governing body (again following a nomination process) appoints sponsor governors from those who have given substantial financial assistance or provided substantial services to the school.

Associate Members

The governing body can appoint associate members to become members of committees established by it. An associate member is not a governor; the intention is that this will give governing bodies flexibility in drawing on expertise outside the governing body itself. They have the right to attend governing body meetings but without voting rights and this entitlement to attend all governing body meetings may in practice be an inhibiting factor in appointing people as associate members as distinct from observers which has been a common practice. Associate members who are over 18 can vote at committee meetings of which they are a member. Pupils can be appointed as associate members, although obviously they cannot vote at a committee meeting until they are aged 18. A compulsory duty (has now been placed upon governing bodies to consult with pupils about decisions that affect them, subject to Guidance to be issued by the Secretary of State. It may well be the case that the appointment of pupil associate members will be a convenient way to achieve this and this was specifically mentioned as an option in the draft Guidance consulted on in 2003.

Composition of Governing Bodies

The instrument of government must specify the size and composition of the governing body, set within rules fixed by regulations according to the type of school.

Community Schools, Maintained Nursery Schools and Community Special Schools

The governing body of a community school, a maintained nursery school or a community special school must have:

- one third or more parent governors;
- at least two but no more than one third staff governors;
- one fifth LEA governors; and
- one fifth or more community governors.

In addition, the governing body may appoint up to two sponsor governors.

Foundation schools and foundation special schools

The governing body of a foundation school or a foundation special school must have:

- one third or more parent governors;
- at least two but no more than one third staff governors;
- at least one but no more than one fifth LEA governors;
- one tenth or more community governors; and
- at least two but no more than one quarter foundation governors or, where the school does not have a foundation, partnership governors.

In addition, the governing body may appoint up to two sponsor governors.

Voluntary controlled schools

The governing body of a voluntary controlled school must have:

- one third or more parent governors;
- at least two but no more than one third staff governors;
- at least one but no more than one fifth LEA governors;
- one tenth or more community governors; and
- at least two but no more than one quarter foundation governors.

In addition, the governing body may appoint up to two sponsor governors.

Voluntary aided schools

The governing body of a voluntary aided school must have:

- at least one but no more than one tenth LEA governors;
- at least two but no more than one third staff governors;
- at least one parent governor;
- as many foundation governors as it takes to out number all the governors listed above by two.

As noted above, at least one fifth foundation governors must be eligible for appointment as parent governors. Those governors, when added to the parent governors themselves, must make up at least a third of the governing body.

In addition the governing body may appoint up to two sponsor governors and the person who is entitled to appoint foundation governors may appoint up to two additional foundation governors to preserve their majority.

The following table summarises the new constitutional requirements by school type.

	Community	Foundation	VC	VA
Parent	1/3+	1/3+	1/3+	1+Foundation = 1/3+
Staff	2→1/3	2→1/3	2→1/3	2→1/3
LEA	1/5	1→1/5	1→1/5	1→1/10
Community	1/5+	1/10+	1/10+	
Foundation		2→1/4	2→1/4	Outnumber above by 2
		OR		
Partnership		2→1/4		
Sponsor	(2)	(2)	(2)	(2)
Additonal Foundation				(2) if sponsors appointed

ELECTION AND APPOINTMENT OF GOVERNORS

The provisions for the election of governors are similar for all types of school. There is no statutory prescription regarding elections. The effect of this is that control of parent governor elections lies with the LEA for community schools and with the governing body for other schools and the process is governed by a view of what constitutes good practice. Parents should be informed of vacancies and of elections and should be given an opportunity to vote either by post or by returning a ballot paper by 'pupil post'. The ballot should be secret but the method of election – e.g. first past the post, proportional representation or otherwise – is for the body organising the election to decide. There is a DfES Circular (7/87) giving detailed Guidance on the conduct of elections and it is wise (although not compulsory) to follow this.

Where insufficient parent governors can be elected the governing body has power to appoint parent governors to fill the vacancies. Any person so appointed must be a parent of a registered pupil at the time of appointment or, if no such person is available, must be a parent of a former registered pupil at the school or the parent of a child of compulsory school age. Slightly different rules apply to community or foundation special schools.

The term 'parent', here as elsewhere in the education legislation, has to be interpreted widely. It includes anyone who has parental responsibility for the child for the purposes of the Children Act 1989 or who has care of the child, so that there may be more than two 'parents' for a given child. It is up to the school to decide who is eligible to vote. Failure to identify everyone who might qualify under the extended definition will not make the election invalid, but reasonable care must be taken.

Staff governors are elected by the staff from among themselves, and the school will organise the ballot, which again should be a secret one.

VA and VC schools and those foundation schools that have a religious character will have a body that has the power to appoint foundation governors. Other foundation schools may have a foundation body set up under the School Standards and Framework Act 1998 for the purpose of holding land for the school and that body will also have the power to appoint foundation governors. That power will include the right to remove such governors and this is dealt with below. An interesting question, known to have arisen in practice but one which has not yet been the subject of a decided case, is whether the foundation body has a duty, compellable by the courts, to appoint foundation governors to fill vacancies. A dispute between the foundation body and the governing body which led to a refusal to make such appointments could seriously affect the ability of the governing body to discharge its functions.

Term of Office

The instrument of government will specify the term of office for each category of governor other than the headteacher. This must be for whole years between one and four and the term of office for each governor in a particular category must be the same. Governors may resign at any time. Elected staff governors cease to be governors when they leave the school, but elected parent governors may serve their full term even though their child may have left. In every case, the term of office will run from the date of appointment or election.

Elected governors cannot be removed from office, although they can be suspended as explained below. Governors who are appointed can be removed, and this is dealt with below.

Foundation Bodies

Those foundation or VA or VC schools that do not have their own foundation body may apply to the Secretary of State for the establishment of a foundation body. To be eligible, the school has to be a member of a group of at least three schools wishing to have a foundation body, or must join a group that already exists. The functions of the foundation body are first (a *sine qua non*) to hold property (which may be land but is not necessarily restricted to land) for the schools; secondly to appoint foundation governors and thirdly to promote co-operation between schools in the group. Since foundation governors are in the minority in foundation and VC schools, and VA schools will almost certainly have their own foundation body, it is difficult to see that the statutory foundation will have any significant function and it may well be that those foundation schools that hold land following acquisition of foundation status will decide not to seek to become members of a foundation body. Some five years after the legislation was introduced, the author remains unaware of any school that is a member of a foundation body of this kind although that, of course, is not conclusive.

The foundation body will have its own Instrument of Government and will be established with formal powers very similar to a governing body. Each participating school will appoint a governor to be a member of the foundation body. It will, additionally, nominate co-opted members of the foundation body. The total number of co-opted members will always be one less than the total number of governor members. Co-opted members must have interests in either or both of business or the local community, must be at least 18 years old and must not be a parent of a child at the school making the appointment or a governor, employee or pupil of any of the schools in the group or a member or employee of an LEA. Members serve for four years and can be reappointed but a governor member will cease to be a member of the foundation body on ceasing to be a governor of the school.

The foundation body may adopt in its Instrument any particular character, mission or ethos for the group of schools that its members accept.

The regulations require the foundation body to be clerked and contain provisions to ensure that no member has a financial interest. Similar disqualification provisions apply as for governing bodies. The quorum for meetings must be at least half the membership, rounded up. Proper minutes and records are to be kept and the foundation body is to produce an annual report for the schools in the group giving details of membership, a summary of decisions and actions from meetings unless minutes are issued, financial information and a statement of disposals, purchases, gifts and any outstanding liabilities. It seems unlikely that the annual report will be lengthy.

The regulations contain detailed provisions for schools joining and leaving the group and for the consequent transfers of property.

COLLABORATION AND FEDERATION

The Education Act 2002 introduced a number of measures designed to be innovative leading to the sharing of good practice between schools. This includes the power for governing bodies to collaborate with others and for schools to federate under one governing body. The Guidance both for collaboration (LEA/0313/2003) and federation (issued in August 2004 to replace LEA/0312/2003 but without a reference number at the time of writing) emphasises the DfES's enthusiasm for innovation in this area; although the regulations do not provide for formal collaboration or federation outside the maintained sector, the Guidance does encourage less formal links within the education sector generally.

Collaboration

Governing bodies can arrange to discharge any of their functions jointly with the governing body of another maintained school, and can set up joint committees. The ability particularly for smaller schools to share functions in this way is likely to be attractive.

The procedural requirements that apply to joint committees are broadly the same as those that apply to committees of non-collaborating governing bodies. Governing bodies must review the establishment of joint committees annually; the joint committee decides its own quorum, subject to a minimum of three governors and the chair is appointed annually. The rules that apply to the appointment of a clerk are similar to other governing body committees. Unusually, (probably because it would be too unwieldy for the collaborating governing bodies to have to reach agreement on appointment) associate members are appointed by the joint committee which also determines their voting rights. It follows logically from this that joint committee associate members have no right to attend governing body meetings of any of the collaborating schools and this makes associate members appointed to joint committees a slightly different breed to others. As with other associate members, appointments are for between one and four years and they cannot vote unless aged 18. They are in any event prevented from voting on admissions, pupil discipline, budgeting and finance matters or on issues about an individual pupil or member of staff which will anyway have led to them being excluded from the meeting – always assuming that any of these issues fall within the remit of the joint committee. Members of joint committees (unless suspended) have the right to attend meetings as do heads, the clerk and others as determined by the committee.

Federation

Federation brings maintained schools even closer together by federating under one governing body. This power was initially available only to VC and community schools but it has now been extended to foundation and VA schools..

Given that federation, at least at present, is likely to be relevant only for a small number of schools anyone wanting the detail of the procedural and constitutional requirements should refer to the Guidance referred to above. Up to five schools can federate, thereafter the consent of the Secretary of State is required. Governing bodies considering federation are required to consult with the relevant LEAs, staff, parents, headteachers, foundation body, foundation governors and trustees. The governing body must be made up of between nine and 20 members (but federations of four or more schools may have governing bodies of up to 28 depending on whether headteachers of the individual schools are governors and whether or not the federation includes VA schools). In addition, all federations may have up to two sponsor governors and in a federation only of VA schools those entitled to appoint foundation governors in VA schools may appoint up to two additional foundation governors to secure a majority of foundation governors on the governing body.

'Guiding principles' apply to the make up of the governing body drawn from the usual stakeholder groups which are dealt with in the regulations, and vary according to the make up of the federation (i.e. whether it is made up wholly of community schools, VC schools, VA schools, foundation schools or any combination of these). The underlying pattern and principle are broadly similar to those applicable to individual school governing bodies.

In general terms, the procedure regulations apply to federated governing bodies as they do to other governing bodies, treating the federation as, in effect, a single school.

GOVERNORS

There is no specific statutory definition of the role of the school governor. Statute places various responsibilities on the governing body, but these relate to particular aspects of the working of the school. Although the responsibility for the tasks in question rests with the governing body, the governors cannot, and should not, attempt to discharge those tasks personally. The responsibility is a formal one, similar in some ways to the responsibility of a Cabinet Minister for a Government Department. Just as the Minister cannot know or be involved in the thousand-and-one decisions of the Department, so the governing body cannot (and should not try to) know everything that goes on within the school. The responsibility for implementation is delegated to the professional and administrative organisation in the school.

The Relationship Between the Governing Body and the School

This delegation of responsibility raises critically the relationship of the governors with the headteacher and the school. How the governing body functions will vary from school to school. The analogy with businesses is overworked and is to be used with caution, but there is a similarity between school governors and non-executive directors of a company. Day-to-day organisation is left to the headteacher/managing director/chief executive, and the governing body/board of directors is an overseer, becoming as involved as is felt appropriate given the skills and time available. It is common to find that governors of small schools, particularly at primary level, act in a very 'hands-on' way, whilst governors of large schools are much more detached. This partly reflects the availability of resources but is also a function of the way the particular institution finds it appropriate to organise itself.

Governors are unpaid but the law makes no concession to the voluntary nature of governors' work in allocating responsibility. This fact leads some governors to feel that they have to protect themselves by seeing as much as possible and having influence in as many decisions as they can. This is misguided: the test of responsibility (particularly on the issue of personal liability of individual governors) will always be whether the governor or the governing body has acted reasonably and this is dealt with in more detail later in this chapter. The organisation of the school should not be dependent upon the governor resource. The effective governing body acts as a monitor and as a determiner of strategy and policy under the professional Guidance of the headteacher and other appropriate advisers. It will stand back to some extent, but will step in where necessary and will be sensitive to the requirements of the school, particularly when difficulties are experienced.

Terms of Reference

The division of responsibilities has now been recognised by legislation in the shape of regulations that seek to define the roles of the governing body and headteacher, at least in general terms. The starting point is that the governing body in exercising its functions shall have as its terms of reference the principles that it shall:

- act with integrity, objectivity and honesty in the best interests of the school; and

- be open about the decisions it makes and the actions it takes and in particular shall be prepared to explain its decisions and actions to interested persons. 'Interested persons' is the term used on the regulations but is not defined. DfES Guidance (0168/2000) clearly contemplates the press as being amongst those to be regarded as 'interested'.

The requirement to be open is qualified by due sensitivity to the need to protect individuals and confidentiality in suitable circumstances. Thus, governing bodies are not required to disclose material relating to:

- a named teacher or other person employed or engaged, or proposed to be employed or engaged, at the school;

- a named pupil at, or candidate for admission to, the school; or

- any matter which the governing body or a committee of the governing body is satisfied should remain confidential.

The regulations then define the respective roles of governing body and headteacher and it is worth quoting the regulations in full:

'A.   The governing body

(1)   The governing body shall exercise their functions with a view to fulfilling a largely strategic role in the running of the school.

(2)   The governing body shall establish a strategic framework for the school by:

(a) setting aims and objectives for the school;

(b) setting policies for achieving those aims and objectives;

(c) setting targets for achieving those aims and objectives.

(3)   The governing body shall monitor and evaluate progress in the school towards achievement of the aims and objectives set and regularly review the strategic framework for the school in the light of that progress.

(4)   In exercising the functions in paragraphs (2) and (3) above, the governing body shall:

(a) (subject to any other statutory provision) comply with any trust deed relating to the school; and

(b) consider any advice given by the head teacher.

(5)   The governing body shall act as 'critical friend' to the head teacher, that is to say, they shall support the head teacher in the performance of his functions and give him constructive criticism.

B.   (1)   The head teacher shall be responsible for the internal organisation, management and control of the school, and the implementation of the strategic framework established by the governing body.

(2)   The head teacher shall advise the governing body in relation to the establishment and review of the strategic framework, and in particular the head teacher shall:

(a) formulate aims and objectives for the school, for adoption, with or without modification, or rejection by the governing body;

(b) formulate policies for the school for achieving those aims and objectives, for adoption, with or without modification, or rejection by the governing body; and

(c) formulate targets for the achievement of those aims and objectives for adoption, with or without modification, or rejection by the governing body.

(3)   The head teacher shall report at least once every school year to the governing body on the progress made towards achieving the aims and objectives set and in particular towards meeting specific targets set.'

CONDUCT OF GOVERNORS

The Terms of Reference regulations require the governing body to act as a 'critical friend' to the headteacher. The expression is one that had come into colloquial use well before the regulations were made and was apt to define a relationship between individuals, i.e. each governor in a one-to-one relationship with the headteacher. Unfortunately, it can also be seen as a licence for unco-ordinated involvement and even meddling, making it potentially very difficult to determine what was individual governor involvement and what was the implementation of governing body policy. Interpreting the regulations literally produces the difficult concept of a corporate and impersonal 'critical friend' which then becomes a concept that is very difficult to analyse or comprehend. However, the idea that the governing body should challenge (with due regard and respect for the professionalism of the headteacher) and not accept information and proposals in an uncritical manner is not difficult and is, perhaps, the synthesis of the 'critical friend' concept. There is a danger that the school comes to resemble a bottom-heavy hourglass, with the school staff and community forming the lower segment and the governing body forming the upper one. The headteacher forms the narrow constriction through whom all matter passes. The risk is that the governing body has no independent way to judge the quality of information that it receives. To avoid this, governing bodies need to ensure that they have a supply of information enabling a proper evaluation of the school's performance. This is, in any event, necessary to enable the governing body to discharge its responsibilities and to deal with the self-evaluation process required in the course of the OFSTED inspection regime dealt with in Chapter 4.

One way in which governors individually acquire information is from their involvement in the activities of the school. This is an area ripe with potential conflict and DfES has now published Guidance on how governors should handle visits to the school. Whilst not a statutory requirement, DfES recommends that the governing body draws up a policy on governors' visits to the school. This policy should take the following into account:

- Governors do not have any rights of access to the school.
- Visits should be undertaken as part of a strategic programme to:
  - improve governor knowledge of the school, its staff, needs, priorities, strengths and weaknesses;
  - monitor and assess the priorities as outlined in the development plan;
  - assist the governing body in fulfilling its statutory duties.

Before visiting the school the governor should:

- inform the school of the visit and seek approval of the arrangements;
- become familiar with health and safety procedures including what to do in the event of a fire.

After visiting the school the governor should:

- complete a visit report outlining the objectives and results of the visit;
- report back to the committee or governing body as appropriate;
- provide constructive feedback as appropriate.

It is important that governors remember that the purpose of governors' visits is not to assess the quality of teaching provision, nor to pursue issues that relate to the day-to-day management of the school other than as agreed with the headteacher or the Senior Leadership Team (SLT). This is especially important when governors see lessons in progress. Governors are not inspectors and generally do not have relevant skills with which to make judgments. A governor who sees a lesson in progress does so as part of the governor's learning process. Note-taking can give a teacher concern. It is better not to take notes but a governor who wishes to do so should get permission from the teacher at the outset and should offer to show the notes at the end of the lesson – before there is any opportunity to sanitise them.

PROCEEDINGS OF GOVERNING BODIES

How governing bodies of maintained schools conduct their proceedings is laid down by regulations and it is important to observe due form. Heads, chairs of governors and, in particular, clerks to governing bodies need to be familiar with the details of the regulations to avoid finding that decisions of the governing body or of a committee are vulnerable to challenge on procedural grounds. Special issues apply to staffing committees, and are dealt with in Chapter 9.

Chair and Vice-chair

The governing body determines the term of office of the chair and vice-chair between one and four years. A governor who is paid to work at the school, or who is a pupil at the school cannot be elected as chair or vice-chair. The governing body must then elect a chair and vice-chair. There is no longer a set procedure or nominations process that must be followed and no requirement that these appointments should be dealt with at the first governors' meeting of the year; vacancies are simply required to be filled at the first meeting after they arise. It is no longer required that the election should be by secret ballot if contested, although candidates must withdraw from the meeting when the election is being dealt with. Governing bodies will therefore need to regulate their own proceedings for these elections.

The appointment ends if the chair or vice-chair resigns, ceases to be a member of the governing body, is paid to work for the school, is removed or the term of office ends. As noted above, when a vacancy arises, the governing body must fill it at their next meeting, having again first determined the term of office between one and four years. A chair or vice-chair may be re-elected. The chair has all the powers of an individual governor, including the power to do anything that has been lawfully delegated, either to the chair specifically or generically to any individual governor, by the full governing body, and also has power to do whatever may be necessary in an emergency where delay might be seriously detrimental to the school, a pupil or parent, or an employee of the school. There is, however and contrary to widely-held belief, no overriding power to take 'chair's action' simply because it is thought that it is in the interests of the school and/or it would ultimately have been agreed to if considered by the governing body or relevant committee. The vice-chair has the powers of the chair if the chair is not available. Any action taken under these powers must be reported to the next meeting of the governing body. This is a standard requirement following any exercise of a delegated power, whether by an individual governor or by a committee.

Delegation of Powers to the Chair

There is no definition of 'seriously detrimental' but it is generally accepted that the chair has wide powers to act where it is not practical to call a special meeting of the governing body or defer action until the next scheduled meeting. In practice, many decisions are taken by way of 'chair's action' despite this potentially being ultra vires as mentioned above. The legality of such action depends on the level of delegation by the governing body to the chair. Some schools will give a detailed delegation; others will be content to leave it to the chair's discretion but this is of questionable legal correctness. Both approaches have advantages and disadvantages. Detailed delegation has the merit of clarity but may inhibit the chair from acting outside the scope of the specific delegation at times when decisive and speedy action is needed. Leaving it to the chair's discretion gives flexibility but relies heavily on the chair's judgment and probity: monitoring is difficult and it may not be possible to reverse a decision that the governing body disagrees with. The chair is also vulnerable if not ultimately supported by the governing body and the governing body's action in giving a broad and unspecified discretion might be challenged if a significant problem arises from a decision taken in that way by the chair. In an extreme case, governors could find themselves personally liable if a commitment entered into by the chair is not ratified. It is, though, important not to be excessively exercised about the problem of delegated authority: the practicality of running a school means that many small decisions are sensibly taken as a result of discussions between headteacher and chair or chair and individual governors without being brought to the full governing body or committee for a ruling. Much will depend on the culture of the school, the trust that the governing body has in the chair and headteacher and the relationship between school and governing body. It is interesting that a DfES Guidance document Guidance on Good Governance (which was published some years ago, appears now to be out of print, but remains a very useful aidé-memoire) does not attempt any Guidance on this issue.

Whichever style is adopted, the chair must feel able to take decisions which affect pupil and employee safety or which are time-critical, without the fear of not being supported by the governing body when the action is reported. Clearly, the chair would be wise to consult with other governors where time permits although this itself brings its own problems if those who are not consulted object. A good working rule is that the chair should, unless it is quite impractical, consult with the chair of any committee of the governing body that has responsibility for the particular area of concern. Thus, the chair of the finance committee or the premises committee could be consulted on a decision involving emergency building works.

However, there are times when consultation is best avoided. For example, if the action relates to possible disciplinary action against an employee it is essential not to involve too many governors. If too many are involved, even on an informal consultation basis, there is the risk that there will be insufficient governors who remain uninvolved to form panels to hear the case and any appeal.

The Chair's Casting Vote

The chair of any meeting of the governing body (except in relation to the election of the chair at the first meeting of the year) or of any committee has a second or casting vote if a vote is tied. There is a convention on the use of casting votes (not limited to schools) that the chair will vote for the status quo. This ensures that changes are made only where there is a clear majority in favour. If amendments to a resolution are being considered and the voting on the amendment is equal, the casting vote should be used so as to preserve the original resolution, i.e. to vote against the amendment. This method of using the casting vote is not obligatory but it is good practice. It can have the odd effect that the chair may vote one way substantively and the other way when using the casting vote. This is appropriate because the casting vote is not intended to give the chair additional personal influence. It is a mechanism designed to prevent a stalemate.

The Chair and the Headteacher

Few individual relationships within a school are more significant than that between the headteacher and the chair of governors. It is the interface between the formal level of control and responsibility vested in the governing body and the day-to-day management of the school. A failure in this relationship can lead to serious problems. Each must have trust in the judgement of the other and each must know the other's role and responsibility.

Nothing is laid down by statute or regulation and again Guidance on Good Governance says nothing beyond defining one of the functions of the chair as 'liaising with the headteacher'. Certain principles can be gleaned from recognised good practice. The effective chair will:

- respect the professional ability and status of the headteacher and support it, particularly in dealings with school staff, parents and other third parties. Any private reservations the chair may have about a particular matter should not become evident: they should be resolved in private discussion and, if necessary, at meetings of the governing body or a relevant committee;

- act as a sympathetic sounding-board for the headteacher who will often wish to canvass ideas knowing that complete confidentiality will be maintained. The chair may be the first port of call when the headteacher has ideas for radical reform;

- avoid getting involved in matters of detail or day-to-day administration. The headteacher must be free to run the school without having to seek approval and without worrying that the chair will intervene;

- avoid too close a personal relationship with the headteacher. The chair must retain independence of thought and must be prepared to be critical of the headteacher (in private unless public comment becomes imperative), if the headteacher's proposals or actions appear unwise. The chair does, however, need at all times to allow the headteacher the freedom to make professional judgements and management decisions. The critical function is normally to ensure that proposals are properly considered and the implications fully understood. The chair may frequently disagree with what the headteacher suggests but that is rarely if ever a valid reason for trying to exercise a veto. The answer in those circumstances, assuming that the issue is one that involves policy, is to bring it to the governing body for further discussion.

The headteacher's role in relation to the governing body is legally defined as part of the statutory conditions of employment. The duty is:

'advising and assisting the governing body of the school in the exercise of its functions, including (without prejudice to any rights he may have as a governor of the school) attending meetings of the governing body and making such reports to it in connection with the discharge of his functions as it may properly require either on a regular basis or from time to time.'

Further specific duties have been added, namely to report to the chair of governors annually on the professional development of teachers at the school, to advise the governing body on the adoption of effective procedures to deal with incompetent teachers and to keep the governing body informed of the general operation of the procedures. The headteacher must make arrangements if required to do so by the governing body for the security and effective supervision of the school buildings and ensuring any lack of maintenance is reported back.

This, however, does not define the relationship with the chair and again one looks to good practice for Guidance. The headteacher should:

- have an open and frank relationship with the chair. Nothing is more likely to damage the relationship than for the chair to believe that relevant information is being deliberately withheld;

- share thoughts regularly with the chair. It is particularly important for the chair to understand the headteacher's strategic thinking because that informs the school's policy-making and impinges directly on the role of the governing body. The timing of when to take a new idea to the governing body can be critical to its proper acceptance and implementation and judging this depends on the chair fully understanding its implications. The chair has a pivotal role in the relationship between school and governing body: the effective chair knows what the governing body is likely to accept and knows how to get the right decision within the parameters of open debate. The effective headteacher will understand this process and work with the chair to secure a proper presentation when the time is ripe;

- warn the chair of problems on the horizon. There is a temptation to avoid giving potential bad news in the hope that it will not materialise. That hope is often unfulfilled and lack of advance warning can mean that the issue cannot be properly contained. Every chair's nightmare is to be telephoned by the Press and asked about something that the chair has not yet heard of. Even a 'no comment' will make its own comment about the internal organisation of the school and in itself is bad publicity;

- stand firm if the chair tries to exercise power, influence or decision-making that cuts across the headteacher's role. Conflict is rarely desirable but it is better for the headteacher to be in conflict with the chair than to lose authority within the school. The relationship must be publicly perceived as one of equals: if the chair appears to be dominant, the effective management of the school is at risk.

Removal of the Chair

The governing body can remove the vice-chair by resolution and (unless the chair has been appointed by the Secretary of State because the school has serious weaknesses or requires special measures) the governing body can also remove the chair by resolution. Notice must be given and the resolution must be specified as an item of business on the agenda of the meeting, i.e. it cannot be taken as 'Any Other Business'. The governor proposing the removal must give reasons for doing so at the meeting, and the chair or vice-chair must be given the opportunity to make a statement in response before withdrawing from the meeting so that a vote can be taken. The requirement for the resolution to be confirmed at a second meeting held no fewer than 14 days after the first meeting has been removed.

DELEGATION OF THE FUNCTIONS OF THE GOVERNING BODY

The workload borne by governing bodies means that much must be delegated to committees and this is provided for in the regulations. The terms of reference, constitution and membership of each committee and the extent to which it can take binding decisions must be clearly defined by the full governing body and reviewed at least once every 12 months. Committees can be set up only by the governing body, and any change of membership is also reserved to the full body. Associate members described above (who, it will be recalled, must be at least 18 years old at the date of appointment to be given any right to vote – no right to vote will accrue on the 18th birthday) may be appointed to committees, but the majority of members must be governors. The governing body will determine whether an associate member has voting rights, although associate members may not vote on resolutions concerning admissions, pupil discipline, the election or appointment of governors or the budget and financial commitments of the governing body. All committees exercising statutory functions must have clerks, although as explained below the clerk to a committee can be anyone other than the headteacher, which could include a governor. Committees are organised in a similar way to the governing body (such as notice, minutes and the requirement to make the minutes and other documentation available for inspection), although the appointment of the chair of the committee by the governing body is for a period of one year and is made either by the governing body or, if the governing body decides so, by the committee. The chair or clerk of a committee may be removed at any time by the governing body. The quorum is determined by the governing body, subject to a minimum of three governors. A vote cannot be taken on any matter unless the majority of committee members present are governors; any vote is decided by majority and the chair (if a governor) has a second casting vote.

All decisions must be reported to the next governing body meeting. The easiest way to do this is to table the minutes of the committee meeting at the governors' meeting. The headteacher is entitled to attend all committee meetings even if not a member of the committee in question.

What Cannot be Delegated

The number of functions which by law cannot be delegated, has now been reduced significantly. The fact that some functions still cannot be delegated does not mean that a committee cannot consider issues relating to those functions but the law restricts them from reaching binding decisions. Committees can have a very significant part to play in the process. Committees can go into issues in great depth in a way that a full governors' meeting cannot do, and then produce a detailed report and recommendations for the governing body to approve.

The governing body cannot delegate:

- functions relating to the constitution of the governing body including the preparation of the instrument of government;
- the appointment or removal of chair, vice-chair or clerk;
- the removal or suspension of governors; or
- the establishment of committees.

The act of delegation cannot itself be delegated (although the fact that powers have been delegated does not prevent the full governing body from exercising those powers). It follows from this that committees and individual governors exercising delegated powers cannot further delegate that responsibility. This is an important principle to keep in mind in running a committee. A committee may set up a sub-group to look at a particular topic, but that group cannot take decisions. It must report back to the committee in the same way as a committee considering an issue that is reserved to the full governing body will report back to a full governors' meeting.

Functions that can be Delegated to a Committee but not to an Individual

The governing body can delegate to a committee (but not to an individual) functions relating to:

- the alteration, discontinuance or change of category of the school;
- the LEA's financial scheme to the extent that it requires the governing body to give its approval to the first formal budget of the financial year;
- discipline policies;
- the exclusion of pupils;
- admissions including the decision to object to the admission arrangements of another admissions authority.

Other Restrictions on Delegation

Generally speaking, anything that can lawfully be delegated can be delegated either to a committee or to an individual governor. There are, however, certain exceptions:

- schools that deal with their own admissions decisions must either deal with them in full governing body (which is impracticable) or delegate them to the admissions committee;
- consideration of whether or not to reinstate an excluded pupil. The make up of what was the Pupil Discipline Committee was prescribed by regulation, but it is now an issue for the governing body to determine. It is probably sensible for the governing body to preserve the old arrangements with the committee having either three or five members. Although again it is not a mandatory requirement of the regulations, the headteacher should not be a member of that committee in order to preserve natural justice;
- although there is no technical restriction on delegation in relation to staffing issues, in practice most schools, even if

they delegate dismissal decisions to the headteacher, will want to delegate the appeal function to a committee rather than to an individual.

In each case, anyone with a personal interest greater than the remainder of the governors, or who has been involved in the matter before it reaches the governors, is ineligible to serve on the committee. This is dealt with in more detail below.

In the Guidance (DfES/0168/2000) referred to previously on the application of the Terms of Reference Regulations, there is useful Guidance on delegation, both in terms of the principles to be applied and the specifics of what should be delegated and to whom. The Guidance includes a Decision Planner which identifies no less than 81 areas in which decisions may be required. The Planner identifies for each area whether delegation is permitted. It also suggests the level to which matters should be delegated where that is possible. Governors do not have to follow the Planner to the letter but it is a sound basis from which to work in reaching decisions. Additionally, Annexe A to the Guidance has a useful table showing a suggested division of responsibility for the majority of issues that governing bodies face between the headteacher and the governing body. This is supplemental to the issue of what can be delegated: there are many aspects that either cannot be delegated to the headteacher or where the governing body wishes to retain the final decision-making power but where the headteacher should be the instigator of a process, provider of information or formulator of a policy or plan. This Guidance was published before the relaxation of the constraints on delegation and the table indicating where decisions can be delegated is, in consequence, somewhat out of date. Nevertheless, the Guidance overall remains very useful.

GOVERNING BODY MEETINGS

All governing bodies are required to meet at least three times in every school year and will often need to meet more frequently. The governing body has the power to decide when it will meet. Community schools will often have meeting dates set by the LEA to facilitate clerking and other administration but these dates are not binding. Committees have no minimum frequency requirement and will meet as necessary. All meetings, both full governors' meetings and committee meetings, must be called with at least seven days' notice except in an emergency (other than to deal with the removal of the chair or vice-chair, the suspension of a governor or the discontinuance of the school) at the direction of the chair. A meeting of the governing body must be convened by the clerk if requested in writing by at least three governors. It should be noted that if the governing body of a foundation or voluntary school decide to close the school, it will not have effect unless it is confirmed by a governing body meeting held not less than 28 days after the meeting at which the decision was made; the item has to be an agenda item and seven days' notice must be given.

Administrative Matters

Notice of Meeting, Agenda and Minutes

An agenda must be sent with the notice of meeting and any reports or other papers to be considered, which should be sent to each governor, associate member and the head (if not a governor already). Meetings must be minuted and (subject to the approval of the governing body) signed by the chair. A record must be kept of those attending any meeting. There is no rule as to the form of minutes, which can vary from brief decision-only minutes to detailed records of discussion. The choice of style is for each governing body to decide on, but detailed discussion minutes have the disadvantage that inevitably the record has to be selective. What appears to be comprehensive usually is not, and disputes can arise over accuracy. It is also not unknown for governors to speak 'for the record', though generally this is not desirable: whatever the differences during discussion, the governing body should corporately accept the ultimate decision, and it weakens the strength of the decision if the minutes disclose detailed disagreement. It is not conducive to effective government for individual governors to be able to distance themselves from a contentious decision by citing the minutes as evidence that they opposed it. Indeed, the Guidance on Good Governance noted previously says that 'once decisions are made by the group' (i.e. the governing body) 'individual governors are bound by them and should be loyal to them'. The minutes must, however, be sufficiently full to show clearly what topics were discussed and what decisions were taken. They form an invaluable part of the permanent record of the school and are of great potential interest to local historians and archivists.

Access to Minutes and Confidentiality

Minutes must be signed by the chair at the next meeting of the governing body or the relevant committee. When they have been signed they must be made available at the school for public inspection. Anyone can ask to see them and no reason need be given. Reports or other papers considered by any meeting are treated as part of the minutes and must be made equally accessible. Certain business – often referred to as 'Part 2 Business' – should, however, be treated as confidential. This may be because it relates to actual or intended pupils or employees or because the governing body regards it as particularly sensitive. Those minutes are not to be disclosed and they are often printed on paper of a different colour so that they are distinctive. These rules apply equally to committees.

Clerking and Conduct of Meetings

Governing bodies must be clerked. Regulations require this and also require that a clerk be appointed to each committee of the governing body which exercises delegated statutory functions. The clerk to the governing body cannot be a governor, associate member or headteacher of the school – although a governor (other than the head) can deputise at a meeting in the absence of the clerk. The governing body appoint and remove the clerk.

There is less restriction in relation to committees. The regulations simply specify that a clerk to a committee must not be the headteacher, and the Guidance indicates (but does not recommend) that clerks to committees could be other governors. The complexity of some of the issues some committees need to consider, particularly exclusions and admissions, may lead governing bodies to conclude that professional clerks are required in some circumstances.

The clerk's principal duties are to convene and attend meetings, ensure minutes are produced and signed by the chair at the next meeting, maintain a register of members of the governing body and of associate members and report any vacancies to the governing body, maintain a register of governors' attendance at meetings (and report on non-attendance) and give and receive notices dealing with expiry of term of office and resignation. The clerk will normally also be given other functions, and will often advise the governing body on legal and procedural issues. Guidance on Good Governance describes the clerk's role as 'central in providing administrative and organisational support'. The extent of those responsibilities is for each school to decide. Frequently, the LEA will discharge the clerking function for community schools although, under financial delegation schemes this is now not universal. Clerking is a highly skilled task: a good clerk will ensure that the meeting remains procedurally correct and, because the clerk is not involved in discussion and remains objective, can help the meeting to avoid making decisions that are technically wrong. The prevalent practice of downgrading the status of the clerk to little more than a minute-taker is potentially a false economy and puts an unreasonable burden on the headteacher and the chair of governors to ensure procedural regularity.

Conduct of Meetings

Subject to some restrictions, governors, associate members, the head teacher and the clerk have the right to attend governing body meetings and committee members, the headteacher and the clerk have the right to attend committee meetings. If the business of a governing body or committee meeting concerns an employee or pupil, the governing body can exclude an associate member from that part of the meeting. The governing body can in addition allow others to attend its meetings. Each governing body will establish its own procedure for the conduct of meetings. Meetings may be held in public and many governing bodies routinely invite observers to represent, for example, parent-teacher associations or the student body. Note that, although there is no express prohibition on students being governors, no one under 18 years old may be a governor. There is, however, no age restriction on observers. There will be certain business which the governing body will consider inappropriate for observers to hear but that will be for each body to decide situation by situation. It is generally accepted that all discussions at governors' and committee meetings are confidential even for business that is not treated as Part 2 Business. The reason for this is that anything else would inhibit frank discussion. This is often also regarded as a reason for not holding meetings in public.

Quorum

The quorum for the governing body is half the actual membership rounded up if necessary. If a meeting of the governing body ceases to be quorate, the chair should consider stopping the meeting for the clerk to convene a further meeting as soon as reasonably practicable. However, if there are no formal decisions to be taken, there is no legal objection to the meeting continuing simply to facilitate discussion although this should not be done where the issues being discussed are of significance and absent governors might have important contributions to make. The minutes should record when people leave and join meetings so that it is clear whether or not the meeting remains quorate.

APPEAL FUNCTIONS

Most governor functions are executive in nature, involving the taking of decisions relating to the running of the school. There are, however, a number of instances when the governing body has to deal with appeals or complaints and must therefore act in a quasi-judicial capacity. This division of functions can lead to tensions and practical difficulties, particularly when the people involved (employees, pupils or parents) are known to many governors. Procedures need to be in place to cover:

- staff disciplinary matters which, as touched on above, are governed by separate regulations;
- permanent exclusion of pupils;
- complaints both in relation to the National Curriculum and generally;
- appeals by parents in respect of the disapplication of the National Curriculum;

Governing bodies may also have to deal with grievances under the staff grievance procedure and appeals in respect of possible redundancies or the operation of the school pay policy.

POLICIES

All schools will have a range of policies in place. A number are required by law, either specifically or as a necessary means of compliance with statutory requirements, whereas others are optional.

The obligatory policies at present are:

- admissions (where the school rather than the LEA is responsible for determining admissions arrangements);
- aims and objectives of the school;
- appraisal;
- bullying;

- charging and remission of charges;
- child protection;
- curriculum;
- health and safety;
- length of the school day;
- pay – this is not a statutory policy but the governing body cannot discharge its obligations in terms of setting and reviewing teachers' pay without a pay policy;
- promoting race equality;
- pupil discipline;
- religious education and collective worship;
- sex education;
- special educational needs;
- staff competence;
- staff discipline;
- staff grievance.

Other policies which schools are likely to adopt may include:

- equal opportunities;
- redundancy;
- school development plan (which, contrary to widespread belief, is not mandatory but which OFSTED will invariably expect to see);
- staff development and in-service training;
- uniform. Guidance was issued by DfES in June 2004, coinciding but not based on the High Court case involving uniform for Muslim girls that is referred to in chapter 14 and chapter 8. This Guidance is dealt with in chapter 13.

REMOVAL, SUSPENSION AND DISQUALIFICATION OF GOVERNORS

Certain governors may be removed from office by the body with the power to appoint. Thus, LEAs can remove their appointed governors and foundation governors can be removed by the body that appointed them. The governing body in certain circumstances can remove any community governor, appointed (as opposed to elected) parent governor, *ex officio* foundation governor or sponsor governor. If it considers it appropriate, the governing body may remove an *ex officio* foundation governor at the request of the person identified as being entitled to do so in the instrument of government. The governing body may also remove nominated community governors or sponsor governors at the request of the nominating body, if the governing body thinks it appropriate.

Removal of Governors

There are constraints on the way an appointing body exercises the power of removal. Governors are not representatives of whoever appoints them (or for that matter, in the case of elected governors, those who elect them). It is, therefore, improper for the appointing body to remove governors simply because they do not act as the appointing body wishes. Thus, in one case, where the governing body of an LEA-maintained school was contemplating a course of action that was contrary to the wishes of the LEA, the LEA tried to bring its appointed governors into line by asking them to support a proposal to extend the relevant consultation period and in the meantime support the LEA policy. Two governors declined to give that confirmation and indicated their intention to act as they thought fit in the interests of the school. When the LEA resolved to remove them as governors the court decided that this was an unlawful exercise of the right of removal.

There is a similar restriction on the power of a foundation body to remove foundation governors, based on the same judicial authority. The right cannot be exercised in such a way as to remove from the governing body its power to run the school in the way that it sees fit. Thus, in another case the trustee, who had the power to appoint, purported to remove two foundation governors who were not willing to support a proposal for reorganisation put forward by the diocese. This was held to be an improper exercise of the power because under the terms of the Trust Deed and the Articles of Government of the school the governing body had the exclusive control of the conduct and curriculum of the school. Cases of this kind will always depend on a detailed consideration of the particular Trust Deed or the arrangements between the appointing body and the governing body. Governors are entitled to exercise their own individual judgements and do not have to vote in accordance with the appointing body's policy. Furthermore, certainly in the case of a governor appointed by an LEA and possibly in the case of foundation governors, a governor who is to be removed for good cause must be treated fairly by being given notice of the intention and an opportunity to be heard.

Governors' terms of office can be terminated by resolution of the governing body in certain circumstances:

- The governing body can remove any community governor, appointed (as opposed to elected) parent governor or sponsor governor.

- If it considers it appropriate, the governing body may remove an ex officio foundation governor at the request of the person identified as being entitled to do so in the instrument of government.

- The governing body may also remove nominated community governors or sponsor governors at the request of the nominating body, if the governing body thinks it appropriate.

In all cases, the reasons for the proposed removal must be given, and the governor concerned must be given the opportunity to make a statement in response. The decision to remove the governor must be confirmed by a second resolution at a governing body meeting at least 14 days after the original meeting, and the removal of the governor must be a specific item of business on the agenda of both meetings.

The governing body cannot remove foundation governors (other than ex officio foundation governors), LEA governors, partnership governors, elected parent governors or staff governors.

Automatic Disqualification

Governors will be disqualified from office if they:

- are aged under 18;

- become bankrupt or make an arrangement with creditors;

- are liable to be detained under the provisions of the Mental Health Act 1983;

- are subject to a disqualification order relating to holding office as a charity trustee or as a company director or are banned from being employed to work with or in proximity to children or are banned from being a proprietor of an independent school or from being employed in any school;

- have been convicted of a criminal offence within five years before appointment or while holding office which resulted in a prison sentence (even if suspended) of not less than three months without the option of a fine. A sentence of at least two-and-a-half years' imprisonment within 20 years before appointment also disqualifies as does a conviction and fine for causing nuisance or disturbance on school premises. Finally, a sentence of at least five years' imprisonment disqualifies an individual from appointment – there is no 'rehabilitation period' for a sentence of this length;

- hold more than one governorship at the same school;

- fail to attend any governors' meeting or a meeting of a committee over a period of six months without consent. The disqualification is automatic but the governor can be reappointed (although with the exception of staff and parent governors, a year must pass before doing so). Governing bodies need to check attendance and make sure that formal consent is given in suitable circumstances. Although the regulations no longer explicitly require the minutes of a governing body meeting to record whether the absence of someone who has sent apologies is consented to or to send a copy of the minutes to the governor concerned, the clerk should keep attendance records and ensure that there is no inadvertent disqualification. Failure to do this may lead to governors who are technically disqualified taking part in meetings. This would not invalidate the meeting in itself but it might give rise to quorum difficulties. It would be especially critical if the disqualified governor took part in disciplinary matters or appeals where the correct constitution of the body is of particular importance;

- refuse a request from the clerk for a Criminal Records Bureau check.

In particular:

- a community governor may not be a pupil at the school, eligible to be a staff governor at the school, or be an elected member of the LEA;

- a parent governor may not be an elected member of the LEA or be paid to work at the school for more than 500 hours a year. However, a parent governor, whether elected or appointed, may continue in office even though his or her child has left school during the term of office;

- a partnership governor may not be a pupil, a parent of a pupil at the school, eligible to be a staff governor at the school, or be an elected member or employee of the LEA;

- a staff governor who ceases to be employed at the school becomes disqualified from being such a governor, although may be eligible for appointment or election to some other category of governor.

Suspension of Governors

The governing body can in certain circumstances suspend a governor for up to six months, although the Guidance says that this should be a tool of last resort. It can do this if the governor:

- is employed at the school and is subject to disciplinary action;

- is subject to court proceedings that could lead to disqualification;

- has acted in a way that is inconsistent with the school's ethos or religious character and is likely to bring the school, the governing body or the office of governor into disrepute; or

- has broken the duty of confidentiality to the school, staff or pupils.

The proposal to suspend must be an item of business on the agenda of the meeting, the governor who is proposing the suspension must give reasons for doing so and the governor who is the subject of the proposal to suspend must be given the opportunity to respond. A suspended governor is entitled to continue to receive notices, agendas and other documentation relating to governing body meetings.

DECLARATION OF INTEREST AND WITHDRAWAL FROM MEETINGS

There are detailed rules requiring governors to declare interests and withdraw from meetings where they have:

- a direct or indirect pecuniary interest in any proposed contract or other matter being discussed;

- other personal involvement.

Rules Regarding Pecuniary Interest

Such interests must be declared as soon as practicable – the issue could arise unexpectedly in the course of a meeting – and the governor must not take part in the discussion or vote on it. The governor must withdraw from the meeting while it is being discussed. Subject to due observance of the rules relating to declaration of interest and withdrawal, there is express provision for a governor to enter into a contract with the governing body for profit. This contrasts with the usual rule relating to charity trustees who cannot normally do this.

The restriction does not just relate to the interest of the governor. It includes any interest of a relative or a spouse, which includes someone living with another person as that person's spouse. It also includes interests that arise to the governor or to a relative or spouse through partnership with or employment by the person or company with whom the contract or arrangement is to be made or by whom the governor was nominated. This would include, for instance, an employee of a service provider under a PFI scheme – although issues of confidentiality would remain. Interests arising through membership of or employment by a public corporation or other body are ignored if the governor has no financial interest in the organisation in question. Ownership of shares in a company, even if that company is a major public company, with whom a contract is to be made could, however, be a financial interest to be disclosed. Some common sense is required here: it would be nonsense to expect a governor holding shares in ICI to withdraw from a meeting considering a building contract because of the possibility that the contractor will use paint manufactured by ICI.

A staff governor is not taken as having a pecuniary interest in a contract or other matter involving employees of the school unless that particular governor has an interest greater than that of the body of employees generally. A staff governor may, therefore, take part in a discussion on the school's pay policy but not on an issue that might alter that governor's personal position in relation to the rest of the staff. An obvious example would be a discussion regarding responsibility allowances for that governor's department which could affect the teacher, or one regarding the promotion or retirement of a member of the department which could affect the governor's own promotion prospects. There is a specific requirement that a governor employed at the school (other than the headteacher) must withdraw from consideration of pay or appraisal of that governor or of another employee at the school and the headteacher must withdraw from any discussion about his or her pay or appraisal. Subject to this, teacher and staff governors are allowed to participate fully in discussions on issues relating to the management of the budget and the curriculum even though there may be financial implications for them. However, a decision to close a school does have pecuniary implications for teachers and in one case the court decided that teacher governors were not eligible to vote. It might be thought that the interest in question was no greater than that of the generality of teachers in the school and therefore within the exception mentioned above. However, school closure might impinge differently on different individuals because some might face redundancy while others might be deployed.

Rules Regarding Other Personal Involvement

A governor who is personally involved in a decision should not, as a matter of good practice, take part in the discussion or vote and would be well advised to withdraw from the meeting even if this was not required by the regulations. The involvement will not necessarily be a direct one. As shown above in relation to staff governors, an employee may be potentially affected by a decision which could have future promotion implications for that person. Governors and governing bodies need to consider carefully whether there is a potential conflict whenever setting up appointment panels: the validity of the appointment process could be challenged even though the failure to disclose and withdraw was inadvertent.

In any circumstance where there may be a conflict between the interests of a particular governor and those of the governing body, or where a fair hearing is required and there is reasonable doubt about the ability of someone to act impartially, that person must withdraw from the meeting and not vote.

Even if there is no express requirement for a governor to withdraw, there may be instances where natural justice requires that a governor does not take part. Where individual rights might be affected, nothing should be done that might give rise to a suspicion of bias. This will, for example, require that governors who have been involved in an investigation should not take part in subsequent action arising out of that investigation. This principle, which if breached can invalidate action taken by the governing body, has to be kept in mind at all times. It is also important not to involve too many governors at too early a stage in matters that may become disciplinary issues. This can lead to insufficient governors without prior knowledge being available for the formal disciplinary steps. It is natural for governors to be concerned with potential problems but it is necessary to erect 'Chinese walls' at times.

PERSONAL LIABILITY OF GOVERNORS

Most public bodies, such as the BBC, Independent Television Authority (ITA) and the Civil Aviation Authority, are constituted as corporations, and the issue of personal liability affects all members (i.e. the senior, non-executive individuals appointed, usually by the Government, to the board) of such corporations. The statutes creating such corporations are silent on the issue of personal liability of the appointed members, and schools are in the same position. There is no clear statement of law establishing when or whether individual governors can be held personally accountable for what happens in their school.

On incorporation, any property, rights or liabilities attributable to the governing body immediately before incorporation were transferred to and vested in the body corporate. Rights and liabilities are 'attributable' to a governing body if acquired or incurred by any person as a member or former member of the governing body and subsist immediately before incorporation. This means that any liability of the governors at the time of incorporation, 1 January 1994, was taken over by the governing body. Governors do not, therefore, have to worry about the past unless circumstances apply that would make them personally liable now, such as personal fraud.

Statutory Protection

There is a limited statutory protection. The governors of a school are not liable for anything done in good faith in the exercise or purported exercise of their powers in connection with a delegated budget.

Analogies with Company Directors and Trustees

Since there is no express law on the subject, we have to look at analogies to gauge the risk of governors being held personally liable. Perhaps the most obvious one is with limited companies, comparing governors to company directors. Under both statute and common law, directors have a degree of personal responsibility to shareholders and to creditors. Governors may have similar common-law liability but cannot have the liabilities that directors have under statute – Acts of Parliament only apply to the specific instances that they deal with and no legislation makes governors equivalent to directors. Generally speaking, the only liability that directors have under common law is a duty to act honestly and in good faith.

The other analogy is that of a trustee and this is a much closer one. All foundation, VA and VC schools are statutory charities. Some will have a foundation body that is in itself a charity with separate trustees. Others will have a foundation body established as outlined above and that will itself be a statutory charity. The trustees or members of the foundation body will not themselves have responsibility for the conduct of the school but school governors, even of community schools which are not themselves charities, may be regarded as having similar obligations to charitable trustees. It will probably surprise no one that charitable trustees have personal liability for their acts and defaults, and the same is probably true of school governors. However, the default must be of the trustee rather than the corporation, i.e. the school. A governor will not automatically be personally liable for the school's contractual obligations or other legal liabilities. There has to be an element of personal wrongdoing which is either negligent or fraudulent. A governor who acts in good faith and without negligence has nothing to fear. A negligent governor may, however, be held liable for loss that arises, and a fraudulent governor will certainly be liable. Negligence has to be significant. Merely getting something wrong is not negligence: there has to be clear carelessness or recklessness in the way a decision is made.

Protection Against Liability

Governors who take care can sleep at night but there is an element of risk, and governing bodies do, therefore, need to protect their position. Apart from insurance (which all governing bodies should have), there are two possible options:

(1) To ensure that all potentially difficult questions and actions of the school are considered by the governing body in detail and a fully informed decision taken.

   The disadvantages of this are:

   - a greatly increased workload for all governors;
   - the inherent difficulty of a large group reaching a clear decision;

- the risk that too many views that are not based on good knowledge or expertise will colour the decision-making and lead to the informed opinion being out-voted;
- that it leads to the governors managing the school instead of governing it.

(2) To establish a scheme of delegation within the school through the committee structure down to the headteacher and senior staff. This should be designed so that each decision is made at an appropriate level and by those who have the necessary expertise.

The disadvantages of this are:

- decisions will be taken by fewer people. By the time they are reported back to the governing body it may be too late to take other action;
- some governors, particularly those who take a close interest in the affairs of the school, will necessarily be excluded from some areas of interest;
- governors may feel that they are not 'in control' and that they are therefore more at risk.

The question of which style of government is likely to produce the better quality decision-making and the better management structure is one for each governing body. From the point of view of liability, however, the test will probably be whether the governors have acted reasonably and in good faith. They are not liable simply because the decision turned out to be wrong, and governors who adopt the second option are, on balance, more likely to be able to establish that they acted reasonably. It may be held not to be a responsible course of action to insist on reserving decision-making where the people making the decisions are not those best equipped to do so.

Outside Advice

One other area of great importance and significance in avoiding personal responsibility is in the employment of specialist advisers. Governing bodies will often have a range of expertise, as their membership may well include professionals such as accountants, architects, surveyors and lawyers. There is a great temptation to rely on them for 'free' advice. This has its dangers, both for the school and for the individual governors. From the school's perspective, the governor in question may not have sufficient expertise to advise specifically on a school-related matter. From the governor's point of view, giving such advice (even if not charged for) may well lead to personal liability if the advice is negligent. If the governor in question practises in partnership then the other partners (or their insurers) may end up with a substantial bill. This is not a burden that a volunteer should take on or have imposed. If governors are asked to comment on matters within their professional expertise, they should make it clear that they are commenting as individuals and as governors, but not as professionals taking on a responsibility for that advice. Schools which need professional advice should obtain it on a formal basis so that the provider accepts full responsibility for it and is backed by professional indemnity insurance.

Schools have to be aware of when they need professional advice. Governing bodies should ensure that the headteacher has expert advisers available, either at the LEA or otherwise. No headteacher should be expected to be an expert in areas other than education. Legal matters, particularly in the technical areas of education law and employment law, should always be referred to solicitors or the LEA's legal department. Premises matters should be referred to architects, surveyors or health and safety consultants as appropriate. Expert consultancy may also be needed in education areas to avoid potential negligence claims. This is particularly important in the prompt identification of and attention to a pupil's special educational needs.

CONFLICT INHERENT IN THE GOVERNORS' ROLE

There are areas where the obligations of governors under the law may appear to bring them into conflict with the role perceived for them within the overall school organisation or with their personal or professional interests. It is easy to identify problem areas and to ask the questions. Finding the answers is more difficult and this will be for each governor and each school to resolve in its individual circumstances.

Personal Knowledge or Financial Interest

There are obvious areas of personal conflict, such as in exclusion or admission cases where a governor has personal knowledge of relevant circumstances. These are relatively easy to deal with because the law will normally require that the governor concerned does not deal with or get involved in the case. Similarly, financial interests are dealt with by withdrawal from the relevant meeting or from voting on the issue.

Personal Issues

Personal conflicts may cause greater problems in specific cases. For example, a staff governor who is a teacher may be involved in a staff appointment and may disagree with the headteacher or other governors over a proposed appointment. How far will that governor be prepared to be in conflict? What might the effect be on that teacher's own career in the school? One cannot assume that all concerned will always act in perfect good faith. Can the issue be avoided by staff governors not being involved in appointments? If so, does this not create a two-tier governing body and a breed of second-class governors?

The Appointed or Elected Governor – Representative or Delegate?

Sometimes conflicts may arise between governors and the bodies which elect or appoint them. In each case, there may be specific interests that those appointing or electing the governors in question may expect them to represent. In making decisions, governors have to reach individual decisions based on each governor's own perception of what is right for the school and without regard for the specific interest or wishes of those making the appointment. Governors are not delegates and cannot be mandated or required to vote in any particular way. A governor who agreed to vote as directed without being independently satisfied that it was in the interests of the school would be acting improperly. It can clearly lead to an individual governor being at odds with the appointing or electing body, particularly where large or dramatic issues arise such as, for example, a proposal to make a significant change in the character of the school. Conflict can arise in other ways: for example, there may be strong parental views regarding school uniform but the elected parent governor may feel that those views are not in the interests of the school. In such a case, the governor must consider the parental views but must not be swayed by them if they are not convincing.

Sitting in Judgement

Removal of the involvement of governors in appeals relating to the admission or exclusion of pupils has significantly reduced the area of potential conflict arising from the need to conduct a quasi-judicial hearing. They may, however, be involved in hearings relating to staff discipline. In exercising this quasi-judicial function they have to act independently of their ordinary role as governors but they are doing so in relation to the school for which they have responsibility. How does the governor reconcile the perceived needs of the school with the claims of the employee? There is no easy answer beyond saying that the governor must act fairly.

The extension of this problem is the conflict between the general role of the governor as a facilitator and supporter of the school and that of adjudicator and arbitrator when things go wrong. The role of employer requires that governors at one and the same time become involved in the activities of the staff to support and encourage, and remain objective and distanced so as to be able to exercise functions in relation to appointment, promotion, pay, pay incentives, redundancies and disciplinary issues in a way that is fair and is felt to be fair.

Finally, there is the potential conflict over the role of the governing body as an unpaid lay body in relation to the professional staff of the school. The governing body has overall responsibility for all aspects of the school that are vested or delegated to it. These are now extensive and include areas, such as curriculum, which the professional staff regard as their province. Where do the governors draw the line? To what extent do they involve themselves in day-to-day activity? If they do so, how do they maintain the necessary detachment mentioned above, and how do they persuade the professionals of their competence? If they do not, how do they monitor what is happening so as to discharge their legal obligations? Again, there is no easy answer, and each school has to develop its own culture to cope with the inherent problem.

OTHER SCHOOL EMPLOYEES

Apart from the headteacher and staff governors, no other members of the school staff have specific roles to play in school government. Frequently, deputy heads and staff representatives are invited to attend as observers and may be appointed as associate members. This is good practice both in terms of the professional development of those observers and in terms of the service given to the governing body.

PUPIL INVOLVEMENT

There is no specific prohibition on pupils being appointed as governors in most categories, but governors must be at least 18 years old. There is now the opportunity to appoint pupils as associate members of committees with the right to attend meetings of the governing body as mentioned previously. Also, there is no legal objection to pupils attending governing body meetings as observers but this, as with care the appointment of associate members, needs to be handled with great care. Much of what is discussed at a meeting of the governing body will be confidential, and a meeting with pupils present may be difficult to manage. There may be a case for allowing pupil observers to attend for specific items on the agenda dealing with pupil matters: it would be sensible to leave to the headteacher the decision on whether and how such observers were to be appointed.

OTHER OBSERVERS

Similar considerations apply to other, adult, observers at governing body meetings, although there may be less concern. Observers need to understand and accept the doctrine of confidentiality and that, even though they may be encouraged to participate in discussion, they are not permitted to vote. It might be considered good practice for observers to withdraw whenever a formal vote is taken. It is permissible to hold governing body meetings in public although this is rarely, if ever, done.

SIGNIFICANT CHANGE TO THE SCHOOL

An important area of concern and responsibility for governors is that of maintaining or changing the character of the school. This may arise in a number of different situations:

- a change in the status of the school e.g. from community to foundation;
- an increase of one form of entry or more;

- a significant change in the basis on which pupils are admitted to the school, particularly where a school wishes to move to a system of banding by ability or where a grammar school ballot requires the ending of selection;

- a change from or to co-educational provision;

- an enlargement of the school premises increasing its capacity (in broad terms) by 30 pupils or more; or

- a transfer to a new site.

Proposals for change for community schools will come from the LEA and the governing body has no power to initiate change (except where it wishes to change from community status to a different status). There is, however, an entitlement to be consulted. The governing body would need to consider such proposals and to respond. In general, the process following the publication of proposals is similar to that described in relation to voluntary and foundation schools. The LEA also has power to propose change to a foundation school but only in respect of a physical enlargement of the school premises.

Proposals for change for voluntary and foundation schools, and proposals for a change of status for any school, may come from the governing body. Those making the proposals must consult with anyone they consider appropriate and must have regard to Guidance given by the Secretary of State. Guidance indicates that consultation should be with (in summary):

- all schools likely to be affected;

- all LEAs likely to be affected;

- parents and teachers in the area who may be affected;

- any relevant diocesan authorities or other connected charitable or foundation body;

- the Learning and Skills Council (where 16–18 education is affected);

- any other interested party.

Proposals requiring the governing body to go through the formal procedure for approval will fall within the category of prescribed (by the Secretary of State) alterations which cannot take place without going through the formal process.

Proposals are to be published in such manner as regulations may prescribe. They must include the proposed implementation date and information as to pupil numbers. They must also set out the rights of objection. In general terms, any 10 or more local government electors in the LEA area affected and the governing body of any school that may be affected by the proposals may object. The proposals go in England to the School Organisation Committee which will consider them in the light of the LEA's school organisation plan and the funding implications. There is no longer provision for the Secretary of State to give consent but if capital expenditure is involved, since the School Organisation Committee will need to know that funding is available, there is still a role for the Secretary of State, at least where VA schools are concerned or where a Public Private Partnership (PPP) scheme is envisaged. If the School Organisation Committee fails to agree the proposals, or fails to deal with them within the prescribed timeframe, they are referred to the Adjudicator.

There are detailed restrictions on changes of status. Thus, apart from any other hoops that it needs to jump through, a school cannot change to VA status unless the governing body satisfies the school organisation committee that it will be able to meet its liabilities for capital works for at least five years. A school seeking to become, or cease to be, a foundation school will also have to consider the regulations relating to foundation bodies. The proposal to change status must state the rationale of the proposal and also deal in detail with any implications for admission, such as a change in the admissions authority, and with other matters such as the outcome of OFSTED inspections, information about proposed numbers and age limits (with five-year forecasts) and property information.

Changes to admission arrangements used to cause particular difficulties. However, the changes effected by the School Standards and Framework Act 1998, in eliminating the right to move to a selective or partially selective intake and in requiring an annual process for agreement of admission policies, will largely remove this from the arena of significant change. In particular, a change to take advantage of the right to select up to 10 per cent of the intake by reference to aptitude in subjects where the school has a speciality is expressly excluded from the ambit of these provisions. A change to a banding system, whereby applicants are tested to establish a broad band of ability as part of the admission arrangements, is to be treated as a prescribed alteration.

There have been many court decisions relating to due process in the area of proposed change to individual schools and to LEA provision generally. These normally arise in applications for judicial review of the decision in question and the cases form part of a much larger corpus of law relating to the obligations on public bodies (which include maintained schools) in their decision-making procedures. Almost all cases turn on their particular facts but there is a common thread: fairness must prevail, those who have a legitimate expectation to be consulted must be consulted and decisions that are taken must have a rational basis. This derives from a general principle of public law known as the Wednesbury principle: in reaching a decision, a public body such as a local education authority must have material before it on which such a body, acting reasonably, could come to that decision. If no such body could reasonably come to the decision, it will be said to be irrational and will usually be referred back to the body for further consideration. If the decision was not irrational, and if procedures have been properly followed, the decision will stand. In this area of law the courts do not interpose their own judgments on issues of policy. The judge may disagree with the conclusion, but that is not relevant in a judicial review case. This has to be distinguished from an appeal process where the appellate body will normally review the decision appealed against on its merits as well as looking at the legal process.

Ballot on Changing the Status of the School

The idea of the parental ballot first arose in connection with GM status. That no longer applies but the idea of balloting continues in connection with the continuation of grammar school status. The complexities were such that it appears that the process became largely unworkable and to all intents and purposes a dead issue. It is not proposed to repeat here the extensive description previously given.

SUGGESTED READING

Publications marked * are available from the DfES Publications Centre (see Chapter 1 for address).

Generally

* *Guidance on Good Governance* (DfES, 1996).

* *Governors' Guide to the Law* (DfES, 2004).

Incorporation

* Circular 15/93, 'The Use of School Premises and the Incorporation of Governing Bodies of LEA-maintained Schools'.

Governor Liability

* Circular 15/93 (above).

Election of Governors

Circular 7/87, 'Education (No 2) Act 1986: Further Guidance'.

Governing Body Constitution

* Six-part Guidance issued by DfES according to school type (2003).

Governing Body Procedures

* DfES Guidance issued 2003.

Chapter 3

CURRICULUM

Introduction – Responsibility for the curriculum – The National Curriculum – The structure of the National Curriculum – 14–19 provision – Changes to Key Stage 4 – Assessment and reporting at Key Stages 1 to 3 – Assessment and reporting at Key Stage 4 – Disapplication of the National Curriculum – Changes in the National Curriculum – The revised National Curriculum – The national grid for learning – Careers education – The Connexions Strategy – Sex education – Religious education – Drug education – Political education – The qualification structure for 16- to 19-year-olds – School development plans – Target setting – Complaints about the curriculum – Education development plans – Education action zones – Relevant guidance

INTRODUCTION

The curriculum can be defined simply as the sum total of all the activities that a school provides for its pupils. As such, the basic curriculum is far broader than the National Curriculum and will include, for example, additional items from an LEA's curriculum statement and a school's own specialisms such as Latin or Greek. It will be supplemented by extra-curricular pursuits, inputs from visitors outside the school, and religious education, which, in denominational schools, will usually be based on the tenets and beliefs of a particular faith.

RESPONSIBILITY FOR THE CURRICULUM

Responsibility for the secular curriculum taught in schools devolves from the Secretary of State, through the LEA and governors, to the headteacher.

The Secretary of State has the duty to prescribe the National Curriculum, but is specifically precluded from laying down the periods (proportions of time) to be spent by schools in teaching the various elements of the National Curriculum or the methodology to be employed.

Governing bodies have a duty to adopt a curriculum policy which must be formulated by the headteacher. The governing body may accept or reject it, but if they reject it the headteacher must reformulate it. It is not open to the governing body to write its own policy. The headteacher must keep the policy under annual review and formulate any necessary changes and must implement the policy. The governing body must monitor, evaluate and review the implementation of the policy. Thus, in practice, the headteacher is firmly in control of implementation, management and organisation of the curriculum in accordance with the policy determined. This freedom is, however, considerably circumscribed by the obligation to comply with the National Curriculum and by other statutory requirements that are dealt with later in this chapter.

All concerned, from the Secretary of State downwards, have a duty to act in a way that secures a balanced and broadly based curriculum which promotes the spiritual, moral, cultural, mental and physical development of pupils at the school and of society (although how a school's curriculum is expected to operate outside the confines of its pupils is not stated) and prepares pupils for the opportunities, responsibilities and experiences of adult life. This is over and above the requirement to teach the National Curriculum, which is subject-based and formal. Unlike the National Curriculum, which is formulated through regulations and has strict legal effect, nothing is prescribed for the teaching of this wider curriculum.

THE NATIONAL CURRICULUM

The statutory basis for the National Curriculum lies in the Education Act 1996, which empowers and requires the Secretary of State to prescribe a curriculum to be followed in all maintained schools. The detail is entirely in subordinate legislation which requires no debate in Parliament and can be (and is) changed from time to time by ministerial action. The Minister is advised by the Qualifications and Curriculum Authority (QCA) and Awdurdod Cymwysterau, Cwricwlwm ac Asesu Cymru (the Qualifications, Curriculum and Assessment Authority for Wales) (ACCAC) in Wales. ACCAC is specifically responsible for curriculum matters in Wales and for Welsh as a language. QCA and ACCAC have been given wide-ranging powers to carry out research, to conduct a review of the curriculum, examinations and assessment processes, to develop a coherent national framework of qualifications and to promote the creation of a learning society.

The National Curriculum applies to all registered pupils of compulsory school age including pupils in special schools. Where it is inappropriate for a particular child to follow the whole or part(s) of the National Curriculum, an exception may be made, either in a statement of special educational needs or by way of a specific (and time-limited) disapplication – which is dealt with in greater detail below and in Chapter 5. The National Curriculum does not apply to pupils in independent schools although there is nothing to prevent such schools from following it (and many do), and the two systems effectively come together at General Certificate of Secondary Education (GCSE) which constitutes a Key Stage in the assessment process.

For the reasons explored more fully below, the delivery of the curriculum for 14–19-year-olds is in the process of fundamental change in order, it is hoped, to lead to the disaffection of fewer pupils and their retention within the education system beyond compulsory leaving age.

It is possible for a school or an LEA or an Education Action Zone (EAZ) to seek the Secretary of State's approval to disapply all or part of the National Curriculum in order to develop their curriculum for particular objectives. This may be for the whole school, a Key Stage group or other groups of pupils but (although technically permissible) it is not appropriate for individual pupils. An application by an LEA or EAZ must be approved by all governing bodies of the affected schools.

THE STRUCTURE OF THE NATIONAL CURRICULUM

The structure of the National Curriculum encompasses the establishment of Key Stages in the course of a pupil's progress through compulsory education, a prescribed syllabus, as contained in the individual subject orders, and assessment arrangements. These elements are treated separately below, but are obviously interconnected.

Key Stages

The five main Key Stages and the associated pupil ages and year groups can be illustrated in tabular form.

Key Stages	Pupils' Ages	Year Groups
Foundation	3–5	Nursery and Reception
Key Stage 1	5–7	1–2
Key Stage 2	7–11	3–6
Key Stage 3	11–14	7–9
Key Stage 4	14–16	10–11

The National Curriculum does now apply to children who are under the age of five, and is defined in terms of early learning goals and educational programmes. The detail of the foundation stage is beyond the scope of this book.

Subjects

The National Curriculum comprises three 'core' subjects, English, mathematics and science, which must be taught throughout compulsory schooling, and other 'foundation' subjects, which have more limited application. The format in which science is to be taught will change significantly in 2006. The other foundation subjects are:

- history and geography to Key Stage 3;

- design and technology to Key Stage 3 (as a full or 'short' course at Key Stage 4);

- a modern foreign language at Key Stage 3 (as a full or 'short' course at Key Stage 4). If only one language is taught, it must be one of the recognised EU languages. Any second language may be drawn from the languages in this list or a range of others;

- information and communication technology to Key Stage 4 (which must now be taught as part of all other subjects except in the non-core foundation subjects at Key Stage 1 and except in PE);

- physical education (PE) to Key Stage 4;

- music to Key Stage 3;
- art and design to Key Stage 3;
- citizenship at Key Stages 3 and 4;
- religious education at Key Stage 4;
- sex education at Key Stage 4;
- careers education at Key Stage 4;
- work-related learning at Key Stage 4.

The information given above applies to England, although the arrangements made for Wales are only marginally different. For example, in Wales, Welsh is a core subject for schools that are Welsh-speaking, but a foundation subject for those that are non-Welsh speaking. English is not a statutory requirement in Welsh-speaking schools at Key Stage 1 and Welsh as a second language has been compulsory in non-Welsh speaking schools since September 1999. Separate Subject Orders, moreover, have been drawn up in Wales for history, geography, art and music.

Subject Orders

Individual Subject Orders contain:

- common requirements;
- programmes of study;
- attainment targets;
- level descriptions.

The English and PE Orders also include some general requirements. In the case of English, they highlight the need for all pupils to develop as effective speakers, listeners, readers and writers, with a proper understanding of the use of standard English and its vocabulary, and the rules and conventions of grammar, spelling and punctuation.

In PE, the main focus is on the promotion of physical activity as being of value of itself and because it is likely to lead to a healthier lifestyle, on the development of concepts such as fair play and sporting behaviour, and on the means whereby pupils' awareness of safety factors and their appreciation of rules, codes, etiquette, etc, might be heightened. The revised 1995 National Curriculum Order lays greater emphasis on competitive sport and traditional team games at all Key Stages and, as a reflection of this, schools have since then been required to provide additional information on their sporting aims and achievements in the prospectus and in the annual report to parents (dealt with in more detail in Chapters 7 (prospectus) and 13 (annual report). There is also a sharper focus, during an OFSTED inspection, on the quality and range of games offered by a school, both as part of the PE curriculum and in its extra-curricular activities.

Common Requirements

Common requirements stress the importance of access to the curriculum for all pupils and of making appropriate provision for pupils who may have visual, sensory or physical disabilities. A key factor, under the heading of 'Use of Language', is the contribution that each individual subject can make to pupils' overall confidence and proficiency in the use of their native tongue. There are similar provisions, in principle, in regard to information and communication technology (ICT) and the way in which the other subjects (apart from PE which is a conspicuous exception) can enhance pupils' ICT capability. There is also a specific reference to the Curriculum Cwmreig and to the opportunities that should be given to pupils in Wales to develop and apply their knowledge and understanding of their country's cultural and historical heritage and its economic, environmental and linguistic characteristics.

14–19 PROVISION

The publication by the government of '14–19: Opportunity and Excellence' marks the start of a very significant process of change in educational provision for 14 to 19-year-olds, with the aim of tailoring the curriculum to the needs of pupils in such a way that will encourage them to remain within education that is appropriate both to their abilities and aspirations. The introduction to the summary of the report reads:

> '14 to 19 marks a critical phase in young people's lives. It is the period when they build on their earlier learning and prepare for adult life and employment. Many young people make this transition well – but too many do not. Too many young people lose interest in learning before the age of 16. As a result, too many of them drop out of formal learning at 16. Moreover, too many of those who remain fail to reach their full potential.'

The longer-term aim, as expressed by the report, is to create a 14–19 phase where:

- all young people can choose from a range of courses and qualifications covering a wide range of subjects and skills from 14;

- they can start to develop their own mix of subjects from 14, combining a broad range with more specialist choices that meet their interests and aspirations. This should help them to move on to more advanced courses at 16;

- they can easily see how their studies will lead to further education and employment, whether they are involved in general education or more specialised vocational courses. Students must be able to switch courses too;

- all young people can develop essential practical skills for life and work. Additionally, the curriculum and assessment arrangements must emphasise and promote competence in analysis, problem-solving and thinking, so that young people have the confidence to explain and defend their conclusions;

- those with special needs or those facing difficult personal, family or social circumstances are helped to overcome any problems these present;

- regardless of where they learn, young people have access to different types of provision, centres of excellence and other relevant expertise; and

- schools and colleges are working in partnership and innovatively to meet the needs of all learners. This is welcomed in principle by many schools. In practice, however, there are a number of practical issues to resolve, e.g:

  - funding (LSCs only fund post-16 courses at colleges, not pre-16. So schools have to pay for the college courses using their LEA-delegated budgets. This is often insufficient to cover the cost of the college courses);

  - supervision (some colleges are unwilling to accept responsibility for the health and safety of pre-16 students because their lecturers are not trained to teach this age group; they therefore expect schools to send along a teacher or other staff to supervise the pupils);

- timetabling (the school, being the smaller institution, usually has to fit its timetable to suit that of the college course);

- reporting to parents (schools and colleges need to agree how and when the college will report to parents about progress on the college course).

The Working Group on 14–19 Reform has been established to address the longer-term implications of this strategy. It published its interim report in February 2004, which will be followed by its final report in the autumn of 2004. The interim report proposes a radical shake-up of curriculum delivery and assessment between the ages of 14 and 19, with the introduction of a new diploma system. The diploma system is intended to be flexible and capable of meeting the expectations both in terms of subject and ability of the wide range of pupils who will be assessed by it – 'unified not uniform'. The proposals are subject to alteration following consultation, but the general principles appear to have been well received both by the profession and the government. It is proposed that the diploma will be structured around four levels – entry, foundation (equivalent to the current GCSE grades D to G), intermediate (equivalent to the current GCSE grades A* to C) and advanced (to cover the equivalent of academic and vocational 'A' levels). Progression through the four levels of diplomas would be at a speed that suited pupils – related to ability rather than age.

It is proposed to include a compulsory 'core' made up of maths, communication and ICT together with extended project work, wider activities and personal planning, review and guidance. The main part of the diploma would be made up of different subjects, chosen by the pupil and determined by whether the pupil had a specialised or an open diploma.

The pupil's performance would be assessed and recorded by using formal transcripts to record details of the pupil's programmes and achievements, grading individual components within diplomas and the grading of diplomas within each level. Performance would be measured by a mix of external public exams, teachers, college lecturers or industry trainers, or via computer 'e-assessment'.

It is intended that any reform will be phased in, probably over 10 years.

The first phase of this change is the implementation of changes to Key Stage 4. Useful Guidance about these changes has been produced by QCA reference QCA/03/1167 and is available through its web-site. The Guidance emphasises that these changes will provide the flexibility needed to meet the needs of all students, and should be seen within the context of what is proposed for 14–19-year-olds more generally. They have a knock-on effect too in relation to the disapplication of the national curriculum for design and technology, foreign languages and science – although regulations for temporary disapplication and disapplication for SEN remain unchanged.

CHANGES TO KEY STAGE 4

Changes are being introduced in two stages. First, some quite general changes were introduced in September 2004, and changes specifically relating to science will be introduced in September 2006. The changes in more detail are:

- With effect from the beginning of the academic year 2004–2005:
  - work-related learning became a required statutory component. 'Work-related learning' is defined by DfES Guidance as 'planned activity that uses work as a context for learning'; it involves learning *through* work, learning *about* work and learning *for* work; it can therefore include work experience, mini-enterprise days, industry days, vocational courses, enterprise education, speakers and so forth. A non-statutory framework has been established that sets out the minimum experience schools should provide for all students and it is stated that this should be delivered across the curriculum and should not require additional curriculum time. The experience of work-related learning is very varied, and some schools have struggled to find suitable placements. The Trident Trust can assist through its Skills for Life programme, and organises about 130,000 placements a year making sure that all health and safety, legal, child protection and data protection requirements are met;
  - foreign languages are no longer compulsory;
  - schools must make available a course in each of the arts, design and technology, the humanities and modern foreign languages for any pupil wishing to study them; and

- the disapplication regulations for design and technology and modern foreign languages have been withdrawn.

- With effect from the beginning of the academic year 2006–2007:

  - there will be a new science programme of study. It will have a smaller core that is designed to be suitable for all pupils although the expectation is that most will take courses that lead to the equivalent of a double award GCSE;
  - the science programme of study will be a statutory requirement for all students. Disapplication regulations for science will be withdrawn from September 2006;
  - there will be a wider range of science options at GCSE – including a new single science award;
  - there will be alternative routes to the double science and separate science awards.

This means at Key Stage 4 the statutory curriculum will be made up of:

- English;

- Mathematics. It is worth noting that the Post-14 Mathematics Inquiry has recommended in its report 'Making Mathematics Count' significant changes to the curriculum and the way in which assessment is structured. It recommends amongst other things creating a flexible set of interlinking pathways the provide motivation, challenge and attainment across abilities.

- Science (subject to the 2006 changes);

- information and communications technology, with an emphasis on developing it through other subjects;

- physical education, with an emphasis on health and fitness;

- citizenship;

- religious education;

- sex education;

- careers education; and

- work-related learning.

In addition:

- schools must provide access to a minimum of one course in:
  - the arts (the minimum expectation being that schools should maintain their current range of courses and offer courses in both music and art and design). Schools may make the arts part of their compulsory Key Stage 4 curriculum if they wish which may be particularly appropriate to specialist arts or music colleges;
  - design and technology (the minimum expectation being that schools should maintain their current range of courses). Again, schools may make design and technology part of their compulsory Key Stage 4 curriculum if they wish which may be particularly appropriate to specialist technology colleges;
  - the humanities (the minimum expectation being that schools should maintain their current range of courses and offer both history and geography). Again, schools may make humanities part of their compulsory key stage 4 curriculum if they wish which may be particularly appropriate to specialist humanities colleges;
  - modern foreign languages (the minimum expectation being that schools should maintain their current range of courses, of which one language must be an official language of the EU). Again, schools may make foreign languages part of their compulsory Key Stage 4 curriculum if they wish which may be particularly appropriate to specialist language colleges; and

- courses must lead to an approved qualification;

- schools must provide the opportunity for any pupil who wishes to do so to take a course in all four areas;

- schools are expected to offer at least two courses in each entitlement area, preferably in two subjects or disciplines. This may be done either by themselves or in collaboration with others.

In itemising the requirements listed above, it is acknowledged that some schools will have difficulty in offering a range of language options so they are encouraged to work in partnership with each other to provide a wide range of courses.

Programmes of Study

Programmes of study essentially represent the precise syllabus that has to be followed in each subject. They also set out the corpus of knowledge, skills and understanding that constitutes the minimum statutory entitlement for each subject at each Key Stage and serves as a suitable foundation for teachers in their planning of teaching and learning, in the formulation of their schemes of work and in the day-to-day assessment of pupils' progress.

Attainment Targets

Attainment targets (ATs), as their name implies, define the standards of performance/achievement expected of the majority of pupils at the end of each Key Stage in terms of the level reached.

ASSESSMENT AND REPORTING AT KEY STAGES 1 TO 3

The statutory assessment arrangements at the end of the first three Key Stages comprise teacher assessment and National Curriculum tests. The two modes of assessment have equal weight and must feature in all forms of reporting, including the school prospectus and the annual report to parents, although the results have to be recorded separately in each case, as they are in the national comparative performance tables. They cover English, mathematics and (except at Key Stage 1) science.

Headteachers of maintained schools are under an obligation to ensure that:

- teachers are aware of their contractual duty to administer the assessment and reporting arrangements;

- all pupils who are in the final year of their Key Stage are properly identified for assessment purposes;

- the test opening and administrative procedures outlined in the instruction booklets are properly adhered to;

- all pupils have their teacher assessment (TA) levels for the core subject attainment targets duly recorded and that the overall subject levels derived from these TAs are calculated;

- all pupils being assessed undertake the relevant tests and tasks at Key Stages 1–3 (and that the tasks – and the tests at Key Stage 1 – are marked within the school);

- all the test materials are securely locked up and regarded as confidential;
- teachers comply with the arrangements for external marking, national data collection and reporting to parents.

The obligations outlined above apply to all three Key Stages. In addition, headteachers must arrange at Key Stage 1 for all those pupils who are deemed capable of achieving level 4 or above in mathematics and/or English to take the appropriate Key Stage 2 tests and for these scripts to be despatched to the relevant external marking agency. Teacher assessments may be recorded at level 4 even if a pupil has not been entered for the Key Stage 2 tests. Pupils should not, however, be permitted to take the Key Stage 2 science test.

Headteachers must comply with the requirements of an external audit of administration and marking conducted by the LEA for LEA-maintained schools and a QCA accredited agency for independent schools. They must also allow the auditors right of access to the school at all reasonable times and provide them with samples of pupils' written work from the tests and tasks on request. The auditors are obliged to inform headteachers whether the marking standards have been accurate or not and, in the event of any inaccuracy, to require the papers in question to be re-marked and then submitted again for verification. In the final analysis, if agreement cannot be secured, the auditors are empowered to substitute their own assessments for the school's.

Assessment and Reporting Arrangements for Key Stages 1 and 2

A baseline assessment has to be carried out on each Key Stage 1 pupil. Additionally, teachers are statutorily required to provide at least one written report annually to parents on the progress of their child. The precise timing and the form of reporting are matters for the headteacher to determine, but a 'normal' report would usually contain some reference to the strengths and weaknesses of a pupil (and how these might be enhanced or remedied as the case may be) in particular areas (or subjects) of the curriculum. Judgements about a pupil's interim progress towards 'levels' can be included, but this is not compulsory. The detail of what has to be reported on is specified below under the relevant Key Stage headings.

Baseline Assessment for Key Stage 1 Pupils

Baseline assessment has been instituted as part of the general drive to raise standards and is intended to serve two essential purposes:

- to provide information to help teachers plan more effectively to meet pupils' individual learning needs;

- to measure pupils' attainment on entry, using one or more numerical outcomes, which can inform later value-added analyses of their progress.

The National Framework specifically requires schemes to:

- ensure an entitlement for all pupils to be assessed, including those for whom English is a second language;

- involve parents in partnerships with the school;

- monitor pupils' later progress effectively and provide outcomes which will facilitate value-added measurement;

- support effective and appropriate planning for teaching and learning, on the basis of a detailed identification of individual pupils' learning needs;

- be manageable for schools;

- focus as a minimum on early numeracy and literacy.

All maintained primary schools are required to use a baseline assessment scheme accredited by the QCA. The assessment applies to all new 4- to 5-year-old pupils, whether they are full-time or part-time, and should normally be undertaken within seven weeks of their arrival in the school. As a bare minimum, the assessment should encompass the basic skills of speaking, listening, writing, reading, mathematics and personal and social development.

The governing body, when considering the adoption of an accredited scheme, should take into account the merits of the scheme selected by the LEA. Having made its decision, the governing body must inform the LEA of the outcome within 10 school days.

The headteacher may exempt pupils from baseline assessment on the following two grounds:

- where a pupil has already been formally assessed at a previous school and the 'new' school is in possession of those results;

- where an assessment would add little to the information provided by other, earlier assessments of the pupil carried out in connection with a statement of SEN.

In such cases, the headteacher must notify the governing body and the LEA each term of any pupils who have been exempted, giving the reasons for the exemption. The headteacher should also provide the parents of exempted pupils with an explanation of why this decision was taken.

Headteachers of maintained schools are also obliged to supply the LEA with a copy of the results of all baseline assessments completed in any given term within 10 school days of the end of that term. Results of assessments processed in the last 10 days of a term should be passed on as soon as possible after completion. The precise format of the returns is open to schools to determine, but headteachers are bound to include:

- the name and address of the school and its DfES number;
- the name of the accredited scheme being used by the school;

and, for each pupil:

- his/her family name and given name;
- his/her sex;
- date of birth;
- whether the pupil was part-time or full-time at the time of the assessment;
- the month and year of the assessment;
- the results of the assessment – disaggregated into its constituent parts, if possible;
- the components in which the pupil was assessed in a language other than English.

Parents should be offered a reasonable opportunity of meeting their child's teacher to discuss the results of the assessment.

Key Stage 2

Pupils who are working at levels 1 and 2 are only statutorily assessed via teacher assessment, whilst those achieving level 3 and above take the tests. Only pupils obtaining level 5 in their other tests can be awarded level 6 on their extension papers.

Teacher assessments at Key Stages 1 and 2 are presented in the form of summaries including:

- a level for each AT in English, mathematics and science;
- an overall subject level, calculated by averaging the AT levels in accordance with prescribed weightings (in mathematics and science only at Key Stage 1).

Reporting requirements at Key Stages 1 and 2

Years 2 and 6 only:

- test and/or task results and teacher assessment levels in the core subjects, together with a brief commentary;
- a statement that the levels have been arrived at by statutory assessment;
- a statement on exemption/disapplication from any AT, if applicable;
- comparative data on teacher assessment and test scores (including the proportion of those working towards level 1, absentees and disapplications), both in relation to other pupils of the same age in the school and in terms of national comparators (the previous year's statistics are normally used) and local comparators, if these are available.

All year groups:

- comments on National Curriculum subjects;
- comments on other subjects and activities;
- observations on general progress;
- attendance record;
- arrangements for discussing the reports.

Assessment at Key Stage 3

Pupils working at levels 1–3 in English and levels 1 and 2 in mathematics and science have been statutorily assessed through teacher assessment alone since 1997. Two tests and an optional extension paper are taken in each subject. Tiers of entry (i.e. where the degree of difficulty of the papers is geared to the particular span of levels being tested) apply at this Key Stage to facilitate appropriate differentiation (in mathematics, paper 1 is a non-calculator test in each tier) as follows:

English

- one tier: levels 4–7;

Mathematics

- four tiers: levels 3–5, 4–6, 5–7 and 6–8;

Science

- two tiers: levels 3–6 and 5–7.

Extension papers are designed to stretch the brightest pupils and permit the award of level 8, but only if pupils have been entered for the highest tier of the tests in that subject and have achieved the highest possible level in that tier.

At the end of Key Stage 3, teachers are required to summarise their assessments in the same format as outlined above for Key Stages 1 and 2 in respect of the core and foundation subjects.

No formal external audit is conducted for teacher assessment at Key Stage 3, but schools are encouraged to establish appropriate, unofficial standardisation and/or moderation procedures with other schools.

Reporting requirements at Key Stage 3

Year 9 only:

- for the core subjects:
  - the pupil's National Curriculum test results and teacher assessment subject levels;
  - comparative information on the results of pupils of the same age in the school (including the proportions of those working towards level 1, absentees and disapplications) and national performance data as provided by the DfES for the previous year;
  - a brief commentary;
- for non-core subjects:
  - the pupil's teacher assessment subject levels or a commentary on the pupil's attainment in relation to the end of Key Stage descriptions;
  - comparative data on the performance of pupils of the same age in the school (not in art, music or PE);
  - a brief commentary;
- other requirements:

  - a statement that the levels have been arrived at by statutory assessment;

  - a statement on exemption/disapplication from any AT, if applicable;

- all year groups:

  - comments on National Curriculum subjects;

  - comments on other subjects and activities;

  - attendance record;

  - arrangements for discussing the reports;

  - observations on general progress.

Administrative Arrangements for Assessment at Key Stages 1–3

National Curriculum tests and tasks should be administered to all pupils in their final year of a Key Stage. This means that at Key Stage 2, for example, most pupils will be in Year 6 and will reach the age of 11 during the course of the school year. Headteachers should also make arrangements for testing those pupils who are not 11, but who are taught in a class where the majority will be 11 that year, and for testing those who will reach their 11th birthday in that year but who are being taught in a class where no single age group preponderates. In exceptional circumstances, headteachers may decide to assess pupils who will become 11 that year, but who are taught in a class where the majority of pupils are in another age group, or decide not to arrange for the assessment of pupils who are being taught with 11-year-olds, but who are not yet 11 themselves. The same principle holds good for 7-year-olds at Key Stage 1 and 14-year-olds at Key Stage 3, with one or two minor differences. At Key Stage 3, however, in the case of a class that is due to take a GCSE subject early, the fast-track pupils concerned may be assessed a year earlier in that subject than other pupils.

Pupils who arrive late for a test may be permitted the full time to complete it. Where a paper is missed through absence or illness, the absence should be recorded on the marksheet. Pupils cannot be awarded a level in these circumstances, but where only one paper (of two or more) is missed, the other(s) may be sent off for external marking, so that parents can at least be presented with an informal assessment of their child's progress.

Where disapplication from teacher assessment applies and only a single AT is disapplied, the overall subject level may still be calculated, but if more than one AT is disapplied, a subject level cannot be awarded. Where a pupil is unable to complete a National Curriculum task owing to absence (usually prolonged), he or she should not be awarded a level unless the headteacher thinks that there is sufficient evidence available for such an award to be made. Where a pupil is disapplied from a test, he or she cannot be awarded a level.

Special Arrangements

The tasks and tests are designed to enable most pupils to take them in their standard format. In some cases, however, teachers will have to adapt them so that pupils with SEN can demonstrate achievement, but it is important to remember that no pupil should secure an unfair advantage (or be treated disadvantageously) as a result of the additional support provided. For example, the nature of the test questions must not be altered and the answer given must be the pupil's own. It should be noted that special considerations cannot be invoked retrospectively and that all applications must be submitted by the deadline set.

The procedures for requiring permission and the Guidance on acceptable school-based adaptations have both been simplified and the procedures for requesting special arrangements are now limited:

- to individual pupils' assessment needs; and
- to the pupil's stage on the SEN Code of Practice.

The above changes apply to Key Stages 1–3. In addition, at Key Stage 3, schools should take account of Guidance on the use of readers, communicators, signers and amanuenses.

Special arrangements may be appropriate for pupils:

- who are statemented or are at the assessment stage of the SEN Code of Practice;
- who are registered as being at the school action plus stage of the Code and whose learning difficulties or disabilities affect their access to the tests markedly;
- for whom English is a second language;
- who are unable to work for a sustained period owing to emotional, social or behavioural difficulties.

Permission is not required for special arrangements (from LEAs or the QCA) in the case of pupils registered at the assessment stage of the Code of Practice. For pupils below this stage, permission must be sought (on the official application form in the QCA booklet) before the deadline in respect of:

- the early opening of test papers;

- allowing additional time (the maximum allowable is 25 per cent, except for pupils using the Braille or large-print papers, when it may be as much as 100 per cent).

A number of other specific arrangements do not require permission.

Emergency procedures may be invoked in cases where the need for special arrangements could not reasonably have been foreseen.

ASSESSMENT AND REPORTING AT KEY STAGE 4

The GCSE regulations and the criteria for specific subjects (which were produced by the SCAA) are intended to ensure that GCSE syllabuses and examinations in the compulsory Key Stage 4 subjects reflect the knowledge, skills and understanding that appear in the relevant National Curriculum Order. In the case of non-compulsory National Curriculum subjects, e.g. history, the criteria are designed to ensure that the syllabuses maintain the continuity and progression of the essential knowledge, skills and understanding required at Key Stage 3.

Key Stage 4 pupils may pursue the more applied and vocationally orientated full General National Vocational Qualification (GNVQ) as the equivalent of four GCSEs. Those pupils who might previously have taken the Part I GNVQs will now consider the new vocational GCSEs (VGCSE). 8 VGCSEs began in September 2004 and are:

- applied art and design;

- applied business;

- applied ICT;

- applied science;

- engineering;

- health and social care;

- leisure and tourism;

- manufacturing.

Approval is also being sought for vocational languages and others which have as yet not been identified.

The final part ones are being staggered over until 2007 as follows:

Final assessment in summer 2005 will be for:

Engineering (OCR), hospitality and catering, land and environment, manufacturing, performing arts (Edexcel), retailing and distributive services, construction and built environment.

For summer 2006:

Art and design (AQA), media (AQA and Edexcel), engineering (AQA and Edexcel), science, performing arts (AQA).

For summer 2007:

Performing arts (OCR), business, health and social care, science (OCR), media (OCR), ICT, leisure and tourism, art and design (OCR and Edexcel).

Schools may not offer any course of study that leads to an external qualification for pupils of compulsory school age unless the qualifications and associated syllabuses have been formally approved by the Secretary of State and QCA respectively. It is the responsibility of the headteacher in the first instance to ensure that any qualification or syllabus has been specifically approved or meets the criteria for general approval (e.g. all non-GCSE community service, awards or sports qualifications). An updated list of approved qualifications and syllabuses is issued annually by the DfES and should be checked. The task of verification may be delegated, e.g. to the school's examinations officer, but the responsibility remains with the headteacher. The DfES Guidance will provide extensive information on:

- the statutory framework and the basis upon which qualifications and syllabuses have been approved;
- the normal arrangements for the approval of qualifications and syllabuses and for the withdrawal of such approval;
- the qualifications and syllabuses that have specific approval for the current year;
- the qualifications that have general approval (these cover all the qualifications and syllabuses on offer to pupils in primary and middle-deemed-primary schools) for the current year;

- the arrangements in respect of the National Curriculum and the use of National Vocational Qualifications (NVQs) and GNVQs;

- the use of Entry Level qualifications; and

- qualifications approved for use in pilot projects funded by the Secretary of State.

Separate Guidance, issued by the Welsh Office Education Department (WOED), provides similar information on the specific requirements that pertain to schools in Wales.

Until the National Curriculum changes to science are effected in 2006, it is expected that most pupils will study a 'double' or 'balanced' science course at Key Stage 4, leading to dual certification (i.e. GCSE passes in two subjects), but the regulations only stipulate single science as a requirement. The regulations can also be met by pupils studying GCSE courses in all three of the separate sciences of biology, physics and chemistry.

Where arrangements have been made for whole classes to take examinations for National Curriculum subject(s) at Key Stage 4 early, i.e. before the start of Year 11 (normally, but not exclusively in the summer term of Year 10) or at any time before the end of Year 11, the regulations allow the pupils concerned to cease pursuing the National Curriculum in the subject(s) in question. PE, however, is a notable exception to such latitude and must be studied in its entirety to the end of the Key Stage. In the case of examinations in the three discrete sciences of biology, physics and chemistry, the exception to completing the course in National Curriculum Science will apply only if a class takes all three subjects at the same time and with the same examining body.

Schools should be fully aware of the finer points of detail in respect of the relative coursework weightings in different subjects in non-modular syllabuses and make the information freely available to parents, pupils and governors. Clear and non-negotiable (except in very rare cases) deadlines, that are suitably staggered, should be set, so that pupils are not overwhelmed by a plethora of simultaneous demands which simply cannot be met. This obviates the perceived need for pupils to take time off school to complete the requisite work.

For most GCSE subjects, there are two tiers available: a foundation tier and a higher tier, encompassing grades G–C and grades D–A* respectively. Parents often feel disappointed if their son or daughter is not automatically entered for the higher tier, and schools should be ready to advance reasoned arguments for their decisions if they are challenged. For example, many heads would say that experience shows that a pupil predicted grade C at GCSE is more likely to achieve this on a G–C tier paper than on a D–A* tier paper. Mathematics is an exception in that there are three tiers (subject to the recommendation of the Post-14 Mathematics Inquiry that they should be reduced to two): foundation (grades G–D), intermediate (E–B) and higher (C–A), whilst in music, art, history and PE, the examinations cover the full grade range.

The limited facility to disapply parts of the National Curriculum at Key Stage 4 without going through the detailed disapplication process referred to below was removed in relation to design and technology and foreign languages in 2004, and will be removed in relation to science in 2006. Schools may currently disapply science to provide a pupil with an extended work-related programme.

Assessment at Key Stage 4

The assessment requirements at the end of Key Stage 4 will normally be met by means of public examinations at GCSE level or via a recognised equivalent organised by the principal examination boards or one of the other suitably accredited bodies.

Governing bodies will have an interest in the school's overall policy in respect of examination entry as this may well reflect the ethos (in the general sense) of the school. A common policy is that all pupils are entitled to be entered for a particular subject, whatever the predicted outcome, if they have tried hard and done their best throughout the course and completed the relevant coursework requirements. The policy will, however, retain the right not to enter pupils who have not been diligent, usually as demonstrated by performance in 'mock' examinations or in their coursework. Governing bodies may, in this eventuality, either refuse to enter the pupil in question for the appropriate examination(s) to avoid wasting public money or decide to charge them for entry under the operation of their charging policy (see Chapter 10), with the additional option of reimbursing them if their actual performance in the examinations warrants it.

Examination entry policies, however, should not generally be dependent on financial considerations. On the other hand, governors should monitor the total examination bill for their school regularly; the introduction of the National Curriculum has generally increased the number of subjects taken by each pupil by some 15–20 per cent and this has clear cost implications. Any increase in the number of vocational courses such as GNVQs will also usually incur additional expenditure.

Pupils not entered for the GCSE in a National Curriculum subject may have their performance or progress measured exclusively by teacher assessment, and the outcomes noted in 'Progress File – Achievement Planner', which is to replace the existing National Record of Achievement (NRA).

Reporting at Key Stage 4

Different arrangements apply at Key Stage 4 and beyond to those applying to the earlier Key Stages, although the essential principles of reporting to parents remain the same. These are dealt with in Chapter 13.

DISAPPLICATION OF THE NATIONAL CURRICULUM

The National Curriculum may be disapplied for individual pupils either by virtue of a statement of special educational needs (dealt with in Chapter 5) or by a specific disapplication in accordance with regulations. There are two types of disapplication: general disapplication and special disapplication. A general disapplication applies where the headteacher considers that the National Curriculum is not appropriate for the pupil but that it is not necessary to seek an assessment of special educational needs. A special disapplication is used when an assessment for a new statement or revision of an existing one is needed and the National Curriculum should be disapplied while the assessment takes place. In each case, the disapplication is temporary, for up to six months with the facility to extend for up to a further two consecutive six-month periods. The process is a formal one and the requirements for both general and special disapplication are set out in detail in Chapter 5.

CHANGES IN THE NATIONAL CURRICULUM

Literacy

All primary schools are encouraged (there is no statutory obligation) to follow the framework for teaching laid down in the National Literacy Strategy (NLS). The objectives of the framework are to give the teaching of literacy greater structure and direction with a view to increasing pupils' motivation and their active engagement during lessons. A wide range of teaching approaches is recommended.

The framework specifies what should be taught in each term throughout the seven-year period in question (Reception to Year 6) in considerable and helpful detail. The three main strands are: the word (phonics, spelling and vocabulary); the sentence (grammar and punctuation); and the text (comprehension and composition), applied through the daily literacy hour. The framework is supplemented by an extensive range of support materials, e.g. 'The National Literacy Strategy: Revision Guidance for Year 6 Pupils', which can be obtained from the DfES.

Numeracy

All primary schools are similarly enjoined to follow the framework for teaching mathematics laid down in the National Numeracy Strategy. Again, this is non-statutory. Numeracy requires a variety of diverse skills: an understanding of the number system; a repertoire of computational techniques; an ability and an inclination to solve problems; and a practical grasp of data-gathering and of the presentation of information in graphs, diagrams, charts and tables.

It is expected that mathematics will be taught for at least 45–60 minutes every day.

Again, the framework is underpinned and supplemented by a range of support materials, e.g. 'The National Numeracy Strategy: Mathematical Vocabulary', again available from the DfES.

THE REVISED NATIONAL CURRICULUM

The new modified version of the National Curriculum was introduced in September 2000. The DfES and QCA jointly published National Curriculum Handbooks. Copies can be purchased from HMSO or the material can be viewed on the HMSO web-site (www.hmso.gov.uk).

In general terms, the National Curriculum has been made more flexible, slimmer and less prescriptive, a more explicit rationale has been developed, coherence across the different phases and Key Stages has been strengthened, the programmes of study in English and mathematics have been brought into alignment with the national literacy and numeracy strategies (to reflect Ministerial priorities), the critical elements (of each subject) that need to be studied in greater depth have been identified, the programmes of study for all subjects include 'ICT exemplars', the programmes of study in the non-core foundation subjects have been re-classified under 'knowledge, skills and understanding', and citizenship has been given formal recognition within the statutory framework. Every effort has been made to maintain stability and continuity and to avoid excessive upheaval and turbulence.

Four key functions are emphasised in the current Order:

- establishing an entitlement – for all pupils irrespective of culture, social background or gender;
- establishing standards;
- promoting continuity and coherence;
- promoting public understanding.

There is, moreover, a clear directive to teachers to make the curriculum more inclusive by:

- setting appropriate learning challenges;
- providing for the diversity of pupils' needs;
- providing for pupils with special educational needs; and
- providing support for pupils for whom English is an additional language.

A number of changes have been incorporated into the subject-specific access statements, for example:

- *English*: attention is drawn to the importance of securing improvement in boys' achievements. Teachers are urged to set high expectations all round, to recognise and build on what boys do well and, in their planning, to ensure that:
  - tasks are carefully structured, with clearly defined goals;
  - boys' ability in spoken language is given an appropriate outlet (e.g. in drama and role play);
  - opportunities for conciseness, analysis and synthesis are provided in the range of written tasks that are set;
  - the range of boys' voluntary reading is duly recognised;
  - reading and writing are integrated into activities which entail action as well as the expression of feeling and imagination;
  - collaborative activities are a regular feature of lessons;

- *Science*: appropriate support should be given to pupils with hearing and visual impairment to help them access the sound and light components of the programmes of study, respectively;

- *Art and design*: proper provision should be made for those pupils whose tactile skills need to be developed;

- *Music*: special consideration should be given to pupils with hearing impairment;

- *PE*: suitable provision should be made for pupils:
    - who need activities to be adapted to enable them to participate;
    - with specific religious and cultural beliefs and practices to help them to participate at times of fasting, in clothing appropriate to their beliefs and in appropriate groupings and settings;
    - so that the size and gender of groupings foster effective learning and promote safety.

The statements on the use of language and the use of ICT have been revised. In language, pupils should henceforth be taught:

- to use the correct spelling and punctuation and to follow grammatical conventions in writing;

- to speak precisely and cogently;

- in reading, strategies to help them to read with understanding, to locate and use information, to follow an argument, and to summarise, synthesise and adapt what they learn from their reading.

In ICT, pupils should be given opportunities to practise and develop their ICT capability by the regular use of ICT as an aid to learning in all subjects.

Headteachers will need to check the detailed changes that have been, and no doubt will continue to be, made in individual subject areas.

Citizenship

Compulsory lessons on citizenship in the curriculum as a means of engendering a greater sense of responsibility *en masse* and in the hope of transforming the community in which we live into a more law-abiding, caring, considerate and moral society were introduced in 2002 in secondary schools. Planning of provision should reflect the need to ensure that pupils have a clear understanding of their roles, rights and responsibilities in relation to their local, national and international communities. The three strands in the programmes of study to be taught are:

- knowledge and understanding about becoming an informed citizen;

- developing skills of enquiry and communication; and

- developing skills of participation and responsible action.

Citizenship does not form a compulsory part of the curriculum in primary schools or nurseries. The section in the *Curriculum Guidance for the Foundation Stage* concerned with personal, social and emotional development provides a starting point for work at the Foundation stage, and the programmes of study described in the non-statutory guidelines for personal, social and health education (PSHE) and Citizenship cover the knowledge, understanding and skills that deal with basic citizenship issues for pupils at Key Stages 1 and 2.

THE NATIONAL GRID FOR LEARNING

The opportunities offered by the development of the information superhighway and networked technologies, which permit ready access to the most up-to-date information and direct electronic links with people all over the world, are now beginning to be appreciated. The creation of a National Grid for Learning will have a profound impact on the future of learning and the way in which schools operate, the full effects of which can still at present only be imagined and perhaps not truly comprehended.

Governors who are keen to increase their awareness of the possibilities afforded by the new technology and in the details of the Grid should obtain their own copy of the DfES booklets *Connecting the Learning Society* and *Preparing for the Information Age*. These provide interesting examples of the networked school and of projects that are already up and running, as well as putting some flesh on the Government's skeletal vision of the way ahead, e.g. in relation to the potential of the Grid, its design and content and how it might be built up, and ICT targets.

CAREERS EDUCATION

The governing body and the headteacher of all LEA-maintained, foundation and voluntary schools and foundation special schools (and the proprietor and the headteacher, and the LEA and the teacher in charge, in the case of city technology colleges (CTCs) and Pupil Referral Units (PRUs) respectively) must:

- provide all registered pupils with a programme of careers education during the relevant phase of their education (defined as Years 9 to 11 inclusive);

- supply accredited careers advisers with the name and address of every relevant (14- to 19-year-old) pupil at the school and any other items of information which the careers advisers may need to enable them to give appropriate advice and guidance on career decisions (unless the parent or the pupil, if he or she is over 18, has indicated that such information should be withheld);

- allow careers advisers access to the relevant pupils:
  - on the premises; and
  - at an agreed time;

- make available to all relevant pupils:
  - guidance materials; and
  - a wide range of up-to-date reference materials relating to careers education and career opportunities.

'Access', it should be noted, includes a personal interview (if the pupil agrees). Careers advisers must submit their requests for information and access in writing, usually to the headteacher of the school/institution in question.

DfES Guidance 0208/2000 'Preparing Pupils for a Successful Future in Learning and Work' is a guide aimed at governors and senior managers who are accountable for careers work and for the development of self-management and decision-making skills of pupils. It explains the purpose of careers work, and sets out legal requirements and expectations of good practice.

Governors should also be aware that OFSTED inspection teams are specifically required to evaluate careers provision in the schools that they inspect in respect of the following:

- impartial guidance, completely devoid of stereotyping and bias;
- clear (and close) liaison with the careers service;
- a well-documented and co-ordinated careers programme;
- well-planned and carefully monitored work experience;
- up-to-date information on the full range of post-16 options;
- proper access to appropriate training for all staff who are involved in the process.

Work Experience

The provision of work experience is a major exercise for all secondary schools. There is extensive DfES guidance 'Work Experience: A Guide for Secondary Schools' which goes into considerable detail. Key legal issues for schools, apart from the major task of securing work placements, relate to health and safety, insurance and child protection. The guidance stipulates the checks that need to be made to cover both aspects and makes it clear that the school has a major responsibility. There is a strong recommendation that each workplace is visited before any placement and that every student is visited by 'teachers, local organisers, governors and/or senior staff' at least once during the placement. Whether governors should be expected to take on such a responsibility is another matter: the assessment of a student on a work placement is a professional matter and arguably not something that an unpaid non-expert volunteer should be expected to undertake. The guidance does recognise this when dealing specifically with health and safety aspects and draws attention to the need to include governors in insurance arrangements.

Parents need to have full information about the placement. The guidance gives a list:

- Purposes and aims of work experience, including links to the curriculum;
- Learning benefits for the student, including skills to be developed;
- When and where it will take place;
- Travel arrangements and any associated costs;
- Nature of the work involved;
- Working hours;
- Any significant risks to health and safety and the control measures in place to protect the young person as identified by the placement provider's risk assessment;

- The name of the work experience co-ordinator in case of emergency or complaint;
- How they can support their child during the placement period; and
- The name and contact details of the person responsible for them in the workplace.

The guidance recognises that parents can often facilitate a work experience placement but stipulates that this does not absolve the school from its overall responsibilities. By implication, this would include a placement in the parent's own workplace.

Child protection is dealt with in summary in the guidance but it makes it clear that employers take on responsibility for 'social' welfare as well as physical welfare. The guidance refers to the legislation relating to the disqualification of people from working in regulated positions, i.e. positions whose normal duties either involve either caring for, training, supervising, or being in sole charge of children or involve unsupervised contact with children but it gives no advice as to the action schools should take. Schools do need to ensure that employers have systems in place that would ensure that pupils are not at risk and this may (depending on the nature of the placement and the level of supervision) involve carrying out CRB enhanced checks.

Work experience can also give rise to (perhaps unexpected) disability discrimination issues. A recent case demonstrating this is examined in Chapter 6.

THE CONNEXIONS STRATEGY

The Connexions Strategy, set out in DfES Guidance 0078/2000, establishes a learning framework for the whole of the teenage years (13 to 19). It is designed to bring together a range of services for young people to provide a coherent whole. Key to the Connexions Service is the network of Personal Advisors drawn from a range of backgrounds: the careers service, Youth Service, social services, teachers, Youth Offending Teams and voluntary and community groups.

Personal Advisors are expected to ensure attendance at school pre-16, then provide information about future learning and work opportunities, and support the gaining of access to education and to training and specialist services. Heads can request three possible levels of support from Connexions: Level 1 is intensive sustained support for young people with multiple problems; Level 2 is in-depth Guidance for a pupil who is at risk of disengagement; and Level 3 is provision of information and Guidance on careers/learning/ employment and personal development.

Personal Advisors are deployed in a variety of locations such as schools, FE colleges and community settings. Those working in schools are appointed and managed by the headteacher but will also operate as part of the integrated Connexions Service. Managers from the Service will have to work closely with the headteacher to ensure that their staff complement the pastoral and other support systems of the school.

'Working with Connexions' and 'Connexions Partnerships: The First Year 2001–2002', offers advice on how schools should carry out their statutory duties in respect of 'careers advisers', how effective partnerships with the careers services might be forged and guidance on careers education provision. Non-statutory guidance 'Careers Education and Guidance in England: A National Framework', was issued by DfES in 2003 and envisages a continuum of careers education provision from age 11 to 19 building on and developing the guidance previously issued.

SEX EDUCATION

Governing bodies of community, VC and foundation primary schools have to decide whether or not to include sex education as part of the secular curriculum, and that decision must be recorded in the school's prospectus. VA schools are not statutorily bound by these requirements, but it is hoped that they will voluntarily adopt a similar approach. Secondary schools do not have the option: they are required to include sex education in the curriculum, as are special schools for those pupils receiving secondary education.

The definition of sex education includes education about AIDS, HIV and other sexually transmitted diseases, but is otherwise remarkably vague. The Secretary of State has no statutory powers to issue any prescription in regard to the content or organisation of sex education. Every governing body must make and keep up to date a separate written statement of policy with regard to the provision of sex education. Parents of registered pupils are entitled to inspect the statement and to receive a copy, free of charge, on request. Information about sex education, including its content and organisation, has to appear in the school's prospectus.

Parents have the right to request that a pupil be wholly or partly excused from receiving sex education at the school, except insofar as such education is specified in the National Curriculum. The Science Order specifically excludes the study of AIDS, HIV, other sexually-transmitted diseases and aspects of human sexual behaviour other than the biological. The effect of this is that the biological dimensions and reproductive processes are taught within the National Curriculum, and pupils cannot, therefore, be withdrawn from this part of sex education on parental request. Schools should remember, however, that they remain responsible for pupils who are withdrawn from sex education lessons and must make some arrangements for them. They should, moreover, ensure that pupils' general education does not suffer as a result of withdrawal.

There is a statutory obligation to teach sex education in a manner that encourages pupils to have due regard to moral considerations and the value of family life. More detail on this is given in DfES Guidance 'Sex and Relationship Education Guidance', which is to be read in conjunction with the PSHE framework introduced in 1999. This Guidance replaces Circular 5/94 and represents a significant change in attitudes towards this area. As did its predecessor, it acknowledges the need to promote the spiritual, moral, cultural, mental and physical development of pupils at school and of society and to prepare pupils for the opportunities, responsibilities and experiences of adult life, but it does so in a less judgmental way. Whereas Circular 5/94 exhorted teachers to emphasise the value of a stable family, marriage and the responsibilities of parenthood, whilst at the same time being sensitive to the fact that some communities do not necessarily subscribe to these values, the Guidance recognises explicitly that there are strong and mutually supportive relationships outside marriage. Whilst stating that pupils should learn the significance of marriage and stable relationships as key building blocks of community and society, it also states that care needs to be taken to ensure that there is no stigmatisation of children based on their home circumstances. The emphasis that still remains on the importance of marriage reflects the statutory provisions that require the Secretary of State to issue Guidance designed to secure that pupils learn the nature of marriage and its importance for family life and the bringing up of children, and to ensure that pupils are protected from teaching and materials which are inappropriate having regard to the age and the religious and cultural background of the children concerned. Also, the OFSTED report 'Sex and Relationships' published in 2002 (reference code HMI 433), has useful material and pointers on good practice.

Governing bodies and others involved are statutorily required to have regard to this Guidance. The legal requirement is to have an up-to-date policy which is made available for inspection and to parents. The Guidance says that the policy must:

- define 'sex and relationship education';
- describe how sex and relationship education is provided and who is responsible for providing it;
- say how sex and relationship education is monitored and evaluated;
- include information about parents' right to withdrawal; and
- be reviewed regularly.

It contains good-practice Guidance on all of these areas and although compliance with the Guidance in all its detail is not obligatory, the effect of the statutory requirement to 'have regard' to it means, as where this phrase is used elsewhere, that schools may not depart radically from the advised framework and need to have clear and articulated reasons (preferably recorded in a governing body minute or headteacher report) for any significant variation.

Sex education is one of those emotive areas where the layman often feels at least the equal of the professional. Governors should remember to maintain a clear distinction between their responsibility for formulating general policy and the exercise by the headteacher and his or her colleagues on the staff of their professional skills and expertise in delivering the school's sex education programme in accordance with that policy.

RELIGIOUS EDUCATION

Religious education (RE) does not form part of the National Curriculum, but it enjoys a special status in the basic curriculum and is compulsory in all maintained schools. It also has its own inspection procedures. The nature of the syllabus will depend on the type of school (see below). In many cases, the syllabus will be developed out of a complex local consultation structure. The requirement to teach RE originates from the Education Act 1944, but has been made more elaborate and hard-edged in recent legislation. Some of the vocabulary used in the DfES Circular 1/94 is emotive, yet the emphasis on supremacy, predominance (both with reference to Christianity) and divisiveness is set against a background of very laudable sentiments, which highlight the respect due to others with different beliefs and the country's long-standing commitment to the preservation of religious freedom and tolerance. Perhaps the wording merely mirrors the tensions that exist in the minds of politicians and legislators and represents an uneasy compromise between a recognition and acceptance of the increasingly multi-ethnic nature of our society and the necessity for RE to reflect the fact that Christianity is the main religious tradition of the country.

Each LEA is required to establish a standing advisory council on religious education (SACRE), although its advice does not carry any statutory force. The composition of the SACRE should reflect the religious tradition of the area in proportion to the strength of the denomination or religion in question and will include representation from the Church of England (except in Wales), teachers' associations and the LEA, but there is no definition of what constitutes a religious tradition. The SACRE has a responsibility for advising the LEA on religious worship and religious education, as well as for certain functions in relation to collective worship which are dealt with below. In addition, each LEA will have a 'local conference', which is similarly representative and is required to establish a syllabus for religious education to apply in county schools. Although each local conference is autonomous, most will adopt one of the two model syllabuses drawn up by the SCAA, with variations to take account of particular local circumstances.

The syllabus to be followed depends on the category of school, as follows.

(1) In the case of community, foundation and voluntary schools which do not have a religious character, the syllabus will be the locally agreed syllabus.

Governing bodies of secondary schools should, however, note that where the parents of any pupil express a formal wish for their child to receive RE in accordance with the tenets of a particular denomination, the LEA is obliged to make facilities available to give effect to such parental wishes, provided that the arrangements do not entail any additional cost to the school or the LEA. Any such arrangements must not interfere with pupils' attendance at the school except at the beginning or end of a session.

For former grant-maintained schools, existing practice may continue until the Secretary of State determines otherwise or the governing body decides to revert to the home LEA's agreed syllabus at an earlier date.

No agreed syllabus shall provide for RE to be given to pupils by means of any catechism or formulary which is distinctive of a particular religious denomination (although the study of such catechisms or formularies *per se* as part of the syllabus is not prohibited).

(2) Foundation or VC schools designated as having a religious character must provide RE in line with the syllabus adapted for the school by the governing body.

Where parents request that their children receive RE in accordance with a trust deed of the school or with the tenets of the religious denomination specified for the school by the Secretary of State, the foundation governors are obliged, if it is reasonable to do so, to arrange for such RE to be provided at the school during not more than two periods a week.

As above, for previously grant-maintained schools, the existing syllabus may be followed until the Secretary of State or the governing body decrees otherwise.

(3) In the case of VA schools designated as having a religious character, RE provision must be in keeping with:

- the trust deed of the school; or

- the religious denomination specified by the Secretary of State; or

- parental wishes.

Where parents request that RE should be provided in accordance with the home LEA's agreed syllabus, the school should make reasonable efforts to comply with their wishes (the LEA will do so, if the governing body is unwilling to make the necessary arrangements). Such RE must be given at the times set apart for RE at the school.

These options are intended to ensure that schools are free to offer an RE syllabus that is in line with the tenets of their foundation. This will in many cases be a specifically denominational syllabus, whereas the locally agreed syllabus will be a non-denominational one and may well involve a greater degree of study of comparative religion.

As can be seen, parents have significant rights in relation to this area of the curriculum. Governors should be aware that each parent has an independent right: if one parent seeks to exercise, for example, the right of withdrawal, the school must acquiesce, even though the other parent may take a different view. Schools have no power to arbitrate between parents in these circumstances, and any discontented parent should seek a court order determining what is in the best interests of the child. The school would, naturally, comply with that order and this would have the effect of overriding parental choice.

A difficult situation may arise in the event of RE being taught in an integrated way together with National Curriculum subjects (from which there is no right of withdrawal), but schools must none the less take care to ensure that parents are allowed to exercise their right of withdrawal. As in the case of collective worship, moreover, schools would normally remain responsible for the supervision of the pupils concerned where withdrawal occurs.

Collective Worship

All maintained schools are obliged to hold a daily act of collective worship: few legislative requirements are so substantially honoured in the breach. Paragraph 141 of the 2002/03 HMCI report states that 'four fifths of schools do not hold a daily act of collective worship for all pupils.' Whereas in the past OFSTED effectively accepted this situation, the new OFSTED framework means that reports issued since September 2003 heavily criticise governing bodies that breach the law. The aim of collective worship according to Circular 1/94 is:

> 'to provide an opportunity for pupils to worship, to consider spiritual and moral issues and to explore their own beliefs and to encourage participation and response, whether through actions, involvement in the presentation of worship or through listening to and joining in the worship offered.'

Although neither 'collective' nor 'worship' are defined in the legislation and there is no specific reference to 'God', the Circular suggests that worship should be 'concerned with reverence or veneration paid to a divine being or power'. This quasi-definition has been considered judicially and, although it was not approved as such, it was accepted as one that a Secretary of State could reasonably employ.

Headteachers and governors might, however, feel somewhat apprehensive about having a duty to ensure that collective worship actually occurs when schools would normally be dealing with large groups of pupils at an assembly and when they could reasonably argue that genuine worship is a free, personal response to God, emanating from deeply held religious beliefs and the dictates of individual conscience. The subtle distinction that is drawn in the Circular between 'collective' and 'corporate' is of little practical use, and the interpretation of 'taking part', which implies a good deal more than passive attendance, is fundamentally incompatible with the definition of worship that is offered above.

The collective worship must be wholly or mainly (the mathematically minded will argue that over 50 per cent will suffice) of a broadly Christian character, which is again a general expression that is not more specifically defined. The requirement is loose enough to allow for acts of worship from time to time that are not at all Christian, but a school cannot opt out totally of the requirement for Christian worship without consent from the local SACRE. That consent can be given for the whole school or for particular sections, so as to enable the school to arrange for specific groups to hold their own acts of worship. It should, however, be remembered that, even if headteachers are successful in invoking the 'determination' procedures, as they are formally called, a determination from the SACRE only lifts or modifies the 'broadly Christian' requirement, and that daily collective worship must still be provided for those pupils for whom a determination has been granted. Voluntary or foundation schools with a religious character do not necessarily have to hold Christian acts of worship. They will act as the governing body may determine or as is required under the school's trust deed. No consent is needed from the SACRE, but it is not permissible for these schools, either, to opt out of the requirement to hold a daily act of collective worship.

Collective worship does not have to involve the whole school at the same time, but every student in the school must participate in such an act each day. It is open to the school to arrange groupings by age or otherwise and to hold acts of collective worship at any time during the school day.

As in the case of the provision of RE, the responsibility for arranging collective worship rests with the headteacher (who can refuse to participate) of a community school or a foundation school that does not have a religious character (although he or she must consult with the governing body) and with the governing body (who must consult with the headteacher) of a foundation (or a voluntary) school with a religious character. Headteachers, in conjunction with their governing body, should ensure that acts of collective worship are appropriate to the family background of their pupils and their ages and aptitudes, and they have a professional decision to make on what constitutes 'appropriate'. Whatever arrangements are made, however, headteachers are not permitted to leave pupils unsupervised and must be aware that nothing can override the school's responsibility for the health and safety of its pupils.

Parents may withdraw their children from collective worship. As with RE, the right is individual to each parent, and the school must comply with a request from one irrespective of the wishes of the other. Parents may, moreover, make alternative arrangements for collective worship for their children. It should be noted that the parental right of withdrawal from both collective worship and RE applies to *all* schools, including those designated as having a religious character. This is so even if faith commitment is one of the admissions criteria. Furthermore, all schools must refer to the right of withdrawal in their prospectuses, again even if the school is designated as having a religious character.

Teachers, unless specifically employed for the purpose, cannot be required to teach RE or to be actively involved in the daily act of collective worship. They may not be disadvantaged, either in the appointment process or during employment, for any refusal or unwillingness to take part in either activity. It is an unresolved question whether a teacher may be required to attend collective worship for supervisory purposes only, i.e. without taking an active part in the worship, but disciplinary action following a refusal would certainly constitute disadvantage and that would arguably breach the statutory right. These provisions do not apply in voluntary or foundation schools with a religious character that provide denominational RE.

It is interesting to note that, whereas strict regulations apply to school sixth-formers in regard to RE and collective worship, the requirements for students of the same age who are educated elsewhere, for example at an FE college, are far looser; RE need only be provided at a time when it is convenient for the majority of full-time students to attend, and collective worship should be held at an appropriate time on at least one day in each week and students may attend.

The first steps may have been taken towards a radical re-shaping of the concept of, and requirement for, daily collective worship. The Chief Inspector of Schools has (April 2004) publicly questioned its validity in today's society and seems to be trying to steer government towards a more relaxed, less prescriptive regime where the concepts of 'worship' and 'collective' may be more flexible and no longer on a daily basis. It is likely, though, to be a lengthy debate with an uncertain outcome.

DRUG EDUCATION

It is recognised that drug misuse is a major threat to individuals, families and the wider community. Schools cannot by themselves 'solve' the problem of drug misuse in society, but an effective programme of drug education can play an important part in raising youngsters' awareness of the risks involved in taking drugs and in helping them to develop the confidence to resist peer pressure.

Certain aspects of drug education have statutory force because they are included in the National Curriculum Science Order, and pupils must be taught:

- at Key Stage 1 about the role of drugs as medicines;

- at Key Stage 2 that tobacco, alcohol and other drugs can have harmful effects;

- at Key Stage 3 that the abuse of alcohol, solvents, tobacco and other drugs affects health and that the body's natural defence may be enhanced by immunisation and medicines; and how smoking affects lung structure and gas exchange; and

- at Key Stage 4 about the effects of solvents, tobacco, alcohol and other drugs on body functions.

Schools also need to take account of their duty to promote 'the spiritual, moral, cultural, mental and physical development of pupils' and to prepare them for 'the opportunities, responsibilities and experiences of adult life'. The difficulty here, of course, is that some pupils, owing to factors entirely beyond the school's control, may not be very receptive to the former and be too ready to participate in the opportunities and experiences of adult life before they are responsible or mature enough to deal with them (and they are positively encouraged to do so by the media). The above, however, represents a statutory minimum, and schools at all levels can and should do much more.

Schools are free to organise drug education as they wish, but such programmes have been found to be particularly effective for example, they:

- are part of a coherent, carefully integrated programme of health education spanning all four Key Stages (secondary schools should note the need to liaise appropriately with their primary colleagues and vice versa);

- focus on the facts, emphasise the benefits of a healthy lifestyle and give pupils the knowledge and skills to make informed and responsible choices (the information provided should include details about the legal position of drugs, their physiological and psychological effects and the implications of their use for the individual, the family and society generally);

- help pupils to cope with the external pressures to experiment (e.g. in local communities where the profits and the 'high life' associated with drug-taking outwardly appear to be extremely attractive and alluring);

- have due regard for the particular needs and concerns of pupils and take appropriate account of their age and maturity (and recognise that patterns of drug misuse vary over time);

- involve parents.

The teaching of drug education should be supported by other interactive approaches to learning and draw on a wide range of imaginative and innovative materials. The new drugs Guidance (that is referred to below) recommends that schools should appoint a designated senior member of staff with overall responsibility for all drug issues within the school. This may be seen to be a burdensome role which creates a tension with the whole-school approach to drug-related issues. The importance of personal conduct and example in this respect should not be underestimated. Where visiting speakers come into a school to help with the delivery of drug education, they should be properly briefed (about the school's aims, values and practices) and vetted in advance, and their contribution carefully planned to fit in with the rest of the programme.

Effective networking in an area can be particularly useful, and schools should endeavour to develop close links with each other, the police and other agencies. LEAs often offer very helpful advice and policy guidelines, as well as providing relevant training for teachers and governors. Governing bodies should be aware of the existence of the hundred or so Drug Action Teams around the country, whose specific remit is to co-ordinate action at local levels. The membership of these teams includes high-ranking representatives of the LEA, the district health authority, the police, HM Prison Service and the probation service.

'Drugs: Guidance for Schools' (which was issued by the DfES in February 2004, and which replaces Circular 10/95 and 'Protecting Young People') and the SCAA publication 'Drug Education: Curriculum Guidance for Schools' are valuable points of reference. The status of the Guidance is 'recommended action' and although there is no statutory obligation for schools to formulate a policy on drug education and drug-related issues, governing bodies need to appreciate that inspection teams have been instructed to monitor schools' policies and practice in drug education and their handling and management of drug-related incidents as part of the formal process of inspection. The Guidance itself says that all schools should have a drug policy (dealing with both legal and illegal drugs) that should be widely distributed through the school, readily available and regularly updated. It exhorts schools that do not have one to develop one as a matter of urgency, and indicates that the date for the next major review should be recorded in it.

There are clear links between policies on drug education and those on discipline and behaviour. Schools should indicate quite unequivocally their attitude to illegal drugs and other substances open to misuse, and what sanctions will be applied in the event of any transgressions, e.g. the possession, use or supply of illegal drugs on the premises. Surprisingly, perhaps, the Guidance states that schools should have a range of responses and procedures for managing drug incidents, implying that, unless the policies say so, exclusion is not perceived to be the inevitable conclusion in any incident involving illegal drugs. That having been said, the Guidance does repeat the exclusions Guidance issued in January 2003 that the Secretary of State would not normally expect the governing body or independent appeal panel to reinstate a pupil permanently excluded for supplying or repeated possession or use of illegal drugs.

The Guidance is very comprehensive, running to 126 pages, and covers drug education, the management of drugs within the school, responding to drug-related incidents and the school drugs policy which are considered in Chapter 8. Schools should review their own drug education and policy within the light of the new Guidance: it includes a checklist (at Appendix 7) which can be useful in doing so.

The Guidance includes a series of appendices which provide useful practical resources including:

- a summary of the curricular requirements of drug education;

- a summary of relevant law including the definition of illegal drugs (and an explanation of the reclassification of cannabis);
- lists of useful organisations and web-sites;
- various checklists;
- suggested procedures to deal with drug-related incidents including medical emergencies;
- Guidance on the use of sniffer dogs; and
- Guidance on drug testing in schools and a pro-forma incident report form.

In dealing with drugs education, the Guidance says that research has indicated that certain models of drug education can achieve modest reductions in the consumption of cannabis, alcohol and tobacco, and delay the commencement of their use. The Guidance requires all schools to have a drug education programme which is developmental and appropriate to the age, maturity and ability of pupils and in doing so should take account of pupil's views. It should also be accessible to pupils with SEN. It should cover the statutory elements included in the National Curriculum Science Order for each Key Stage, starting in primary schools and developing to achieve continuity and progression. Drug education should be delivered as part of PSHE and citizenship and, the Guidance says, is most effective when supported by a whole school approach. Drug education should cover all drugs and, when appropriate, should focus on drugs of particular significance to pupils such as alcohol, tobacco, cannabis, volatile substances and Class A drugs. The programme should be based on pupils' existing knowledge and understanding and in secondary schools it should be provided by a team of specialist teachers trained to provide it.

Schools are required to assess their pupils' learning and provide parents with information about it (who should, within a whole-school context, be given the opportunity to be involved with developing the policy and education programme).

'The Right Approach' should be regarded as essential reading as it sets out the quality national standards for the successful implementation and delivery of drug education in schools. It provides extremely detailed, practical advice and Guidance on each of the four main headings:

- co-ordination, staffing and organisation (if time is at a premium schools are advised to concentrate on this standard first and to move on to the others later);

- teaching and content;

- monitoring, evaluation and review;

- the wider context.

The annexes are also very helpful and cover:

- the statutory context of drug education;

- the discretionary content of such educational programmes over and above the minimum requirements of the National Curriculum;

- an example of basic drug knowledge at Key Stage 1 — i.e. what every pupil should know by the time he or she reaches the age of seven;

- the fundamental principles of drug education;

- relevant national documents; and

- a list of the names and addresses of useful contacts.

POLITICAL EDUCATION

Headteachers, governing bodies and LEAs are expressly enjoined to prohibit:

- the pursuit of partisan political activities by any registered pupils who are junior pupils (this is usually assumed to mean those of primary age, i.e. up to age 11, but the term is not defined);

- the promotion of partisan views in the teaching of any subject in the school.

If political activities for junior pupils take place off-site, the same strictures apply, provided that the activities have been managed by a member of staff or by anyone acting on his or her or the school's behalf. LEAs, governing bodies and headteachers must also take all reasonable steps to ensure that pupils, either at school or in the course of extra-curricular activities organised by or for the school, are given a balanced presentation of opposing views when political issues are discussed or raised. The term 'partisan' should, in this context, clearly be taken to mean biased or one-sided. What constitutes a 'balanced presentation' is, again, as in so many of these sensitive areas, left to professional judgement to determine. Headteachers should, however, institute appropriate monitoring procedures to check that what is forbidden is not, in practice, happening.

THE QUALIFICATION STRUCTURE FOR 16- TO 19-YEAR-OLDS

As touched on above, the whole structure of 14–19 provision including examinations and qualifications is on the cusp of radical change. The post-16 structure described below was introduced with effect from September 2000. The structure reflects the then Secretary of State's commitment to lifelong learning and his deeply held view that broader, more flexible and more coherent post-16 arrangements are essential for the nation's future economic prosperity and that the opportunities for combining academic and vocational studies should be enhanced, without in any way sacrificing rigorous standards and quality.

SCHOOL IMPROVEMENT PLANS

Schools are not legally obliged to produce a school improvement plan (SIP), (formerly known as school development plans), but the DfES recommends that they do and it can clearly serve as a useful management tool. OFSTED inspectors, moreover, will expect to see evidence of its existence and its implementation. The identification of key issues for action at the end of an inspection, and the requirement on schools to draw up their action plans in response (and to send a copy to OFSTED, parents and other interested parties) again presuppose that planning takes place and that its details are formally recorded.

The governing body must be involved in the formulation of the SIP to the extent that this forms part of the process of establishing the strategic framework for the school and the subsequent monitoring and evaluation of progress towards achieving the defined aims and objectives of the school. The SIP will be generated by the headteacher and, whilst it would be normal (and good practice) for governors to see and discuss the detail (preferably in an appropriate committee rather than at a full governing body meeting), it is important that the formal division of responsibility between governing body and headteacher is maintained. It may well be helpful if the SIP can flow out of the governing body's strategic framework which should identify the school's aims and objectives. Part of the SIP's function should be to establish key strategies and actions for achieving those aims and objectives.

TARGET SETTING

Governing bodies are obliged to set and publish targets, which should be realistic and challenging, by 31 December each year for the achievement of pupils at the end of Key Stages 2 and 3 and in the final year of compulsory education. During the period from September to December, governors will have to review the outcomes of the previous school year and consider both the progress made towards the targets already set the previous autumn term and the setting of targets for the following school year.

Once they have been determined, the targets cannot be altered.

The statutory targets are:

- the percentage of registered pupils who, in the opinion of the governors, will in the following year be in their final year of Key Stage 2 and achieve:

  - level 4 or above in the National Curriculum tests in English; and
  - level 4 or above in the National Curriculum tests in mathematics;

- the percentage of registered pupils who, in the opinion of the governors, will in the following year be in their final year of Key Stage 3 and achieve:

  - level 5 or above in the National Curriculum tests in English; and
  - level 5 or above in the National Curriculum tests in mathematics

  - level 5 or above in the National Curriculum tests in science;

  - level 5 or above in the National Curriculum tests in ICT;

- the percentage of registered pupils in the relevant year group who, in the opinion of the governors, will be aged

15+ in the following year and achieve five or more A–C grades (or equivalent) in the GCSE examinations, equivalent vocational qualifications or a combination of both; and

- the average points score for the school to be achieved by that group of pupils in GCSE and vocational qualifications.

Secondary schools' performance against the targets they have set themselves will be published in the Secondary School and College Performance Tables.

Headteachers and governors should be mindful, when setting targets for their schools, of the need to relate these to the targets set nationally by the Government for the year 2002 (e.g. under the National Literacy and Numeracy Strategies: see earlier in this chapter). They must also keep in mind the new targets for 2007, and need to be working towards these when setting their targets. The targets must be published in the governing bodies' Annual Report to Parents each year for four years, including the year in which they are set: in the first two years they will appear as targets alone; in the third and fourth years, details of actual performance will also be included and parents will be in a position to compare outcomes achieved against targets set. Circular 11/98 gives useful Guidance on the issue generally and Annexes 1 and 2 delineate the precise reporting format to be used (according to whether the Report is produced during or after the year to which it relates) and a framework for calculating the average GCSE (or equivalent) points score, respectively.

Schools will, moreover, have to liaise closely with their LEA with a view to securing agreement on the targets set. LEAs are expected to assess whether schools' targets are realistic and sufficiently challenging (and to suggest appropriate amendments if they are not). LEAs have an important role to play in the process, both as a source of support and as a provider of up-to-date performance data and training. LEAs are, besides, required to include schools' targets in their EDPs and to ensure that cumulatively these targets add up to or exceed the targets which the DfES has set for them individually.

Schools may choose to set themselves other targets in addition to the statutory ones described above, e.g. the percentage of pupils achieving level 5 in English, mathematics and science at the end of Key Stage 3 (in the case of secondary schools) or the proportion of pupils with special educational needs attaining National Curriculum levels 1, 2 or 3 in English and mathematics, or the percentage of more able pupils who are likely to achieve higher levels.

The DfES has produced two booklets on the topic ('From Targets to Action: Guidance to Support Effective Target-setting in Schools' and 'Setting Targets to Raise Standards: a Survey of Good Practice') which governors might find a useful means of gaining a greater insight into the process.

COMPLAINTS ABOUT THE CURRICULUM

There is a statutory right of complaint in relation to the curriculum. This is not limited to the National Curriculum, and anyone, not only parents, may complain. The area open for complaint is very wide and covers any complaint that a school or LEA has acted, or proposes to act, unreasonably or has failed to discharge a duty in relation to the curriculum, the provision of information about the curriculum, and religious education. It does not, however, encompass complaints relating to individual teachers or pupils which are dealt with separately under the complaints procedures introduced by the Education Act 2002. The Secretary of State will not entertain any complaint relating to curriculum issues unless the complainant has already used the specific curriculum complaints process. It is a relatively little-used procedure, largely because people are not aware of its potential. Hard-pressed schools and LEAs may regard this as fortunate, given its scope. It is likely that many complaints that are made to schools ought, in truth, to be channelled through the formal process. For LEA-maintained schools, the complaints procedure is established by the LEA after consultation with all of its schools.

DfES Circular 1/89 gives Guidance to LEAs on the procedures to be adopted, and a model form has been produced jointly by the Association of Metropolitan Authorities and the Association of County Councils. Most LEAs follow the model form with only minor variations of detail. The Circular stresses that efforts should be made to settle complaints informally within the school and that the formal procedures should be invoked only if these fail. The model form adopts this approach with a three-tier process of initial discussion with the school, followed by representations to the governing body and thereafter to the LEA. Complaints which are not school-specific or which may be of a general nature can be taken directly to the LEA. The Guidance and the model form require that a detailed investigation should be undertaken and that the complainant be kept informed of progress at all stages.

There is no statutory entitlement for the complainant to be heard at a formal consideration of a complaint, but the model form does allow for this. Each LEA will adopt its own detailed procedures for any hearing and these should spell out who is entitled to be heard and what representation is to be permitted. The rules of natural justice will not necessarily apply to a hearing of this kind, but it is good practice to follow them, at least to the extent of ensuring that the complainant sees all documents considered by the panel hearing the complaint and has an opportunity to comment on them. It may not be appropriate for witnesses to be called or for cross-examination to be allowed.

The LEA cannot deal with complaints relating to collective worship or denominational religious education in VA schools. These schools must, however, have a procedure in place for handling such complaints, which will probably be dealt with by the diocesan authority.

EDUCATION DEVELOPMENT PLANS

LEAs are under a statutory duty to promote high standards of education and, to this end, are required to produce an EDP. The EDP must outline the authority's strategies for raising the standards of education provided for its pupils and for securing improved performance in its schools. When preparing its EDP, an LEA is obliged to consult the headteacher and governing body of every school maintained by the authority, the appropriate diocesan authority (Church of England, Church in Wales or Roman Catholic) for any foundation or voluntary school in its area and any other appropriate persons.

LEAs must submit their EDPs to the Secretary of State for approval. He may give the EDP full or qualified approval, approve the plan for a limited period or subject to certain conditions or require the LEA to modify it or reject it altogether. In the case of modifications or rejection, he must notify the LEA of his decision and give his reasons for it; the LEA must then revise its statement and resubmit it by the prescribed date.

After gaining approval, LEAs must publish their EDPs and distribute copies of the plan (or a summary) to such persons as may be prescribed in regulations. The Secretary of State will keep the implementation and delivery of all such EDPs under review and may, as a result, impose further modification or withdraw approval temporarily if he feels dissatisfied with developments.

EDPs are likely to be extremely bulky documents because they will include a vast array of background data and detailed descriptions of all the various dimensions and subsections of LEAs' strategies for improvement. As a result, governing bodies may find the prospect of having to become familiar with such a wealth of information so daunting that they refrain from reading the EDP altogether – but this would be a grave error. An EDP constitutes 'eligible expenditure' (i.e. funding may be retained centrally for this purpose within the local schools budget) and it is important for heads and governors to scrutinise the provisions of the EDP, so that they are in a position to question the amounts of money allocated to each heading. Otherwise, LEAs will effectively be able to keep back as much money as they want at the centre on these grounds – and it will be progressively more difficult to claw this back as the pattern for future years will have been set. In this matter, as in so many others, there is no substitute for doing one's homework, and the time invested, although considerable, will have been well spent.

EDUCATION ACTION ZONES

EAZs were an essential part of the Government's programme for raising standards. However, their effectiveness and the likelihood of their future development have been questioned and it is now known that they will not be renewed when they expire.

EAZs consist of a cluster of schools (usually 15 to 25, with a suitable mix of primary, secondary and special schools), working together in a new partnership with local and national businesses, parents, the LEA, the LSC and others. They are sited in areas (urban and rural) of educational underperformance and disadvantage, where schools (and the whole community) need targeted support to succeed. They are instituted for three years in the first instance, but their life-span may be extended for another two years by an Order of the Secretary of State. Each zone has a guaranteed level of additional annual funding and is eligible for extra of (capped) grant aid per annum on a matched funding basis. An EAZ is designated as an exempt charity for the purposes of the Charities Act 1993.

RELEVANT GUIDANCE

Circular 2/99, 'Statutory Approval of Qualifications under section 400 of the Education Act 1996'.

Circular 6/98, 'Baseline Assessment of Pupils Starting Primary School'.

Circular 5/98, 'Careers Education in Schools: Provision for Years 9–11'.

Circular 5/94, 'Sex Education in Schools'.

Circular 1/94, 'Religious Education and Collective Worship'.

Circular 11/98, 'Target-setting in Schools'.

Circular 1/89, 'Local Arrangements for the Consideration of Complaints'.

DfES Guidance, DfES 0208/2000, 'Preparing Pupils for a Successful Future in Learning and Work'.

DfES Guidance, DfES 0116/2000, 'Sex and Relationship Education Guidance'.

DfES Guidance, SPD/WES/01/02/02, 'Work Experience: a Guide for Secondary Schools'.

DfES Guidance, DfES/0076/2003, 'Disapplication of the National Curriculum (Revised)'.

DfES Guidance, DfES/0163/2003, 'Careers Education and Guidance in England: A National Framework 11-19'.

DfES Guidance, DfES/0092/2004, 'Drugs: Guidance for Schools'.

DfES Guidance, DfES 0019/2002, 'Working with Connexions'.

QCA Guidance, 'Changes to the Key Stage 4 Curriculum', reference QCA/03/1167.

'Connexions Partnerships: The First Year 2001–2002', OFSTED

HMI 521.

www.teachernet.gov.uk/14to19 summarises all 14–19 issues.

Full details of national curriculum requirements can be found at http://www.teachernet.gov.uk/citizenship/section.cfm?sectionId=5& hierachy=1.5.

Chapter 4

INSPECTION

*Introduction – Some implications of change – The current regime – Purpose –
Composition of the inspection team – Code of conduct – Quality assurance
requirements – Types of inspection – Initial steps – During the inspection –
Re-inspection – The inspection report – Complaints – Denominational inspection –
Pupil referral units – Post-inspection – Schools requiring special measures – Schools
with serious weaknesses – The inspection of LEAs – Relevant guidance*

INTRODUCTION

OFSTED is a non-ministerial government department that is
responsible, under the direction of Her Majesty's Chief Inspector of
Schools (HMCI), for arranging the regular inspection of schools.
OFSTED works in close co-operation with the DfES and is also
responsible for advising (and reporting to) the Secretary of State on
all aspects of the quality and standards of education in schools. It
does not generally undertake inspections itself, but trains and
registers independent inspectors (mainly LEA advisers) and issues
contracts for the inspection of schools to registered inspectors.
HMCI is additionally empowered to make arrangements for schools
to be inspected by members of Her Majesty's Inspectorate (HMI),
particularly when he deems it impracticable for a school to be
inspected by a registered inspector.

The *Framework for the Inspection of Schools* forms the basis of
quality control in the standards of inspections. It is produced by
HMCI, and updated regularly. Inspection teams must adhere to its
specifications scrupulously. Although the *Framework* is published as
a separate booklet, all of its elements are also incorporated into the
OFSTED Handbook, which is available in separate versions
appropriate to the institution being inspected – although the
differences are not significant. The Handbook provides essential
advice on the conduct of inspections and general Guidance on the
inspection of subjects and areas of learning of the curriculum.
Although primarily designed for inspectors, the Handbook is also an
invaluable reference point for schools.

With a change in the chief inspector, OFSTED indicated both a change of emphasis in what it is looking for under the existing regime, and introduced quite radical changes to the inspection regime itself. There was a change of emphasis introduced from September 2003, intended to focus upon leadership throughout the school: how well the governors, head, senior management team and other leaders perform, and how well the school was managed (including evaluation and monitoring). A key issue was the degree to which the school had improved following the previous inspection. The framework was intended as a challenge to complacency.

This had barely come into force before consultations started for further change and proposals published jointly by OFSTED and DfES in Summer 2004 presaged major changes to take effect in September 2005. That consultation gave rise to further consultation which was not available in time to comment on. However, it is unlikely to have altered the main features and the changes foreshadowed can be summarised as follows:

- 2–5 days' prior notice of inspection instead of 6–10 weeks;

- small teams inspecting for two days rather than large teams in school for a week;

- three years rather than six between inspections;

- judgements will be graded on a four point scale rather than the seven point scale currently in use. The four grades will be described as 'outstanding', 'good', 'satisfactory' and 'inadequate'.

- inspections will start from the school's self-evaluation and there will be a concentration on core systems and key outcomes rather than collection of masses of information from extensive lesson observation and other sources;

- HMI will lead many inspections and be involved in all of them;

- the present accountability regime, under which the Registered Inspector has responsibility for contracted inspections, will change so that the Chief Inspector will take responsibility for all;

- reports will be severely shortened – characteristically six pages rather than 30 – and will be produced in draft for the governing body within a week;

- instead of an Action Plan, schools will feed their intended actions in the School Development (or Improvement) Plan;

- in place of the several categories of schools presenting 'problems' there will be two categories, schools requiring special measures and schools that will be subject to an improvement notice.

SOME IMPLICATIONS OF CHANGE

Perhaps these changes will help reduce the stress of inspection, although many schools will find it challenging to have to be on a constant state of alert, at least before the first inspection of this kind and indeed OFSTED reports that schools that have piloted the new style of inspection have been positive and the responses to the initial consultation were similarly favourable.

The consequences for schools caught unprepared by short notice of an inspection will be serious, especially if the inspection is not, as at present, an in-depth inspection. There is great potential for damage to a school and its community by adverse judgments that may be based on 'snapshot' evidence. We know the camera can, and often does, lie. Schools subject to special measures will be re-inspected in two years and those served with an improvement notice will be re-inspected in a year but by then the school may be dammed in the public eye and face an uphill struggle to rehabilitate itself. The Chief Inspector is well aware of these issues and the detached observer might well say that a school that is not prepared for inspection deserves whatever follows.

Certain questions at present remain as issues. In particular, how will the new framework deal with parent and governor involvement. If the inspection report will be written within a week of the inspection, how will the inspection team gather information? It is thought that the meeting with parents will disappear (although legislation will be required before this can happen). Instead, parents will have the opportunity to make comments in writing to the inspection team. The inspection team will try to meet with one or more governors but this may not be easy. The pilot programme has not identified this as a particular problem but it seems that in a high proportion of instances the governors seen have been parent governors. It is unlikely, therefore, that a great deal of weight will be placed on what is said by individual governors and judgements on the governing body will be made largely on the self-evaluation material.

This puts pressure on the governing body to keep ahead of the game. The Form S3 self-evaluation process is time-consuming in the context of normal governing body meetings and business and governing bodies would be well-advised to establish a committee representative of the different interests of the governors to work actively and constantly on the self-evaluation exercise. Monitoring this could then be routinely on the agenda once a year which could in itself be a valuable exercise. Overall, if the governing body is well-organised, the intended new regime will be less burdensome for governors than the current framework which bears quite heavily on governing bodies and can lead to harsh judgements being made.

With the new emphasis on self-evaluation, headteachers would need to complete Form S4 (or the form that will replace it) whether or not they expect an inspection in the near future and to update it thereafter on a regular basis. Headteachers that have done so have found it to be a worthwhile management exercise, particularly when linked with the school development planning cycle.

THE CURRENT REGIME

What follows in this chapter is based on the framework introduced in September 2003.

Schools Covered

Inspection is a statutory requirement and applies to all:

- nursery, foundation, community, voluntary and special schools maintained by LEAs;
- non-maintained special schools;
- CTCs and City Colleges for the Technology of the Arts (CCTAs);
- independent schools approved by the Secretary of State as being suitable for children whose statements of SEN are maintained by an LEA;
- other independent schools. If an independent school is a member of the Independent Schools' Council, the inspections may be undertaken by the Independent Schools' Inspectorate rather than by OFSTED, but the inspection will be conducted within the same framework, albeit a different one to that applicable to the maintained sector.

Separate arrangements exist for the inspection of further education (FE) and sixth-form colleges under the auspices of the Adult Learning Inspectorate (ALI) (for post-19 education and 16–19 training) or OFSTED (for 16–19 education). There is a joint inspection framework between ALI and OFSTED.

PURPOSE

The essential purpose of an inspection is to identify the strengths and weaknesses of a school with a view to:

- improving the quality of education offered; and
- raising the standards achieved by its pupils.

COMPOSITION OF THE INSPECTION TEAM

The size of the inspection team will vary according to the size of a school and the number of pupils on roll, but will normally consist of:

- a Registered Inspector (RgI) – the team leader;
- a core group of inspectors (looking at whole-school issues and some individual subjects);
- a lay inspector;
- subject specialist inspectors (usually only in secondary schools and some very large primary schools).

An inspection encompasses all aspects of a school's educational provision, including its extra-curricular activities and boarding, where this is offered, but will focus primarily on the aspects of the school outlined in the *Framework*, the subjects of the National Curriculum, and religious education (in schools that are statutorily required to teach the subject in accordance with an agreed syllabus). Inspection teams, therefore, must collectively contain sufficient all-round expertise to be able to discharge their functions effectively (and must include one or more members with the specific brief of inspecting or co-ordinating equal opportunities issues and, where relevant, SEN and the education of pupils for whom English is a second language). Primary inspection teams must be competent to inspect the full age range in a school, including nursery provision.

The RgI is required to be open in his or her dealings with a school and to provide the governing body with the curriculum vitae of each member of his or her team prior to an inspection, as a means of establishing its credibility and of inspiring confidence.

CODE OF CONDUCT

It is assumed that inspection will be a humane process, and inspectors must observe a strict Code of Conduct during the course of their visit to a school. RgIs, moreover, are charged with the specific responsibility of ensuring that team members abide by the Code. *Inter alia*, inspectors should:

- carry out their work with professionalism, integrity, sensitivity and courtesy;

- evaluate the work of the school objectively and impartially;

- report honestly and fairly;

- act in the best interests of the pupils at the school;

- respect the confidentiality of personal information received during the inspection.

QUALITY ASSURANCE REQUIREMENTS

As the Code implies, inspection should be carried out to the highest professional standards, and those contracting for inspections must provide OFSTED with details of their quality assurance arrangements. These will be expected to cover:

- the induction, support, selection and deployment of inspectors;

- liaison with schools;

- the review and analysis of inspection evidence;

- ensuring that judgements about the school are corporate;

- ensuring the consistency, clarity and accuracy of reports and their compliance with requirements;

- the use of feedback from the monitoring of inspections by OFSTED.

TYPES OF INSPECTION

The type of inspection will depend upon the type of school: for instance, there are different inspection models for primary and nursery schools. Whilst under the current arrangements, schools have to be inspected once every six years, those that are considered to be less effective will be inspected more regularly.

INITIAL STEPS

Schools will normally be notified by OFSTED of their inclusion in the inspection programme at least six to ten weeks before an inspection is due to take place.

Schools are required to provide electronically information about the school, its pupils and self-evaluation, using four forms:

- S1 includes basic information about the school, which is used to prepare a specification for the inspection;
- S2 includes more detailed information about the school and its pupils;
- S3 is completed by the governing body and includes its assessment of how far statutory arrangements and policies are in place;
- S4 allows the school to evaluate itself. This is an important opportunity both for the school to make explicit reference to those aspects of the school and its development since the last inspection and to emphasise what it regards to be its strengths or special features. Where the school's self-evaluation systems reveal weaknesses, OFSTED expects that these will be acknowledged in the S4, together with the action that the school is taking in response.

Governors, especially those with clearly identified responsibilities, e.g. the chair of the finance committee, the 'outdoor governor' (the governor designated to take a particular interest in, for example, school expeditions), and the 'responsible person', must be fully aware from the outset, quite apart from their statutory duties, that they are an integral part of the inspection process. Their involvement in the life of the school, the way they formulate policy and monitor its implementation, their structures etc. will come under the inspectors' microscope. It is not simply a question of governors looking in from the outside whilst the inspection is 'being done' to the school. They should, moreover, take time to familiarise themselves with the detailed Guidance outlined in the Handbook on subject areas and whole-school aspects.

Secondary schools, for example, might wish to include the items listed below in their specification:

- vocational courses, both pre-16 and post-16 (if the school has a sixth form);

- a sample of the subjects, but not necessarily all of them, taught outside the National Curriculum, for example:

   - economics;
   - politics;
   - classics;
   - general studies;

- community provision;

- link courses (offered off-site at the local FE college or in conjunction with other institutions);

- any other features which might entail a modification of the standard specification.

Arrangements can be made for provision that is not included in the specification to be inspected at the same time, but the outcomes will not form part of the official report and the governors will have to bear the additional costs from their own resources.

OFSTED will decide the programme of inspections to be carried out in each academic year which must be put out to tender to inspection providers. Once the contract has been awarded, the RgI will contact the appropriate authority to agree the dates of the inspection. Where agreement cannot be reached, OFSTED will decide when an inspection is to take place.

The governors, headteacher and senior postholders, in particular, of a school that is to be inspected should give serious thought at the preparatory stage to the following issues:

- the benefits to be gained from the experience (e.g. confirmation that the school is doing well; good publicity; how the process might help to develop a renewed sense of teamwork and common purpose, etc);

- how the school will use the inspection findings (e.g. to speed up its development; to inform future priorities);

- how to create a positive climate and use the time available most expeditiously in preparing the ground for the inspection.

In addition, a governing body has certain statutory obligations to fulfil once it has been notified that an inspection has been arranged. These include arranging the meeting for parents, ensuring that the required documentation reaches the inspection team, inviting outside organisations involved with the school to comment and various obligations in connection with the distribution of the report and the action plan that they are required to produce following the inspection. These are dealt with in more detail below.

Parents' Meeting

The governing body must also arrange a meeting between the RgI and parents of pupils at the school ('parent' in this context means every person known to have parental responsibility for, or care of, a child who is a registered pupil at the school). They should choose a date and a time for the meeting which is likely to be convenient for the majority of parents and inform them of the details in writing at least three weeks beforehand. The formal notice of the meeting should contain a statement from the RgI explaining the purpose of the meeting, and an agenda. A standard pro forma may also be included, inviting parental responses to particular questions to ascertain their level of satisfaction with the education being provided for their children. This is obviously of particular value to those parents who are unable to attend the meeting, but would still like their views to be taken into account by the RgI. The pro forma, the formal letter of notification and the agenda may be translated into other languages if appropriate and distributed by pupil post.

The purpose of the meeting is to elicit parents' views on:

- pupils' attainment and progress;
- the attitudes and values which the school promotes;
- the information which the school provides for parents, including reports;
- the help and Guidance available to pupils;
- homework and the contribution that it makes to pupils' progress.

The summary of the pre-inspection commentary may usefully be introduced into proceedings as a means of stimulating discussion.

The RgI should provide feedback on the meeting as soon after the event as practicable to the headteacher and chair of governors.

It should be noted that, although the headteacher and the chair of governors may welcome parents at the outset and introduce the RgI and some of his or her colleagues, attendance at the meeting itself is confined to *bona fide* parents of registered pupils, and that, consequently, only staff and governors who are parents of registered pupils are allowed to attend. The arrangements are obviously designed to encourage parents to raise points of concern without being inhibited by the presence of those with direct responsibility for running the school. The RgI and, indeed, all members of the inspection team might also wish to make themselves reasonably accessible to parents during the inspection period and to take advantage of any opportunities that may arise to discuss issues with, for example, members of the parent–teacher association (PTA), parent governors and other interested groups or individuals.

Where parents raise any significant concerns either before or during an inspection, inspectors are duty bound to refer to them in their feedback to the senior leadership team (SLT) and the governing body and in the published report (both in the full version and in the summary). A 'concern', it should be noted, may be regarded as 'significant', if at least 20 per cent of the parental responses to the questionnaire circulated to parents by the school (which is common practice, but not demanded by legislation) indicate disagreement or strong disagreement with one (or more) of the statements contained in it, or if a significant number of parents raise the concern at the pre-inspection meeting. In the case of the latter, inspectors will be expected to use their professional judgement, expertise and experience to determine 'significance' in relation to the balance of views expressed.

The RgI must make a preliminary visit to the school to familiarise himself or herself with the site and to meet the headteacher and chair of governors at an early stage in proceedings, normally before the parents' meeting. The RgI may be accompanied by one or two members of the core team on this occasion, and it would be beneficial to arrange a meeting with the staff as a whole and some of the other governors at the same time if convenient, or later, to clarify points of procedure, reduce stress and allay anxieties.

Advance Documentation

The RgI will require the school to provide the following documentation in advance of the inspection:

- the school prospectus;
- the school development plan or an equivalent planning document;
- the most recent LEA monitoring report on the school's progress against its targets;
- a timetable of the work of the school for the period of the inspection;
- a plan of the school (ideally with the main subject suites, offices and toilets marked).

All such documentation is returned to the school as a matter of routine after the inspection.

DURING THE INSPECTION

The prospect of some 16 'visitors' (often the case in a large secondary school) descending on a school with a particular agenda – namely to form judgements, which will be made public, on every single aspect of its performance and *modus operandi* – is guaranteed to send some shivers down the proverbial spine and to cause a few flutterings of the heart. An OFSTED week is, therefore, always likely to prove a stressful experience, no matter how well prepared the school is or how good a job it may genuinely think it is doing. It should, moreover, be remembered that the inspection week will usually reflect, albeit in an accentuated form, the spirit, atmosphere and ethos, etc, that normally pervade the school and that a conspicuous or strange departure from what is expected, for example on the part of the headteacher, may of itself give rise to additional stress and confusion. Where difficulties are likely to be encountered or known shortcomings highlighted, it is important to engender a positive frame of mind and to emphasise the steps that have already been taken to remedy the weaknesses in question.

The headteacher should endeavour to maintain daily contact with the RgI (preferably before the school day begins) to discuss how the inspection is progressing and to be on the alert to nip in the bud any difficulties or problems that may arise. The headteacher will, moreover, need to be on hand to provide any additional information which the inspection team may seek. It is sensible to keep in close touch with the chair of governors throughout the week and to set aside a time at the end of each day, for example from 5 pm to 6 pm, for senior management to review progress and discuss plans or approaches for the remainder of the inspection period.

Practical Arrangements

Schools should provide the inspection team with:

- a secure, lockable room with adequate information technology (IT) facilities, in which inspectors may store confidential items and conduct private meetings and discussions (make prior arrangements with the caretaker to enable team members to stay late!);

- visitors' name badges;

- access to telephone and photocopying facilities;

- suitable car parking;

- refreshment facilities and details of the lunch arrangements.

Additional Documentation

Inspectors will require access to the following documents during the inspection in addition to those which were provided beforehand:

- departmental schemes of work;

- teachers' lesson plans and records;

- pupils' records, reports and correspondence with parents;

- registers of attendance;

- statements of SEN;

- individual pupil education plans;

- other similar documents or policies.

Schools will want to ensure that the data contained in their pre-inspection commentary is accurate in advance of an inspection and to draw the inspectors' attention to any errors or inaccuracies that may have been identified. The inspector will have access to the previous inspection and performance and assessment reports (PANDAs) of the school.

Evidence

In addition to a careful analysis of the available documentation, the members of an inspection team will take account of a whole range of supporting evidence in formulating their opinions. This evidence must include:

- observation of lessons and extra-curricular activities and seeing how the school runs on a day-to-day basis;
- tracking school processes such as evaluation and performance management;
- joining meetings such as school council or management meetings and observing management processes (such as monitoring) directly;
- scrutiny of a sample of pupils' current and recent work;
- discussion with pupils;
- discussion with teachers, governors, parents and others involved in the work of the school;
- analysing records of pupils with special educational needs (SEN) including individual education plans (IEPS), statements, annual reviews and transitional reviews.

The Framework emphasises that in considering school policies, it is their effectiveness that is central. It indicates that it should be unnecessary to analyse policies in detail because it is the practice that stems from them that is important.

Feedback

It should be remembered that, although the judgements of an inspection team are not negotiable, the evidence upon which such judgements are based may be challenged – which in turn may lead to a modification or a retraction of some of the judgements. It is, however, impossible for schools to challenge evidence if they have to rely entirely on the memory or impressions of their staff: they must, therefore, be ready to collect their own evidence in a systematic way. Pro formas should be devised for staff to complete as soon as possible after they have had a lesson visit from an inspector, for example, or following a discussion with a member of the team. The same principle applies to the parents' meeting, and those staff and governors who are entitled to attend should be primed to take notes. Initially, the use of tape recorders at any stage of the inspection process was strictly prohibited, but this is now a matter for the RgI's discretion and OFSTED is prepared to accept the tape-recording of feedback sessions, if the RgI agrees.

Feedback has often been called the 'breakfast of champions' and it is incumbent on all members of an inspection team, but especially the RgI, to ensure that any feedback they give reflects careful preparation, affords sufficient scope for clarification, is unequivocal in its judgements (on what has gone well and where there is room for further improvement), and takes place in a climate conducive to a proper professional dialogue.

Feedback must be provided to individual teachers and other staff in respect of the work the inspectors have seen. The Framework says that 'Inspectors must be clear in explaining their judgements about the quality of teaching and any identified strengths and weaknesses, so that teachers will know how to improve their work'.

In addition, inspectors will give feedback during the course of the inspection to leaders and managers responsible for areas of learning, subjects or curriculum areas.

The lead inspector will produce for the headteacher a confidential profile of the quality of teaching for the whole school. The profile will show the number of lessons seen taught by each qualified teacher which were graded in accordance with a 1–7 scale. It would normally be given to the headteacher no later than the formal debriefing referred to below.

The lead inspector should give a brief interim feedback to the headteacher ideally before leaving the school at the end of the inspection. At this stage, the inspector should inform the headteacher if the inspection team has judged or might judge the school to require special measures, has an inadequate sixth form, shows serious weaknesses or is underachieving. This interim feedback will be followed by a more formal and considered debriefing once the team has had time to reflect on the evidence and its judgments. This meeting is likely to be attended by senior staff. The LEA would not be represented except in exceptional circumstances, examples given in the Framework being where the headteacher is holding a temporary appointment or where the headteacher may be distressed by the findings.

Formal debriefing is then provided to the governing body. The headteacher would normally be present and the governing body (whose meeting it is) may invite the LEA to be represented. This debriefing will be less detailed than that to the headteacher.

The feedback will be concerned with the significant judgements of the team in relation to, for example:

- the effectiveness of the school's management and leadership (middle and senior);
- standards of achievement and progress;
- the main strengths and weaknesses of the teaching observed (and the prime factors that account for these);
- the key issues for improvement.

Schools may not readily appreciate at the time of their feedback or debriefing sessions that they will not normally have another chance of querying the evidence or judgements contained in the subject reports until the draft version of the full report appears. If, therefore, after receiving any feedback, staff remain uneasy about the justification of some of the statements which have been made, they should inform the SLT so that the issues can be specifically raised preferably in the debriefing to the headteacher or, failing this, in the debriefing to the governing body. The opportunity may otherwise be lost for ever, because both of these meetings are usually devoted exclusively to the presentation of the main findings and key action points (as indicated above). While the use of visual aids is encouraged, the draft report itself will not be available at the feedback or debriefings. The draft will be submitted subsequently and the school then has only five working days in which to comment on factual accuracy. The school cannot at that stage challenge any judgment that is made unless the judgment depends for its validity on facts that are successfully challenged.

Celebration

The end of an inspection is an opportunity for celebration, at least for those that are not totally exhausted or traumatised by the process. A post-inspection party will gives staff an opportunity of relaxing, unwinding and sharing their week's experiences in an informal, convivial setting. This should be well publicised in advance so that governors can attend and share in the corporate feelings.

RE-INSPECTION

Inspection is a routine cyclical event. A school can currently expect to be inspected every six years. Those that are adjudged to be performing poorly or to be deteriorating significantly are inspected more frequently. The precise timing is determined by HMCI. In drawing up the programme for each school he will:

- ensure that the schools due to be inspected in each year constitute a properly balanced sample in terms of geographical location, size, performance and type;

- ensure that the sample includes schools that might on the evidence of previous inspections serve as models of good practice;

- include schools that are regarded as performing poorly in respect of the five main criteria listed below:

  - low attainment by pupils or a significant decline in the school's performance in terms of pupil attainment;
  - poor progress by pupils in relation to their prior attainment;
  - weaknesses in the quality of education (particularly teaching) which the school provides;
  - weaknesses in pupils' behaviour and personal development or poor attendance;
  - weaknesses in the management and efficiency of the school (in the case of nursery and special schools, the first of the five criteria listed above does not apply and reference is only made to the findings of the previous inspection);

- have regard to circumstances which may make it necessary or desirable to include particular schools that:

  - are failing to fulfil their statutory duties;
  - are linked (e.g. infant and junior schools on the same
  - site) and would, therefore, benefit from a co-ordinated inspection;
  - have been opened as new establishments or have
  - experienced a significant change of character or status;
  - exceptionally, are deemed to warrant closer investigation in the light of information received from the headteacher, the governing body or the LEA.

The inspection team will start from the previous inspection findings and has access to all the data provided by the previous inspection. Inspectors will not only evaluate the school's current standards, provision and performance, but will also analyse the 'progress' that the school has made in the intervening period and establish the extent to which it has improved, maintained its earlier excellence (which is regarded as the equivalent of improvement), or deteriorated, as well as identifying the main reason(s) for that 'progress'. Inspectors are, besides, obliged to assess whether the school has the capacity (i.e. the leadership, structures, strategies and systems available) to secure improvement or to maintain high standards. When completing the school's profile, the RgI is required to summarise judgements on both improvement and capacity on a 1–7 scale, where 2 = very good, 4 = satisfactory and 6 = poor.

When formulating their judgements, inspectors will take particular note of:

- improvements in performance since the last inspection. This is a key feature of the new reporting format;
- the school's own priorities for improvement;
- any self-evaluation reports (including details of the school's internal monitoring processes), analyses of the school's performance over time and any data available to the school from the LEA or other sources;
- changes in the school's characteristics (e.g. the attainment of pupils on entry, the admissions criteria and socio-economic circumstances, and high pupil mobility) and other factors, including changes in staff, senior management and accommodation that might affect the way in which the school operates.

THE INSPECTION REPORT

The report is in two parts, a summary followed by a commentary.

The summary, which must contain all statutory reporting requirements and required judgements, will cover:

- information about the school;
- how good the school is;
- what the school does well;
- what could be improved and whether the school is underachieving or is identified as having serious weakness or requiring special measures;
- improvement or otherwise since the last inspection;

- pupils' attitudes and values;
- teaching and learning;
- school leadership and management;
- parents' and carers' views of the school;
- any other aspects.

The commentary will effectively provide the backing evidence for the conclusions shown in the summary. It will vary according to whether the inspection is a short one or a full one. In a short inspection, the commentary will concentrate on what the school does well, what could be improved and what the school can do to achieve that improvement. The commentary in a full inspection will naturally take a wider and more comprehensive view of the school and will comment particularly on overall standards, leadership and management, relationships with pupils and parents and the quality of teaching. Both forms will have data relating to the school and a summary of parental responses to their questionnaire.

Seriously Misleading Reports

These may be conveniently defined as reports which essentially paint a false picture of the school and present the quality of education provided in a substantially better or worse light than the evidence warrants.

The procedure for dealing with seriously misleading reports is as follows:

- the report is assessed against OFSTED's usual quality assurance criteria;
- if it is accepted as being seriously misleading, both the contractor and the RgI are asked for an explanation. Where the report fails to match up to the required standards, but is not seriously misleading, the RgI is contacted in the normal way and warned that he or she may be de-registered if the standard of reports continues to fall below par;
- if the RgI's explanation is regarded as reasonable, the matter rests there. Although OFSTED states quite unequivocally that each case will be treated on its merits, it would normally consider an explanation to be reasonable if the RgI was under particular personal pressure or happened to be ill at the time of the inspection, or if the report had been altered by the contractor without the agreement/knowledge of the

RgI or if the school being inspected had provided misleading or inaccurate data which the RgI had, therefore, been obliged to accept at face value;

- if the RgI's explanation is not accepted, a decision has to be made about his or her status and whether he or she should be de-registered. When coming to such a decision, OFSTED takes into consideration the individual's previous track record, the extent to which the report under investigation is seriously misleading, the explanations advanced by the contractor and the RgI, and any other factors which may be deemed relevant.

In cases where OFSTED concludes that a report is seriously misleading, the school in question is normally afforded the opportunity of a full inspection within 18 months or a short follow-up inspection (which could be undertaken by HMI) as soon as possible after the event.

COMPLAINTS

There are three basic ways of lodging a complaint about the conduct of an inspection and other related issues. The first, and in many respects the fairest, is to raise the complaint directly with the RgI and the contractor as soon as it has arisen. This approach has the additional merit, apart from natural justice, that the precise details can be recalled fairly accurately because of their proximity to events (before memories fade) and because the cause(s) of the grievance(s) have not had a chance to harden with the passage of time. In most cases, one would hope that the difficulties could be resolved without going any further. The other possibilities are:

- to telephone the OFSTED helpline;
- to make a formal written complaint to Inspection Quality Division, OFSTED.

Complaints are not considered when more than a year has elapsed since the date of the inspection.

Unfortunately, from the school's point of view, even if a complaint is subsequently upheld, it can often be too late to redress the injustice, because the inspection will have been completed and the report published.

It is helpful from OFSTED's point of view if:

- one person co-ordinates all aspects of a complaint;

- the complaints are grouped under headings that correspond to the various sections of the *Framework*;

- the presentation of the evidence is succinct, yet sufficiently detailed to permit the exercise of sound judgement.

Where complaints refer to the conduct of the RgI or a team inspector, it will often be difficult for OFSTED to come down on one side or the other because of the differing perceptions of the same event, although, when the RgI is not the subject of the complaint, he or she may be in a position to support the complainant. Where the complainant claims that erroneous judgements have been made, it is open to OFSTED to carry out an internal investigation of the evidence to see if, for example:

- the requirements of the *Framework* have been observed;

- the wording of the report properly reflects the judgments which have been formed;

- the judgments are firmly rooted in the evidence.

Where the substance of a complaint has been upheld, an addendum slip may be issued to rectify any factual inaccuracies in the report, which can then be sent out by the school to all interested parties, or a new, amended report produced in the event of grave errors, or, in extreme cases, a report may be declared null and void. The school may in this case also be offered the opportunity of a fresh inspection.

If the complainant remains dissatisfied, the matter may be referred to the OFSTED Complaints Adjudicator within three months of the final response to the school's complaint.

Identifying Team Inspectors on Inspection Reports

The following requirements are intended to increase the accountability of individual team members and to enhance the quality of their work:

- the inspection report must include the name and address of the inspection contractor and a list of all the members of an inspection team;

- the list of inspectors will show the subjects or courses for which each inspector had a lead role in inspecting or co-ordinating evidence and judgements. The inspectors responsible for co-ordinating the team's evidence, judgments and inspection findings on the under-fives, English as an additional language, equal opportunities, and special educational needs will also be identified;

- the summary report for parents will include the names of the RgI and the inspection contractor and the latter's address.

Compliance

Governors need to be aware of their obligation to comply with the statutory regulations on several counts. Inspectors are required to check that compliance is being observed in respect of, for example:

- the National Curriculum;
- religious education and collective worship;
- financial arrangements (especially value for money);
- appraisal;
- health and safety aspects;
- the Children Act 1989;
- copyright;
- attendance;
- the SEN Code of Practice;
- sex education;
- information in the prospectus.

Whilst governors are not bound by any statutory requirements to produce an SIP (see Chapter 3 for a detailed explanation), there is a *de facto* supposition that it should exist (because it is indicative of good management), and inspectors will expect to be shown a copy, and, indeed, see evidence of its implementation.

Governors are under an obligation to afford the inspection team every opportunity of making a full and fair assessment of their school throughout the inspection period, by giving ready and easy access to all the relevant documentation (apart from personal appraisal statements), lessons and discussions with key members of the governing body, staff and pupils. No part of a school's premises is off limits and potentially every nook and cranny may be investigated – and governors should be aware that wilful obstruction in this context is an offence in law.

DENOMINATIONAL INSPECTION

Governing bodies of VA, VC or foundation schools which have been designated as having a religious character by the Secretary of State and which provide denominational RE have the additional responsibility of making arrangements for the inspection of RE, and are obliged to indicate on Form S that they offer denominational education when they are consulted about their school's specification for inspection.

It is clearly sensible from a practical viewpoint to arrange for denominational inspection to occur at the same time as the main OFSTED inspection. Indeed, governors are positively encouraged to do so by the fact that grants for the cost of the additional inspection arrangements are not normally payable if denominational education is not inspected in the same academic year as the whole school curriculum. It should be noted that payment of the grant (which is cash limited depending on the type of school) will be authorised only when governors produce documentary proof of the expenditure incurred, i.e. a copy of the report and the summary, together with the relevant receipts for payments made.

When making arrangements for denominational inspection, governing bodies should be aware that:

- in the case of VC schools, the choice of inspector is the responsibility of the foundation governors only, even though they may not constitute a majority on the governing body;

- there is no requirement for the inspector chosen to be OFSTED trained or registered, but if the inspector is to be an integral part of the RgI's team, rather than to work alongside the team at the same time, then the inspector would naturally have to possess the same qualifications;

- the main school inspection will none the less cover the spiritual, moral, social and cultural development of pupils;

- the RgI must report on whether the school complies with the requirement to provide a daily act of collective worship, but not on the contents of acts of worship;

- they should consult those who appoint the school's foundation governors on the choice of an appropriate inspector (different practices operate in different areas, but in the case of a Roman Catholic school, for example, it is not unusual for the diocesan authorities to provide a shortlist of suitable candidates enabling governing bodies to select the inspector that best fits their particular bill);

- they will have to enter into a formal contract with the chosen RE inspector which meets the statutory requirements for the inspection of denominational education. The chosen inspector must report on RE and on the content of acts of collective worship (including how they are conducted) and may also comment on pupils' spiritual, moral, social and cultural development;

- they do not have to organise a meeting with parents in advance of the inspection of denominational education, although there is a clear expectation that the chosen inspector will endeavour to ascertain parental views in this context;

- the reporting arrangements for the inspection of denominational education are broadly similar to those for the main OFSTED inspection and are dealt with later in this chapter. The inspector is, however, only required to deliver his or her report to the governing body and not to OFSTED.

Non-denominational schools, and schools that have a religious character but which do not offer denominational RE are dealt with as follows:

(1) foundation/voluntary schools that are not formally designated as having a religious character, special schools, community schools and any other school will have their RE and collective worship inspected as part of the ordinary OFSTED inspection;

(2) foundation/voluntary schools that are designated as having a religious character, but do not offer denominational RE, will similarly have their RE inspected as part of the ordinary OFSTED inspection unless parents at the school have opted for their children to receive denominational RE, in which case the denominational inspection scheme applies. That scheme applies to the content of collective worship in any event for schools in this category.

PUPIL REFERRAL UNITS

PRUs were established as schools under the Education Act 1996. They are administered/managed directly by education authorities and serve as one of the means whereby LEAs carry out their statutory duties to provide suitable full-time or part-time education otherwise than at school for pupils who, by virtue of illness, exclusion from school or some other reason, would not otherwise receive suitable education. It should be noted that PRUs are not bound by all of the statutory requirements which apply to mainstream schools, and OFSTED does not produce a comparative pre-inspection context and school indicator report (PICSI) for Pupil Referral Units (PRUs).

In particular, PRUs are not required:

- to teach the subjects of the National Curriculum or RE;
- to undertake assessment at the end of the Key Stages;
- to report annually to parents on pupils' progress in the subjects of the National Curriculum (although a report must still be issued).

The curriculum of a PRU should none the less:

- satisfy the requirement of being broad and balanced;
- comply with the LEA's curriculum policy laid down for PRUs;
- give reasonable attention to the National Curriculum programmes of study;
- provide for sex education in accordance with its published policy;
- be planned so as to enable its pupils to be reintegrated after a relatively short period of time into mainstream or special schools or to proceed to further education or employment.

POST-INSPECTION

As already mentioned, an RgI is statutorily bound to discuss the main findings of an inspection with the headteacher and other members of staff (usually the SLT) whom the headteacher wishes to be present at the meeting, and separately with the governing body as soon as possible after the inspection (normally in the following week) and before the report is finalised. The RgI now has six weeks rather than five for the completion of the report, to allow the school more time to consider the factual accuracy of the draft report. The onus is on the contractor to ensure that the appropriate authority at the school is given at least one week for such reflection.

Distribution of the Report

The report of the inspection, together with a summary, must be produced within six weeks of the end of the inspection (i.e. the last day on which the inspection team completed its work on the school site) and sent by the RgI to:

- the appropriate authority (normally the governing body, or the proprietor of a CTC or CCTA);

- OFSTED;

- the LEA (in the case of maintained schools with delegated budgets);

- those who appoint the foundation governors (if relevant);

- the headteacher;

- the LEA or the governing body, whichever is not the appropriate authority (in the case of foundation, community, VC, VA or maintained special schools);

- any person identified as a sponsor of the school in the instruments of government;

- the LEA (in the case of non-maintained special schools where the LEA is funding a pupil).

On receipt of the report and the summary, the governing body must:

- send a copy of the summary to the parents of every registered pupil;

- make arrangements for a copy of the report and the summary to be made available to any member of the public who wishes to see it at a time and place as may be deemed reasonable;

- provide any person who asks for it with a copy of the documents.

Single copies of the summary must be provided free of charge, but a charge may be levied for multiple copies and copies of the full report, provided that it does not exceed the cost of reproduction, although the governing body may decide to provide all the documentation free of charge, especially for parents.

Schools should, in general, try to ensure that the existence of the report is widely known and should arrange for copies to be sent as a matter of routine to:

- the local press;
- public libraries;
- all the local businesses which were notified of the inspection at the outset.

Clearly, feeder primary schools (and prospective parents) would also be interested in the outcome of an inspection of a secondary school, and governing bodies may wish to make copies of the report available to these institutions, too, as part of their initial circulation.

In schools where there are parents whose first language is not English, the governing body will need to decide whether to translate the summary or the full report (or both) into a language other than English (or Welsh).

Action Planning

The governing body must draw up its response to the key issues for action identified in the report in the form of an action plan within 40 working days (which exclude holidays of one week or more) of receiving the report. Governing bodies of schools judged to be failing or in need of special measures, owing to the urgency of the situation, are often given less time to draw up their responses. Although schools are able to use the full statutory period for devising their action plans, it is advisable for them to begin working on their response to the report as soon as they have been given their formal feedback in the week following the inspection.

There are, however, several ways in which they could approach their task. One suggestion is to distribute each of the key issues for action to a small group to work on. Each of the sub-groups might consist of a deputy head, a senior teacher and one or two governors, but clearly a whole range of permutations is possible. A series of meetings would then be held at the school, where the issues could be debated at some length. Other members of staff might be invited to attend such meetings to add their particular views. When all the groups have completed their task and produced some draft recommendations, they should report back to a full meeting of the governing body. The separate parts of the plan should be discussed in detail to eliminate any inconsistencies or misunderstandings and then drawn together into a coherent entity. After the finished article has been formally approved and sanctioned by the governing body as a whole, it can be sent off to OFSTED as required.

Schools should also be ready to manage the media and to prepare a carefully considered press release, which will highlight all the good points that are mentioned in the report, and include some personal celebratory comments from the headteacher and/or chair of governors: this is not a moment to stand back in due modesty and let nature take its course! The steps which the school has already taken to tackle or implement some of the key issues might also usefully be mentioned.

The action plan will normally specify for each of the key issues:

- the definition of the issue;
- a specific target or outcome;
- a strict time-frame;
- the success criteria (i.e. how schools will know that they have achieved what was wanted);
- who will do what, when, etc;
- the person predominantly responsible for its implementation;
- the resources required;
- the procedures for monitoring and evaluation.

An inspection represents a snapshot of schools at a particular point in time and it is normal practice to incorporate the key issues identified for action into the ongoing plans for development which schools have previously formulated, instead of abandoning these and concentrating exclusively on the OFSTED issues. Whichever approach is adopted, however, the governing body is obliged to state in its plan the date(s) by which action will be taken on each item mentioned in the report as a key issue for action.

Once the action plan has been drawn up, the governing body must send a copy of it within five working days of its completion to:

- the parents of all registered pupils at the school;
- all those employed at the school;
- OFSTED;
- the LEA (if the school is LEA-maintained);
- the LEA or the governing body, whichever is not the appropriate authority;
- those who appoint core, sponsor or foundation governors (or the diocese, if different);

- the LEA (in the case of a non-maintained special school where the LEA is funding a pupil).

In addition, copies of the action plan must be made available for inspection by any member of the public, and a single copy provided free of charge on request to anyone living within a three-mile radius of the school (the provisions for 'charging' in this context are those outlined earlier in this chapter in relation to the full report). As with the report and its summary, action plans may be translated into a language other than English. Governing bodies must, moreover, include in each subsequent annual report to parents a statement of the progress made towards implementing the latest action plan.

An interesting review of action plans has been conducted by OFSTED and published in a report entitled *Planning Improvement – Schools' Post-Inspection Action Plans*. The report provides useful Guidance on:

- effective preparation;
- good action plans:
  - addressing key issues;
  - clarity of plans;
  - targeting improvements;
  - measures for monitoring progress;
  - resource and financial implications;
  - effective implementation:
- managing improvement;
- improvement through inspection;
- monitoring and evaluating outcomes,

as well as setting out a number of recommendations.

Governors should also take account of the joint DfES/OFSTED publication *Setting Targets to Raise Standards: A Survey of Good Practice*. The obvious connection between planning, school improvement and school effectiveness is highlighted, and the booklet offers helpful advice on:

- the nature of target-setting;
- target-setting within the school development plan;
- target-setting in primary and secondary schools (with suitable exemplars on the use of, for example, departmental indicators of success, baseline assessment, standardised reading tests, and the targeting of specific pupils);

- target-setting and the role of the governing body;
- the role of the LEA in target-setting.

SCHOOLS REQUIRING SPECIAL MEASURES

Special measures are required if a school is failing or is likely to fail to provide an acceptable standard of education for its pupils. It is unlikely that schools will be categorised in this way on the basis of a single adverse feature or characteristic, but rather on the balance of the available evidence, and those that are adjudged to be in need of special measures usually fall down on several counts. For example, inspection teams might reach such a conclusion where there is widespread and significantly poor attainment and progress, the breakdown of discipline is imminent, staff are demoralised and have lost confidence in the headteacher, and the pupils are at serious and/or physical risk. Some 3 per cent of schools nationally qualify for inclusion in the special measures category.

Factors to be Taken into Account

The factors which inspectors have to take into account when formulating their judgements in this context are:

(1)   Educational Standards Achieved

- low attainment and poor progress in the subjects of the curriculum by the majority of pupils or consistently among particular groups of pupils. This will be evident in poor examination, National Curriculum assessment and other accredited results;
- regular disruptive behaviour, breakdown of discipline or high levels of exclusions;
- significant levels of racial tension or harassment;
- poor attendance by a substantial proportion of pupils or by particular groups of pupils or high levels of truancy.

(2)   Quality of Education Provided

- a high proportion of unsatisfactory teaching, including low expectation of pupils;
- failure to implement the National Curriculum;

- very poor provision for pupils' spiritual, moral, social and cultural development;

- pupils at physical or emotional risk from other pupils or adults in the school;

- abrasive and confrontational relationships between staff and pupils.

(3)   The Management and Efficiency of the School

- ineffectiveness of the headteacher, senior management or governors;

- significant loss of confidence in the headteacher by the staff, parents or governors;

- demoralisation and disenchantment among staff or high levels of staff turnover or absence;

- poor management and inefficient use made of the resources, including finance, available to the school;

- poor value for money provided by the school.

When, as a result of an inspection, an RgI believes a school to be in need of special measures, he or she must:

- inform the headteacher at the end of the inspection;

- offer an oral report to the governing body soon after the inspection has finished;

- send a draft copy of the report to HMCI within six weeks of the inspection.

Within three weeks of receiving the draft copy, a small team (comprising a minimum of two inspectors) of Her Majesty's Inspectorate will pay a two-day visit (normally) to the school to inspect the areas which were adjudged to be particularly weak in the draft report and to check the validity of the RgI's opinions. This is to ensure that such an important decision is not reliant merely on the internal evidence provided in the report, but is corroborated by additional independent verification. When the HMIs in question have concluded their visit and reported on it to HMCI, he will decide whether or not to support the RgI's judgements and will inform the RgI accordingly. HMCI can agree or not as the case may be. HMCI is also empowered to extend the period for the preparation of the inspection report up to a maximum of three months beyond the date when the report should have been issued. The RgI may publish his or her report only when HMCI has declared whether or not he agrees with the judgement that the school requires special measures. The RgI must incorporate HMCI's verdict into the report. If HMCI concurs with the RgI's viewpoint, the provisions relating to special measures will be triggered.

The same principles hold good in the case of a school inspected in the first instance by HMIs, except that their judgement does not need to be confirmed by HMCI.

Any report which contains an opinion that special measures are required must be sent to HMCI and the Secretary of State, as well as to all those on the 'normal' distribution list.

Where a report expresses the opinion that special measures are needed (and the report has been produced by an RgI) and HMCI agrees with that opinion, the appropriate authority, i.e. the governing body of a school with a delegated budget, and the LEA in other cases, must prepare an action plan within 40 days (not counting weekends, bank holidays or school holidays totalling more than five working days). Once the action plan has been prepared, it must be distributed to all interested parties (essentially the same as those outlined earlier). The Secretary of State may impose a tighter time-scale if the urgency of the situation warrants it. Each subsequent annual report to parents of the affected school must state the extent to which the proposals set out in the statement have been carried into effect.

Remedial Options

In the case of a school that is failing to provide an acceptable standard of education for its pupils and is deemed to require special measures, several options are available to rectify the weaknesses which have been diagnosed. The different approaches which are permissible in different contexts and types of school are described later in the text, but in general the range depicted below reflects those most commonly adopted:

- the governing body:
    - formulates its action plan;
- the LEA:
    - issues a commentary on the appropriate authority's action plan;
    - produces a statement of any course of action it proposes to undertake;
    - may suspend a school's delegated budget;

    – may appoint additional governors;

- the Secretary of State:

    – may appoint additional governors;

    – may decide to close the school (although it may subsequently re-open as a Fresh Start school).

The School's Action Plan

Action plans formulated in this context clearly have much in common with those described above. The fundamental aim of the plan should be to remove the school from special measures at the earliest opportunity and certainly within two years of receiving the inspection report. The action plan must address all of the key concerns and specify:

- what is going to be done;
- who is going to do it;
- when it will be done;
- what additional resources are needed;
- the success criteria against which progress will be measured;
- how progress will be monitored and evaluated.

It should be noted that it is the LEA's responsibility to formulate the action plan where financial delegation has been withdrawn prior to the receipt of the inspection report.

The LEA's Action Plan

The LEA must produce its own commentary on the governing body's action plan within 10 days of receiving it. This should assess the effectiveness of the plan put forward and the school's ability to implement it. It should also indicate any areas which the governors may inadvertently have omitted to include and how long the LEA has been aware of the school's difficulties. The LEA must also prepare a statement of any action that it proposes to take. This statement and the accompanying commentary should be sent to the DfES, the governing body of the school and HMCI. The LEA is bound to consult the appropriate authority, i.e. the Bishop of the Diocese in the case of a Roman Catholic school or the Diocesan Board of Education for a Church of England school or the person (body) appointing the foundation governors, before producing these documents.

The statement of action should focus primarily and in some depth on the future options for the school. LEAs are expected:

- to assess whether or not the school should be closed;

- to specify, if it is to stay open, a target date for its removal from special measures;

- to outline the nature and scale of support to be provided;

- to put forward alternative proposals where the commentary has identified any ineffectual aspects of the governors' action plan;

- to state whether the LEA's reserve legal powers (e.g. the appointment of additional governors or suspension of the school's right to a delegated budget) will be invoked.

Suspension of Delegated Budget

If the LEA's statement of action and commentary have been sent to the Secretary of State and duly acknowledged, and 10 days have elapsed since the acknowledgement, the LEA may decide, after informing the governing body and the headteacher, to suspend the school's right to a delegated budget. LEAs will thereby be in a better position to exercise greater (and more direct) influence over staffing and other financial aspects of the school.

The Appointment of Additional Governors

The LEA is empowered to appoint as many additional governors as it thinks fit. If several additional governors are appointed, the composition of the governing body could be altered quite radically. Such an eventuality, however, may be deliberately engineered by the LEA to enable the new governors to exercise a significant influence over the school's affairs and bring about the desired improvement. Governors appointed in these circumstances are not subject to the normal restrictions that limit membership to the governing bodies of a maximum of two schools. The duration of their term of office is not clear; the Guidance offered in Circular 17/93 states only that they will remain in office until their term of appointment expires.

The appropriate authority in the case of VA schools may exercise similar powers (so as to preserve its majority).

The Secretary of State may decide to appoint additional governors of his own – in which case neither the LEA nor the diocesan authorities (if applicable) are permitted to make any additional appointments. Similarly, if the Secretary of State has appointed additional governors, the LEA is not entitled to proceed with the suspension of a delegated budget; if it has already done so, the suspension will have to be revoked.

Closure

The Secretary of State may decide at any stage to issue directions that a school under special measures should be closed. Statutory proposals do not need to be published in such instances. He must, however, consult the governing body of the school concerned, the LEA, the diocesan authorities (in the case of a denominational school), or the body which appoints the foundation governors in the case of non-religious foundation or voluntary schools, and any other persons or groups as he may see fit, before giving a direction to discontinue the school.

Monitoring

HMI will usually visit a school under special measures some six months after the school was first inspected to check on the progress that has been registered in the interim and to assess:

- the quality of the governors' action plan and the LEA's statement;

- the target date for removal from special measures (i.e. whether or not the school is still on track as scheduled);

- the effectiveness of the LEA's programme of support.

After the visit, HMI's considered findings will be reported to the headteacher, the Secretary of State, the governing body, the LEA, and the diocese (if applicable). If the weaknesses have persisted in a material sense, a revised action plan (and a revised LEA statement of action) may be deemed necessary; if this is the case, the relevant documentation must be sent to HMI within 25 working days of the visit. If HMI is still dissatisfied, it will communicate its concerns to the DfES, which will then convene an urgent meeting to discuss the steps that need to be taken to achieve an acceptable rate of improvement.

Thereafter, HMI will normally visit the school once a term. The school is required on each occasion to produce in advance a brief summary of progress against each key issue since the last visit, with details of the improvements which have been made and any important changes that may have occurred. This must be sent to HMI at least one week before the HMI is due to arrive at the school. After each visit, HMI will comment on:

- progress since the last visit;
- progress since the original inspection.

When eventually, following a monitoring visit, HMI is of the opinion that the school no longer requires special measures, a two-day mini-inspection, usually involving two inspectors, will be arranged to confirm the judgement. All being well, a report is produced, giving the school a clean bill of health.

SCHOOLS WITH SERIOUS WEAKNESSES

There is a marked tendency for schools with serious weaknesses to drift into the number of those requiring special measures. For this reason, even if they have judged that a school is providing an acceptable standard of education, inspectors must go on to consider whether it nevertheless has serious weaknesses. If they decide that the school does have serious weaknesses, the RgI must inform the school's senior management team and the appropriate authority and the judgement must be stated in the main findings of the report using the following, prescribed, wording: 'In my judgement this school is giving its pupils an acceptable standard of education, but it nevertheless has serious weaknesses'. The action, moreover, deemed necessary to remedy the weaknesses diagnosed must be clearly specified in the key issues. The RgI must also notify the School Improvement Division in OFSTED of the judgement, initially by telephone, before the school is informed, and subsequently on Form 2, a copy of which is reproduced in the text of the OFSTED booklet.

Schools falling into this category (which constitute an additional 10 per cent nationally) usually exhibit serious shortcomings in certain areas, i.e. where one or more of the following factors are in evidence:

- standards are unsatisfactory in four or more subjects either across the school as a whole, or at particular Key Stages, especially where poor performance in English, mathematics and science has been identified;
- the quality of teaching and learning is unsatisfactory or poor in more than 25 per cent of lessons;

- the standards of pupils' behaviour and conduct, or relationships generally, are giving cause for concern;

- the management is ineffective;

- the school does not give value for money;

- the level of attendance is below 90 per cent;

- fewer than 20 per cent of pupils achieve five or more GCSE grade A–C passes (in a secondary school);

- there are more than five or 25 exclusions (presumably per annum) in a primary or secondary school respectively (it is not clear whether this refers to permanent or fixed-term exclusions).

The response in the case of schools exhibiting serious weaknesses is essentially the same as that outlined above for those requiring special measures, except that the timetable should be designed to eliminate the causes of weakness within one year of the school receiving the inspection report. Where, after analysis by HMI, the DfES and HMI are satisfied that the school's action plan and the LEA's statement will be able to rectify the weaknesses, the school will simply assume its place in HMI's monitoring cycle and the LEA will arrange to review progress with the school formally roughly once a term. If, however, the proposed measures are thought inadequate, a revised action plan may be demanded, as before, and, in extremis, an urgent meeting of all interested parties may be summoned.

HMI will usually go to the school some six months or more after the event, to see whether any significant improvement has been effected. Where the school has managed to remedy the weaknesses identified, or is well on the way to doing so with the implementation of its action plan, it is likely to be left alone to conduct its affairs, although all schools with serious weaknesses are inspected by an RgI about two years after their initial inspection, as a matter of routine. If, however, a visit by HMI reveals that the school has deteriorated in the interim or made very little progress towards a recovery, the LEA will be exhorted to employ its powers of intervention. If it has already intervened to little effect, HMI will be sent in to assess progress – and it may determine that the school requires special measures. In this event, the procedures outlined previously will apply, except that a more rapid rate of progress (than over two years) is likely to be insisted upon in view of the support the school will already have received.

The DfES Circular 6/99, as well as dealing in considerable detail with schools under special measures and those with serious weaknesses, provides useful Guidance on the issue of a formal warning and Circular 10/2002 'Schools Causing Concern' is also useful.

As well as the categories of schools requiring special measures and schools with serious weaknesses, OFSTED also now has a third category of schools described as 'under-achieving schools'. This is a judgement that may be made in either a short or a full inspection. It will be made on the basis of performance data and inspection judgements taken together and will consider:

- the effectiveness of the school;
- improvement since the last inspection;
- the performance of the school in comparison with schools in similar contexts.

The performance data that will be taken into account, looking at the highest Key Stage in the school (up to age 16), will be:

- the school's results, compared with all schools nationally;
- the school's results, compared with schools in similar contexts using QCA benchmarks;
- whether the school's average National Curriculum levels are improving over time, compared with the trend in national average National Curriculum levels.

In most cases, the comparison with other schools will be based on QCA free school meals banding.

The most significant indicator of under-achievement in sixth forms will be the extent to which the value-added figure from GCSE to A level or Advanced Vocational Certificate of Education (AVCE) (which has replaced Advanced GNVQ) is significantly below the national average figure.

Under-achievement is a judgement that may be made even about schools that seem to be flying high in the league tables. It may be seen as an indication that the school may be moving towards having serious weaknesses, perhaps because results are not improving sufficiently well or because there are concerns about aspects of teaching, learning, leadership or management that at present fall short of a judgement that the school has serious weaknesses.

THE INSPECTION OF LEAs

Inspections of LEAs are carried under the terms of the Education Act 1997. They must be conducted by HMI, who may be accompanied by 'additional inspectors' and other nominees of HMCI, including representatives of the Audit Commission. The purpose of such inspections is to gauge the quality of the services provided by LEAs in relation to their educational provision for:

- pupils of compulsory school age (including pupils educated otherwise than at school);

- other pupils who are registered at schools maintained by them.

The services that come within the inspection's purview are grouped into three main categories:

- advisory/inspection and curriculum support;

- management services, including legal, financial, administrative, personnel, premises and grounds maintenance, health and safety, cleaning, transport and catering;

- pupil-centred services, e.g. education psychologists, education welfare officers (EWOs), learning behaviour support, minority group services and those for pupils who do not have a school place – all of which are intended to facilitate access and improvement.

A key feature of future inspections will be the LEA's education development plan and its approach to the promotion of school improvement.

Schools are not part of the LEA inspection process, but visits will be made to schools to check on the effectiveness of the LEA's support mechanisms to improve the standards, quality and management of its schools on the ground. Such visits will usually take the form of discussions with the headteacher, staff and governors, the observation of some lessons, and the sampling of pupils' work. The headteacher and the chair of governors of the participating schools will be given an oral report of the inspectors' findings. Individual schools will not be named in the published report. Schools are not entirely free from risk, however, even if the inspectors' prime purpose is not to pass judgement on them; if, for example, serious concerns emerge during the course of a visit, in respect of a school's financial practices, the Audit Commission members are duty bound to refer these to the Appointed Auditor, whilst members of

HMI, if they find that standards or the quality of a school's education, management or pupils' development are below par, must notify the LEA and report their discoveries to OFSTED's School Improvement Team.

RELEVANT GUIDANCE

HMCI, *The Framework for the Inspection of Schools*.

The OFSTED Handbook:

Guidance on the Inspection of Secondary Schools (HMSO)
Guidance on the Inspection of Primary/Nursery Schools (HMSO)
Guidance on the Inspection of Special Schools and PRUs (HMSO)
Guidance on the Inspection of Nursery Education Provision in the Private, Voluntary and Independent Sectors (HMSO).

Circular 06/99 [10/2002], 'Schools Causing Concern'.

Chapter 5

SPECIAL EDUCATIONAL NEEDS

Introduction – SEN Code of Practice – Responsibility for special educational needs – Special educational needs policy – Modifications to and disapplication from the National Curriculum – Financial considerations – Future developments – Guidance

INTRODUCTION

It is generally estimated that approximately 20 per cent of all children may have some form of SEN or a learning difficulty at some stage during their school career. For about 17–18 per cent of children, such needs are specific, possibly temporary and relatively minor. These fall to be met within the normal compass of a school's educational provision and, most importantly, from the school's basic delegated budget with no additional financial provision. Some, however, will have such severe and complex learning difficulties that special educational provision will be required to meet their needs. This usually takes the form of a statutory statement of SEN issued by the relevant LEA – which is the LEA where the child lives and not necessarily the LEA that maintains the school – which is funded additionally according to the level of additional provision that is required. There is nothing absolute about these figures – they are broad national estimates – and the proportion of children with SEN varies considerably from one part of the country to another, and from time to time, although there has been a perceptible increase in the percentage of children with statements in recent years.

The expression 'special needs' encompasses physical disability, learning problems and emotional and behavioural difficulties, but does not include difficulties arising from the fact that English (or, for that matter, Welsh in schools where lessons are taught in Welsh) is not the language of the home.

A child has special needs if:

- he or she has a significantly greater difficulty in learning than the majority of children of the same age; or

- he or she has a disability that prevents or hinders access to educational facilities generally provided in the LEA for children of the same age.

Children over the age of two but under the age of five may also be regarded as having SEN if they are likely to fall within either category when they reach the age of five. In this case, educational provision of any description is regarded as special educational provision.

SEN may be identified in a number of different ways: a physical disability will often be self-evident; the family GP or hospital staff may diagnose a condition which indicates the possibility of SEN; or parents may suspect that a problem exists as far as their child's learning is concerned and ask for an assessment. Alongside this, schools have a residual diagnostic responsibility, and failure to discharge this properly might lead to claims for negligence being brought against the school (for further details, see Chapter 12).

SEN CODE OF PRACTICE

A Code of Practice was promulgated for dealing with SEN and has now been extensively revised. The Code is intended to serve as a model of good practice in terms of the procedures to be followed and the approaches to be adopted, and is supported by the SEN Toolkit which seeks to provide practical suggestions on the ways in which the Code of Practice could be implemented. Whilst slavish adherence to the Code is neither mandatory nor always desirable, all those responsible for dealing with special needs must have regard to it. There will be a strong expectation that the Code will be followed so far as circumstances permit. It follows, therefore, that any decision to deviate from the Code must be carefully thought out, and the person or persons making the decision should, for self-protection as much as for any other reason, record it formally in the minutes of a meeting, as well as the reasons for that decision. Governing bodies must, however, ensure that any arrangements they may make for SEN in their schools conform to the Code. This will still allow flexibility in dealing with individual cases.

The Code is very long – over 200 pages including the supporting regulations – and what follows is only a summary of those provisions that most directly affect schools.

Certain key principles explicitly underpin the Guidance offered:

- a child with special educational needs should have his or her needs met;

- the special educational needs of children will normally be met in mainstream schools or settings;

- the views of the child should be sought and taken into account;

- parents have a vital role to play in supporting their child's education;

- children with special educational needs should be offered full access to a broad, balanced and relevant education, including an appropriate curriculum for the foundation stage and the National Curriculum.

Whole-school Context

Most of these principles, however, are capable of far wider application than their immediate and specific SEN context and would normally form the basis of whole-school approaches to teaching and learning. The involvement of parents in their children's education, for example, and the development of co-operative links with the home confer benefits across the board. The provision of appropriate and suitably differentiated curricula fosters the learning of all children, not just those with SEN. Accurate record-keeping and assessment procedures which register and diagnose an individual child's strengths and weaknesses will enable schools to use the information gained as a means of planning further progress in respect of knowledge, skills and understanding. These, together with systematic monitoring and review processes, are essential tools for the advancement of all children's learning. The involvement of pupils in their own destiny via negotiated and agreed targets that are set out in their records of achievement has rightly been given increasing prominence. Effective management, clear policies and well-established disciplinary and pastoral arrangements can do much to prevent some special needs arising and reduce the impact of others. Any approach to SEN, therefore, can be successful only if it is not regarded as an esoteric bolt-on extra which must be seen to be in place because of the statutory requirements but, rather, is fully integrated into a coherent whole-school framework which is designed to meet the learning needs of all children.

In addition to the strategies appropriate in the whole-school context, however, schools will undoubtedly wish to espouse certain specific strategies that are generally accepted as being conducive to high-quality provision of education as far as pupils with SEN are concerned. These include, *inter alia*, the development of good teamwork and co-operative practices, such as joint planning, between class teachers and support staff, to ensure that pupils with SEN receive the same curricular experience as the rest of the group, but at an appropriate level, and are properly integrated into the activities of the whole class. Where pupils with SEN are withdrawn from their normal classes, it is essential that the work undertaken in small groups or on an individual basis is closely linked to that of the main class, whilst being suitably targeted and challenging of itself, and that appropriate additional support materials are devised.

A number of factors are identified as being critical ones:

- the culture, practice, management and deployment of resources in a school or setting are designed to ensure that all children's needs are met;

- LEAs, schools and settings work together to ensure that any child's special educational needs are identified early;

- LEAs, schools and settings exploit best practice when devising interventions;

- those responsible for special educational provision take into account the wishes of the child concerned, in the light of his or her age and understanding;

- special education professionals and parents work in partnership;

- special education professionals take into account the views of individual parents in respect of their child's particular needs;

- interventions for each child are reviewed regularly to assess their impact, the child's progress and the views of the child and his or her teachers and parents;

- there is close co-operation between all the agencies concerned and a multidisciplinary approach to the resolution of issues;

- LEAs make assessments in accordance with the prescribed time limits;

- where an LEA determines a child's special educational needs, statements are clear and detailed, made within prescribed time limits, specify monitoring arrangements, and are reviewed annually.

These points will immediately be seen to be highly aspirational, and inevitable questions will arise in practice over the availability of resources. Nevertheless, although they are described as 'factors', they are perhaps better treated as 'targets' by all who are involved. Schools that have to battle for their share of resources may feel the need constantly to remind the LEA of its obligations.

The importance of SEN is recognised by the requirement that all the objectives set by the governing body for the headteacher under the performance management framework include SEN. It is also noted that governors play a major part in school self-review and the governing body is exhorted to establish mechanisms to ensure that it is fully informed about the school, including the systems for and the outcomes of in-school monitoring and evaluation. The specific requirements for governors are that:

- they are fully involved in developing and monitoring the school's SEN policy;
- all governors, especially any SEN governors, are up to date and knowledgeable about the school's SEN provision, including about how funding, equipment and personnel resources are deployed;
- SEN provision is treated as an integral part of the school development plan;
- the quality of SEN provision is continually monitored.

The Code notes the duties of governing bodies to publish information about, and report on, the school's policy on special educational needs and stipulates that the SEN policy should be subject to a regular cycle of monitoring, evaluation and review. It is suggested that governing bodies must, on at least an annual basis, consider, and report on, the effectiveness of the school's work on behalf of children with special educational needs perhaps in consultation with support services used by the school, other schools and parents.

The Code makes the point that the school is often the first point of contact for parents and stresses again the importance of fully involving them in the school-based response for their child, so that they understand the purpose of any intervention or programme of action, and are told about the parent partnership service when SEN are identified. A new duty in the revised Code is that schools must tell parents when they first identify that a child has SEN and the schools' policies must ensure that they encourage active partnership with parents and do not present barriers to participation. Schools should seek to work actively with their local parent partnership service.

Parents also have responsibilities:

- to communicate effectively with professionals to support their children's education;

- to communicate regularly with their child's school and alert them to any concerns they have about their child's learning or provision;

- to fulfil their obligations under home–school agreements which set out the expectations of both sides. Schools may find it necessary to reinforce this, as most parents probably do not keep the terms of the home–school agreement in the forefront of their minds.

The involvement of the child is critical, and may be thought to have become more significant in the light of the human rights legislation. Children who are capable of forming views have a right to receive and make known information, to express an opinion, and to have that opinion taken into account in any matters affecting them. The views of the child should be given due weight according to the age, maturity and capability of the child. The Code contains Guidance on how to handle this, noting that children and young people may feel anxious and confused about the purpose of an assessment. The Code says that schools and professionals need:

- to provide clear and accurate information about the child's special educational needs and the purpose of any assessment, individual education plan or intervention;

- to help the pupil to understand the agreed outcomes of any intervention and how he or she can be a partner in working towards the goals. Pupils who play an active part in assessment and in developing and monitoring agreed targets will also have greater self-esteem and feel confident that they are making progress;

- to explain clearly what additional support or assessment arrangements are being made and how the pupil can contribute to them;

- to consult pupils who need individual support (whether through equipment or a learning support assistant) to ensure that such support is provided in a timely and sensitive way and enables them to participate fully in learning;

- to recognise the potential stress of assessment and review arrangements and do their best to ensure that the pupil understands the role and contribution of any other professionals from the educational psychology service, child health or social services or Connexions Service who may be involved;

- to draw upon the experience of any local pupil support or advocacy services for children which might offer additional advice and assistance;

- to ensure that the pupil has access to a designated member of staff with whom he or she can discuss any difficulties or concerns.

Record keeping, as ever, is critical. This is the responsibility of the SEN co-ordinator (SENCO) and the Code has much to say about the SENCO's role, worth quoting at length – the extract is from the section dealing with the primary school but the same Guidance applies at all levels:

- The SENCO, in collaboration with the headteacher and governing body, plays a key role in determining the strategic development of the SEN policy and provision in the school in order to raise the achievement of children with SEN. The SENCO takes day-to-day responsibility for the operation of the SEN policy and co-ordination of the provision made for individual children with SEN, working closely with staff, parents and carers, and other agencies. The SENCO also provides related professional guidance to colleagues with the aim of securing high quality teaching for children with SEN.

- The SENCO, with the support of the headteacher and colleagues, seeks to develop effective ways of overcoming barriers to learning and sustaining effective teaching through the analysis and assessment of children's needs, by monitoring the quality of teaching and standards of pupils' achievements, and by setting targets for improvement. The SENCO should collaborate with curriculum co-ordinators so that the learning for all children is given equal priority, and available resources are used to maximum effect.

- In mainstream primary schools the key responsibilities of the SENCO may include:

  - overseeing the day-to-day operation of the school's SEN policy

  - co-ordinating provision for children with special educational needs

  - liaising with and advising fellow teachers

  - managing learning support assistants

  - overseeing the records of all children with special educational needs

  - liaising with parents of children with special educational needs

  - contributing to the in-service training of staff

  - liaising with external agencies including the LEA's support and educational psychology services, health and social services, and voluntary bodies.

    ...

- Governing bodies and headteachers will need to give careful thought to the SENCO's timetable in the light of the Code and in the context of the resources available to the school. Experience shows that SENCOs require time for: planning and co-ordination away from the classroom; maintaining appropriate individual and whole school records of children at School Action and School Action Plus and those with statements; teaching pupils with SEN; observing pupils in class without a teaching commitment; managing, supporting and training learning support assistants; liaising with colleagues and with early education settings and secondary schools. Access to a telephone and an interview room is also desirable where possible. In many schools the governing body has been able to allocate some administrative staff time to help the SENCO, thus releasing the SENCO to use their expertise more effectively.

- In schools the SENCO duties will be a specific responsibility for one member of staff. In terms of responsibility the SENCO role is at least equivalent to that of curriculum, literacy or numeracy co-ordinator. The role is time consuming and therefore it is usually inappropriate for the SENCO to have other school-wide responsibilities. Many schools find it effective for the SENCO to be a member of the senior leadership team. However, although in very small schools the head or deputy may need to take on the role of SENCO, such a decision should be considered very carefully.

- It is good practice for the costs of the SENCO (or those parts of the post-holder's work devoted to SENCO duties) to be set against the core or base budget of the school rather than against additional funds delegated to the school for the purpose of meeting the particular needs of children with SEN.'

SENCOs will, no doubt, latch onto the recommendations regarding facilities and responsibility allowances, and schools will take this Guidance into account in determining their staffing and pay structures.

The In-school Process

As indicated above, the Code introduces two stages, School Action and School Action Plus, in place of the previous three stages that preceded assessment for a statement. Again, it is worth quoting from the Code on these stages (this time taken from the section on secondary schools).

`School Action

- When a subject teacher, member of the pastoral team or the SENCO identifies a child with SEN they should provide interventions that are *additional to* or *different from* those provided as part of the school's usual differentiated curriculum offer and strategies (*School Action*).

- The triggers for intervention through *School Action* could be the teacher's or others' concern, underpinned by evidence, about a child or young person who, despite receiving differentiated learning opportunities:

  - makes little or no progress even when teaching approaches are targeted particularly in a pupil's identified area of weakness
  - shows signs of difficulty in developing literacy or mathematics skills that result in poor attainment in some curriculum areas
  - presents persistent emotional and/or behavioural difficulties, which are not ameliorated by the behaviour management techniques usually employed in the school
  - has sensory or physical problems, and continues to make little or no progress despite the provision of specialist equipment
  - has communication and/or interaction difficulties, and continues to make little or no progress despite the provision of a differentiated curriculum.

- If staff conclude, after consulting parents, that a pupil may need further support to help them progress, they should seek the help of the Head of Department or SENCO and consider their reasons for concern alongside any information about the pupil already available to the school.

- The school SENCO should facilitate the further assessment of the pupil's particular strengths and weaknesses; planning future support for the pupil in discussion with colleagues; and monitoring and subsequently reviewing the action taken. The pupil's subject and pastoral teachers should remain responsible for working with the pupil on a daily basis and for planning and delivering an individualised programme.

- An important part of *School Action* is the collection of all known information about the pupil and seeking additional new information from the parents and others. The school SENCO should facilitate this process through either the pastoral system or the identified link workers (link SENCOs) as appropriate. In some cases outside professionals from health or social services may already be involved with the child. In such instances it is good practice for these professionals to liaise with the school and keep them informed of their input. If these professionals have not already been working with the staff, the SENCO should contact them. This information will act as a baseline on which to plan an appropriate intervention.

- Co-ordinating the planning of the pupil's individual education plan, especially setting appropriate targets, should be the responsibility of the school or link SENCO. On the other hand devising strategies and identifying appropriate methods of access to the curriculum should lie within the area of expertise and responsibility of individual subject teachers. All staff should therefore be involved in providing further help to pupils through *School Action*. For this reason the arrangements for devising and recording Individual Education Plans should be planned and agreed with all the staff, and endorsed by senior management.

- Parents should always be consulted and kept fully informed of the action taken to help the pupil, and of the outcome of this action. Indeed parents may often be the prime source of further information about their child. The information collected can be maintained as part of the pupil's individual record that will also include previous observations on the child made as part of the assessment and recording systems in place for all pupils.

Nature of intervention

- The SENCO and the pupil's subject teachers should decide on the *Action* needed to help the pupil to progress in the light of their earlier assessment. There is sometimes an expectation that this help will take the form of the deployment of extra staff to enable one-to-one tuition to be given to the pupil. However, this may not be the most appropriate way of helping the pupil. A more appropriate approach might be to provide different learning materials or special equipment, to introduce some group or individual support, to devote extra adult time to devising the nature of the planned intervention and to monitoring its effectiveness or to undertake staff development and training aimed at introducing more effective strategies. Speedy access to LEA support services for one-off or occasional advice on strategies or equipment or for staff training may make it possible to provide effective intervention without the need for regular or ongoing input from external agencies.

Individual Education Plans

- Strategies employed to enable the pupil to progress should be recorded within an Individual Education Plan (IEP). Information on managing IEPs and Group Education Plans can be found in the SEN Toolkit. The IEP should include information about:

  - the short-term targets set for or by the pupil
  - the teaching strategies to be used
  - the provision to be put in place
  - when the plan is to be reviewed
  - success and/or exit criteria
  - outcomes (to be recorded when IEP is reviewed).

- The IEP should only record that which is *additional to* or *different from* the differentiated curriculum provision, which is in place as part of provision for all pupils. The IEP should be crisply written and focus on three or four individual targets, chosen from those relating to the key areas of communication, literacy, mathematics, and behaviour and social skills to match the pupil's needs. Strategies may be cross-curricular or may sometimes be subject specific. The IEP should be discussed with the pupil and the parents.

- Where a pupil with identified SEN is at serious risk of disaffection or exclusion the IEP should reflect appropriate strategies to meet their needs. A Pastoral Support Programme should not be used to replace the graduated response to special educational needs. [This is dealt with in more detail in Chapter 8 on School Discipline.]

Reviewing IEPs

- The IEP should be reviewed at least twice a year. Ideally it should be reviewed termly, or possibly more frequently for some pupils. At least one review a year could coincide with a routine parents' evening, although schools should recognise that some parents might prefer a more private meeting. Reviews need not be unduly formal, but parents' views on their child's progress should be sought and they should be consulted as part of the review process. The pupil should also take part in the review process and be involved in setting the targets. If the pupil is not involved in the review meeting, their ascertainable views should be considered in any discussion ...

School Action Plus

- A request for help from external services is likely to follow a decision taken by the SENCO and colleagues, in consultation with parents, at a meeting to review the child's IEP. Schools should always consult specialists when they take action on behalf of a pupil through *School Action Plus*. But the involvement of specialists need not be limited to such pupils. Outside specialists can play an important part in the very early identification of special educational needs and in advising schools on effective provision designed to prevent the development of more significant needs. They can act as consultants and be a source for in-service advice on learning and behaviour management strategies for all teachers.

- At *School Action Plus* external support services, both those provided by the LEA and by outside agencies, will usually see the child, in school if that is appropriate and practicable, so that they can advise subject and pastoral staff on new IEPs, with fresh targets and accompanying strategies, provide more specialist assessments that can inform planning and the measurement of a pupil's progress, give advice on the use of new or specialist strategies or materials, and in some cases provide support for particular activities. The kinds of advice and support available to schools will vary according to local policies.

- The triggers for *School Action Plus* could be that, despite receiving an individualised programme and/or concentrated support, the pupil:

  - continues to make little or no progress in specific areas over a long period
  - continues working at National Curriculum levels substantially below that expected of pupils of a similar age
  - continues to have difficulty in developing literacy and mathematics skills
  - has emotional or behavioural difficulties which substantially and regularly interfere with their own learning or that of the class group, despite having an individualised behaviour management programme
  - has sensory or physical needs, and requires additional specialist equipment or regular advice or visits, providing

direct intervention to the pupil or advice to the staff, by a specialist service
- has ongoing communication or interaction difficulties that impede the development of social relationships and cause substantial barriers to learning.

• Where schools seek the help of external support services, those services will need to see the pupil's records in order to establish which strategies have already been employed and which targets have been set and achieved. They can then advise on new and appropriate targets for the pupil's IEP and on accompanying strategies. They may also provide additional specialist assessment that can inform planning and the measurement of a pupil's progress.

• The SENCO, link workers or subject specialists, and the literacy and numeracy co-ordinators, together with the external specialists, should consider a range of different teaching approaches and appropriate equipment and teaching materials, including the use of information technology. The external specialist may act in an advisory capacity, provide additional specialist assessment or be involved in teaching the pupil directly. In some instances better management or alternative arrangements in school, based on advice from health professionals, may considerably reduce the pupil's special educational needs.

• The resulting IEP for the pupil will set out new strategies for supporting the pupil's progress. Although developed with the help of outside specialists, the strategies specified in the IEP should usually be implemented, at least in part and as far as possible, in the normal classroom setting. Hence delivery of the IEP will be the responsibility of subject teachers.

• If the SENCO and the external specialist consider that the information gathered about the pupil is insufficient, and that more detailed advice must be obtained from other outside professionals, then the consent of the pupil's parents must be sought.

• The SENCO should note in the pupil's records what further advice is being sought and the support to be provided for the pupil pending receipt of the advice.'

The third stage of the process normally comes when School Action Plus has failed to deal with the pupil's special educational needs although, exceptionally, a pupil may need immediate referral without passing through the school-based stages. At this assessment stage, the process moves away from the school and into the hands of the LEA. However, before being prepared to embark on the assessment process, the LEA will seek evidence from the school that any strategy or programme implemented for the child in question has been continued for a reasonable period of time without success and that alternatives have been tried, or find out the reasons why this has not occurred. The LEA will wish to see reports of advice from external agencies but the Code makes the point that the LEA should not insist on such reports being obtained if they do not exist. None the less, resource-strapped LEAs will, no doubt, use any deficiency in the information supplied by the school to defer dealing with the matter in preference to those cases where the paperwork is in order. This, again, is a strong incentive to schools to keep good records. Schools should bear in mind that they can seek an assessment from the LEA themselves. It is a tool that should be used, not least because in legal terms it moves a potential problem relating to the level and appropriateness of provision from the school to the LEA. This, of course, is additional to the parental right to seek assessment.

If the LEA concludes that a statutory assessment is required, it must inform the parents of the child concerned by issuing a formal notice of its proposal to conduct an assessment, and the Code goes into detail on the content of that notice and the subsequent process of assessment and statementing. If the LEA decides not to issue a statement, it should consider providing the parents with a formal 'notice in lieu', outlining the reasons for its decision. The notice in lieu should include all the supporting evidence used in the assessment, Guidance on the special educational provision that might none the less be made, and a description of any non-educational needs and of the provision that might be available to meet them. From the school's perspective, the most significant aspect, assuming a decision to issue a statement, is the specificity of the identification of the needs to be addressed by the statement and the degree of provision that the statement makes.

The Special Educational Needs and Disability Tribunal

If the LEA decides not to draw up a statement, it must notify the child's parents, within two weeks of the date on which the assessment was completed, of its decision (and the reasons for it) and of the parents' right to appeal to what is now known as the Special Educational Needs and Disability Tribunal (SENDIST, formerly the Special Educational Needs Tribunal). The Tribunal was set up initially to hear parental appeals against the decisions of LEAs about a child's SEN, where parents and the LEA concerned have been unable to secure agreement, and its scope has been widened, as the new title indicates, to include matters relating to disability discrimination, dealt with in Chapter 6. The Tribunal is independent, having no connection with any LEA, and consists of a panel of three people, one a legally qualified chair, and two lay members with experience of either SEN or local government or both. The Tribunal seeks to be relatively 'user-friendly' and informal. Legal representation for parents is permissible, but legal aid is not available. Parents and/or voluntary representatives may, therefore, find themselves at a disadvantage when facing LEAs which have the benefit of legal support or of specialist personnel who have developed considerable expertise in dealing with such cases.

There is an increasing number of cases passing through the Tribunal. The Tribunal's own statistics confirm this trend, and show an average annual increase of just over 15 per cent; this figure is likely to increase significantly with the introduction of disability claims. This means that headteachers are being called upon to give evidence (usually on behalf of the LEA) more regularly. The Tribunal will normally want to hear from a headteacher about the ability of the school to make the provision specified in the statement. In preparing to give evidence at a Tribunal, the headteacher should therefore be familiar with the statement as a whole (including its appendices) but pay particular attention to the special educational needs of the child as identified in it, and be able to comment in detail upon how the school will be able to meet those needs, taking into account any additional resources that are to be provided. It is almost bound to be the case that the parents will seek to challenge this (which will probably have given rise to the appeal in the first place), hence the need to consider these issues in detail.

Tribunals will order their own proceedings and the responsibility for preparing a Tribunal case rests with the LEA. As a rough guide, the procedure that is used is as follows. The case will usually be conducted on behalf of the LEA by an experienced member of the SEN department or a member of the legal department. There will have been an exchange of a considerable volume of documentation between the LEA, the parents and the Tribunal's office before the hearing much of which a headteacher as a witness will not (and need not) see. It is advisable for a witness to liaise closely with the advocate concerned, and to attend early on the day of the hearing itself in order to be fully appraised. On the basis of the information that it has received, the Tribunal on the day of the hearing will usually try to draft a form of agenda to identify the issues it believes it will need to address through the course of the hearing. This is an important document because it will indicate the way in which the minds of the Tribunal members are working. Normally the Tribunal will deal with each point on the agenda sequentially inviting the LEA to comment first followed by the parents. A witness may be questioned by their own advocate, any member of the Tribunal and the parents or their representative – and sometimes, if appropriate, by other witnesses. Hearings can themselves be lengthy: at least half a day should be put aside, and (depending upon the complexity of the case) it is not uncommon for hearings to take longer. Tribunal decisions are usually communicated in writing to the LEA and parents between seven and 14 days after the hearing.

The Final Statement

The LEA must issue a final statement within eight weeks of drawing up its proposed statement. The whole process, therefore, from the time that the LEA first informs parents of its intention to undertake a formal assessment to the production of the final statement should be accomplished within a period of 26 weeks. This strict timetable, which is represented diagrammatically in the figure below, was introduced specifically to combat any dilatoriness, perceived or real, on the part of LEAs in addressing parental concerns and the needs of children with SEN.

Time-limits for Making Assessments and Statements

Time Scale	Processes
6 weeks	The LEA issues a notice or recieves a parental request
	Decision to assess
	Yes No
10 weeks	Decision to make a ← statement
	LEA seeks advice 6 weeks advice
	Yes No
2 weeks	Proposed statement Notice in lieu with supporting reasons for decision
8 weeks	
Total 26 weeks	Final statement

The Form and Content of a Statement

The format and content of a statement are determined by statutory regulations. A statement is composed of six parts, plus appendices, and must include certain specific information.

- *Introduction* – the name, address and date of birth of the child and other family details.

- *SEN* – a description of the child's SEN in respect of his or her learning difficulties.

- *Special Educational Provision* – such as is considered necessary to meet the child's SEN. This part comprises three subsections:
  - the objectives which the special educational provision should aim to meet;
  - the actual special educational provision that is to be made in order to achieve the objectives, including the requisite staffing, equipment, etc, and whether any modification or exclusion of the National Curriculum applies;
  - the arrangements for monitoring and review.
- *Placement* – the type and name of the school where the provision recorded in Part 3 is to be made.
- *Non-educational Needs* – e.g. any medical treatment which may be specified.
- *Non-educational Provision* – provision that should be made available in accordance with an agreed, co-ordinated approach between the LEA, the health authority and/or social services.

Where parents are dissatisfied with the terms of their child's statement, particularly in regard to Parts 2, 3 and 4, either when the statement is first drawn up or if it is changed or amended later, they have the right of appeal to the SEN and Disability Tribunal. This right also applies if the LEA refuses to re-assess a statemented child or it decides to stop maintaining a statement. Parents should, however, be aware that they must exercise their right of appeal to the Tribunal within two months of the publication of the final statement, and that this time-limit is extended only in extremely rare cases. Parents may also refer their complaints to the Ombudsman, who is empowered to investigate allegations of injustice arising from local authority maladministration, e.g. when the provision stipulated in a statement has not been made. They may, moreover, as a final resort, take their grievances or complaints to the Secretary of State in cases where, for example, an LEA has unreasonably disregarded the instructions of the SEN and Disability Tribunal.

Naming a School

Parents of children with statements of special educational needs are not entitled to seek a place at a maintained school through the normal admissions process. Their right is to express a preference for a school in the maintained sector to be named in the statement. The LEA must comply with their wishes unless:

- the school is unsuitable for the child's age, ability, aptitude or special educational needs; or

- the placement would be prejudicial to the efficient education of other children with whom the statemented child would be educated; or

- to do so would be incompatible with the efficient use of resources.

There are clearly tensions here between the absolute rights of an individual child and the impact of those rights on the majority of children and on the equitable distribution of finite resources.

If the parents exercise their option in favour of an approved non-maintained special school or independent school, the LEA should arrange a meeting with them to discuss their reasons for choosing such a school, especially if residential education is requested. Where it is agreed by the parents and the LEA that a child should attend an independent school that is not approved, the Secretary of State's sanction for the placement must be sought by the LEA before it names the school in the final statement.

The Requirement to Consult the Governing Body of a 'Named School'

Before including the name of any maintained school in a statement, the LEA must consult the governing body of the school in question and the school's LEA, if the school is maintained by a different authority. It should be noted that the admission criteria for the school are not relevant to the decision save to the very limited extent that they may indicate that the school is unsuitable or, where the preferred school is selective, where the statemented child does not meet the ability level that the school requires. Although technically, the child cannot be required to take the same test as non-statemented applicants, in practice failure to do so will support the objection by the governing body that the school is not suitable for the child's ability. Apart from this, an argument based on suitability will rarely be accepted because the test of suitability relates only to the child's special needs. This applies even to admission to a denominational school where some form of religious or faith commitment is a first criterion for entry for non-statemented pupils and the school is normally full with pupils who meet that criterion. Governing bodies of such schools should note that they cannot refuse to admit a child with a statement on grounds of religion or faith. They should ensure during the consultation process that the LEA is aware that the child in question would not normally qualify for entry on the basis of the admission criteria and they should assert quite unequivocally that the LEA would be acting unreasonably in naming the school in a statement.

There is no formal appeal route for the governing body where the school is named in face of opposition by the school. If the LEA persists, all the school can do is to refer the matter to the Secretary of State for adjudication on the grounds that the LEA is acting unreasonably. To succeed, the governing body would need to show that the LEA is acting irrationally or has totally failed to consider relevant facts. There is no parallel right to seek review where the school has been named by the SEN and Disability Tribunal following a parental appeal. The fact that, even if the LEA accedes to the school's views and refuses to name the school in the statement, the parent has the right of appeal to the Tribunal places great pressure on the LEA to comply with parental wishes. Not to do so simply involves the LEA in defending an appeal with its consequent resource implications.

Similar considerations apply to any proposed placement where the school feels strongly that, perhaps because of the severity of the special needs, the child should not be in mainstream education or, for other reasons, there will be prejudice to other children or inefficiency in the use of resources. It should be noted that the DfES appears to take the view that even if the issue has been referred to the Secretary of State, the Department cannot take any action once the child is admitted, implying that prior to actual admission some action by the Department is possible. This is a view that is debatable, as is the line taken by the Department that the school should refuse to admit the child until the Department's decision has been made. Once, as may often be the case, the statement has been issued and the school is named in it, a refusal to admit puts the governing body in the position of having to breach the legal requirement to admit a child where the school is named. It also puts the governing body in the position of potentially having to defend judicial review proceedings by the parent in circumstances where, if it is challenging a decision of its own maintaining LEA, it may not be able to look to the LEA for the usual support. All a school in this position can do, therefore, is to indicate at an early date to the LEA and the parent that it will act in accordance with DfES practice by not admitting until the issue has been resolved and make sure that the DfES is aware of this at the outset.

When a statement for a child is issued after the allocation of places has already been completed by an over-subscribed school and the relevant year group is full, the LEA, after consulting the governors, has to weigh up in making its decision the wishes of the child's parents against the deleterious effect on the education of other children of having an extra child in the class.

If any of the three considerations mentioned above, i.e. unsuitability, incompatibility and inefficiency, applies, the LEA is not obliged to comply with parental wishes and may name an alternative school which fits the bill better. It should, however, take care to explain the rationale for its decision sensitively in writing to the parents to assuage their feelings of disappointment, in the hope, at least, that this may stave off an appeal.

For most schools, the naming process probably works reasonably well. However, in some areas, where there is heavy pressure on some schools for places for both statemented and non-statemented pupils, the absence of any formal process to enable schools and LEAs to control the admission of statemented pupils works to the detriment of both schools and statemented pupils. Schools that are in demand because of their success in dealing with SEN are, paradoxically, penalised for that success by having to admit unreasonable numbers of statemented pupils or pupils with special educational needs that do not fall within the school's particular areas of expertise. Schools in that position need to have strategies in place to deal with this problem, trying to agree protocols with their home LEA and those that regularly maintain statements for pupils in the school to prioritise applications and by establishing detailed responses to the consultation process. This will not prevent a determined parent from pursuing an appeal to SENDIST but laying the paper trail will help the school in its attempt to persuade the Tribunal that the school should not be named.

One further point should be noted. The parental right is to express preference for 'the' school to be named in the statement. That means that it is at least arguable that the parent may not name or approach a range of schools as alternatives within the scope of the statutory provisions. It is often evident that an LEA is consulted with more than one school. In those circumstances, where the school feels unable to agree to the placement, it might decline to respond to the consultation until the LEA confirms that the school is the one school that the parent is proposing in exercise of the statutory right.

It should be remembered that the contents of a statement should not be disclosed without the consent of the child's parents except when:

- statutory purposes require it, for example to an SEN and Disability Tribunal or an OFSTED inspection team;

- it is in the interests of the child to do so, for example to the teachers at his or her school to enhance their knowledge of the child.

The Annual Review

Whilst an LEA, having drawn up a statement, is entitled to review it at any stage, it has a statutory obligation to review all statements annually. The LEA is also responsible for monitoring a child's progress towards the targets set on a regular basis.

The purpose of the formal review is:

- to collate and record the information that the school and others can use to plan their future support for the child;

- to gauge the extent to which the targets that were set previously have been achieved;

- to assess the appropriateness of any special equipment provided – and its continuing need;

- to determine whether the statement should be maintained in its existing form (with the incorporation of new targets for the following year) or amended or whether the statement should cease to operate altogether.

It is the LEA's responsibility to initiate the review by asking the headteacher to convene a meeting of all interested parties and to prepare a review report. At least two months' notice must be given to enable proper preparations to be undertaken. Those invited to the review meeting must include:

- an LEA representative;

- the parents of the child (or his or her carer if the child is under the care of the LEA);

- a relevant teacher.

Prior to the meeting, the headteacher must request written advice from the child's parents, all those specified by the LEA and anyone else that the headteacher deems appropriate. The headteacher must also circulate copies of all the advice received to everyone who is due to attend the meeting, inviting further comments. It is particularly important that detailed responses are submitted by those who are unable to attend the meeting. It is not unusual in the case of a large school for these tasks to be delegated to the SENCO, who would also chair the meeting, but, in smaller schools, the arrangements are likely to be made by a deputy or the headteacher in person.

In the case of a family whose first language is not English (or Welsh) it is expected that consideration will be given to:

- the translation of any relevant documentation into the family's mother tongue;

- the availability of an interpreter and a bilingual support teacher or teacher of English or Welsh as a second language both before and during the review meeting;

- access on the part of the child's community professionals to interpretation and translation facilities.

Similarly, where a child or a member of the child's family has a visual impairment, the relevant information should be made available in Braille, in large print or on tape for easy access. The time-scale for the review may have to be lengthened in such circumstances.

At the review meeting, the views of all those present should be solicited and account taken of the written advice that has been received, so that a thorough assessment of the child's progress can be carried out. The meeting should conclude with a clear set of recommendations that are based on unanimity or at least a consensus, but dissenting recommendations can be advanced. The same principle holds good in the case of a child who is educated otherwise than at school or is being taught through home tuition or in a PRU, but the precise practical details of the review arrangements may differ from those outlined here.

After the annual review, the headteacher must produce a report of the meeting, summarising its outcomes, including any specific recommendations that have been made and any educational targets set for the following year, and circulate it to all the parties involved by the date specified by the LEA in its original letter. The LEA concludes the review process by considering the headteacher's report and any other relevant information and drawing up its own recommendations. A copy of these recommendations must be sent to the school, the parents and all those invited to the review meeting before the statutory deadline for review.

Where an LEA proposes to amend a statement – and there is a firm expectation that it will accept the unanimous recommendations of a review to amend a statement, unless there are good reasons to the contrary – it must inform the child's parents in writing of its intention and of their right to make representations within 15 days of receiving the proposal. The LEA must then consider any such representations before coming to its final decision. An amendment must be made within eight weeks of the date on which the letter of proposal was sent out and a copy must be provided for parents. The parents should also be informed of their right of appeal to the SEN and Disability Tribunal. If the authority decides to cease maintaining a statement, it must again inform the parents of its decision and the reasons for it and draw attention to their right of appeal to the Tribunal. Where, after an annual review, a statement is left unaltered, no right of appeal exists.

Annual Review in Year 9 and subsequently

LEAs remain responsible for statemented pupils who stay on at school post-16 until they are 19. Some, however, will leave school at 16 and proceed to a college of FE or become the responsibility of social services. Because of the increased significance of the annual review as a statemented pupil approaches the statutory leaving age, the first review after a child's 14th birthday must involve all the agencies which will play a major role in the post-16 years, so that the move towards adult life can be planned more coherently. In particular, the Connexions Service must be involved. The same procedure as outlined above for a normal review should be followed in this instance, apart from the exceptions listed below.

- It is the LEA's duty to convene the review meeting.
- Other agencies such as the social services department must be informed and invited to attend.
- A representative of the careers service must be invited.
- The LEA must prepare the review report and draw up a Transition Plan after the meeting.

Copies of the report and the Transition Plan must be circulated to the young person's parents, the headteacher, all those from whom advice was sought, those who attended the meeting and anyone else the LEA may consider appropriate.

Transition Plans

The Transition Plan should address certain critical issues involving the school, other professional agencies, the family and the young person concerned, for example:

- What are the young person's curriculum needs during transition?

- Does the young person have any special health or welfare needs which will require planning and support from health and social services now or in the future?

- What do the young person's parents expect of their son's or daughter's adult life?

- How can young people be encouraged to contribute to their own Transition Plan and make positive decisions about the future? What information do they need?

Schools should clearly do all they can during the transition period to encourage a young person to take more direct responsibility for his or her own destiny and to become increasingly involved in the decision-making process, and to lay greater emphasis on the development of personal skills at this juncture. Schools might also consider forging close links with their local FE colleges and establishing link provision.

The Code of Practice specifies that transition planning should be participative, holistic, supportive, evolving, inclusive and collaborative. The Connexions Service is responsible for overseeing the delivery of the Transition Plan, and the Connexions Personal Adviser should co-ordinate its delivery.

Where a young person with a statement of SEN transfers to an FE college post-16, LEAs should ensure that a copy of the statement, the most recent annual review and the Transition Plan are sent to the social services department and the college – and to the LSC in relevant cases – although they should seek the consent of the young person and his or her parents to the transfer of such privileged information beforehand. Although not statutorily bound to do so, schools may adopt similar approaches to the transfer of pupils with SEN who are not statemented, but who receive additional support at one of the school-based stages – even to the extent of compiling their own Transition Plans.

RESPONSIBILITY FOR SPECIAL EDUCATIONAL NEEDS

The statutory provisions relating to SEN apply to children under 19 who are registered pupils at a school. Since the obligation to register pupils extends to independent schools, the SEN 'net' covers pupils in such schools, although there is no obligation on an LEA to fund provision in an independent school if the provision can be made more efficiently within the maintained sector. An LEA is empowered to arrange for a part or all of a child's SEN provision to be made otherwise than in a school – although it should consult the child's parents before taking such a step. Where an LEA decides that SEN provision might most appropriately be offered in an institution outside England and Wales it may contribute towards or pay in full:

- the fees;
- expenses reasonably incurred in maintaining the child while he or she is at the institution or travelling to or from it;
- the child's travelling expenses;
- the expenses of any person accompanying the child whilst the child is travelling to or from or staying at the institution.

The specific responsibilities that are imposed on the relevant bodies in regard to meeting the needs of children with SEN are outlined below.

LEAs' Responsibilities

LEAs must:

- keep their arrangements for special educational provision under review and consult on this as necessary, with, for example, the governing bodies of maintained schools in the area;
- exercise their powers so as to identify those children who have SEN and for whom special provision is needed;
- use their best endeavours to see that any child in a maintained nursery school who has SEN receives appropriate provision and that the child's needs are made known to all likely to teach the child. LEAs must also secure that teachers in such a school are aware of the importance of identifying such children;
- have regard to the Code of Practice when discharging their duties in relation to SEN;

- provide the resources necessary to implement any statement of SEN.

District Health Authorities' Responsibilities

District health authorities are also under a duty:

- to notify parents and, after consultation with the parents, the LEA if they identify a child under five as having SEN or potential SEN. They must also advise the parents of any voluntary organisation that may be able to help with the particular problem. This duty is also imposed on NHS Trusts;

- where necessary and reasonable, to provide help to the LEA in exercising its SEN functions. This will frequently include examining and reporting on children who are being assessed for SEN. This duty also extends to local authorities.

Governing Bodies' Responsibilities

Governing bodies are obliged:

- to use their best endeavours to see that any child with SEN receives appropriate provision and that the child's needs are made known to all likely to teach the child;

- to secure that teachers in the school are aware of the importance of identifying such children;

- to designate a person (who may be the headteacher or a governor) as the 'responsible person' to liaise with the LEA on all appropriate SEN issues;

- to maintain a policy on SEN and keep it under review;

- to include in the annual report to parents a report on special educational needs in the school covering:

  - a statement about the school's policy, indicating its success during the year with particular reference to the effectiveness of its approaches to identification, assessment, provision, monitoring and record-keeping, and the use made of outside agencies and any significant changes made to the policy;
  - details of any consultation on special educational needs with the LEA and, where appropriate, with the other schools in the area (to ensure effective co-operation) during the course of the year;

- to have regard to the Code of Practice when discharging their duties in relation to SEN;

- to apply any resources made available under a statement of SEN in making the specific provision required under the statement;

- to ensure that, as far as is practicable, children with SEN are integrated into school activities with other pupils;

- to notify their LEA of children who may need a statement.

Governing Bodies' Accountability to Parents

The requirement for governing bodies to account in the annual report for the way in which the monies nominally assigned to their school for SEN purposes or under an SEN heading have been spent is not unreasonable, nor should it prove too difficult, and the topic should be formally discussed at a governors' meeting and the outcomes duly minuted. The requirement to publish information on the success of a school's SEN policy, however, and the identification of suitable measures of effectiveness, represent a far taller order.

It is interesting to note in this context that the main findings of a survey carried out by HMI and published under the title *The Implementation of the Code of Practice* underline governors' apprehensions about reporting to parents on the implementation and effectiveness of their school policy. Most governors seem to find it difficult to acquire the requisite knowledge and experience to discharge their functions properly, and very few are familiar with the finer details of the Code. It is acknowledged that reporting to parents on the success of a school's policy is extremely demanding and that most schools are 'a long way away from being able to do this'. In the absence of any clearly identified national criteria, members of the Senior Management Team (SMT), the SENCO and the governing body might find the suggestions outlined below helpful.

- Compare the reading ages of pupils on entry with subsequent test scores.

- Monitor the percentage increase or reduction in the number of pupils with SEN at the school-based stages over time (although care should be taken with the interpretation of results, because an increase might be indicative of more effective diagnoses).

- Issue a questionnaire to parents of pupils with SEN to gauge their level of satisfaction.

An analysis of individual education plans (IEPs), or the time notionally allocated to the SENCO or SEN support staff, or the percentage of targets which pupils with SEN have managed to achieve, or the enthusiasm of teachers for this aspect of their work might permit other valid (if subjective) conclusions to be drawn.

SPECIAL EDUCATIONAL NEEDS POLICY

It is the responsibility of governing bodies in conjunction with the headteacher to draw up a school's overall policy for SEN provision. A review of the implementation and success of the policy must be included in the annual report to parents, as already indicated, and a summary published in the school prospectus. Depending on their normal practice in regard to policies generally, schools may decide to distribute a copy of their SEN policy to parents, but in any case a copy must be made available for parents to see on request. This follows from the general rule that policies approved by the governing body form part of the public documentation of the school in the same way as minutes of governing body meetings.

The content of a policy is not prescribed, but it must address certain key issues as itemised in the Code of Practice and provide information under the following three main categories.

(1) The school's special educational provision:

- the objectives of the school's SEN policy;
- the name of the school's SENCO or teacher responsible for the day-to-day operation of the SEN policy;
- the arrangements for co-ordinating educational provision for pupils with SEN;
- admission arrangements;
- any SEN specialism and any special units;
- any special facilities which increase or assist access to the school by pupils with SEN.

(2) The school's policies for identification, assessment and provision:

- the allocation of resources to and amongst pupils with SEN;

- identification and assessment arrangements, and review procedures;
- the arrangements for providing access for pupils with SEN to a balanced and broadly based curriculum, including the National Curriculum;
- how children with SEN are integrated within the school as a whole;
- the criteria for evaluating the success of the school's SEN policy;
- the arrangements for considering complaints about special educational provision within the school.

(3) The school's staffing policies and partnerships:

- the school's arrangements for SEN in-service training;
- the use made of teachers and facilities from outside the school, including support services;
- the arrangements for partnership with parents;
- the links with other mainstream schools and special schools, including arrangements when pupils change schools or leave school;
- the links with health and social services, educational welfare services and any voluntary organisations.

All mainstream schools must designate a named teacher as the SENCO, who will have specific responsibility for the day-to-day implementation and operation of the school's SEN policy, the co-ordination of the school's SEN provision, liaison with colleagues, parents and external agencies and the maintenance of the SEN register. He or she will also have a major part to play in advising colleagues on suitable strategies to adopt, in contributing significantly to their in-service training and in the preparation of appropriately differentiated materials and worksheets. The Guidance in the Code of Practice, noted above, should be kept in mind in defining the role of the SENCO and allocating resources.

A governing body may wish to appoint a committee or an individual governor to develop a particular interest and expertise in SEN matters to take the lead in offering advice at meetings and to monitor the school's work for children with SEN on its behalf. Where such delegation occurs, the precise remit of the group or individual should be clearly established and minuted. It should not, moreover, be forgotten that any arrangements that are made relating to SEN provision, including the measures taken to ensure that all staff have ready access to relevant and up-to-date in-service training (and to a wide range of reading matter to enable them to keep abreast of developments), should be firmly rooted in the school development plan and carefully costed.

In framing their policies on SEN, governing bodies should bear in mind the obvious link between this policy and policies on behaviour and discipline, including the range of sanctions employed and how these sanctions, e.g. exclusions, are applied.

During an OFSTED inspection, the inspecting team will subject all aspects of a school's *modus operandi*, including its policies and procedures in regard to SEN provision, to careful scrutiny to ensure that the statutory requirements are being observed (one member of the team will be given a specific SEN brief). The inspectors will also want to determine how effective the school's SEN policy is in practice and whether, for example:

- all staff work in close co-operation with the SENCO;
- the resources allocated to pupils with SEN are well managed;
- there is effective use of any additional external specialist support; and
- progress is properly assessed, recorded and monitored.

MODIFICATIONS TO AND DISAPPLICATION FROM THE NATIONAL CURRICULUM

Headteachers are statutorily bound to ensure that the National Curriculum is provided for all pupils of compulsory school age on their school roll as an entitlement, and there is a clear expectation that departures from the norm will be very few and far between. In certain specific cases, however, it is recognised that exceptions should be permitted and all of these relate to pupils with SEN. Those children, for example, who are visually impaired or physically handicapped, either individually or as a group, may have certain attainment targets, programmes of study, assessment arrangements or the requirement to study one or more foundation subjects modified or disapplied by the Secretary of State, especially where involvement in practical work or experiments which might put their own or other pupils' safety at risk is entailed.

For individual pupils with SEN, modification or disapplication may operate through their statement of SEN. The statement should indicate quite unequivocally, in section 3, the nature and extent of any modification to the National Curriculum which is deemed desirable to meet the child's SEN or the precise details of any exemptions from one or more foundation subjects. This should happen in only extremely rare instances in a primary school, but may occur more frequently in a secondary school, where the effective removal of one or two subjects from a child's curriculum allows greater concentration on other subjects in terms of depth and/or time.

General and Special Directions

Headteachers are also permitted by the regulations to issue a General or Special Direction to modify or disapply the National Curriculum for individual pupils on a temporary basis, where they are satisfied that a child's needs cannot be met appropriately in any other way.

It should be noted that temporary exceptions cannot be made to the provisions of the Education Act 1996 relating to:

- a balanced and broadly based curriculum;
- approved qualifications and syllabuses;
- religious education and collective worship;
- the publication of information;
- arrangements for the consideration and resolution of complaints.

Headteachers, however, are expected to use powers to issue General or Special Directions sparingly and only in exceptional circumstances. Thus, it would not be appropriate to issue Directions for short-term contingencies, for example where a pupil needs to concentrate for a few weeks on bringing a particular area of weakness up to scratch.

A General Direction could be issued when, for instance:

- a pupil comes from such a different educational background that a period of adjustment to the National Curriculum is deemed essential;

- a pupil who has spent a lengthy spell in hospital, has been educated at home or has been excluded needs time for re-integration;

- a pupil is temporarily experiencing severe emotional problems.

Headteachers are still responsible for the education of registered pupils who are in receipt of home tuition or are being taught in a hospital school or in an off-site unit and, if it is impossible to offer pupils the full National Curriculum in such circumstances, a General Direction should be issued. A General Direction should be given:

- separately for each child; and

- only after appropriate consultation with, for example, a child's parents and teachers and an educational psychologist.

The headteacher should normally allow one calendar month after giving a Direction before it comes into effect, although in cases of extreme urgency it may be activated sooner.

To comply with regulations, the direction must be in writing, and must include brief particulars of:

- those provisions of the National Curriculum which are to be modified or disapplied;

- the operative date of the direction and, if that date is less than one month after the date on which the direction is given, the reasons why it is less than one month;

- for how long the direction is to apply;

- the reasons for the direction and whether it is general or special;

- the change in provision for the pupil's education that will apply;

- how the headteacher will secure a return to the full National Curriculum, if the direction is a general one, or a statement that in the headteacher's opinion the pupil has special educational needs requiring an assessment, if the direction is a special one.

The direction must also advise the parent of the parent's right to appeal to the governing body against the direction.

A copy of the direction must be kept on the pupil's file and it must be sent by first class post within three school days to the chair of governors, the LEA, at least one of the pupil's parents and, if the direction is a special one, to the LEA where the pupil lives if that is not the school's LEA. The headteacher should arrange for the direction to be translated, if appropriate.

A direction may be varied or revoked following the same procedure.

A parent may at any time request the headteacher to give a direction (or a further direction), or to revoke or vary a direction currently in force. The request can be oral or in writing but must give reasons why it is being made. A request to revoke or vary a direction can only be made once during the currency of the original direction and once during any extension. The headteacher must deal with the request within two weeks and give reasons for a refusal to comply with the request together with a statement of the right to appeal to the governing body. The parent has the right to appeal if the request is not responded to within the two-week period. Similar notification rules apply.

Headteachers may vary, revoke or renew Directions and in all cases go through the same procedure as for an initial Direction. A General Direction may be renewed twice for up to six months in each instance, although in each case subject to notification and the parent's right of appeal. As indicated in more detail below, a Special Direction can only be renewed once unless a statement has been issued but is under appeal to the SEN and Disability Tribunal, in which case it may be renewed for successive periods of up to six months until the appeal has been determined.

There is little practical difference between a General Direction and a Special Direction in terms of procedures, but the Special Direction is used as a temporary expedient pending the assessment of a pupil with SEN with a view to issuing a statement. Because the LEA retains the ultimate responsibility for assessment and statementing procedures for all pupils with SEN, the headteachers of all schools must consult with their LEA before giving a Special Direction and specify their reasons for the assessment. Special Directions cease to be operative as soon as a statement is issued (or amended). Where an LEA decides not to undertake a formal assessment or draw up a statement, the headteacher must arrange for the pupil to receive the National Curriculum provision in full within one calendar month of being notified by the LEA of its decision. If, after six months, an LEA has not responded to a Special Direction by issuing (or amending) a statement or has failed to inform a headteacher of its intention not to do so, the Special Direction automatically expires, but the headteacher may renew the Direction once to run consecutively. The renewed Direction will cease to have effect within one calendar month of a statement being issued or automatically after the second six-month period has elapsed.

Parents have the right to ask a headteacher to give a temporary Direction for their child or to vary, revoke or renew one that is already in force. Headteachers must reply to such requests within two weeks of receiving them and, if their decision is to reject the request, provide reasons in writing for their rejection, as well as informing parents of their right of appeal to the governing body. After hearing such an appeal, the governing body must notify both the parents and the headteacher of its decision in writing. The headteacher must comply with any decision that is made, but the parents, if they are still dissatisfied, may invoke the normal complaints procedures.

Avoiding the Need for Directions

There is no doubt that the process of giving Directions is cumbersome, although less so than in its original form. This may have been an intentional design fault to discourage headteachers from embarking on it except in the rarest of cases, because of the importance of ensuring that all children as far as possible receive their full entitlement under the National Curriculum. The relaxation of the rules governing disapplication, particularly at Key Stage 4 (as detailed in Chapter 3 on the curriculum) has reduced, at least partially, the need for the requirements to be modified or disapplied, either temporarily by a headteacher's Direction or in the longer term by means of a statement of SEN. The access statements in the section on common requirements at the head of each of the Subject Orders are particularly helpful in this respect in that they permit the use of materials from earlier or later Key Stages, as appropriate, and draw attention to the various technical aids available to pupils with SEN, particularly those who are visually or physically impaired. The broader range of levels, which were introduced at that stage, has, moreover, allowed pupils with SEN to work at levels below those previously associated with their age group, for instance, at level 1 at Key Stage 1 and at levels 1 and 2 at Key Stage 2.

It should also be remembered that children with SEN are, in certain circumstances, entitled to additional support (such as extra time, a person to read an exam paper or the use of an amanuensis) when taking public examinations. Schools may, therefore, wish to try to arrange for these support mechanisms to be incorporated into a pupil's statement to lend greater strength to their arguments when seeking concessions from examination boards on behalf of their pupils.

FINANCIAL CONSIDERATIONS

Mention has already been made of the tensions and conflicting pressures that are inherent in the current 'system' in regard to the funding of SEN, and these have not been eased by the Department's assumption that the introduction of the SEN Code of Practice has been 'cost-neutral'. These tensions, moreover, are compounded by the absence of any clear agreement on suitably differentiated cut-off points that would automatically trigger additional resources when reached or exceeded, despite the demarcations of the school-based stages of the Code of Practice.

The essential difficulty is that the demand for additional financial support for SEN is potentially limitless and absolute (the provisions identified in a statement must be funded), whilst the resources available to meet the need are finite. Similarly, schools are expected to develop general resource strategies to meet the needs of all their pupils, whilst the Code of Practice emphasises individual identification of need and, by implication, the targeting of resources on individual pupils. Schools, moreover, are funded on an individually based mechanism of resource allocation in their local schemes of financial delegation.

It is obvious that any re-allocation of resources at the LEA or school level within a finite budget to a particular item can only be undertaken at the expense of other budget headings, but it is perhaps less palatable when this principle is applied to children. Certainly it is an inevitable consequence of any increase in the funding assigned to statemented pupils that the amount available for the general provision for all pupils will be proportionately reduced. The advent of local management and the pressure for greater/maximum delegation on local authorities have undoubtedly made matters worse; LEAs' scope for manoeuvre has been considerably curtailed, whilst schools are not always readily able to contend with the added responsibility of meeting the needs of all their non-statemented SEN pupils. Although the assumption of such responsibility is an inevitable and perfectly reasonable concomitant of full-scale financial devolution, headteachers and governing bodies will always be afflicted, especially at times of economic stringency and budgetary cuts, by the thought that insufficient funds have been channelled through the LEA's formula to schools to enable them to meet the costs of their SEN provision. Under these circumstances, therefore, it is not surprising that, despite what has been said above, schools should often, with the support of parents, push more and more of their pupils forward for statutory assessment in the hope of securing additional funding from the ensuing statements.

These issues also highlight the frustrations felt by those involved in the SEN scheme and which were expressed in two reports issued by the Audit Commission in 2002. Whilst the Audit Commission concluded that improvements could be effected within the existing regime by taking steps such as promoting consistent practice and early intervention and by further delegating SEN resources and developing rigorous monitoring arrangements, it acknowledged that there was a limit to what can be achieved by doing so. It identified what it described as a number of tensions in the statutory framework that lie behind its key shortcomings. In particular:

- LEAs are held responsible for arranging provision to meet the needs of children with statements − but resources are increasingly controlled by schools;
- some children require the support of health and social services, but these agencies are only required to respond in so far as their resources and priorities allow; and
- statements place unlimited demands on limited LEA budgets.

The key recommendation of the Audit Commission was that government should establish a high-level independent review, engaging all key stakeholders (young people and parents, schools, local authorities, health services, voluntary organisations and others) in considering options for future reform. Given the resource implications of the changes such a wholesale review would be likely to recommend, it is perhaps not surprising that the Government has not acted on this recommendation.

Measures of SEN and Accountability

The requirement of the Code of Practice (repeated in Circular 6/94) that governing bodies must account in their annual report to parents for the way in which they have allocated resources to and amongst pupils with SEN over the year means that they must do their homework. It is incumbent on them to ascertain the precise basis of SEN funding in their formula allocation by asking some fundamental questions. For example, governors may not be aware that free school meals (FSM) are often used as a proxy indicator for SEN.

Although FSM is essentially an economic measure rather than an educational one, the relevant data can be collected easily and there is a statistical correlation between the overall percentage of the school population with SEN and the percentage of pupils on FSM. If FSM is being used as a proxy for SEN, governing bodies should probe further and ascertain whether the operative number of pupils in the formula reflects entitlement or take-up, and whether the figure itself is accurate. The main issue here is that if schools are funded on the basis of take-up (i.e. the number of meals actually consumed) rather than entitlement, they will receive less money than would otherwise have been the case – and could even argue that they have not been funded for some SEN pupils at all.

Growing dissatisfaction with the use of an indicator (FSM) that has no overt connection with education has led many authorities to switch to an audit-type approach, which relates directly to SEN processes and provision. Audits will normally take account, for example, of the overall numbers of pupils with SEN in a school at each stage of the Code of Practice. In its simplest form, this is merely a mathematical exercise that quantifies the extent of the provision being made. More refined approaches will also specify the criteria to be employed for assigning pupils to the different stages. In the case of learning difficulties, these might include standard reading tests (vital in the interest of fairness and universal application), and pupils would only be allowed to move, e.g. from School Action to School Action Plus, if they had a reading age below the agreed threshold. Governors should be aware that totally separate criteria may be established in regard to sensory and physical disabilities and behavioural difficulties.

Where audits of SEN are used to determine funding levels, they are invariably accompanied by moderation procedures. The composition of a moderation panel will vary from authority to authority, but will usually include representatives of the authority's heads of service and headteachers. Moderation is essential to ensure that a school adheres to the 'rules' and that the SEN criteria have been correctly applied. Without these checks, consistency across the whole authority cannot be achieved and the credibility of the system will be called into question, as there will always be a lingering suspicion that the schools are 'doctoring' their figures to secure an unfair financial advantage.

Governing bodies should be sure to study not only their own budget statement but also that of the LEA which covers all its schools to ensure that they are fully aware of what the unit rate of resource per pupil is, how much has been allocated under various individual headings (including statemented provision) and how much the school has notionally received *in toto* for SEN purposes (and its entitlement). It should be noted that some LEAs do not identify any additional funding for Stage 1 pupils, but claim that the standard Age Weighted Pupil Unit (AWPU) already includes an element for such costs, whilst others operate differently. An additional allowance is made for socio-economic factors in some formulae in recognition of the known link between poor or low attainment and social disadvantage, often on the basis of FSM as the indicator of need.

Assessment of the Costs of SEN

Having established the total 'income' in their budgets, governing bodies must assess the costs of their SEN provision. It is a relatively easy matter to calculate the salaries, plus on-costs, of those who are employed purely in an SEN capacity and to quantify the school's liabilities for meeting the needs of statemented pupils. But is it fair to assign the whole of this expenditure to the SEN budget? To what extent do pupils without special educational needs benefit from the expertise of SEN staff? Have welfare assistants been included in the calculations or has any account been taken of administrative salaries? This is particularly important where large numbers of annual reviews have to be organised and reports produced. What about 'teacher time' at the various school-based stages? With a mixed-ability class of 30, for example, in a one-hour lesson, each pupil has a notional allocation of two minutes. If, however, the teacher spends 20 minutes on two SEN pupils, the others only receive 1.42 minutes of teacher time, a significant reduction. How should these costs be estimated? These are all issues which must be properly addressed in open and sharply focused debate.

Recoupment and School/LEA Contracts

It should be remembered that the responsibility for funding a statement rests with the LEA in which a child lives, and in many cases this will not be the same as the LEA in which the school that the child attends is situated. According to the Guidance given in Circular 1/96, 'The Belonging Regulations', in a subsection on the subject of inter-authority recoupment (i.e. reimbursement of expenditure incurred), arrangements which schools have entered into with authorities other than the 'home' LEA will need to be revised. It appears that schools have no legal standing to enforce recoupment claims against authorities and that authorities are not permitted to adjust the budgets of schools so as to take account of recoupment income which should accrue to authorities (i.e. authorities are not legally able to pay recoupment directly to a maintained school). Schools should, therefore, negotiate such agreements with their home authority which will then act as a 'middle-man' or agent (perhaps even making the process more expensive by imposing a surcharge for its services). The need, however, for schools to enter into such specific financial contracts with their LEA to provide the support delineated in a statement was substantially reduced under the Fair Funding arrangements, because funding for this purpose has usually been included in their individual school's budget.

Where financial contracts of this kind continue to operate or where schools have taken on additional staff to meet their obligations to their statemented pupils from the funding delegated to them, care should be taken that tenure is specifically tied to the delivery of such provision. Otherwise, schools could be saddled with the burden of salary costs for which they do not receive any income – although the fact that employees have employment protection and other permanent rights after one year in post is likely to make matters even more difficult to manage. Whatever the precise circumstances, such arrangements, and those that involve contracts with outside agencies for supplying the same provision, should be carefully monitored at regular intervals to ensure that a deficit is not incurred unwittingly. Where necessary, schools must also be prepared to issue invoices promptly (termly or half-termly, depending on the arrangement) and to follow up non-payment assiduously.

These issues should be formally considered by all governing bodies at one of their main meetings as a separate agenda item, and both the substance of the discussion and the outcomes should be minuted. It is also sensible for financial decisions to be clearly related to a policy, which might state, for example, that the amount to be spent on SEN should not exceed the funding normally available through the formula allocation. All of this entails a great deal of work, but, as a result, governing bodies will be in a position to render a full and detailed account of their SEN stewardship to parents, and this aspect of the annual report should hold no fears for them.

FUTURE DEVELOPMENTS

Improving the SEN Framework

The Code of Practice on Special Educational Needs is part of the Government's commitment to improving the accountability of LEAs by requiring them to provide more detailed information about their SEN policies and by monitoring their performance closely against critical indicators.

Developing a More Inclusive Education System

The Government is committed to a policy of greater inclusion, which is underpinned by an expectation that children will generally spend most of their educational lives during the compulsory years in a mainstream setting. The following measures, designed to foster the development of inclusion, have been given prominence in the programme:

- greater collaboration between mainstream and special schools. This applies to staff and pupils. The proposals envisage an enhanced role for special schools as centres of excellence, but operating under more flexible arrangements, which might entail that they, for example, serve as a source of professional expertise for mainstream teachers or admit pupils from mainstream schools on a temporary, rather than a permanent, basis or re-integrate pupils into mainstream education more speedily; and

- a requirement that LEAs:

  - promote inclusion in the fullest sense;
  - support projects which raise the aspirations of pupils with emotional and behavioural difficulties;
  - improve access to the schools of their choice (and, therefore, to better educational opportunities) for pupils with SEN under the statutory provisions of the Code of Practice governing admissions.

Decisions on the pattern of special school provision in the area are determined locally by School Organisation Committees (and Adjudicators if their involvement proves necessary). They pay particular attention to whether there is a real need for a particular type of provision in the locality, parental preference, the cost-effectiveness of any proposals put before them and whether the proposals foster post-16 collaborative arrangements.

It is of course generally accepted that the earlier the intervention for a child with SEN, the better. The implementation of the Disability Discrimination Act 1995 within the field of education has focussed some attention upon such issues for disabled children, and the DfES and Department of Health have issued Guidance 'Together From the Start' which advocates a more co-ordinated, family-centred approach to multi-agency working when addressing the needs of disabled children, and applies to health, education and social service professionals. The DfES has also issued Guidance which it has produced in conjunction with the RNID called 'Developing Early Intervention/Support Services for Deaf Children and their Families', which is designed to address the consequences of the increasingly early diagnosis of deafness in children.

Target Setting

Many of the general target-setting principles are also applicable in the case of pupils with special educational needs, but the DfES publication, *Supporting the Target-Setting Process: Guidance for Effective Target-setting for Pupils with SEN*, offers particularly relevant advice for such pupils and is to be recommended. The booklet suggests that schools which have a preponderance or a substantial number of pupils with SEN should tailor the target-setting process to their own context and:

- institute time-scales and measures of assessment that are able to gauge the rate of school improvement and the progress registered by their pupils more appropriately and accurately. The normal National Curriculum level descriptions may not be particularly helpful and other, more differentiated, assessment criteria may have to be devised;

- identify other schools (in cases where the national benchmark data is inadequate for their circumstances and meaningful comparison with other schools cannot be drawn), which exhibit similar characteristics, with a view to sharing good practice and employing common measures of pupil performance;

- set targets in addition to those which are required by statute, which reflect their priorities and needs with greater precision, e.g. quantifiable improvement in basic number or communication skills or being able to work more independently;

- take appropriate action to achieve the targets which have been determined;
- review progress and adjust targets as necessary;
- repeat the cyclical process.

GUIDANCE

Circular 1/96, 'The Belonging Regulations'.

Circular 1/98, 'LEA Behaviour Support Plans'.

Special Educational Needs Code of Practice (DfES, 2001).

Supporting the Target-Setting Process: Guidance for Effective Target-setting for Pupils with SEN (DfES, 2001).

Chapter 6

DISABILITY DISCRIMINATION

Introduction – Disability – Discrimination – Employment issues – Provision of non-educational services to the public – Enforcement – Accessibility planning – Publication of information – Guidance

INTRODUCTION

Initially, the Disability Discrimination Act 1995 applied to schools only in certain areas, i.e. as employers, in the provision of non-educational services, and in imposing obligations to give information about arrangements for disabled pupils. The Special Educational Needs and Disability Discrimination Act 2001 extended the requirement not to discriminate against people with disabilities generally to the provision of education. Despite its title, the Act is not restricted to pupils with special educational needs. It applies potentially to all pupils, even if the disability in question is not related to any ability to learn or access the curriculum. In short, the non-discrimination provisions cover essentially the whole range of a school's activities.

The main new sections of the Act, extending the non-discrimination obligations to pupils, were implemented on 1 September 2002. They apply specifically to:

- admissions arrangements, so that the admissions policy of the school must not in itself discriminate against people with disabilities and the terms on which an offer of a place is made must not be discriminatory. Furthermore, a school may not refuse to accept an application from a disabled pupil although this does not change the position of pupils with statements of special educational needs whose admission to a school comes through the statementing process and not through the application of the ordinary admissions policy. Schools that recruit by reference to ability will be relieved to know that selection by ability is specifically declared not to be discrimination, although care is needed in determining what steps are taken to assess that ability for the reasons touched on below. Admission to courses involving dance or drama may also be dependent on reaching a specified standard even though this may discriminate against pupils with disabilities;

- the exclusion process;

- the provision of education generally, and related services. Those services are not defined but regulations are to be made that will establish (to avoid scope for argument) that certain services are to be treated as education services and which, therefore, must be made available without discrimination except where the discrimination can be justified. The following will be important for schools in dealing with disabled pupils:

  - extra-curricular activities in and out of school;
  - arranging field trips;
  - arranging study or work placements abroad;
  - arranging outings and trips;
  - finding of work placements;
  - providing leisure and sports facilities;
  - providing catering.

Discrimination arises by treating a disabled person less favourably than others. In addition, schools will be required to provide certain types of reasonable adjustments to provision where disabled students or other disabled people might otherwise be substantially disadvantaged. Schools and LEAs are also required to plan for physical change, although there is no requirement for them to provide auxiliary aids and services (on the footing that if these are required, the pupil should have a statement of special educational needs that will make specific provision and carry appropriate funding) or to make alterations to the physical features of the premises. Governing bodies must prepare an accessibility plan in relation to access to education (to be implemented over time) which must improve access to the curriculum, make improvements to the fabric of the school to improve access to education and improve the provision of information in a range of formats for disabled pupils. OFSTED will monitor the implementation of the planning duty through inspections, and the Secretary of State can intervene when a school is not complying with the duty, and can be directed to do so.

The non-discrimination provisions take effect in two distinct ways. First, there is the general negative obligation not to discriminate against disabled people by treating them less favourably than others. Secondly, and in a more restricted way, there may be an obligation to take positive steps to make reasonable adjustments to the way in which the school provides its services. Each of these aspects apply already to employment, so that schools have been required for some time not to discriminate against disabled employees and to make reasonable adjustments to accommodate their needs.

The DfES has issued Guidance, Circular 20/99 and 'Accessible Schools: Planning to increase access to schools for disabled pupils'. In addition, the Disability Rights Commission (DRC) has drafted a Code of Practice for Schools which is extremely well written and of real practical value and application. It can be referred to in relevant proceedings potentially as evidence of failure to avoid discrimination and any adjudicating body, i.e. a Tribunal or court must take into account any provision of it that it considers relevant to the issue it is deciding. Schools should therefore be extra cautious about deviating from it, and should consider seeking specialist legal advice before doing so.

DISABILITY

Not all discrimination against disabled people will be unlawful. The definition of 'disability' and 'disabled' is restricted and it is necessary to look closely at some definitions.

For the purposes of the legislation, for a person to be treated as disabled, that person must have, or have had, a physical or mental impairment which has a substantial and long-term adverse effect on the ability to carry out normal day-to-day activities. Long-term means that the impairment has lasted or is expected to last for at least 12 months or for the rest of the life of the person concerned. It follows from this that a short-term but incurable impairment (i.e. an impairment which results in a short life expectancy) constitutes a long-term impairment.

A disability may be said to affect the ability to carry out day-to-day activities if it affects one of the defined categories of capacity listed in the legislation, namely:

- mobility;
- manual dexterity;
- physical co-ordination;

- continence;
- ability to lift, carry or otherwise move everyday objects;
- speech, hearing or eyesight;
- memory or ability to concentrate, learn or understand; or
- perception of the risk of physical danger.

Any physical, sensory, or mental (provided it is a clinically well-recognised illness) impairment, including a learning disability, qualifies as an impairment for non-discrimination purposes, as do any progressive conditions, such as cancer, multiple sclerosis, muscular dystrophy, HIV infection and severe disfigurement. However, for reasons that make commercial if not medical sense, not every adverse condition constitutes an impairment, even though it may in colloquial terms be said to impair the ability of the person concerned to perform his or her functions as employee or student. Addiction to alcohol, nicotine, or any other substance (except as a result of it being medically prescribed), seasonal allergic rhinitis, e.g. hayfever (unless it aggravates the effect of another condition), exhibitionism, voyeurism or tendencies to set fires, to steal or to physical or sexual abuse of others are excluded.

Disfigurements such as tattoos, non-medical body piercing and objects attached through such piercing are treated as not having a substantial adverse effect on the ability to carry out normal day-to-day activities. Other severe disfigurements do constitute long-term impairments and it is not necessary for the affected person to demonstrate that this has a substantive adverse effect – it is assumed that it does.

If someone is undergoing medical or other treatment that alleviates or removes the effect of the impairment (rather than curing it), that treatment (unless it merely involves wearing spectacles or contact lenses) is ignored in deciding whether the impairment is one that would have a substantial adverse effect. In other words, one looks at the nature of the impairment rather than its physical manifestations at any given time. The rationalisation for this, presumably, is that the effect of treatment may be uncertain, erratic or short-term, and the affected person's conditions in the workplace or in the school should not change as a result of the treatment ceasing to be effective.

The requirement that the adverse effect be substantial means that minor or trivial conditions can be ignored. The Guidance suggests that a test might be whether or not the disability causes a difficulty that goes beyond the normal differences in ability which might exist among people.

An impairment that ceases to have a substantial adverse effect is nonetheless treated as though it continues to have that effect if the effect is likely to recur at least once within 12 months. This is intended to cover conditions that may go into remission or be temporarily alleviated.

In considering the application of the legislation to any particular person, it is essential to be able to establish when the right not to be discriminated against arises. This involves defining when the disability itself arises. The test is that the right not to be discriminated against arises from the moment the condition leads to an impairment which affects the ability to carry out normal day-to-day activities if the effect is eventually likely to become substantial. This poses an obvious difficulty for schools, in that it may not be immediately obvious that someone has a relevant condition. Reasonable lack of knowledge is a defence, but the fact that no one had made the school aware of the condition will not necessarily be enough. Schools will need to consider how they will monitor their pupils and staff. One small step that schools can take to protect themselves is to include in their home–school agreements a parental obligation to keep the school informed of any medical condition that may not be temporary. This is not foolproof, in that schools cannot claim to be exonerated from the legal duty simply because the parent has not complied with the terms of the home–school agreement, but it may be useful evidentially if there is a dispute over whether the school should have become aware of the disability. If the parent did not think it important enough to mention, why should the school have noticed? It is not an argument likely to succeed where the parents are themselves disadvantaged in some way. Staff should also periodically be reminded that they should advise the school if they consider that the terms of the legislation may apply to them, although they cannot be compelled to respond and the school cannot use a lack of response as a justification for not acting where the disability is known or should be known.

DISCRIMINATION

Discrimination occurs when:

- a disabled person is treated less favourably than someone else;
- the treatment is for a reason relating to the person's disability;
- that reason does not, or would not, apply to others; and
- this treatment cannot be justified.

It should be emphasised that there may well be occasions when discriminatory treatment may be justified because the nature of the disability goes to the root of what is needed to perform the job. Thus, it is plainly permissible to discriminate against an unsighted person when recruiting bus drivers. It may be reasonable to discriminate against an unsighted teacher where it is an essential part of the job that the teacher drives the school mini-bus. However, in that case, the question will also arise as to whether by making a reasonable adjustment, i.e. moving the driving requirement to another teacher with the candidate for appointment taking on a suitable alternative duty. This demonstrates the second limb of discrimination, namely that discrimination also occurs when:

- the school has a duty to make reasonable adjustments to cater for the disability;
- it has failed to make those adjustments; and
- that failure cannot be justified.

In deciding whether it is reasonable for a school to be expected to make an adjustment, the following factors should be considered:

- What improvement will the adjustment produce?
- How easy is it to make the adjustment?
- What will it cost, financially and in terms of disruption?
- What resources (including available grants) does the school have for the purpose?

These tests apply to discrimination in all areas. Ultimately, value judgements will need to be made and schools would be well advised to consult with those affected and take professional advice based on the particular facts, particularly if it is decided not to make a particular adjustment. It would be prudent for a decision not to make an adjustment to be considered by the governing body or a committee to whom powers have been delegated.

EMPLOYMENT ISSUES

Apart from Circular 20/99, there is a useful good practice guide by SKILL, the National Bureau for Students with Disabilities, entitled *Employing Disabled Teachers*. It makes the positive point that disabled people represent a largely untapped source of talent. At a time of teacher shortage, there are sound commercial reasons, quite apart from any moral or legal ones, for a school to take a positive approach towards catering for the disabled. The guide also highlights the opportunities that may arise for pupils, with or without disabilities, to develop an unprejudiced view of disability and to see disabled people overcoming difficulties and achieving a professional career.

The requirement not to discriminate against an employee with a disability has wide implications. It applies, of course, to all employees and not just teachers and to a wide range of employment issues such as:

- recruitment processes, including job specification, advertising, the process of application and interviews;
- appointment;
- promotions and transfers;
- workplace conditions;
- other conditions of employment;
- benefits; and
- employment protection.

Not all employers are affected but, in practice, all but the smallest of schools will be because the legislation applies to all those who employ more than 15 people. Certain types of employee are excluded but none that are relevant to schools.

The Appointment Process

Discrimination may occur in:

- job advertisements. Do they make it clear that the school welcomes applications from disabled people?

- the application process. A requirement that an application be handwritten may be discriminatory;

- the selection criteria used. Are the criteria focused on the needs of the post or do they reflect non-essential aspects? A school may feel that it would be an advantage that a physics teacher is able to referee a football match but unless refereeing is to be a specific part of the job specification, applying that as a differentiator may well be discriminatory;

- the interview procedure. Each applicant should be asked in advance whether the school needs to cater for any disability. A disabled parking space or wheelchair access may be required. Questions about the disability must be restricted to determining whether or not the disability would affect the candidate's ability to do the job and whether any adjustment would be required. The question of adjustment should always be explored and in deciding between candidates the school should assume that reasonable adjustments would be made. It would be discriminatory to engage a non-disabled person in preference to an equally qualified disabled one simply to avoid the cost of a reasonable adjustment. This does not mean that the school must consider making all adjustments that would be necessary to enable the disabled person to be employed: if the nature of the adjustment, for example installing a lift, was disproportionately expensive or inconvenient it would not constitute a reasonable adjustment and an unwillingness to make it would not be unlawful discrimination. If, on the other hand, accessibility to upper floors was the key issue and there was a lift serving part but not all of the building, the school should consider whether timetabling or adjustment of the job requirements could enable the person to work only within those accessible areas. If that could be done without significant cost or disruption (bearing in mind the impact of the change on others) then the school might be at risk if the reason for rejecting the candidate was to avoid that adjustment. Failure by the school to ask itself the relevant questions may in itself be discrimination;

- the terms of employment offered. It goes almost without saying that it would be discriminatory to offer terms to a disabled person that were less favourable than those that would have been offered to a non-disabled person;

- deliberately not offering the job because of the disability;

- not adjusting the job reasonably to meet the disability.

It is impossible to give a complete list of what would constitute reasonable adjustments because these will depend in every case on the exact nature of the disability and the physical conditions of the school. Modern premises should be substantially equipped to cope with disabilities and adjustments may well be minor or not needed. An old Victorian or Edwardian building may present quite different, and often impossible, challenges. It cannot be said too often that schools are not required to go beyond what is reasonable in all the circumstances and they are not required to make adjustments where the disability causes only minor disadvantage. Examples of reasonable adjustments will be found in Circular 20/99 and in the SKILL Guide. The latter is particularly useful, with specific examples of small adjustments that can readily be made.

Adjustments need to be considered in specific contexts, relative to the particular disability. They may involve:

- altering premises;
- allocating some duties to another employee;
- altering working hours;
- changing the person's place of work;
- allowing absences during working hours for rehabilitation, assessment or treatment;
- supplying additional training; and
- acquiring or making changes to equipment.

It must be kept clearly in mind that the obligation not to discriminate does not relate only to those who are disabled when their employment commences. It applies just as much to those who become disabled during their employment, and the financial consequences of discriminating against long-serving employees may be greater than those of discriminating in the appointment process.

Remedies

Disabled or prospective employees may complain to an Employment Tribunal if they believe an employer has:

- unlawfully discriminated against them; or
- refused to make reasonable adjustments.

The Employment Tribunal may recommend appropriate action (such as making an adjustment) or order compensation.

PROVISION OF NON-EDUCATIONAL SERVICES TO THE PUBLIC

Schools that provide goods, facilities and services of a non-educational nature are required not to discriminate against disabled people by unjustifiably refusing to provide a service which they provide to non-disabled members of the public, or by providing a service that is worse or of a lower standard or on less favourable terms. There is also a duty to make reasonable adjustments if that is necessary to prevent it being impossible or unreasonably difficult for the disabled person to take advantage of the service in question. The requirement in relation to reasonable adjustment to premises came into force on 1 October 2004. At present, schools must take reasonable steps to change any discriminatory practice, policy or procedure, to provide auxiliary aids or service, and to deal with physical barriers which make it impossible or unreasonably difficult for disabled people to use a service. The DRC has drafted a further Code of Practice which applies to providers of services, and is again very useful.

Circular 20/99 specifies a number of services which the DfES regards as being within the category of non-educational services even though they may be provided for parents or pupils. These are:

- services offered to pupils which are not related to their studies, such as skiing holidays;

- services offered to parents, such as governing body meetings to present the annual report;

- admissions appeal hearings where the school organises the appeal by the parents;

- fund-raising events organised by PTAs, such as jumble sales, boot sales or dances;

- leisure time activities for children or adults without any element of educational development; and

- the use of school sports facilities by the local community or the hiring of school accommodation to members of the public.

It will be noted that the responsibility is not necessarily limited to the school. There will be a responsibility on the PTA for events that it organises and the PTA may well rely on the school for advice and Guidance.

The Circular and Code of Practice give a number of examples of unlawful discrimination. Those relating to the provision of services are self-explanatory. Thus, if the school lets a hall for weddings or other functions, it would be unlawful for the school to refuse to let it to a disabled person, at least if there were no other sound reasons for not entering into the contract: for example, if the disabled person were under some legal disability that would make any purported contract unenforceable. It would be unlawful for the school to refuse to allow a disabled person access to a meeting organised by the school for parents generally. It would be unlawful for the PTA to refuse a disabled person access to a fund-raising event held on school premises. These examples are, however, subject to the proviso that there should be no health and safety issues.

The Circular and Code of Practice also give examples of possible adjustments that might reasonably be made to make the service in question accessible to disabled people. Here, as distinct from employment obligations, the duty is an anticipatory one in that schools need to consider in advance how they may make the service in question more accessible. The examples given in the Circular relate to:

- a dogs policy that makes no allowance for guide dogs;
- a complaints procedure that does not allow for the complaint to be made verbally;
- the provision of newsletters and other information in Braille or cassette form – which, although the Circular does not specifically mention the point, must be considered within a resource context in deciding whether this would be a reasonable service to provide;
- the location of meeting places either for general meetings or for individual appointments so that disabled people are not presented with reasonably avoidable difficulties.

ENFORCEMENT

The Special Educational Needs and Disability Tribunal has jurisdiction to deal with claims of unjustifiable discrimination by or on behalf of disabled pupils. Although it does not have the power to award financial compensation, it does have the power to make an order as it thinks reasonable in the circumstances of the case. This may take the form of directing further training, adaptation of policies, adaptation of premises by, for example, relocating facilities within the school to improve accessibility, or the provision of extra tuition to make good the learning deficit caused by the unlawful discrimination. The Tribunal does not have jurisdiction in cases relating to an admissions decision or an appeal against permanent exclusion but even here the Tribunal may claim jurisdiction over the arrangements that are made for dealing with admissions, as distinct from the decision whether or not to admit. The case referred to below relating to the sitting of a secondary school selection test is indicative of the distinction.

Disability discrimination cases are now beginning to make their way through the tribunal process and to the courts. An important decision concerns the case of a boy on the autistic spectrum. The school appears to have managed his transition into year 7 effectively with the use of a strategy developed by an educational psychologist that recommended the use of buddies, direct questioning techniques in lessons, the production of subject-specific word banks and the repetition of instructions in lessons to help his understanding. Problems arose when transferring into year 8 because it was no longer possible to support the pupil in the same way as the year group moved from mixed ability groups into sets for each subject, meaning that the buddy system was no longer operable and that the boy was placed in groups of lower ability children. The pupil's behaviour deteriorated through the course of the autumn term, and he became the victim of what are described as bullying incidents. Matters came to a head when the pupil appears to have become largely uncontrollable, and was given a fixed-term exclusion when he became physically and verbally abusive to members of staff including the headteacher. Although the Tribunal did not find against the school on most of the points raised, it did conclude that the school could have done more because the pupil had not been afforded sufficient pastoral care and Guidance particularly through the course of the transition to year 8. The discontinuance of the buddy system was not in itself discriminatory but the failure to put adequate alternative support in place was. It would appear that the school took exception to this, perhaps feeling that it had done everything that could be reasonably expected of it, and appealed to the High Court on that point. The High Court dismissed the appeal, concluding that the Tribunal's decision could not be impugned which demonstrates the need to leave no stone unturned when considering what adjustments should be made for a disabled pupil. An important point to note is that the Court will not change a Tribunal decision simply because the judge feels that a different decision was possible. If there was evidence on which the Tribunal could reasonably base its decision, the Court will not interfere with it. It follows, therefore, that schools must ensure that their case is fully presented to the Tribunal: there will not be a second chance.

Of greater significance was the Court's conclusion that, in determining whether a disabled pupil suffering from autistic spectrum disorder had been treated less favourably, comparison should be made with a pupil who is not disabled *and who behaves properly*. This decision is likely have a profound impact upon the way in which schools draft and apply their behaviour and discipline policies and the way in which they approach exclusion. Schools are already exhorted not to exclude pupils because of their disability. Where challenging behaviour is a symptom of that disability schools should take particular care. Schools should seek to manage that behaviour by the use of appropriate pastoral support and reasonable adjustments, and only resort to disciplinary sanctions when all avenues of this sort have been explored. This is not to say that such pupils cannot be disciplined or excluded: such action must however be justified and constitute a material and substantial reason. A useful example, endorsed by the court in this case, is included at examples 5.7C, 5.10C, 5.15C and 5.16A of the DRC Code of Practice for Schools which is reproduced below:

'A pupil with Tourette's Syndrome is stopped from going on a school visit because he has used abusive language in class. The school has a policy of banning pupils from trips and after-school activities if they swear or are abusive to staff.

The reason for not allowing the pupil to go on the school visit is his use of abusive language. His involuntary swearing is a symptom of his Tourette's Syndrome. This is less favourable treatment for a reason that relates to the pupil's disability ...

In the example of the pupil with Tourette's Syndrome who was banned from a school visit because of abusive language, the reason was directly related to his disability. The comparison has to be made with others who had not used abusive language. In this case, the pupil who used abusive language, which is directly related to his disability, was treated less favourably than pupils who had not used abusive language. So, for a reason that relates to his disability, this boy is being treated less favourably than another child to whom that reason does not apply ...

In the example of the pupil with Tourette's Syndrome who was banned from a school visit because of abusive language, is the less favourable treatment justified? In this case the responsible body might argue that the inclusion of the disabled pupil on the visit would make the maintenance of discipline impossible. This may constitute a material and substantial reason. However, the responsible body would need to have considered the extent to which the disabled pupil's behaviour could have been managed. It would also need to have considered whether reasonable adjustments could have been made to its policies and procedures before it could attempt to justify less favourable treatment ...

In the case of the pupil with Tourette's Syndrome there were reasonable adjustments that were normally in place; the introduction of new ideas was carefully managed, as were time pressures. Left unmanaged, both of these tended to exacerbate the effects of the pupil's impairment. In this case, a supply teacher was taking the class and failed to make the adjustments that were normally made. Reasonable adjustments might have been made but were not, and therefore the responsible body is unlikely to be able to justify the less favourable treatment.'

Another recent court decision relates to a placement for work experience which, as indicated in Chapter 3, now forms part of the Key Stage 4 curriculum. The school used an external provider to find and organise the placements. It had a process designed to elicit information to enable the provider to do so appropriately to need. Parents were asked to complete a form which included a question about medical condition. In this case, the pupil had a visual impairment but this was not disclosed on the form. The medical question was not answered at all because, as was well-known to the school and as appeared in the pupil's statement of special educational needs, the pupil did not like attention being drawn to her disability and did not like to be treated differently. The school did not notice the absence of a response to the medical question but in discussions with the provider the school did mention that the pupil was visually impaired and that the employer would need to be consulted. None of the pupil's stated choices were considered suitable, although for reasons not connected with the disability. The provider took the view that unless the medical condition question was answered, no placement could be made since employers needed the information in order to make proper provision. The parent refused to complete the form or provide any further information on the somewhat conflicting grounds first of confidentiality and secondly that the school had all the relevant information to pass on. In consequence no placement was made.

The claim of discrimination was upheld, although the reasoning is compressed and not entirely easy to follow. The school seems to have assumed that the refusal by the parent to give information about the disability absolved the school from any further responsibility but the court did not accept that. The judge felt that the school could have dealt with the lack of information on the form by way of a covering letter which would have meant that the provider and therefore any employer would have the information that was needed. The judge did not deal with the question of how that meshed with the claimed right to confidentiality but reading a bit between the lines, it may be that the parent was simply exasperated by what may have seemed to be petty bureaucracy. The parent's relationship with the school seems to have been strained anyway. At all events, the case demonstrates the need for schools to be alert to specific disability issues when dealing with work experience placements.

It is difficult to get a feel for the decisions that are going through the Tribunal because they are not widely reported, and do not have a binding effect upon subsequent decisions. However, the DRC does keep a note on its web-site of a number of cases (some of which have received media attention) which are useful for illustrative purposes. They include a pupil with learning difficulties and developmental delay whose exclusion from school activities (including the Christmas play, assemblies and school trips) was found to be discriminatory. The school concerned apparently sought to justify the action it took on the basis that it believed the pupil would not benefit from these activities, and would disrupt other children. Another case, in which a child with eczema was prevented from wearing cotton trousers to school, was settled: although the report does not make it clear, one assumes that agreement was reached on the basis that the child's mother obtained what she had been seeking – an apology, a change to the school's uniform policy and staff training in disability awareness. In another case, a girl with specific learning difficulties who was afforded reasonable adjustments (extra time and a reader) when sitting SATS exams, was not given the same facilities when sitting a secondary-school selection examination. The DRC indicated that it felt it had good prospects of success. Similarly, a candidate for a selective examination who suffered from Chronic Fatigue Syndrome who tired very easily and could only concentrate on school work for

Running a School 2004/05

approximately 20 minutes at a time was initially refused a request from his parents for the exam to be split into 20-minute sections because the school felt it would be unfair to other candidates. This case was settled with the school agreeing for the exam to be split in to three sections sat on three separate days. It is now generally accepted that when using competitive exams such as this, admission authorities should have policies to address issues relating to disability and adopt procedures to consider the merits of each case on an individual basis.

Schools may feel that if a claim of discrimination is made and is taken to the Tribunal, it is enough for the school to meet the claimant's demands. That will not necessarily stop the case going ahead if the claimant wants a formal ruling that there had been disability discrimination. The Tribunal can still make a finding against the school and can order the school to change its practice even though (as was the situation in the case referred to above) the child in question is no longer at the school. This is another reason why disability discrimination issues, and allegations of discrimination, must be taken seriously at the outset. There is no obligation on the LEA to meet the costs incurred by the school and no guarantee that it would do so. Furthermore, Tribunal hearings are very draining in terms of time and stress.

ACCESSIBILITY PLANNING

As touched upon above, schools must now have an accessibility plan which must be published in its annual report to parents. The initial plan was required to run for a period of three years from 1 April 2003 until 31 March 2006. Schools have a duty to review their plan, revise it if necessary, and implement it. They are also required to allocate adequate resources for implementing the plan. As ever, the legislation is silent as to where those resources are to come from.

The Guidance contained in 'Accessible Schools: Planning to increase access to schools for disabled pupils' has been written with a deliberately light touch. It is not prescriptive, but provides pointers and useful checklists to assist schools in meeting their obligations.

The Guidance suggests that in improving access to the curriculum, reference to:

• The National Curriculum 2000, which incorporates a statement on 'Inclusion: providing effective learning opportunities for all children';

- The Qualifications and Curriculum Authority's general and subject guidelines on planning, teaching and assessing the curriculum for pupils with learning difficulties; and

- *Supporting The Target Setting Process* (revised March 2001) published by the DfES and QCA

will assist compliance. It also emphasises that curricular activity is expected to include activities such as participation in after-school clubs, leisure, sporting and cultural activities and school visits. It recommends the use of flexible grouping arrangements including those where pupils with disabilities can work with their peers, and encouraging peer support by, for example, setting up buddying or mentoring arrangements. It also emphasises the need to ensure that staff training needs are met.

The Guidance's comments about improving the physical environment are very limited but do emphasise the need to consider this issue within the resources available to it. These issues should be dealt with by the LEA except in the case of VA schools where it will be a governing body obligation, albeit with capital grant where appropriate. The Guidance suggests that schools might consider accessibility in all purchasing decisions, which might include decisions for instance about the choice of carpet for wheelchair users or lighting, colour contrasting décor and signage.

The format in which information including handouts, timetables and information about school events is delivered should be considered. The Guidance indicates that plans could include provision of more information pictorially and orally and the use of lip speaking so that disabled pupils can access material more easily. The Guidance indicates that schools should consider how all information normally provided in a written format could be made more accessible over time.

When developing the plan, schools are encouraged to link it in with other plans, so that the point is eventually reached where disability planning simply forms another strand of the overall planning processes schools follow. Initially however, the Guidance recommends using the following stages:

- Access audit and review of current activities

    - The school needs to know from where it is starting. Therefore the Guidance recommends a review of access including the physical environment, the provision of auxiliary aids and services, teaching and learning practices, the curriculum, staff training, the culture and ethos of the school and the provision of written information.

- Schools need to be able to take account of future need and LEAs are encouraged themselves to obtain relevant information from other sources (such as, for instance, the local Health Authority) to do so. This information should then be shared.
- The Guidance includes helpful checklists to assist in this process.

- Devise actions

  - These should include realistic costs estimates.
  - The Guidance suggests breaking this down into staff training, teaching and learning practices, refurbishment and maintenance (such as the use of colour when redecorating and replacing floor coverings or furniture), minor capital expenditure, and major capital expenditure. Schools are then encouraged to draw up short, medium and long-term priorities and devise strategies to address these priorities with clear implementation arrangements and a timeframe for the work.

- Set goals and targets

- Consult on the plan

  - The Guidance suggests that it may be appropriate to consult with staff, which could be broadened to include parents, pupils other bodies.

- Publicise the plan

  - The plan must be publicised in the governors' annual report to parents.

- Implementation
- Evaluate the plan

  - This is intended to include a process of review and revision.

PUBLICATION OF INFORMATION

Schools are required to publish in their annual reports:

- a description of the admissions arrangements for pupils with disabilities;

- details of the steps taken to prevent pupils with disabilities from being treated less favourably than other pupils;

- details of facilities provided to assist access to the school by pupils with disabilities; and

- information about the accessibility plan which the governing body is required to prepare and implement.

GUIDANCE

DfES Circular 20/99, 'What the Disability Discrimination Act (DDA) 1995 Means for Schools and LEAs'.

Disability Rights Commission 'Code of Practice for Schools'.

Disability Rights Commission 'Code of Practice: Rights of Access: Goods, Facilities, Services and Premises'.

DfES Guidance (reference LEA/0168/2002), 'Accessible Schools: Planning to increase access to schools for disabled pupils'.

'Guidance on matters to be taken into account in determining questions relating to the definition of disability', available from The Stationery Office.

Chapter 7

ADMISSIONS

The right to a school place and admissions information – Admissions policies – Co-ordination of admissions arrangements – Infant class sizes – The provision of information – Extent of parental entitlement – Appeals against refusal to admit – Appeals by governing bodies – Relevant guidance

THE RIGHT TO A SCHOOL PLACE AND ADMISSIONS INFORMATION

The most significant and critical area of school organisation relates to the admission of pupils to schools and the nature, extent and limitations on parents' rights. Probably no single area causes more concern, confusion and individual distress. Radical changes were made as part of the reorganisation of the framework of State school education. The essential entitlement that parental preference be met, and the circumstances in which it need not be met, were left largely as they had been since 1980, but the mechanics were changed, with added powers given to the LEA and certain schools to object to individual admissions policies. It is, though, doubtful that the changes have succeeded in making the admissions jungle less impenetrable and the problems that arise from the mismatch of supply and demand, and public perception as to which schools are 'good' schools, remain intractable. The government continues to try to make admissions more responsive both to parental and other local concerns by the now compulsory introduction of Admissions Forums and the co-ordination of admissions arrangements. Given the intention for all parents to be given one school place offer for their children, parents may gain the impression that admission arrangements have simplified. Time will determine the extent to which this may be illusory, because the underlying rules relating to the formulation and content of admissions policies remain largely unaltered.

The Codes of Practice

The Secretary of State has issued two Codes of Practice. One deals with the admissions process and the other with appeals. All concerned with the administration of admissions must have regard to the Codes and they will be referred to here as they relate to the different aspects of the process. The observations made in Chapter 1 about the extent to which admissions authorities and appeal panels should 'have regard' to the Codes of Practice has particular resonance in school admissions.

ADMISSIONS POLICIES

Admissions policies are set by the admission authority for the school. This will normally be the LEA for community and VC schools and the governing body for VA and foundation schools. It is, however, possible for the LEA to agree that a community or VC school be its own admission authority.

Each admission authority must determine its admissions arrangements each year and must normally consult with each admission authority and community or VC school which is not its own admissions authority in its area. Church of England schools must consult the relevant diocesan board before consulting others. An admissions authority need only consult every other year if the LEA has notified the Secretary of State that all admissions authorities in its area consulted in the previous year, it is not proposing to change the admission arrangements from the previous year and no objections have been made to the adjudicator in any of the preceding five years. Primary schools that are admission authorities must consult with all other primary admission authorities. Secondary-school admission authorities must consult with both primary and secondary admission authorities. The area will never be less than the area of the LEA and may be more extensive, particularly for school admission authorities that are within two (for primary schools) and three (for secondary schools) miles of the LEA boundary. It is the LEA's responsibility to decide on the relevant area.

Any admission authority or the governing body of a community or VC school has the right to object to any proposals and parents have certain objection rights in relation to partially selective schools and to proposals to reduce the proposed admissions number below the indicated admissions number. The governing body of a community or VC school also has the right to object to the admission arrangements of other schools in the area, except other community and VC schools whose admission arrangements have been determined by the LEA. The governing body of a community or VC school can only object to the admission number for its own school, and not in respect of other aspects of the admission arrangements for its own school.

If the admission number determined by an admissions authority is less than the school's current indicated admission number, it must be published. Parents can object and if 10 or more parents make substantially the same objection (the same applies to pre-existing partial selection arrangements) the Adjudicator, appointed by the Secretary of State, must then consider the situation. The Adjudicator has discretion over most matters and can rule on any objection or refer it to the Secretary of State. However, any issue involving admission criteria that relate to a person's religion or religious denomination must be referred to the Secretary of State. The Secretary of State has power to lay down other categories of dispute which the Adjudicator must refer for decision, but has not yet done so.

VA and foundation schools with a religious character can no longer seek to include criteria that are intended to preserve the religious character of the school, and therefore can no longer keep places empty if faith criteria are not met. However, schools with a religious character can give preference in their admission criteria to members of a particular faith or denomination.

The Code of Practice stipulates that admissions arrangements enable parents' preferences to be met to the maximum extent possible and that admission criteria are clear, fair and objective for the benefit of all children, including those with special educational needs, disabilities or in public care. The Code does not prescribe any particular forms but it does have some general Guidance. For example:

- criteria must not infringe discrimination or equal opportunities legislation;
- giving priority based on the date order of receipt of applications before a deadline is not acceptable;
- schools giving priority on religious grounds must make the criteria clear. They must state whether a statement of religious affiliation or commitment is sufficient and if, and how, that is to be tested. Parents must be told what

evidence they need to provide. Until the admissions round leading to 2005 intakes, the Code of Practice indicated that schools with a religious character could interview to test religious commitment. As touched on in Chapter 1, the Code of Practice now indicates in quite prescriptive terms that parents and children should no longer be interviewed to establish religious or denominational commitment. However, an admissions authority is simply required to 'have regard' to the Code. Provided it has done so, and is able to produce cogent reasons for doing so, an admissions authority may depart from the Code of Practice. The Code stands as an indicator of good practice and if an objection were taken to the Adjudicator there would need to be very compelling reasons for departure. It then becomes a matter of judgment whether or not the departure is justifiable, and this applies to interviewing as it does in any other area where there is no express statutory prohibition. Indeed, there is no legal objection to any school including interviewing in its admissions procedure. Having said this, the Adjudicator has ruled against interviewing in the only case that has been referred since the new Code of Practice came into force. The Adjudicator held that interviewing was neither necessary nor desirable in the light of the clear guidance in the Code. It is understood that this decision may be challenged by judicial review.

- Faith schools are now encouraged by the Code of Practice to reserve places for local children, even if they are not of the relevant faith, but again this is not mandatory;

- academic selection should not be used for entry to primary schools and where it is used elsewhere it must conform to what is permissible by law. In practice, that restricts selection by ability to grammar schools and those schools that were partially selective in September 1997 and which have been able to continue partial selection because their admissions arrangements have continued to be approved year by year. These aspects, and admission by reference to banding, are dealt with in more detail below;

- schools may admit up to 10 per cent in total of the intake by reference to aptitude in one or more prescribed subjects where the school has a specialism in the subject concerned. This again is subject to the overall annual approval of the admissions policy and again the admission criteria must be explicit and clear;

- the Code requires testing for both ability and aptitude to be accessible to disabled and SEN pupils. This could, for instance, have an impact upon issues such as the size of print on examination papers or the amount of time allotted to take the examination itself. Issues of disability discrimination are explored more fully in Chapter 6.

- non-statemented children with special educational needs, and children with 'challenging behaviour' are to be treated in the same way as other applicants. It is for the school to deal as best it can with the problems once the child is in school. The Code recognises that seriously and persistently disruptive children may then be subject to disciplinary action.

Selection

As mentioned, existing grammar schools can continue to select pupils by reference to ability. Their right to do so, however, can be challenged by parental ballot, although these provisions have proved unworkable in practice and can be regarded very much as a dead letter. Those schools that select a proportion of pupils by reference to ability can continue to do so provided that they do not increase the proportion above that applying in September 1997. The right for these schools to continue to select pupils in this way is subject to their admissions arrangements being approved each year. There is no provision for ballot but the Adjudicator can rule on objections from other admission authorities or from at least 10 parents. It is not necessary for the parental objections to come in a single group of 10 or more or for the objections to be couched in the same words; it is sufficient if the Adjudicator receives objections from different sources that raise substantially the same issue. Partially selective schools will, therefore, be vulnerable to challenge year by year and to secure stability will need to reach a *modus vivendi* with their local community. One way to do this may be through the Admissions Forum referred to below.

Schools that already operated a banding system, under which all applicants are tested to establish into which band of ability they fall, can continue to do so but the system used must give equal weight to each ability band that is used. Schools that wish to adopt such a system in order to achieve a balanced intake must obtain consent from the School Organisation Committee. A change of this nature is one that is prescribed as an alteration that requires publication of formal notices, consultation with interested parties (who have a right of objection) and final determination by the Adjudicator. The banding must be used only to allocate pupils within the relevant bands and not to rank the pupils by ability within the band. At that stage, the objective criteria, such as location of the home, will be applied if the band is over-subscribed.

CO-ORDINATION OF ADMISSIONS ARRANGEMENTS

LEAs must establish Admissions Forums which can be undertaken jointly with other LEAs. They must meet twice a year. The forums are made up of 'stakeholder' groups including LEA representatives, representatives (who can be a headteacher or governor) from each *category* of school (not individual schools), representatives from dioceses, representatives from academies, City Technology Colleges, and representatives of service personnel if appropriate. The purpose of the forums is to consider how well existing and proposed admission arrangements serve the interests of children and parents in the area, to promote agreement on admissions issues, and to consider the effectiveness of the LEA's proposed co-ordinated admissions arrangements, by means of a consensus if possible. They should consider how admissions procedures can be improved and review how comprehensible they are – the Code suggests that parent-governor representatives may be particularly helpful in doing so. The Code of Practice also sees a particular function for forums in seeking to address difficult issues such as ensuring that admission arrangements provide effectively for what it describes as 'vulnerable children' (including looked-after children and children with special educational needs), the allocation of such children outside the normal admissions rounds, and the accommodation of children with challenging behaviour. Admissions authorities must have regard to advice given by the forum for the area.

The Code of Practice requires that:

> 'Forums must be consulted on the co-ordinated scheme being proposed by the LEA. They should consider how effective these arrangements would be and advise the LEA accordingly, ensuring they advise on how decisions will be made on a place offer, in circumstances in which, potentially, a parent could be offered more than one place, or none.'

and goes on to say:

'... The purpose of co-ordinated admission schemes is to establish mechanisms for ensuring, so far as reasonably practicable, that every parent of a child living in the LEA area who has applied for a school place in the "normal admission round" receives an offer of one, and only one, school place on the same day ... Schemes should also address how late applications, and arrangements for handling admissions outside the "normal admission round", will be handled.'

This objective is clearly very welcome and should reduce the frustrations felt by schools and parents alike when offers are not accepted or made as the case may be. The practical difficulties of doing so are considerable, as demonstrated by the fact that the introduction of compulsory co-ordinated admissions arrangements for primary schools was put back by a year. The hope is that LEAs will be able to negotiate agreement for the co-ordinated scheme with all schools in its area, although the Secretary of State can impose a scheme if necessary which has happened in at least two cases. Primary and secondary schools are regulated separately, and the scheme does not apply to special schools. After the initial adoption of a scheme, it does not need to be redrafted each year. Once the scheme has been adopted, it is for the LEA to publish a composite prospectus including both the details of the co-ordinated scheme and the admissions policy for each school, and then to administer the scheme. The Code of Practice includes Guidance about formulation and administration of schemes, with model schemes and timetables included. All secondary offers are to be made on 1 March in any year; primary offers will be made on a date that is designated by the LEA concerned.

The different possible co-ordinated schemes, and the way one LEA's scheme may interact on that of other LEAs, present complexities that are outside the scope of this book. London, with its particular difficulties of numerous quite small LEAs and a significant willingness of parents to cross LEA boundaries in their quest for the 'best' school, has introduced a pan-London secondary scheme which may well stand as a model for future inter-LEA co-operation. The difficulties of co-ordination, though, are demonstrated by the very long lead time. To enable offers to be made on 1 March, applications are required by 22 October. That in turn imposes great pressure on schools and parents to hold open days and visits in the first six weeks of the autumn term. Some schools are even holding open days towards the end of the summer term, which is not the most characteristic time to see a secondary school.

The outline of the operation of a co-ordinated scheme is as follows. Parents must be invited to express at least three preferences (which stand as applications for places) on the common application form, with room to give reasons for applying to their preferred schools and ranking the preferences. Forms from individual schools that are their own admission authority (i.e. Foundation and VA schools) and that require further information (usually described as 'Supplementary Information Forms') can supplement, but not replace, the common application form. The LEA will then inform each school that is its own admission authority of applications made together with relevant supporting information. This could include ranking details and it must do so where the ranking of preferences is relevant to the application of the policy, i.e. where an admission authority gives priority to those who specify the school in question as first choice, as is often the case with schools that are in high demand or which require a level of religious commitment. There are clear signs of pressure from LEAs on such schools to cease giving priority to those who make the school their first choice and it is highly likely that in the course of settling secondary admission policies for September 2006 formal objections will be made. Also, the Secretary of State (who has jurisdiction over questions relating to religious issues in the admissions context) has directed that a number of Roman Catholic VA schools drop their priority for first choice applicants. This decision may well be challenged as the principle is considered by a number of Dioceses to be an important factor in maintaining the Catholic character of the school.

Each application must then be considered by the admissions authority concerned, and listed in rank order according to the priority the application has under the school's admission arrangements. The list should then be sent to the LEA which will assimilate all the information it has obtained from all admissions authorities with the intention of making one offer of a place for each child, usually at the available school ranked highest by the parent on the common application form. Neighbouring LEAs are required to share information where parents resident in one LEA area apply for a place in a school in another.

One function identified by the Code of Practice for Admissions Forums is an attempt to address the issues that can be presented by the fact that some undersubscribed schools are required to admit a disproportionate number of pupils who have exhibited challenging behaviour in part because oversubscribed schools cannot accommodate them. Admissions Forums are required to discuss these issues (which the Code explicitly considers could include the admission of some pupils above the admission number during the year in popular schools), and admissions authorities are required to heed their Admissions Forum's advice.

INFANT CLASS SIZES

The general principle is simple, namely that in infant years (Reception and Years 1 and 2) no class shall be larger than 30, or be taught in a ratio greater than one qualified teacher to 30 pupils. This goes to some extent against the concept of parental preference and, in particular, the idea that the appeal panel can override the school's admission number. The effect of the legislation is that the duty to keep to the class limit overrides parental preference and the appeal panel can only allow appeals in very limited circumstances. This is dealt with in more detail below.

THE PROVISION OF INFORMATION

As indicated, the LEA must make arrangements to give parents the opportunity to express a preference as to the desired school and to give reasons for that preference. The right to express a preference is of only limited use if the parent cannot get relevant information about the available schools and the basis on which admissions will be organised. Essentially, there are two sources of information available to parents, that from the LEA and from the schools. LEAs and schools are each required to publish extensive information and this must be available at least six weeks before the last date on which parents have to express their preference for entry in the normal admission round.

LEA-wide Information

LEAs are required to publish both details about admission arrangements in a composite prospectus and other information relevant to admissions. Those details will be supplied to parents on demand and will normally be issued as a matter of routine to all parents whose children are due to transfer from primary to secondary school (or to and from middle schools in those authorities that have such schools). Parents are, however, entitled to apply to any school. They may have to make their own enquiries to get details of the admissions arrangements made by other LEAs.

The composite prospectus must include:

- Contact information for both the LEA and the schools it maintains and an indication about the sources of other general information relating to the school.

- The classification of each school and the expected number of pupils at each school, and their age range.

- The particulars of the admissions policy determined for each school in relation to each age group at the school including:

  - arrangements made for parents to express a preference and to co-ordinate the admission of pupils;
  - admissions appeal arrangements;
  - admission arrangements which give priority to children with special educational needs but without a statement;
  - admission arrangements which give priority to looked-after children. The Code of Practice places particular emphasis upon looked-after children and recommends that admissions authorities give them first priority
    in oversubscription criteria;
  - oversubscription criteria;
  - the admission number determined for each age group and, if the admission number is lower than the indicated admission number for that age group (calculated by the LEA according to net capacity assessment), the reasons for determining that number; and
  - the expected timetable for the process and, in particular, the date and time by which applications for admission must be received.

- The LEA's arrangements for transfer between schools maintained by it outside the normal admissions round.

- The affiliations of each such school with a particular religious denomination.

- In respect of secondary schools, the number of places available at the start of the preceding school and the number of applications made for places at the start of that preceding year.

- The additional information the LEA must publish each year includes the authority's general arrangements and policies in respect of:

  - transport for pupils of compulsory school age and below;

- catering, including the remission of charges;
- the provision of school clothing and the making of grants to obtain clothing;
- the making of grants to defray other expenses and the granting of allowances for pupils over compulsory school age;
- entering pupils for public examinations;
- special educational provision including detail about the identification and assessment of need and provision made to meet those needs.

The key part of the information will be the admission criteria. These set out how admissions decisions will be made. Selective schools will usually indicate the general nature of the entrance examination. If the school is non-selective, the admission criteria will normally give priority to those few for whom there are special social or medical reasons for admission to the particular school. The next in order of priority will then usually be siblings of children already at the school, and the remaining places may be offered either to those who live nearest to the school or to those who have no more convenient school to go to: the exact criteria will vary from LEA to LEA and from school to school. Frequently, there will be an express priority for children with statements of special educational needs naming the school. This can be misleading to parents who may think that the route into a school for a statemented child is via the ordinary admissions policy. This is not the case, and statemented children get their place through the statementing process, described in Chapter 3, leading to the school being named. The reason for including statemented children as a priority in the procedure for admission of non-statemented children is to ensure that, when calculating the number of offers to be made, the statemented cohort is taken into account. Otherwise, there is a risk of the school being over-subscribed once the special educational needs statements are included. Admission authorities should make it clear that the ordinary policy does not apply to statemented children and should indicate what the correct method of application for a place is.

As previously mentioned, many VA and some foundation schools have a religious foundation, and there may be a religious qualification required to gain priority for entry. Such schools can no longer refuse places to children who do not qualify if the school is undersubscribed. The Code of Practice seeks to prevent admissions authorities from interviewing to test faith commitment and this has already been commented on.

School-specific Information – the School Prospectus

All schools are required to publish a prospectus containing extensive prescribed details about their organisation, curriculum and examination performance. Some of the mandatory items (particularly in relation to the curriculum) have been removed as part of the attempt to reduce bureaucracy, but the list is still a formidable one. Furthermore, Departmental Guidance suggests that schools should consider voluntarily publishing some at least of the previously required information. The information which must be published falls under the following main headings:

- the name, address and telephone number of the school and the names of the headteacher and chair of governors;

- the classification of the school as:

  - a community, VC, VA, or foundation school or a special school within the appropriate category;
  - a primary, middle or secondary school;
  - a comprehensive, secondary modern, grammar or bilateral school;
  - a co-educational or single-sex school;
  - a day school or boarding school, or a school taking both day and boarding pupils;

- unless the LEA has agreed to publish it, particulars of the admissions policy adopted by or for the school;

- a statement of the ethos and values of the school;

- particulars of any arrangements for visits by parents considering sending their child to the school;

- unless the LEA has agreed to publish it, in the case of a secondary school, and where the information is available, the number of places for pupils in the entry year for the school year prior to the year of publication of the prospectus and the number of written applications for those places;

- a summary of the school's policy in relation to pupils with special educational needs;

- any particular religious affiliations that the school has;

- particulars of religious education and rights of withdrawal;

- a very wide and detailed range of information about the school's achievements in relation to National Curriculum attainment targets and its entry for and achievements in external examinations;

- information about national examination performance. The way in which the examination results are published is specified by the Secretary of State by regulations. The requirements change year by year and care must be taken to report in the current format;

- information regarding the destination of school-leavers in the age range 15 to 18;

- the number of pupils on roll prior to the school-leaving date – the Friday before the last Monday in May. The school can choose the date used for this purpose;

- the number of authorised and unauthorised absences during the year up to the school-leaving date. This is limited to those of compulsory school age and is to be expressed as a percentage of the total possible attendances in the year being reported on. There is no scope for the school to distinguish between absences for which no permission was sought and those for which the school refused permission. The figures will include all those absences for which school permission has not been given or for which acceptable parental explanation has not been forthcoming. Apparently poor figures may reflect a strict line regarding term-time holidays, or the unwillingness of parents to write notes to explain quite proper absence, or the lack of time for teachers to make telephone calls to establish reasons for absence.

The intention is that parents should have a coherent body of information that will enable an informed preference to be expressed. The Secretary of State has the power to add to or alter these requirements. It is, therefore, necessary to check each year whether or not any changes to the requirements have been made. Generally, the DfES will issue Guidance documents that give the necessary information.

EXTENT OF PARENTAL ENTITLEMENT

Once parents have expressed their preference, there comes the question of whether or not that preference is to be complied with.

The principle is a simple one. It is the duty of the body that decides on admissions to comply with parental preference unless:

- compliance with the preference would prejudice the provision of efficient education or the efficient use of resources ('the prejudice test'): prejudice is deemed to arise in infant schools if the ratio of 30 children to one qualified teacher in a class would be exceeded, but otherwise it has to be proved; or

- the arrangements for admission to the preferred school are based wholly on selection by reference to ability or aptitude, and compliance with the preference would be incompatible with selection under these arrangements. In other words, the school in question (which invariably will be a secondary school) is a selective school or admits its intake on specified criteria relating to ability or aptitude;

- the child has been permanently excluded from two or more schools, and the most recent one must have been within two years. For this purpose, an exclusion is treated as taking effect on the day the headteacher takes the decision, although for all other purposes it does not take effect until the date on which the pupil can lawfully be removed from the school roll, i.e. when the appeal process is exhausted. Naturally, if the child is reinstated by the governing body or the appeal panel (or the appeal panel determines that the child would have been reinstated were it not for the impracticality or exceptional circumstances of the case) the exclusion does not count, nor does an exclusion that happened before the child reached compulsory school age. The admission authority is not precluded from offering a place, but if the admission authority is not the school, the school has a right of appeal to the appeal panel;

- where another place has been offered, as identified under co-ordinated admission arrangements.

Many schools admit up to 10 per cent of the intake by reference to aptitude. This is specifically sanctioned by the legislation, subject to the provisions relating to approval of admissions arrangements, provided:

- the admission authority for the school is satisfied that the school has a specialism in the subject or subjects concerned;

- the total number admitted does not exceed 10 per cent of the relevant year group.

The specialisms must fall within one or more of certain subjects:

- physical education or one or more sports;
- one or more of the performing arts;
- one or more of the visual arts;
- one or more modern foreign languages;
- technology.

The school may test for aptitude in the subjects concerned but the test must not be a test of ability – the distinction can be difficult to discern (for instance, a case concluded that requiring a musician to have attained grade 3 was not by itself an appropriate test of aptitude) – and the school may not link that test to any other aspect of selection.

Even schools that are fundamentally non-selective may wish to use a selection process in an attempt to balance the spread of ability of their intake. This reflects the problem that non-selective schools face if they have a number of competing selective schools in their natural catchment areas. In these cases, what can happen is that the selective schools take a disproportionate number of the local higher ability pupils, to the disadvantage of the non-selective school that admits pupils mainly by reference to where the family lives. Higher ability children living at some distance away may not be admitted because there are too many other children living nearer. A means, therefore, has to be found to enable the distance test to be applied separately to those children. This may be done by testing all applicants to rank them in broad ability bands. Places are then offered to the bands proportionately: characteristically, there will be 25 per cent higher ability, 50 per cent average ability and 25 per cent lower ability places offered. The school's admission criteria will then be applied to each band independently: for example, the first places in each band may be offered to siblings and the remainder according to the location of the home. It is, of course, a process that will only achieve its objective if the school is oversubscribed: a non-selective school with spare places would have to admit all applicants irrespective of ability bands. Schools with this system in place before the 1998 legislation came into force may retain it, subject to the process ensuring that no level of ability is substantially under- or over-represented. That, if taken literally, suggests that the testing should be designed to produce roughly an equal number of pupils in each band, which the example given above does not. The Code of Practice, however, appears to sanction the 25–50–25 split, presumably on the grounds that the highest number represents the middle or average ground.

Usually, the only question facing a parent seeking entry to a community non-selective school is whether admission meets the 'prejudice' test. Selective schools present the additional hurdle of establishing that the applicant reaches the required standard for entry. It is an additional hurdle, because the 'prejudice' test still applies if there are more pupils reaching the required standard than the school is willing to admit.

The detailed admission criteria that apply to an individual school are critical. There is no legislation setting out how these should be arrived at or what they should be. However, some rules can be gleaned from litigation, as illustrated by the following examples:

- in determining admissions policies, an LEA may not distinguish between those who live within and those who live outside the authority. The obligation to meet parental preference is not constrained by borough boundaries;

- the fact that a parent may have reasons that are racially based for making a preference is not relevant in determining an application for admission to a particular school. On the other hand, LEAs and schools may not adopt admission criteria that discriminate on the grounds of race.

Admissions policies must be reasonable. This, however, is not as great a protection for parents as it may seem at first sight. The courts would only declare a particular policy unlawful if it were so unreasonable that no reasonable body could have adopted it: this is very hard to establish. The attitude of the courts shows a reluctance to upset policies that have been determined and acted upon. The remedies, therefore, in respect of an existing policy which is thought to be unreasonable are to lodge an objection with the Adjudicator at the next annual round of admissions policy consultation and approval or to apply to the Secretary of State for a ruling under the general procedure giving the Secretary of State supervisory powers over schools and LEAs. Given the right of objection to the Adjudicator, it seems most unlikely that the Secretary of State would be prepared to intervene. To do so would contradict the expressed wish for local issues to be determined locally. A further limitation is that parents do not have a direct right to object to the Adjudicator except when at least 10 raise substantially the same objection either in relation to pre-existing partially selective admission arrangements or where the admissions number determined by the admissions authority is lower that the school's current indicated admission number calculated by the LEA using the net capacity formula. They would need to find a sympathetic admission authority (i.e. the LEA or a VA or foundation school) willing to take up the issue.

Other Issues

The Code of Practice on Admissions, replacing previous Departmental Circulars, gives Guidance on a number of other issues:

- admission authorities can refuse places in years other than the normal admission years even if the admission number has not been reached under the 'prejudice' test. The Code says that this should be done only if the school has 'a particularly high concentration of pupils with challenging behaviour, or the child is particularly challenging'. The Code limits this to schools which are then, or within the previous two years have been, under special measures or identified as having serious weaknesses, subject to a formal warning notice, a Fresh Start school or Academy open for less than two years or a secondary school where less than 25 per cent of whose pupils are achieving five or more GCSEs at grades A* to C. An admission authority which decided to refuse a place when those conditions were not met would have to justify its decision to an appeal panel and this is not likely to be easy;

- there is no legal obligation to have a waiting list, but if one is used the school's admissions policy should make this clear and indicate for how long the list will be maintained. The Code advises that the waiting list should be applied according to the oversubscription criteria (and not, for instance, the order in which names were added to the list). This reflects general current practice in that policies usually say that as places become vacant they will be filled from the waiting list in accordance with the school's criteria. Where difficulty and ambiguity often arise is in deciding how to deal with late applications. Do they take their place among the other applications to be treated equally under the criteria or should they be required to wait until all 'in-time' applicants have been offered places, have had any appeals dealt with, or have accepted places elsewhere? A clear admissions policy will address this issue and the co-ordinated admissions scheme should do so as well although the Code indicates that where school places become vacant before any admission appeals are heard, they should be filled from the waiting list. The Code also indicates that where a school is asked to admit a pupil outside the normal admission round under co-ordinated arrangements or by agreement through the Admission Forum, it should take precedence over applicants on the waiting list: again, the policy should make this clear;

- no fees may be charged for or in connection with admission to a school and that includes contributions to the cost of administration even if they are refundable to successful applicants. Furthermore, the practice of inviting parents to give financial support to the school (however conditional) before the admission decision is taken is frowned upon. There may be a fine line between an invitation to give and informing parents that the school has a practice of inviting contributions once the child enters the school. It is lawful to approach parents for contributions once the place has been offered and accepted, but it must be made clear that the offer of the place (and the way the child will be treated when in the school) will not be affected by a decision not to contribute. It would also be good practice not to cash cheques or implement bankers' orders until the child has actually started school, and to make it clear to parents that this is the school's practice;

- it may 'in very limited circumstances' be lawful to withdraw an offer, for example if the place was offered on the basis of a fraudulent or intentionally misleading application. This addresses the problem, familiar to oversubscribed schools giving priority to those living nearest the school, of false addresses being given – grandparents', aunts' or even accommodation addresses being used instead of the true normal residence of the child. Admission authorities whose admissions policy makes it clear that proof of residence may be required could rely on this Guidance to justify withdrawal of a place where there is cogent evidence that a false address has intentionally been given. Some successful schools find this to be an increasing problem and schools in that position should make express provision for verification of addresses. The policy should also be clear as to which address is the relevant one especially where the child does not live with both parents – is it the address of the parent or carer with whom the child lives for the majority of the school week, the address of the parent or carer with any relevant court order or the address recorded at the primary school? What is the relevant date? Is it the date of application, the date on which the admission policy is applied or the date on which the offer is actually to be made? What, if anything, happens if the address changes between application and offer, or between offer and the place being taken up? There may be other circumstances that could justify withdrawal of an offer, for example if deliberately false information was given suggesting that a pupil met specific entrance qualifications to a denominational school when that was not the case;

- it may also be justifiable to withdraw an offer if it is not responded to within a reasonable time. 'Reasonable' is not defined. Admission authorities can pre-empt the question by specifying a time (which should be a reasonable one) within which the place should be accepted. Ideally, the admissions information supplied before applications are made should make it clear when offers will be made and the time allowed for acceptance. Parents should also be invited to inform the school if it is likely they will not be able to respond in that time (for good reason such as absence abroad) so that the school can consider extending the period;

- if the child has started at the school, the place should be withdrawn only if it was fraudulently obtained. Swift detection and action will be vital. The Code says that the length of time that the child has been in the school must be taken into account in deciding whether to withdraw the place. The Code also says that if the place is withdrawn, the application must be reconsidered by the admission authority and, if (as presumably will inevitably happen) it is decided not to offer a place at the school, there is a right of appeal to the appeal panel. The logic, and the legal basis, for a reconsideration is questionable: it is presumably intended to give the parents an opportunity to appeal against the decision to withdraw the place which can only arise if a place is refused.

Admission and Indicated Admission Numbers and the 'Prejudice' Test

The right to express a preference and to have it complied with would be potentially illusory without some constraint on the ability of a school or LEA to declare that a particular school was full and that admission would prejudice the efficient use of resources.

Accordingly, we have the concept of 'admission numbers' which set a minimum capacity for every school. In simplest terms, a number is set for each school as the number of pupils intended to be admitted in any school year. The effect is that an admission cannot be refused on the 'prejudice' test if the relevant number has not been reached for the age group in question. In other words, if that year group is not 'full', a place cannot be refused.

The process for determining and changing admission numbers forms part of the overall planning function and comes within the purview of the Adjudicator. The LEA must determine the indicated admission number of a school by using the net capacity formula. If an admission authority for a school determines an admission number that is lower than the indicated admission number, the admission authority must publish prescribed information including notification of a parent's right to appeal to the Adjudicator.

APPEALS AGAINST REFUSAL TO ADMIT

Parents have a right to appeal to an independent appeal panel against a refusal to admit, including where a pupil is refused permission to transfer to the sixth form of the school he or she is attending. Under co-ordinated admission arrangements, parents have the right to appeal for a place at any of their preferred schools even though they may have received an offer of a place at one of their preferred schools. The decision of an appeal panel on any appeal is binding on the school and the LEA, although the parent cannot be compelled to take up the place if the appeal is successful. An appeal panel must consist of three or five members made up of lay members and individuals with experience in education. Individuals who might be considered not to be independent (for instance because of their connection with the school or the LEA) are ineligible. If a panel member dies or becomes unable because of illness to continue, the panel can still sit provided it has at least three members, and a representative from each class of member. The general procedural rules relating to admissions appeal panels are similar to those for independent appeal panels dealing with appeals against permanent exclusion. The LEA is responsible only for arranging appeals for community and VC schools. The responsibility for appeals against admission refusals in VA and foundation schools rests with the governing body.

The appeal panel should satisfy itself that the admissions policy has been correctly applied. If it has not, and the panel considers that the place would have been offered if it had been, the appeal should be allowed, although the panel does have a discretion. The way in which an appeal panel approaches admission issues where the policy has been correctly applied has been laid down by the courts. It is a two-stage process. The first stage is for the panel to decide whether it is satisfied that admission would prejudice the provision of efficient education or the efficient use of resources. If it is not satisfied on this then the appeal must be allowed. If it decides that there would be prejudice, the panel goes on to the second stage and has to do a balancing act. It has to weigh up the extent of the prejudice against the advantage to the parent (and pupil) of complying with the parent's preference. This is not necessarily a question of strict proof. The panel can look at all factors and will often take its own knowledge into account.

There is no definition of what constitutes prejudice to the provision of efficient education or the efficient use of resources. It will always be a question of fact for the appeal panel to consider. A school that wishes to establish prejudice will need to put forward a detailed case. Getting past the first stage will generally be straightforward, because most appeal panels will accept that even the addition of one extra pupil will cause a degree of prejudice. However, the appeal panel must form its own view. The fact that the school or LEA considers that prejudice will arise from even one extra pupil is not evidence on its own of actual prejudice. One appeal panel that accepted the school's view without examining or questioning its validity found itself subject to judicial review, and the appeal had to be heard again by a differently constituted panel. The second stage needs more consideration: a well-briefed parent will want to probe the nature of the problem, and the school needs to identify the difficulties quite clearly. Questions of space, health and safety, pressure on staff, efficient teaching groups, available books and other resources will all need to be looked at to counter the obvious argument by the parent that accepting just one more child to the class can be coped with.

The power of the appeal panel to allow appeals for places in infant schools is very restricted. If the 30:1 ratio mentioned above would be exceeded by allowing the appeal, then the grounds on which it can be allowed are either:

- the decision to refuse a place was not one that a reasonable admission authority would make; or

- a place would have been offered if the admissions policy had been properly applied.

In deciding an infant appeal, the appeal panel may only consider the material that was actually available to the admission authority or which the admission authority ought to have taken into account. However, the obligation to produce evidence rests firmly with the parent: the appeal panel is not required to make its own independent enquiries. The appeal is not a re-hearing of the original application, but a review of the admission authority's decision. In other words, it is very largely concerned with whether or not due process was observed. If it was, the appeal is bound to fail. Experience shows that very many appellants do not appreciate the limitations on the powers of an infant appeal panel and come to the hearing (despite clear Guidance from the LEA or school) with quite unrealistic expectations. Nonetheless, it is always open to parents to argue that their special circumstances are such that a place should be offered. It may be difficult to envisage circumstances in which this would lead to an appeal being allowed within the parameters mentioned but an appeal panel that refused to allow the matters to be raised would be acting unlawfully. Guidance to appellants may indicate the realistic position but it should not tell parents that special circumstances are irrelevant or may not be raised before the panel.

It is worth noting that although a child who is admitted in either of these circumstances does not count in the 30:1 ratio in the year of admission (so it is not necessary to provide extra resources immediately), that exemption only applies to the initial year and the school will have to organise its resources in any following infant year to keep within the ratio. This applies also in relation to other pupils who are admitted as exceptions, mid-year arrivals in the area and certain categories of other pupils.

The decision of the appeal panel must be given in writing. There is no need to set out reasons for allowing the appeal and giving a place. If the appeal is dismissed, however, then reasons must be given and the appeal panel must show that the formal requirements have been duly considered. Thus:

- if the reason for rejection is that the child does not meet the specific criteria for admission, for example if the child has not passed the examination for entry to a selective school or does not have a religious qualification that is required by the school, the letter should state this. In strict terms, if an appeal is rejected on that ground, the appeal panel need not consider the 'prejudice' test. It is good practice, though, to do so, and if the appeal would have been rejected on the prejudice test, the letter should say so. The reason for this is that there may be a dispute over whether the appeal panel came to the right conclusion over the specific criteria: this becomes academic if the appeal would have been turned down on the 'prejudice' test anyway;

- if the appeal is rejected on the 'prejudice' test, then the decision letter must show:
  - that the appeal panel was satisfied that prejudice would arise if the child were admitted; and
  - that it had considered the balance of hardship as between school and child and had decided that the hardship caused to the school by allowing the appeal outweighed that caused to the child by refusing it.

Frequently, the decision letter outlines the factors that the parent puts forward as indicating hardship. Although that is not legally necessary, it is good practice, because it shows on the face of the decision letter that the appeal panel has considered the parent's case in detail. This is particularly important where an appeal panel may be hearing several appeals for admission to a single school and may otherwise be exposed to the criticism that it took a 'blanket' view.

The School Admission Appeals Code of Practice summarises the law on the subject and contains Guidance on how appeals should be organised and conducted and how the decision letter should be written. It is noteworthy that those responsible for the Code feel that, in order to maintain an informal atmosphere, legal representation for the appellant will usually be unnecessary although the right to representation is acknowledged. The Code goes into great detail on how parents should be advised on the procedure, how the hearing should be conducted, and on the need to be sensitive to ethnic and language issues. It emphasises the general principles of natural justice, including the requirement that the parents see all written material that is to be put before the appeal panel, and the requirement to set out the two-stage decision process referred to above. It also deals specifically with the roles of the clerk, the members of the appeal panel, the chair and those presenting the case. It has comments on particular aspects, in many respects duplicating and mirroring the Guidance contained in the related Code of Practice on Admissions.

All those involved in admissions appeals have a statutory duty to have regard to the Code of Practice. Deviation from the minutiae of the suggested procedures may be permissible if there are cogent reasons, but most of what appears in the Code is sensible and practicable. Deviation from the overriding principles would be most unwise and would expose the school or LEA or appeal panel to judicial review or criticism from the Local Government Ombudsman. The Code of Practice emphasises the need for panel members to be properly trained. The Council on Tribunals has been particularly critical of the performance of admissions appeal panels, and has suggested that they should come under the umbrella of SENDIST. Whilst this may not prove to be politically or financially acceptable, panels must be meticulous in their approach to appeals if nothing else to try to reduce the risk of decisions being appealed to the High Court.

The Code of Practice reflects a number of court rulings on admissions and admissions appeal processes. A number of points have emerged from those rulings:

- admissions arrangements must be structured so that parents have to express a preference for a school. An arrangement that purports to give parents automatic priority if their child lives within a given area or attends a given school is not lawful and will not work as intended: a parent who positively expresses a preference, even though not qualifying for priority, must in law be given priority over those who say nothing;

- admissions policies will be strictly interpreted and must be followed even if the result is not what the admission authority intended or wanted. Thus, where a policy says that places will be offered in specified proportions or specified numbers, those proportions or numbers must be observed. Great care is needed in drafting admissions policies and criteria to ensure that they are clear and straightforward to apply;

- where there is more than one appeal for a particular year group in a school, the appeal panel may have to rank the claims of the appellants before deciding which appeals to allow. A recent attempt to persuade the court that this meant that every parent should have the right to hear and comment on every other case failed. The appeal panel should consider each case separately on its own merits but will need to have regard to all the cases to decide which show the greatest degrees of hardship. This does not mean that each appellant must know the details of the other cases or have the right to comment on the ranking. Each appeal is to be dealt with individually and privately. Having heard each case, the panel can then consider the extent to which it is proper to allow one or more parental cases to override the prejudice to the school;

- where the appeal turns on issues of parental preference and the location of the home in relation to the school, the appeal committee must, where the parents do not live together, consider any evidence that is put to them by either parent and consider each parent's preference before reaching a conclusion. This would be particularly relevant where parents are separated, but the child spends a significant amount of time with each.

APPEALS BY GOVERNING BODIES

Where the LEA is the admission authority for a community or voluntary controlled school, it must make arrangements that allow the governing body to appeal against a decision by the LEA to admit a twice-excluded pupil. The panel must have regard to the reasons for the LEA's decision that the child should be admitted and those advanced by the governing body as to why the admission would be inappropriate.

RELEVANT GUIDANCE

Code of Practice on Admissions.

Code of Practice on School Admission Appeals.

Chapter 8

SCHOOL DISCIPLINE AND INCLUSION

Introduction – Social inclusion – Drugs – Management of drugs within the school – Responding to drug-related incidents – Drugs policy – Responsibility for school discipline – Corporal punishment and restraint – Home–school agreements – Truanting penalty notices and parenting orders – Truancy notices – Parenting contracts – Exclusions – Types of exclusions – The exclusion guidance – Exclusions and the governing body – Right of appeal – The appeal panel – What is reinstatement? – The future – Relevant guidance

INTRODUCTION

With the publication in September 1999 of the two DfES Circulars, 10/99 for schools ('Social Inclusion – Pupil Support') and 11/99 for LEAs ('Social Inclusion: the LEA Role in Pupil Support') relating to social inclusion, issues of school discipline became inextricably linked with a range of other issues and from that time onwards, behaviour and discipline issues have had to be considered in that wider context. However, government policy has changed over the period reflecting significant professional concerns from schools feeling themselves disadvantaged by what was felt to be undue concentration on the needs of the individual against the needs of the wider school community, together with media attention and the intervention by the Secretary of State in a number of high-profile cases. Also, there have been a number of court cases dealing with reinstatement considerations and the way governing body committees and appeal panels were required to deal with the hearings. New regulations were issued and Guidance published replacing Chapter 6 and Annex D of 10/99, although the rest of 10/99 remained in force. In particular, the composition of independent panels was been altered in a way that was perceived to be weighted in favour of the school, and their powers were extended to allow panels not to reinstate in circumstances where it would otherwise be justified if there are exceptional circumstances that make reinstatement impractical. This would include, for instance, if the relationship between pupil and staff had broken down to the point that staff were considering taking industrial action not to teach the pupil concerned. That revised Guidance has itself been further revised and re-issued and in addition the education-related provisions of the Anti-social Behaviour Act 2003 (and its accompanying Guidance) deal with both truancy and exclusion at some length and offer a new vehicle in the parenting contract to seek to address them.

The introduction of both parenting contracts and the power for schools to issue penalty notices to the parents of truanting pupils marks another significant shift in the responsibilities of schools. These changes put significant law enforcement powers (that are usually the responsibility of the police, LEA and courts) into the hands of schools, which are not always welcome. Schools will wish to be careful in the exercise of these powers not only because they represent completely new territory, but also because they could put the school into a position of direct conflict with parents in circumstances where that relationship is already delicate.

SOCIAL INCLUSION

The two Circulars and Guidance encompass a very wide range of issues, e.g. increasing attendance at school – which is a pre-requisite for pupils' progress – reducing disaffection, disenchantment and, above all, pupils' sense of failure, and the cumulative impact of such factors on the individual and society at large.

Headteachers and governors should familiarise themselves with the general scope of Circular 11/99 to understand the key legal and administrative role of the LEA in relation to:

- the management of attendance (including legal powers to enforce attendance by means of school attendance orders, prosecution, parenting orders and education supervision orders);
- pupils at risk of exclusion (and the importance of pastoral support programmes);
- the education and reintegration of excluded pupils (LEAs are committed to ensuring that all permanently excluded pupils receive full-time education);

- the provision of education otherwise than at school;
- PRUs.

Circular 10/99, relating directly to schools, is essential reading for headteachers and governors. The Guidance covers all the key elements of pupil support and the illustrative case study exemplars are extremely helpful. Headteachers need to be aware of the entire Circular as will governors with special responsibility for or involvement with curriculum, discipline and special educational needs issues. From the perspective of the whole governing body, however, the annexes and the replacement Guidance about exclusions are the key parts because they describe in detail the governing body's legal responsibilities relating to:

- attendance registers (which is supplemented by the Guidance published to support the introduction of truancy penalty notices and parenting contracts);
- school discipline;
- detention;
- exclusion;
- school reports to courts.

The prime objective of the Circular is to reduce pupils' disaffection, but it should also be viewed in the context of the measures adopted nationally to prevent social exclusion, such as supporting local communities, encouraging employment and reducing crime. Early intervention and working closely with parents in the interests of their children are always vital ingredients of any course of action that a school may wish to take.

The Circular stresses the importance of establishing good habits of regular attendance and appropriate behaviour from the outset so that parents are left in no doubt about the school's position on these issues. Successful strategies will normally include the positive recognition of good behaviour and the application of rewards, as well as sanctions, supportive behaviour management (e.g. 'Assertive Discipline' and 'Circle of Friends') and the provision of study support through, for example, homework clubs.

A wide range of pupils are identified as being particularly at risk. These include traveller children (for whom Guidance has been specifically issued – 'Raising the Achievement of Gypsy Traveller Pupils – A Guide to Good Practice', young carers who have to stay at home to look after a sick or disabled relative (although schools should set a time limit for such absences and provide work for pupils to do whilst they are away from school), children from families under stress (for example, because of parental unemployment, bereavement, divorce, separation or the formation of new adult relationships), children who feel particularly apprehensive or anxious when starting school or when transferring from primary to secondary school, refugee children and others who may join a school outside the normal year of entry. In the case of pupils with special educational needs, the early identification and accurate diagnosis of such needs, including emotional and behavioural difficulties, can often play a crucial part in preventing the escalation of such difficulties and securing the desired improvement.

Children in care constitute a particularly vulnerable group in that up to 75 per cent of them leave school without any qualifications and, as adults, they are much more likely than their peers to be unemployed, homeless or involved in criminal activities. Schools should liaise closely with social services in such cases and should ensure that a named contact is available to deal with problems that may arise or to provide appropriate support as and when required.

Black-Caribbean pupils, especially boys, tend to be excluded from school much more frequently than other pupils. Schools should check that their anti-racist policies are working effectively and monitor regularly their use of sanctions against ethnic minority pupils. Close co-operation with representative community groups is also recommended.

When dealing with pregnant schoolgirls and teenage mothers, schools should aim to work closely with social services and the LEA to bolster such youngsters both during pregnancy and after the child is born and to provide suitable childcare support so that they can return to school as soon as possible after the birth. The Guidance emphasises that these are not appropriate grounds *per se* for exclusion.

The section dealing with the handling of signs of disaffection covers irregular attendance and truancy, the management of disruptive behaviour, the use of curricular flexibilities, and behaviour that needs to be dealt with sensitively. Schools are in a position to adopt a wide range of strategies to combat irregular attendance and truancy, such as first day contact with the home, the use of information technology to improve the monitoring of attendance, frequent written reminders to parents of the school's policy and procedures, regular attendance checks, the appointment of a senior member of staff with specific responsibility for pupils' attendance, close monitoring of unauthorised absence, and referral to the Education Welfare Service (EWS). The establishment of a Truancy Watch Scheme in the local community is often an effective deterrent against truancy.

The school's behaviour policy should spell out in no uncertain terms the standards of behaviour that are expected (and acceptable) and what will happen in the event of any deviation from the norm. Sanctions must be applied fairly and consistently by all staff – and within a context of positive reinforcement of good behaviour.

Schools should have an attendance policy (upon which parents and pupils should be consulted) which includes systems and procedures to encourage regular school attendance and investigate the underlying causes of poor attendance. The attendance policy should also include the circumstances in which the school will consider entering into a parenting contract and issuing a penalty notice, although schools are encouraged to seek to deal with problems informally before doing so. These systems should be reviewed regularly and modified where necessary. The policy should set out staff roles and responsibilities for dealing with attendance, and should link to the school's behaviour and bullying policies. It should reflect the LEA's attendance strategy and its code of conduct for issuing penalty notices, and should be endorsed by the governors. The Guidance encourages schools to use ICT or radio communications systems to record attendance on the basis that it is both more effective and can be used easily to identify trends.

It may be useful to set up learning support units to provide pupils who are particularly at risk of exclusion with a separate base in which to pursue a carefully structured programme, under close supervision. As the prime aim of the temporary withdrawal from normal lessons is to improve the behaviour and learning of disruptive pupils in mainstream classes, the development of social skills, anger management and individual counselling, as well as targeted literacy and numeracy work, might also be incorporated into such a programme. The attachment of older pupils (or supportive adults) to disruptive youngsters as role models can often pay dividends, especially when there is a good match in terms of background and experience.

The curricular flexibilities available to schools include the use of materials from earlier or later Key Stages than a pupil's notional Key Stage, disapplication from (parts of) the National Curriculum, the provision of work-related courses for 14- to 16-year-olds, co-operative arrangements with a college of FE, whereby pupils at

Key Stage 4 are able to pursue individually customised programmes on a full-time or part-time basis, and the opportunities offered for participation in character-building ventures, such as those available in the Duke of Edinburgh's Award Scheme or from the Prince's Trust.

A section is devoted to pupils who do not respond to action to combat disaffection. It specifies that a longer-term action plan – including the formulation of a Pastoral Support Programme (PSP) – will invariably be needed in such cases. A PSP is intended as an intensive individual programme lasting typically 16 weeks designed (with external agency and parental support) to move the pupil away from the brink. These remedial measures should focus on specific and attainable short-term behavioural outcomes and should be developed in connection with external agencies (e.g. social services, housing departments, voluntary organisations, the youth and careers services and, where appropriate, ethnic minority community groups). In some instances, joint registration of the pupil at a PRU – or a managed transfer to another school – may prove beneficial. It is important for schools to keep in mind that the LEA has a responsibility to work with the school and to provide resources. It follows from this that schools should be alert to the need to involve the LEA at an early stage with any pupil showing clear signs of disaffection and to document the steps taken, particularly if help is not forthcoming. This is of special importance in relation to permanent exclusion. First, it will be difficult to justify permanent exclusion (except where it is the only justifiable response to the particular incident) where a PSP has not been used, although the explicit linkage between PSPs and the entitlement to exclude permanently has been dropped. Secondly, and by contrast, the Circular and Guidance envisage that, where alternative strategies (of which a PSP is likely to be a part) fail, permanent exclusion may be the only response to continued breaches of discipline. It is worth looking at the role of the LEA in relation to PSPs and exclusions in a little detail.

The LEA has no independent function in relation to exclusions beyond the right to make representations to the governing body and the appeal panel (in which case the representative should not express an opinion about whether exclusion is justified in the case being considered but be objective and provide accurate and neutral assistance to the governing body or panel by advising them of the situation in other schools in the area or providing other factual information) and the obligation to make arrangements for appeals against permanent exclusion. However, Circular 10/99 and the related Circular 11/99 indicate significant areas of LEA responsibility in helping schools deal with disaffected pupils and in dealing with the reintegration of permanently excluded pupils. There is a clear requirement for LEAs to participate fully in the process by providing personnel and additional resources for the school, particularly in supporting PSPs. Schools will find the detailed Guidance on the role of the EWS and EWOs of particular use. To quote Circular 11/99:

'1.4 EWOs should work closely with schools and families to resolve attendance issues, arranging home visits where necessary. The key to success is an effective working relationship between schools and the EWS including:

- shared policies and operational practices between the EWS and the schools;

- clearly defined roles of school staff and EWOs;

- how much time the EWO will devote to the school;

- expectation of the quality of EWO service;

- arrangements for referral, regular review, monitoring and evaluation;

- procedures for resolving enquiries.

1.5 To achieve this, LEAs should draw up service level agreements, while schools may appoint a senior member of staff to co-ordinate attendance issues as part of the whole school approach.

1.6 Each school maintained by the LEA should have a named EWO responsible for the attendance of all the pupils in the school. Where a child lives in a neighbouring LEA, follow-up action will require co-operative working with the relevant EWS. Any necessary legal action is the responsibility of the LEA where the child lives.'

The Guidance on PSP support is equally useful:

'3.1 Pupils who have had several fixed period exclusions that may lead to a permanent exclusion, or who risk failure at school through disaffection, or rapidly deteriorating behaviour, need a school-based Pastoral Support Programme (PSP). Further details are given in Section 5 of Circular 10/99. Schools setting up a PSP must alert LEAs as the PSP is a multi-agency intervention. The school should invite the parents and an LEA representative to discuss the causes of concern and what the pupil needs to do to improve, both academically and socially. Occasionally the LEA, from its record of fixed period exclusions, may prompt a school to set up a PSP.

3.2 LEAs should help schools with pupils who have PSPs. This may be done in various ways by:

- offering support free to the school;

- supplementing the school's budget so it can buy the extra support outlined in the PSP;

- supporting the child in a move to another school; or

- joint registration at a Pupil Referral Unit and mainstream school.'

The use of exclusion is put into the context of general behaviour, particularly stressing the need (except in exceptional cases) to have tried other strategies (including PSPs) first, and consideration should be given to the use of a parenting contract after a first fixed-term exclusion. The Guidance emphasises that the decision to exclude is a serious one in response to serious breaches of the school's behaviour policy; and when allowing the pupil to remain in school would seriously harm the education or the welfare of the pupil or others in the school. The exclusion process is dealt with in detail below.

Reintegration of permanently excluded pupils is the responsibility of the LEA, but schools have their role to play. The successful reintegration into a mainstream or special school of excluded pupils must be the prime objective in all cases. Ideally, such pupils should be reintegrated within days or weeks (the Secretary of State firmly expects that most children excluded from primary school will be reintegrated within one term at the most) of being excluded. Schools should not refuse to admit pupils on the basis of their previous disciplinary record (including exclusions) – except where the pupil in question has already been permanently excluded from two or more schools.

As mentioned above, the Annexes set out the legal requirements on the aspects covered by Circular 10/99.

Annex A: Guidance on Attendance Registers

The Guidance given in Annex A states that schools are obliged to register pupils twice a day (at the beginning of the morning session and once during the afternoon), using the appropriate codes. The register must show whether pupils are in school, pursuing an approved educational activity off-site or absent. If a pupil is absent, the absence must be marked as authorised or unauthorised. The following are listed as types of authorised absence:

- illness, or medical or dental appointments;

- days of religious observance;

- official interviews;

- study leave;
- exclusion;
- absence of traveller children, when the family is travelling;
- funerals;
- absence due to the responsibilities of young carers;
- special occasions (e.g. family weddings);
- public performances (where pupils are properly licensed by the LEA);
- birth of a child (up to 18 weeks' absence may be authorised to cover the period before and after the birth).

Headteachers and governors should pay particular attention to what is said on the vexed question of taking children on holiday during term time:

- parents should not normally take their children out of school for holidays during the school term;
- if schools do not support such absences, they must be recorded as unauthorised (in the author's experience, over 95 per cent of unauthorised absences can be explained on these grounds);
- schools should only exceptionally agree to an absence of more than 10 school days in any one school year – and should not regard 10 days as the norm (parents will need to be disabused of the fundamental misconception that they are entitled to take their children out of school for two weeks every year);
- a pupil who fails to return within 10 days of the agreed return date, unless there is good reason for the continued absence (e.g. illness), may be removed from the school roll.

Annex A has been supplemented (but not replaced) by the Guidance that accompanied the introduction of truancy penalty notices and parenting contracts and includes, among other things, the requirement for a school to adopt an attendance policy. Parenting contracts and truancy penalty notices are new tools that can be used by schools within the context of the strategy they adopt to deal with truancy, and are explored more fully below.

Annex B, Annex C and Annex D

These cover specific issues relating to school discipline. Annex B covers the legal responsibilities of the governing body and the headteacher for school discipline. Annex C deals with detention, and Annex D, which dealt with the exclusion process, has been replaced by new Guidance on exclusions. These topics are covered in detail later in this chapter.

Annex E: School Reports to Courts

Such reports may be prepared by the headteacher of a school or other members of staff (although in this case the report must be countersigned by the headteacher). They should be succinct, balanced, factual and written in user-friendly language and will usually cover the areas listed below:

- pupil achievement: this section will include a fair assessment of the pupil's strengths, weaknesses, motivation, application, comparative academic and social progress, and extra-curricular contributions;

- attendance and punctuality record (with specific details to back up any judgements that may have been made);

- behaviour;

- health;

- family circumstances (e.g. illness, bereavement or any other special difficulties);

- the involvement of external agencies.

Schools should be suitably cautious and circumspect in the comments that they make when writing such reports because, although the reports are unlikely to be made public by the court, they will almost certainly be divulged to the pupil's parents (and, possibly, the pupil). It may even be sensible to show a draft version to the parents in advance to allay any fears and to check any factual inaccuracies.

DRUGS

Drugs have become the focus of a number of initiatives from the DfES, which has also issued new Guidance. Schools should have anti-drugs policies in place which make it plain that drug-taking will not be condoned. The exclusions Guidance emphasises that a key factor in determining whether a permanent exclusion is justified will be by reference to the assessment of a particular incident against criteria set out in the school's policy. The policy should be clear in terms of the expressions it uses (for instance, what it means by the word 'supply'), what sort of penalty particular conduct is likely to attract and deal both with legal as well as illegal drugs. Schools are strongly advised to maintain close links with the local Drug Action Team as a source of invaluable advice. They must also establish clear guidelines on the unacceptability of any form of bullying or sexual or racial harassment – and specify how such offences will be handled.

'Drugs: Guidance for Schools' was issued by the DfES in February 2004, which replaces Circular 10/95 and 'Protecting Young People'. It is very comprehensive, running to 126 pages and covers drug education (which is dealt with in Chapter 3), the management of drugs within the school, responding to drug-related incidents and the school drugs policy. Schools should review their own drugs and behaviour policies within the light of the new Guidance: it includes a checklist (at Appendix 7) which can be useful in doing so. The status of the Guidance is 'recommended action' and although there is no statutory obligation for schools to formulate a drug policy, the Guidance itself says that all schools should have a drug policy (dealing with both legal and illegal drugs) that should be widely distributed through the school, readily available and regularly updated. It indicates that schools that do not have one should develop one as a matter of urgency.

The Guidance emphasises the importance of treating all issues relating to drugs on a whole-school basis, consistent with the ethos and values of the school and developed by all members of the school community. The school's approach should always be consistent irrespective of the context within which the drug-related issue arises.

MANAGEMENT OF DRUGS WITHIN THE SCHOOL

The Guidance says that all school staff should receive drug awareness training, understand the school's drug policy and their role in implementing the policy. Schools should appoint a designated senior member of staff with overall responsibility for all drug issues within the school. Staff should have access to support and continuing professional development and schools should identify pupils who are vulnerable to drug misuse (including those at risk of exclusion and those excluded; the Guidance exhorts schools to address gaps in the drug education programme of a pupil who has missed a substantial amount of schooling when that pupil returns to school and includes a school-refuser. The Guidance identifies as being particularly vulnerable individuals who are:

- homeless;
- looked after;
- school truants;
- pupils excluded from school;
- sexually abused;
- prostitutes;
- in contact with the mental health and criminal justice system;
- children of parents with drug problems.

Staff should receive appropriate support either from within the school through the curriculum or pastoral system, or through referral to others. Schools are required to be aware of and establish referral protocols with the range of relevant agencies providing support to pupils vulnerable to drug misuse. Drug Action Teams have been established locally and are responsible for co-ordinating local drugs strategy. Schools will need to have procedures for taking possession of and if appropriate disposing of drugs (which is covered below); in the case of illegal drugs, schools should inform the police immediately who will deal with destruction. Consistency with the drug policy is central; both in determining what constitutes a drug incident and dealing with it.

The Guidance recommends that schools make 'significant progress' towards smoke-free status.

RESPONDING TO DRUG-RELATED INCIDENTS

Clearly, all responses by a school to a drug-related incident within school should be consistent with the drugs policy. The Guidance requires priority to be given to safety, meeting any medical emergencies with first aid and summoning appropriate help. As touched upon in the policy section below, schools should develop a range of responses to drug incidents that are clearly set out in the policy including referral to other agencies when required – taking care over any issues of confidentiality. The drugs Guidance echoes the exclusions Guidance, saying that any response should balance the needs of the individual with those of the wider community and should be determined after a full and careful investigation.

Schools are recommended to involve parents in any incident that involves illegal drugs, unless this could jeopardise the pupil's safety. The Guidance emphasises that schools have no obligation to report an incident involving illegal drugs to the police, but does state that failing to do so may be counter-productive: an individual judgement will need to be made depending upon the circumstances of the case. As already mentioned, the police should be called to deal with the destruction of suspected illegal drugs, but in the meantime the Guidance advises schools to:

- ensure that a second adult witness is present throughout the process of handling what is suspected to be an illegal drug;

- seal the sample in a plastic bag and include details of the date and time of the seizure/find and witness present. Some police forces provide schools with drug bags for this purpose;

- store it in a secure location, such as the school safe or other lockable container with access limited to two senior members of staff;

- notify the police immediately;

- record full details of the incident, including the police incident reference number;

- inform parents, unless this would jeopardise the safety of the pupil.

DRUGS POLICY

All schools should have a drugs policy (dealing with both legal and illegal drugs) that should be widely distributed through the school, readily available and regularly updated. The importance of dealing with all drugs is highlighted by the Guidance's reference to a recent survey which found that 24 per cent of 11–15-year-olds had consumed alcohol in the previous week and so the Guidance identifies educating pupils about the effects of alcohol and how to reduce alcohol-related harm as an important priority for all schools. The policy should interrelate with the school's medicines policy.

Section 4.5 of the Guidance is useful in assisting to draft a medicines policy and highlights that schools should be aware of the potential misuse of prescribed medicines: they should not be given or passed to a third party, and responses to the misuse of medicines should be included within the school's drug policy. The Guidance emphatically advises schools not the give non-prescribed medication to pupils.

The Guidance indicates that the policy should set out the school's role in relation to all drug matters – both the content and organisation of drug education, and the management of drugs within school.

The drug policy should be developed in consultation with the whole school community including pupils, parents, staff, governors and other relevant organisations such as the police and drug referral agencies. Schools should have a range of responses and procedures for managing drug incidents, which are understood by all members of the school community, and recorded within the policy. It is important that it is consistent with the school's behaviour and discipline policies: for instance, many schools consider that they have a 'zero tolerance' policy towards the supply of illegal drugs when on closer analysis it is clear that they do not.

The Guidance says that schools should make clear that the possession, use or supply of illegal and other unauthorised drugs within school boundaries is unacceptable, and as touched on above it should be clear what the potential disciplinary sanctions are if this is broken. It recommends that schools and police should establish an agreed policy which clarifies roles and mutual expectations before incidents occur, dealing with when:

- an incident can be managed internally by the school;
- the police should be informed or consulted;
- the police should be actively involved; and
- a pupil's name can be withheld and when it should be divulged to the police.

The procedures for and circumstances where searches may be considered appropriate should be made explicit in the school drug policy. It is not appropriate for a member of staff to carry out a personal search: the police should be called who will then be able to enforce relevant powers of search. The Guidance indicates that personal property cannot be searched without prior consent; consent should also be sought for searches of school property such as lockers, but such a search may be conducted even where consent to it is withheld.

RESPONSIBILITY FOR SCHOOL DISCIPLINE

The strategic responsibility for school discipline rests with the governing body, with the headteacher having the responsibility for securing effective discipline in the school.

The governing body must ensure that policies designed to promote good behaviour and discipline on the part of pupils are pursued in the school. In other words, the governing body cannot merely establish the policies: it must keep implementation of those policies constantly under review. The governing body must, in particular:

- make a written statement of the general principles to which the headteacher must have regard in formulating detailed measures for securing proper discipline;

- notify the headteacher of any particular measures that it thinks desirable;

- give the headteacher such Guidance as it thinks appropriate.

The governing body does not have an entirely free hand. It must have regard to any Guidance given by the Secretary of State and it must consult the headteacher and parents on its written statement. It is not, however, required to consult on the other aspects mentioned.

The headteacher is required to determine measures (including rules and sanctions) that will:

- promote self-discipline and proper regard for authority;

- encourage good behaviour and respect for others. Measures under this heading must be designed to prevent all kinds of bullying;

- secure an applicable standard of behaviour;

- generally regulate the conduct of pupils.

The headteacher must frame these measures within the context of the governing body's general statement and must have regard to any governing body Guidance. If the governing body does not determine what is to be an acceptable standard of behaviour, the headteacher must do so. The measures must be in writing and must:

- generally be made known to pupils and parents;

- at least once a year be brought to the attention of pupils, parents and all persons employed or otherwise engaged to provide their services at the school. Presumably this last requirement must be interpreted with a degree of common sense; it is difficult to see what benefit would derive from bringing the measures to the attention of, say, the school architect.

The LEA has wide powers of intervention in all maintained schools if there is, or if it fears that there may be, a breakdown of discipline. If the LEA believes that either the behaviour of pupils at the school or any action taken by them or their parents is such that the education of any pupils in the school is, or is likely in the immediate future to be, prejudiced, it can inform the governing body in writing of its fears. It can, either at the same time or later, take such steps as it thinks fit to deal with the perceived problem. This power is linked also to the powers of the LEA to intervene generally in failing schools. If the LEA has served notice on the governing body expressing concern for the safety of staff or pupils as a result of a breakdown of discipline and the governing body has not dealt satisfactorily with the issue, the LEA can exercise its intervention rights in relation to discipline whether or not it exercises its other rights of intervention. The legislation does not specify what the LEA may do; the power is a general one but it does include the power to give directions to the governing body and/or to the headteacher.

CORPORAL PUNISHMENT AND RESTRAINT

Corporal punishment is not permitted in schools, although the legal way of securing this, by denying the right to argue an entitlement to punish based on the *in loco parentis* rule, is arcane to say the least. What constitutes corporal punishment has always been a grey area and recent legislation allowing the use of force to control or restrain pupils in certain circumstances was welcome. In summary, reasonable force may be used by teachers and others authorised by the headteacher to have control of children to prevent:

- the commission of what would be a criminal offence. It does not matter that the pupil may be under the age of criminal responsibility;

- injury to the pupil or others;
- damage to property of the pupil or others;
- behaviour prejudicial to maintaining good order and discipline at the school or among any pupils. This applies wherever the behaviour occurs, in and out of the class.

The legislation applies in school and also where pupils are in the charge of an authorised person out of school. It is a moot point as to whether it applies to a situation out of school other than on a school visit or out-of-school activity but it almost certainly would apply, for example, to breaking up a fight outside the school or where the pupils are in school uniform and the school discipline and behaviour policy makes it clear that school rules apply in those circumstances.

It is important to keep in mind that this enables a particular course of action: it does not require action to be taken and no one is obliged to face personal risk by intervening in a dangerous situation.

Circular 10/98 amplifies the statutory provisions and makes it clear that they add to rather than limit individual rights. Thus, they do not take away the right to act in self-defence even if that involves a necessary degree of force. It advises that the headteacher should draw up a policy setting out guidelines about the use of force to control or restrain pupils, and discuss these with the staff who may have to apply them, and with the governing body. It suggests that headteachers should refer to any model policy that the LEA has developed about touching, holding or restraining pupils.

The Circular also gives examples of how, and how not, to exercise the right. It stresses the need not to act in a way that might reasonably cause injury to the pupil except in extreme circumstances. One example is restraining a young child who would otherwise run into a busy road. It advises keeping full records of any incident, with the person involved making a written report to the headteacher as soon as possible. This is clearly sensible for the protection of the member of staff and in the interests of child protection procedures.

The statutory provisions protect those working with children in school from prosecution for assault in those cases where the force used was reasonable, but what is reasonable is not, and cannot be, defined. It will depend on the circumstances of the case, but clearly any force used has to be proportionate to the incident. The problem, made evident by high-profile prosecutions and subsequent staff discipline action, is that reasonableness is judged with hindsight and what may seem reasonable in the heat of the moment may be judged differently when put under the forensic microscope in a court. Inevitably, people will be reluctant to use force except where it really is the only way to resolve a situation.

HOME–SCHOOL AGREEMENTS

Following on from what had become an increasing practice, all schools are now required to adopt a home–school agreement and a parental declaration to be used in connection with the agreement. This is seen as a means of impressing on parents and pupils the need to comply with school discipline and to behave in a proper manner in school.

A home–school agreement must specify four things:

- the school's aims and values;
- the responsibilities that the school intends to discharge in relation to pupils of compulsory school age;
- the responsibilities that parents are expected to discharge in connection with the education of their children;
- the school's expectations as to the conduct of the pupils.

The parental declaration is a document to be signed by parents recording that they have taken note of the school's aims and values and its responsibilities and that they acknowledge and accept the parental responsibilities and the school's expectations of its pupils.

The governing body has to take reasonable steps to ensure that the parental declaration is signed by all registered parents of pupils of compulsory school age, but they need not do so if there are special circumstances (not defined) that make it inappropriate. The pupil can be invited to sign the parental declaration if the governing body thinks that the pupil has a sufficient understanding of the home–school agreement.

The governing body must keep the agreement under review and must consult with parents before making changes.

The Secretary of State has issued Guidance on this topic and the governing body must have regard to that Guidance. The Secretary of State can also direct that certain words or phrases shall not be used and the Guidance elaborates on this. The agreement should not include terms or conditions that are either unlawful or unreasonable 'in the strict legal sense' such as requiring financial contributions or refusing to waive uniform requirements that parents cannot meet for religious reasons. It is also suggested that they should not impose terms that parents might regard as unreasonable or unacceptable. Examples given are requiring parents to attend an excessive number of parents' evenings, or ones held at unreasonable times, or requiring them to make 'voluntary' financial contributions towards the cost of expensive books or equipment.

The Guidance suggests that the agreement should cover the following areas:

- the standard of education to be provided, indicating the targets that the school is aiming for;
- the ethos of the school;
- regular and punctual attendance;
- discipline and behaviour;
- homework;
- information that school and parents will give each other;
- complaints procedures.

The agreement will not be legally enforceable in the courts. That is not quite the same as saying that these agreements have no legal effect. It would, for example, be quite proper for breaches of a home–school agreement to be taken into account in considering disciplinary action against a pupil, although DfES Guidance indicates that a breach would not in itself be sufficient grounds for exclusion. A pupil may not be excluded because of parental failure or refusal to sign the parental declaration. Parents cannot be required to sign a parental declaration before a place at the school is offered or as a condition of admission to the school, and the admission authority (the LEA or governing body depending on the type of school) cannot make an admission decision based on whether or not the parent will, or is likely to, sign an agreement.

TRUANTING PENALTY NOTICES AND PARENTING ORDERS

New provisions have been introduced as a part of the government's initiative to try to reduce truancy and exclusion and improve anti-social behaviour. There is a close correlation between orders available to youth courts within the criminal justice system and the steps that schools can take, which may lead to schools potentially assuming a law enforcement and behaviour management function that is completely new. This could have a direct impact upon what is already likely to be a delicate relationship between school, pupil and parent. The new provisions are:

- an extension of the circumstances in which an LEA can apply to a youth court for a parenting order (which is beyond the scope of this book). The Guidance suggests that it may be appropriate to apply for an order if a child is permanently excluded or excluded for a second time within 12 months (meaning that a headteacher may wish to liaise closely with the LEA if he or she wishes to request the LEA to apply for one in those circumstances);

- the introduction of a parenting contract between school or LEA and parent; and

- the introduction of a penalty notice system (similar in many respects to those issued for road traffic offences) for truancy, seen by some cynics as reflecting the unspoken governmental view of headteachers as ranking alongside traffic wardens.

Guidance has been issued by the Secretary of State about the implementation of these provisions to which schools should have regard unless there is a good (and recorded) reason not to.

TRUANCY NOTICES

If the governing body agrees (and the school's attendance policy has been amended accordingly), headteachers (or a deputy or assistant headteacher who has been authorised by the headteacher to do so) may issue penalty notices in circumstances where a pupil has truanted.

LEAs are required to draw up a Code of Conduct (taking account of the Guidance issued by the Secretary of State) about the issuing of penalty notices with which heads or their authorised deputies are required to comply. This should ensure some degree of consistency by, amongst other things, including Guidance about the occasions upon which it is appropriate to issue a penalty notice and the maximum number of penalty notices that may be issued to a parent in any one year.

The power to issue a penalty notice arises when a pupil fails to attend regularly at school, and so care needs to be taken in assessing whether a parent has actually committed an offence: obviously, not all absent pupils are truanting. In addition there is no definition of what 'regularly' means, and that will always be a matter of judgement – although the Code of Conduct issued by the LEA is likely to provide Guidance on this point. This means that an investigation should be undertaken before any penalty notice is issued, and the Guidance recommends allowing 15 school days before issuing a notice to give the parent an opportunity to improve the situation. The investigation need not be extensive, but at least should include writing to the parent concerned explaining that issuing a penalty notice is being considered, and inviting an explanation about the absence concerned. If it appears that an offence has been committed, consideration should then be given to whether it falls within the Guidance issued by the Secretary of State, and so should be dealt with by means of a parenting contract or penalty notice.

Particular issues may arise when dealing with holidays that are taken in term time. Headteachers have the discretion to authorise up to 10 days' (or more in exceptional cases) absence for holidays. The Guidance emphasises the need for headteachers to consider each application individually, and not apply inflexible policies (such as a blanket ban).

The legislation itself specifies that an offence does *not* arise when the pupil:

- is absent with leave;

- is unable to attend because of sickness or some unavoidable cause (which is not defined, and so again is a matter of judgement); or

- is absent on a day set apart for observance of the pupil's parents' religion.

Additionally parents are afforded defences if they do not live within walking distance of the school or their work requires them to lead an itinerant lifestyle. A parent will not be guilty of an offence if he or she can establish that:

- the school is not within walking distance (meaning two miles for pupils who are under eight or three miles for others); and

- the LEA has not made suitable arrangements for the pupil to travel to the school concerned, enrol at a nearer school or to accommodate the pupil nearer to the school

and so a penalty notice should not be issued.

Although the 'walking distance' defence is not available to an itinerant parent, such a parent does have a defence if:

- he or she has work that requires travel from place to place;
- the child has attended at a school as regularly as that work permits; and
- if the child is six or older, has made at least 200 attendances during the preceding year;

and so again a penalty notice should not be issued.

The Guidance indicates that:

'... The key consideration in deciding whether to issue a penalty notice will be whether it can be effective in helping to get the pupil who is truanting back into school.

A penalty notice is a suitable intervention in circumstances of parentally condoned truancy, where the parent is judged capable of securing their child's regular attendance but is not willing to take responsibility for doing so, for example where the parent has failed to engage with any voluntary or supportive measures proposed. It will be particularly useful as a sanction at an early stage before attendance problems become entrenched and where the LEA consider that a prosecution would be too heavy-handed.

The normal response to a first offence should be a warning rather than a penalty. However, authorised officers have the discretion to issue a penalty notice for a first offence in exceptional circumstances. This could be where the unauthorised absence was for an extended period and condoned by the parent, for example where the parent has chosen to take their child on holiday during term time without authorisation.

It is for LEAs to set out in their local code of conduct the levels of unauthorised absence above which a penalty notice may be issued and in doing so, they should take into account the level of unauthorised absence at which they will be willing and able to prosecute for the offence of irregular attendance ...'

If a decision is taken to issue a penalty notice, regulations specify what is required, and the Guidance includes a pro forma that may be used, although LEAs are responsible for drawing up pro forma penalty notices and distributing them to schools. A penalty notice must contain:

- the name and address of the recipient;
- the name and address of the child who is failing to attend school regularly, and the name of the school where he or she is a registered pupil;
- the name and official particulars of the authorised officer (meaning for a school the headteacher or authorised deputy) issuing the notice;
- the dates of the offence and of the issue of the notice;
- the amount of the penalty which is to be paid, and any variation in the amount;
- the name and the address of the local education authority to which the penalty is to be paid and to which any correspondence relating to the penalty notice may be sent;
- the method or methods by which payment of the penalty may be made;
- the period for paying the penalty;
- a statement that payment will discharge any liability for the offence;
- the consequences of the penalty not being paid before the expiration of the period for paying it; and
- the grounds on which the notice may be withdrawn.

The notice must be sent to the parent (either by giving it to the parent, leaving it at the parent's last known address or posting it by first-class mail) and a copy sent to the LEA.

The amount of the penalty is £50 if paid within 28 days or £100 if paid within 42 days of receipt of the notice, and is payable to the LEA. If the penalty is not paid, the LEA must either:

- prosecute the parent; or
- withdraw the notice if it considers that the notice should not to have been issued, or it ought not to have been issued to the recipient concerned.

PARENTING CONTRACTS

A parenting contract is similar to a home–school agreement, except that it is addressed to particular parents to address particular issues that arise as a result of either truancy or exclusion. A parenting contract is a document which contains:

- a statement by the parent that he agrees to comply with specified requirements (which may include a requirement to attend a counselling or Guidance programme) for a specified period; and

- a statement by the governing body (or in appropriate cases the LEA) that it agrees to provide support to the parent for the purpose of complying with those requirements.

The intended purpose of a parenting contract is, in an exclusions case, to improve the behaviour of the pupil, or in a truancy case to ensure that the pupil attends school regularly. It must be signed by the parent, and signed on behalf of the governing body or LEA, although like a home–school agreement, does not create any obligations that can be enforced in court, and schools cannot require prospective parents to sign a contract as a condition of admission. Although the Guidance aims to create a situation where school and parent work in partnership to improve the behaviour or attendance of the pupil concerned, the consequences of breach are such that it will be very difficult for a governing body to foster such a feeling of partnership. The Guidance emphasises that a parental contract is voluntary, and parents, a governing body or LEA cannot be compelled to sign. However, failure to sign (or failure to abide by the terms of a contract) may precipitate other action such as issuing a penalty notice or prosecution in the case of truancy or an application to a court for a parenting order in an exclusion case; the failure to sign or comply with its terms may be relevant evidence in any proceedings that may follow. The Guidance therefore does emphasise the need to follow up breaches of the contract with the parent concerned so that a clear pattern of performance under it can be demonstrated.

Looking at this from the opposite end, clearly obligations are placed upon governing bodies and so it remains to be seen whether parents will seek to use a failure on the part of a school to use a parenting contract as, for instance, an argument against permanent exclusion (on the basis that it should form part of the strategies a school will usually try before moving to permanent exclusion).

In deciding whether a contract should be considered, the Guidance emphasises the need to be responsive to the needs of parents, and acknowledges the need for co-operation on both sides, saying that a contract may be appropriate where a parent is willing but in need of support to address the issues presented by the behaviour of the child concerned. The Guidance reads:

'In deciding whether a parenting contract might be appropriate, the ... governing body should consider all the issues behind the [exclusion/non-attendance], in particular whether [the pupil's behaviour/attendance] may be improved through working with the parent and providing support to them and, if so, what form this support should take.'

It suggests that an assessment of the need for a contract should be made over a four-week period in the case of truancy or once the review process (which will depend upon whether and when any exclusion is challenged) has been concluded in the case of exclusion. The Guidance recommends that before deciding whether to enter into a parenting contract, a school should establish:

- whether other agencies are already involved in working with the child and family (and consult with them if appropriate);
- whether a parenting contract would complement this work;
- the type of support that might be helpful to the parent; and
- how a parenting contract would be funded, although the school will be responsible for bearing the cost of such an arrangement.

The Guidance suggests that support might include family group conferencing, peer mentoring, parenting classes, literacy classes, benefits and drugs/alcohol advice, provision of a key link worker for the parent and help with transport to and from school.

If the school does decide to suggest a parenting contract, it should arrange a meeting with the parents. Whilst indicating that ideally it would expect all parents to be invited to such a meeting, the Guidance does make it clear that the school can exercise discretion in the way in which this is done and in particular whether parents with whom it is difficult to engage should be invited to the meeting at all. If possible, the pupil should be involved in the process too by being involved in the discussions that lead up to a meeting about a contract, and the meeting itself. The parents should outline their views about their child's behaviour, any underlying issues, how they should be tackled and their view of a parenting contract. They should be given the opportunity to indicate the kind of support that they would find useful and be told what support the school is able to provide. The discussion should also be clear about the requirements that the contract will make of the parents. The contract should include specified requirements designed to prevent further truancy or poor behaviour which could include attending meetings with the school, signing weekly behaviour reports and ensuring that the pupil does not contact certain pupils. The Guidance does indicate that it will be a normal expectation that parents attend some form of Guidance or counselling (based on an assessment of the parents' needs). There is no specified period for a contract to last, but the Guidance recommends that it should not exceed 12 months and that requirements relating to the child's behaviour or attendance in addition to the provision of some sort of support should not usually exceed three months – and it also suggests that parents may require further support after the contract has expired.

EXCLUSIONS

Exclusion is the last, sometimes the only, sanction available to a school or PRU to deal with behaviour that is totally unacceptable, either because of the seriousness of one event or because it represents a culmination of lesser incidents that have become intolerable. Exclusion raises conflicts in several areas. The school feels the need to protect itself and its community and has a legal obligation to do so. It may also be sharply aware of its reputation in the locality and the fact that its success in attracting pupils, with the consequent financial implications, depends on this. For the pupil, a permanent exclusion may represent the end of any opportunity for a coherent education the consequences of which can be, as a judge has recently expressed it, more serious than a criminal conviction. PRUs are still a less than adequate substitute for full-time schooling and the opportunity for a pupil who is twice excluded to get into another school may be limited by restrictions on the right of appeal against a refusal to admit even to a school with spare capacity. This is dealt with in Chapter 7. There are also significant discrepancies in the way different schools approach the issue and there is strong evidence that boys, and in particular those with an Afro-Caribbean background, are disproportionately subject to exclusion. A number of initiatives have been introduced to reduce the exclusion rate but ultimately it remains a matter for the headteacher and the governing body. Indeed, one change that came into effect in 1999, the removal of the right of the LEA to direct reinstatement to community schools, took away a significant check on what the school can do. As, perhaps, a counterbalance, headteachers, governing bodies, LEAs and appeal panels have a statutory duty to have regard to Guidance issued by the Secretary of State, although the current Guidance is generally perceived to have shifted the balance towards schools and away from pupils.

There are two factors controlling how schools exercise the right to exclude. One is the detailed Guidance issued by DfES, coupled with the parental right of appeal to an appeal panel that is independent of the school, and the other is the overriding jurisdiction of the courts to control the way in which schools (and appeal panels) approach and deal with their functions. Both require detailed examination, but it must be kept in mind that while the Guidance effectively controls the way in which schools apply the discretion that they have, the courts control only the formal process. The Guidance in its original form within Circular 10/99 radically changed the way schools were required to approach the issue of exclusion and proved very controversial particularly when dealing with one-off cases of violence or drug abuse. The Circular did not directly change the law, but the fact that schools and others had to have regard to it meant that the detailed process and criteria laid down by the Circular became in effect new law. This proved to be too great a constraint on the ability of schools to manage difficult cases and the Secretary of State subsequently reduced the rigour of the Circular. The power of the independent appeal panel to reinstate in contentious cases (sometimes leading to conflict within the school as to the manner of reinstatement) led in part at least to the introduction of the new regulations and the complete re-drafting (and further re-drafting) of the Guidance in its current form.

The requirement of decision-makers within the exclusions process 'to have regard' to ministerial Guidance does not absolve them of the requirement to reach an independent decision in relation to the facts of an individual case. The Guidance should be treated as a list of the factors to which headteachers, governing bodies, LEAs and appeal panels ought in general to consider, without indicating any preferred outcome. These issues are explored in rather more detail in Chapter 1.

The approach of the courts has always shown a reluctance to intervene in day-to-day issues that involved educational or management issues. If procedures were correctly followed it was considered to be up to the school to make its own judgements: the courts would only step in if those judgements were irrational, i.e so unreasonable or perverse that no reasonable person could reasonably be expected to come to that conclusion on the basis of the evidence or material that was being considered. In general, therefore, a school that 'went by the book' in following the formal process was likely to be immune from legal challenge whatever the findings were. This remains the case, but while the old cases are still instructive as a guide to how the judges approach factual situations, the court's approach to the exercise of school powers has become significantly more rigorous, not least because the courts are now required to ensure that everything that is done is human rights compliant.

The old cases, however, remain in substance good law in relation to the powers that schools may exercise. For example, schools were held entitled to exclude permanently for:

- bad behaviour outside school hours and off school premises. How far this extends is not established but it does extend to behaviour of pupils towards other pupils of the school, at least where there is an element of bullying or assault. The Guidance does acknowledge this, stressing that it will be a matter of judgement for the headteacher if there is a clear link between the bad behaviour and maintaining good behaviour and discipline within the pupil body as a whole;

- behaviour that transgresses a strict behaviour code adopted by the school. The courts clearly felt that it was for the school to set its own standards, but nowadays a court will probably take upon itself the power (and duty) to consider whether those standards are reasonable and also whether they are consistent with the human rights legislation. The case that upheld the right of a school to permanently exclude a member of the sixth form with an unblemished discipline record for refusing to apologise for swearing at a teacher – the swearing itself being denied – might well be decided differently today;

- parental behaviour that makes it impossible for the school to work constructively in the interests of the child. This can only arise where there has been a breach of discipline by the pupil: the pupil cannot be disciplined for misconduct, however serious, by a parent or other third party. One such case involved a very young child and the school's position was that it could not keep the child in the school when the parent was hostile, aggressive and apparently not willing to work with the school. In those circumstances, the court would not say that permanent exclusion was bound to be unlawful. Similarly, in a quite exceptional case, a school was held to be entitled to permanently exclude a pupil for a breach of discipline which in itself might not be regarded as sufficient to justify that step because the act in question arose in the context of a serious, acrimonious and long-standing dispute between the father (who was the previous headteacher) and the school, which the pupil was furthering on his behalf;

- single incidents of gross bad behaviour. One case of this kind involved a street fight which produced complaints from members of the public and a number of exclusions, some permanent and some fixed period. The judge refused to allow the parent of a permanently excluded pupil to challenge the dismissal of an appeal and did not even require the school or the appeal panel to present a case in support of the exclusion. It would, however, now be necessary for the school to demonstrate that the single incident was of a kind that permitted permanent exclusion as a response within the terms of the current Guidance.

The courts accept the proposition of proportionality in relation to the offence, i.e. that the punishment should fit the crime, but have generally come down on the side of the school whenever this is an issue. Consistency of treatment of offenders will be relevant where a number of pupils are involved in the same incident or where the school has a particular policy on, for example, drugs. The courts seem more likely to accept a challenge to a decision where pupils in similar circumstances are treated differently. There is no requirement that all are treated alike but the school needs to be able to show why there are differences and that those differences are justified by the particular circumstances of the facts or the individual pupil.

The procedure for exclusion is complex. As mentioned, the most recent cases have demonstrated, on the one hand, support for the school in its definition of what is unacceptable behaviour but, on the other hand, a much greater willingness to explore the process of investigation and hearings to see that they were fair. If they were not, the court will usually require the school (or the appeal panel) to go through the process again. If that cannot be done without causing further unfairness, or if there is a real urgency, such as impending public examinations, the court might simply declare the exclusion to be a nullity, which means that the pupil is reinstated.

The implications in terms of how the headteacher and then the governing body should conduct an investigation and review of an exclusion decision are considered in detail below.

It is important that schools comply with the law, and in particular with the limitations on exclusion that the law imposes. A recent case demonstrates the need for this when it was held that an exclusion that was plainly unlawful – in this case an exclusion for an unlimited period – could give grounds for a claim for damages against the school. The claim essentially is for breach of human rights by virtue of the denial of the right to education. Further, it was held that the headteacher could properly be included in the claim because for human rights purposes the headteacher of a school is a public authority just as are the governing body and LEA. No doubt the headteacher would expect to be indemnified by the governing body for any damages awarded but this cannot be taken as automatic. Indeed, if the damages claim succeeds because of action taken by the headteacher that the governing body had no opportunity to put right one can see the force of an argument that the governing body should not have to meet the resultant cost. An unlawful exclusion that did not come to the notice of governors could fall in that category. Headteachers and governing bodies do, therefore, need to be aware of the constraints on them. This has been made the more important by changes to the Guidance which give added clarity on the subject of what is and is not an authorised exclusion.

TYPES OF EXCLUSIONS

The headteacher or the teacher in charge of a PRU may exclude a pupil, and the Guidance indicates that, in the absence of the headteacher or teacher in charge, the most senior teacher who is acting in that role may do so. An exclusion must either be for a fixed period or be permanent. Lunchtime exclusions have now been introduced and are treated as the equivalent of exclusion for half a school day.

Fixed-period Exclusions

As the term implies, a fixed-period exclusion is for a specified period and should be stated in terms of school days with a specific date given as the date for return. An exclusion expressed to be until such time as the parents come into school for a discussion, which is still quite often seen, is an unlawful exclusion because it is not for a fixed period. The exclusion can be of any length up to 45 school days in any one year, so long as the aggregate of fixed-period exclusions for the pupil does not exceed that total. The headteacher can decide at any time before a fixed-period exclusion expires that it be turned into a permanent one. This is a useful strategy in complex cases, to give time for consideration and investigation. It is also possible to use a long fixed-period exclusion in cases where it is felt that the pupil cannot be allowed to return to the school but that a managed move to another school might be feasible. Whilst the Guidance does acknowledge this practice, it should be used with care: it may need a degree of co-operation from the LEA and it should not simply be left to the parent to find another school with the threat of permanent exclusion hanging in the air. It is laudable to try to avoid a permanent exclusion appearing on a pupil's record, but the line between seeking this and the charge that the school is using fixed-period exclusions so that the school's record of permanent exclusion is not adversely affected is a thin one.

The parents (or the pupil if 18 or over) must be notified immediately, ideally by telephone and followed up in writing within one school day, of the exclusion, the reason for it and its length (including the return date), and must also be told of the entitlement to make representations to the governing body about the exclusion and the person they should contact if they wish to do so. The letter should also mention the latest day by which the governing body must meet (unless the exclusion is for five days or less), the parent's right to see and have a copy of the pupil's school record, the arrangements for setting and marking work through the course of the exclusion and contact details for the LEA and Advisory Centre for Education (ACE). Useful standard letters for this and other purposes are contained within the Guidance. Schools also have to notify the governing body and LEA within one school day if the exclusion will lead the pupil to miss the opportunity to take a public examination or if it will bring the aggregate number of days' exclusion in the term to more than five days. Exclusions for five days or less must be reported to the governing body and LEA once a term. The reports must include details relating to the pupil's gender, ethnicity and whether the pupil is subject to the SEN Code of Practice or is in care, as well as identifying the pupil and specifying the nature of the exclusion and the reasons for it.

Schools should give consideration to the possibility of entering into a parenting contract (as outlined above) in the case of the parents of a pupil excluded for a fixed period. The Guidance suggests that the contract could run once the review process (meaning the date upon which the Discipline Committee endorses the headteacher's decision to exclude, or the date upon which the exclusion began if it is not considered by the Discipline Committee) is complete.

Permanent Exclusions

Again, the phrase speaks for itself. A pupil who is permanently excluded from a school remains on the school roll until the exclusion is confirmed and any appeal has been dealt with. Until then, the school retains responsibility for the pupil's education and should provide work to be done at home, although the Guidance acknowledges that for both permanent and longer fixed-term exclusions the assistance of the LEA may be necessary. Thereafter, the responsibility passes to the LEA until the pupil is admitted to another school. The pupil-related funding for that pupil is withdrawn from the school when the decision to exclude is confirmed by the governing body and 'follows' the pupil according to the alternative provision that is made. If a pupil is reinstated by the Independent Appeal Panel, the LEA will return the funding to the school.

As with fixed-period exclusions, parents (or the pupil if 18 or over) must be notified and told the reasons for permanent exclusion (and any relevant previous history), informed of their right to make representations to the governing body and the person they should contact if they wish to do so. Again, the letter should also mention the latest day by which the governing body must meet, the parent's right to see and have a copy of the pupil's school record, the arrangements for setting and marking work through the course of the exclusion process and contact details for the LEA and ACE – and again, there are useful standard letters for this purpose contained within the Guidance. The governing body must also be notified, as must the LEA.

THE EXCLUSION GUIDANCE

The exclusion process was previously seen by many as a discrete element in the discipline process, but as mentioned above, Circular 10/99 brought it into the overall process of handling behaviour problems and disaffection. The link between the two remains despite the publication of the new Guidance ('Improving Behaviour and Attendance: Guidance on Exclusion from Schools and Pupil Referral Units') although the relationship between them is now less cohesive. The eight parts of the new Guidance (three parts up on the January 2003 Guidance under the same name) deal with:

- promoting positive behaviour and early intervention;
- removing pupils from a school site and exclusion;
- procedure for excluding a pupil and the role of the headteacher;
- responsibilities of the governing body;
- independent appeal panels;
- police involvement in parallel criminal proceedings;
- LEA responsibility to provide full-time education and reintegrate permanently excluded pupils; and
- arrangements for money to follow pupils who have been permanently excluded from school;

together with, as touched upon, containing useful standards letters for the school, governing body or independent appeal panel to use.

All concerned are required to 'have regard' to the Guidance. This means that any deviation from the Guidance must be justified by the circumstances.

The Guidance starts from a position that effective policies, procedures and training will minimise the number of pupils at risk of exclusion and lists a wide range of additional measures designed to secure this. Before excluding a child, in most cases a range of alternative strategies such as those included in Section 1 of the Circular should be tried, and could include the use of a parenting contract. The Guidance suggests that restorative justice, mediation, internal exclusion and managed moves are also alternatives that schools may wish to consider. This is not meant to prevent immediate action to protect pupils and staff, including fixed-period exclusion. A permanent exclusion can be given for a first offence, if the conduct concerned is serious enough to justify it.

A decision to exclude a child should be taken only in response to serious breaches of a school's behaviour policy and if allowing the pupil to remain in school would seriously harm the education or welfare of the pupil or others in the school.

A new passage deals with the removal of pupils from a school site, identifying three 'exceptional circumstances' where this may be done. One is through the formal exclusion procedure to be dealt with below. The second is where a pupil is accused of a serious criminal offence but the offence took place outside the school's jurisdiction. The Guidance says that in these circumstances the headteacher may decide that it is in the interests of the individual concerned and of the school community as a whole for that pupil to be educated off-site for a fixed period, subject to review at regular intervals and it goes on to say that this is not an exclusion. The third is where a pupil's presence on the school site represents a serious risk to the health or safety of other pupils or school staff. The Guidance says that in these circumstances a headteacher may send the pupil home that day after consultation with the parents. This is said not to be an exclusion and that it may only be done for medical reasons.

There is specific Guidance on the use of exclusion which is worth quoting in some detail:

'9.   A decision to exclude a pupil should be taken only:

  (a)   in response to serious breaches of the school's behaviour policy; and
  (b)   if allowing the pupil to remain in school would seriously harm the education or welfare of the pupil or others in the school.

10.   Only the headteacher, or teacher in charge of a PRU, (or, in the absence of the headteacher or teacher in charge, the acting headteacher or teacher in charge) can exclude a pupil.

11.   A decision to exclude a child **permanently** is a serious one. It will usually be the final step in a process for dealing with disciplinary offences following a wide range of other strategies, which have been tried without success. It is an acknowledgement by the school that it has exhausted all available strategies for dealing with the child and should normally be used as a last resort.

12.   There will, however, be exceptional circumstances where, in the headteacher's judgment, it is appropriate to permanently exclude a child for a first or 'one off' offence. These might include:

  (a)   serious actual or threatened violence against another pupil or a member of staff;
  (b)   sexual abuse or assault;
  (c)   supplying an illegal drug;
  (d)   carrying an offensive weapon (for advice on what constitutes an offensive weapon, please refer to the advice in School Security: Chapter 6.
        (http://www.dfes.gov.uk/schoolsecurity/dwt6offensive_weap ons.shtml)

Schools should consider whether or not to inform the police where such a criminal offence has taken place. They should also consider whether or not to inform other agencies, e.g. Youth Offending Teams, social workers, etc.

13. These instances are not exhaustive, but indicate the severity of such offences and the fact that such behaviour can affect the discipline and well-being of the school community.

14. In cases where a headteacher has permanently excluded a pupil for:

    (a) one of the above offences; or
    (b) persistent and defiant misbehaviour including bullying (which would include racist or homophobic bullying) or repeated possession and/or use of an illegal drug on school premises;

    the Secretary of State would not normally expect the governing body or an Independent Appeal Panel to reinstate the pupil.

Drug-related exclusions

15. In making a decision on whether or not to exclude for a drug-related offence the headteacher should have regard to the school's published policy on drugs and should consult the school's drugs co-ordinator. But the decision will also depend on the precise circumstances of the case and the evidence available. In some cases fixed period exclusion will be more appropriate than permanent exclusion. In more serious cases, an assessment of the incident should be made against criteria set out in the school's policy. This should be a key factor in determining whether permanent exclusion is an appropriate course of action. The Department has issued revised Guidance on drugs in schools and this can be accessed on the Teachernet web-site at: http://www.teachernet.gov.uk/wholeschool/behaviour/drugs/.

16. Schools should develop a policy that covers not only illegal drugs but also legal drugs – volatile substances (those giving off a gas or vapour which can be inhaled), and over the counter and prescription medicines – which may be being misused by pupils. This might say, for example, that no drug should be brought in to school without the school's knowledge and approval. Where legal drugs are concerned, again an assessment of the seriousness of the incident is necessary before deciding what action to take.

Factors to consider before making a decision to exclude

17. Exclusion should not be imposed in the heat of the moment, unless there is an immediate threat to the safety of others in the school or the pupil concerned. Before deciding whether to exclude a pupil, either permanently or for a fixed period, the headteacher should:

    (a) ensure that a thorough investigation has been carried out;

(b) consider all the evidence available to support the allegations, taking account of the school's behaviour and equal opportunities policies, and, where applicable, the Race Relations Act 1976 as amended and the Disability Discrimination Act 1995 as amended;
(c) allow the pupil to give his or her version of events;
(d) check whether the incident may have been provoked, for example by bullying, including homophobic bullying, or by racial or sexual harassment; and
(e) if necessary, consult others, but not anyone who may later have a role in reviewing the headteacher's decision, for example a member of the governing body.

18. The standard of proof to be applied is the balance of probabilities, i.e. if it is more probable than not that the pupil did what he or she is alleged to have done, the headteacher may exclude the pupil. However, the more serious the allegation, the more convincing the evidence substantiating the allegation needs to be.

Where a police investigation leading to possible criminal proceedings has been initiated, the evidence available may be very limited. However, it may still be possible for the headteacher to make a judgment on whether to exclude the pupil. Part 6 on page 47 of this Guidance deals with such circumstances in detail.

...

When exclusion is not appropriate

21. Exclusion should not be used for:
(a) minor incidents such as failure to do homework or to bring dinner money;
(b) poor academic performance;
(c) lateness or truancy;
(d) pregnancy;
(e) breaches of school uniform rules or rules on appearance (including jewellery and hairstyle), except where these are persistent and in open defiance of such rules;
(f) punishing pupils for the behaviour of their parents, for example where parents refuse or are unable to attend a meeting.'

The Guidance on uniforms took on special significance when a Muslim pupil who wished to wear a particular form of dress on religious grounds challenged the right of the school to insist on her wearing the school uniform. When the pupil appeared at school not wearing the approved uniform (which had been developed in consultation with the local Muslim community and which was well publicised) she was told to go home and return in correct uniform. She refused to do so and the resultant stand-off led to a well-publicised court case. The human rights element of this case are dealt with in Chapter 14 but the case is of significance in relation to exclusions. It justifies the following propositions:

Requiring a pupil to go home and change into school uniform does not constitute exclusion in any circumstances:

- If the pupil then stays away from school rather than comply with uniform requirements, the school cannot be said to have excluded. The absence from school does not follow from an act of exclusion by the school but from the refusal of the pupil to comply with the school's uniform policy.

- If the pupil insisted on coming to school wearing clothes that did not comply with the uniform policy, the school might be justified in excluding. That exclusion would not breach the Guidance because it would not be for failing to wear school uniform in itself but for persistent breach – specifically contemplated by the Guidance as cited above.

- It is not essential for the uniform policy to specify sanctions for non-compliance

A new section in the Guidance deals with what are described as 'unofficial exclusions' – a new concept in this territory:

'22. If the headteacher is satisfied that, on the balance of probabilities, a pupil has committed a disciplinary offence and the pupil is being removed from the school site for that reason, formal exclusion is the only legal method of removal. Informal or unofficial exclusions are illegal regardless of whether they are done with the agreement of parents or carers.

...

Length of fixed period exclusions

25. The regulations allow headteachers to exclude a pupil for one or more fixed periods not exceeding 45 school days in any one school year. The limit of 45 school days applies to the pupil and not to the institution. Therefore, any days of fixed period exclusion served by the pupil in any school or PRU in the same school year will count towards the total. It is important therefore that, when a pupil transfers to a new school during the academic year, records of the fixed period exclusions a pupil has received so far during the current academic year are also transferred promptly to the new school. However, individual fixed period exclusions should be for the shortest time necessary, bearing in mind that exclusions of more than a day or two make it more difficult for the pupil to reintegrate into the school. Ofsted inspection evidence suggests that 1–3 days is often long enough

to secure the benefits of exclusion without adverse educational consequences. Exclusions may not be given for an unspecified period, for example until a meeting can be arranged. Such a practice amounts to an indefinite exclusion for which no legal arrangements exist.

Considerations following a fixed period exclusion

26. The school's obligation to provide education continues while the pupil is on the roll, and must be met during a fixed term exclusion. In all cases of more than a day's exclusion, work should be set and marked. A headteacher considering whether to exclude a pupil for a longer fixed period, for example for more than 15 school days, should plan:

    (a) how the pupil's education will continue during the period of exclusion;

    (b) how the time might be used to address the pupil's problems;

    (c) together with the school's maintaining LEA, what educational arrangements will best help with the pupil's reintegration into the school at the end of the exclusion. The school will usually be expected to meet some of the costs for this but the exact arrangements will need to be agreed with the LEA.

27. The headteacher should arrange a reintegration meeting with parents following the expiry of a fixed period exclusion. This should be an opportunity to discuss how best the pupil can return to school and can be a useful forum to consider with parents the possibility of a parenting contract (see paragraph 28 below). However, a fixed period exclusion should not be extended if such a meeting cannot be arranged in time or the parents do not attend, as such a meeting is not a statutory requirement.

28. If the school or LEA considers that parental influence could be better brought to bear in improving the behaviour of the pupil who has been excluded, they should consider whether it may be appropriate to offer a parenting contract. A parenting contract is a two-sided voluntary agreement between the school or LEA and the parent under which the parent agrees to comply with certain requirements and the school or LEA agrees to provide or help the parent access the support that they need. Parenting contracts are appropriate where the parent is willing to engage with the school or LEA but needs support. A school may not require a parent to sign a parenting contract as a condition of their child being reinstated in the school.

29. If the exclusion is the second fixed period exclusion (for serious misbehaviour) within a twelve month period and the parent is unwilling to engage with the school or LEA to bring about improvements in the pupil's behaviour, the LEA may consider applying to the court for a parenting order to compel the parent

to comply with certain requirements including attendance at parenting classes.

30. For further information on parenting contracts or orders, please refer to the Guidance on the Education-related Provisions of the Anti-social Behaviour Act (http://www.dfes.gov.uk/behaviourandattendance guidance/parentingcontracts/index.cfm).

Lunchtime exclusion

31. Pupils whose behaviour at lunchtime is disruptive may be excluded from the school premises for the duration of the lunchtime period. A lunchtime exclusion is a fixed period exclusion (deemed to be equivalent to one half of a school day) and should be treated as such, and parents have the same right to be given information and to make representations. A lunchtime exclusion for an indefinite period, like any other indefinite exclusion, would not be lawful. Arrangements should be made for pupils who are entitled to free school meals to receive their entitlement which may mean, for example, providing a packed lunch.

32. The Secretary of State does not expect lunchtime exclusion to be used for a prolonged period. In the long run another strategy for dealing with the problem should be worked out.

Parental co-operation

33. If a parent does not comply with an exclusion, for example by sending the excluded child to school, or by refusing to collect, or arrange collection of, him or her at lunchtime, the school must have due regard for the pupil's safety in deciding what action to take. An exclusion should not be enforced if doing so may put the safety of the pupil at risk. If efforts to resolve the issue with the parents are unsuccessful the school should consider whether to contact the Education Welfare Service and seek the advice of the LEA about available legal remedies.'

It follows from this that a headteacher considering an exclusion, whether fixed-period or permanent, needs to use the Guidance as a checklist. It has always been good practice, and it is now essential, for the headteacher to record the detail of that consideration so as to be able to produce it to the governing body and any appeal panel because those bodies must, in discharge of their obligation to 'have regard to' the Guidance, not only consider the school's policies and the parity of treatment with others involved in the same incident, but also satisfy themselves that the headteacher has gone through that process. Indeed, the headteacher needs to be meticulous in noting every step that is taken in the course of investigation and consideration of the issues, including such elementary points as noting the time, date and the names of those present. If any part of an investigation is delegated to others, those people should also be made aware of the need to keep good-quality records. Whilst it is no longer the case that the governing body and independent appeal panel are exhorted to reinstate if there has been some procedural irregularity, the Guidance does emphasise that independent appeal panels should take account of defects in procedure that are so significant that important factors were not considered or justice was clearly not done.

When applying the 'balance of probabilities' test, the headteacher should include consideration of the potential likelihood or otherwise of the deed having been done, and the more serious the allegation (in the sense that it might amount to a criminal offence), the more convincing the evidence needs to be. Generally speaking, 'balance of probabilities' means 'more likely than not', i.e. a 51 per cent likelihood. However, it is really not possible to assess evidence in this mathematical way and the only satisfactory way for the headteacher to approach the issue is to take the whole of the evidence, assess the extent to which what is said to have happened is corroborated, consider the way the 'defence' is put and assess its likelihood and take a view on the reliability of witnesses and the degree to which what they say may be motivated by self-interest, including animosity towards the claimed perpetrator. It is especially important to try to assess the extent to which witnesses may be biased or be making assumptions based on preconceptions. This is a particular danger when members of staff who did not witness events base themselves on what they believe to be characteristics of the parties involved. They may be quite right to do so and their judgements may be sound, but the headteacher needs to be able to tell governors and an appeal panel that these issues were considered.

Particular care should be taken when dealing with statemented pupils (or pupils who are going through the SEN process), disabled pupils, pupils from an ethnic minority or pupils who are in care.

The Guidance says that statemented children should only be excluded in the most exceptional of cases and that every effort should be made to avoid excluding children who are otherwise involved in the statementing process: effectively, efforts should be made to address the issues raised through the statementing process perhaps by getting the LEA involved or initiating an interim annual review. It goes on to say that if a pupil is permanently excluded, the headteacher should liaise with the LEA before the governing body meet to consider it, to see whether more support can be made available, or another school can be named in which case the exclusion should be withdrawn.

Schools must not discriminate against disabled pupils by excluding them because of their disability, and the Guidance specifically requires consideration of disability discrimination issues in appropriate cases. Disability discrimination issues, including the defence of justification, are explored more fully in Chapter 6. Schools are required not to discriminate against disabled pupils in the sense that they treat a disabled pupil less favourably or place the pupil at a substantial disadvantage because of the pupil's disability. In the context of exclusions, it is likely that the principal issue for the headteacher to consider will be whether there has been less favourable treatment of the pupil concerned. However, the headteacher should also consider whether there were reasonable steps (short of providing auxiliary aids or removing or altering a physical feature) that could have been taken which may have prevented the pupil being placed at a substantial disadvantage when compared with non-disabled peers. The most thorny area revolves around whether a behavioural problem amounts to a disability – and therefore whether an episode of unacceptable behaviour is a symptom of a disability or not. Great care needs to be taken in circumstances such as this, and the issues are explored more fully in Chapter 6.

Similar requirements apply to race relations: schools must not discriminate against pupils on racial grounds when making a decision about whether to exclude a pupil. This requirement arises out of the fact that statistics reveal that exclusion is more prevalent in a number of ethnic groups. A Code of Practice and Guide for Schools has been produced by the Commission for Racial Equality, which the Guidance recommends.

The Guidance finally urges schools to be sensitive when dealing with children in care; it states that every practicable means should be used (including reference to the LEA and professional advice as appropriate) to maintain such a pupil in school.

Each case will have to be taken on its own merits but if the conduct concerned does justify exclusion, a headteacher is likely to see that as the appropriate step to take irrespective of other issues that may affect the pupil concerned.

EXCLUSIONS AND THE GOVERNING BODY

The governing bodies of all schools have to hold special meetings to consider:

- all permanent exclusions;

- all fixed-period exclusions of more than 15 days;

- all fixed-period exclusions which will result in the pupil losing the opportunity to sit a public exam; and

- any other fixed-period exclusions of between six and 15 days where the parents have expressed a wish to make representations.

The governing body must also consider parental representations made in respect of a pupil excluded for five days or less in a term, although there is no requirement to hold a special meeting for that purpose and the parent (or pupil if appropriate) has no right to attend that meeting. This is an important point: many parents (and some advisors) persist in the view that they are entitled to meet with governors no matter how short the exclusion and many schools accede to this wrongly thinking that it is a parental entitlement. It represents a significant waste of governor and headteacher time over issues that will usually be relatively trivial.

It is a matter for the governing body concerned to determine how best to meet these requirements, but it is likely to find that it makes sense to replicate the old compulsory model of the pupil discipline committee. They must hold a meeting not less than six nor more than 15 school days after being notified of a permanent exclusion or a fixed-period exclusion for more than 15 days in total for the year. If the exclusion is for between six and 15 days in total for the year, the governing body has up to 50 school days in which to meet. This applies even though by the time the representations are heard the exclusion will have taken effect. If a pupil could lose the chance to sit a public exam, the governing body must if practical meet before the date of the exam. There is no specific time limit for governing bodies to consider exclusions of five days or less, although the headteacher must notify the governing body and LEA of them on a termly basis, and so it makes sense for the governing body to consider these on a termly basis too. There is no requirement for the school to suspend operation of the exclusion until representations are heard – indeed, that would in most cases defeat the object of the exclusion. A governing body may direct the headteacher to reinstate any pupil excluded if it is practical to do so and must consider whether reinstatement is to be immediate or at a later specified date, and the headteacher must comply with any such direction. The governing body must inform the LEA of the reinstatement.

As touched upon above, schools may feel that it is appropriate to set up a committee comprising three governors, and it would be sensible for the governing body to nominate a pool of governors from which to select such a committee. Non-governors and the headteacher should not be members; it is often wise for other staff governors not to be members too. The usual rules relating to withdrawal by governors apply, so that no governor who has a prior involvement with the exclusion or the circumstances leading to it or who has a material connection with the pupil or family concerned should take part in the process. It is not enough actually to be fair: the governing body must be *seen* to be fair so that anyone whom the pupil or parents might believe (on reasonable grounds) to have some degree of involvement or partiality should not take part.

Parental Representations

There is a procedure laid down for consideration by the committee of exclusions and parental representations:

- the pupil discipline committee must consider the circumstances in which the pupil was excluded. This must not be a 'rubber-stamp' exercise. It involves a proper consideration of the facts and how they were established and this is considered in detail below;

- the committee must consider any representations made by the parents (or pupil if 18 or over) and the LEA;

- the pupil discipline committee must allow the parents (or pupil if 18 or over) and an LEA representative to attend a meeting of the governing body and make oral representations. The committee must consider any such oral representations.

It is worth making the point (even if it is somewhat academic) that the parental entitlement is to make representations which governors will consider along with their own review of the exclusion. It is not an appeal and one implication of this is that technically the parents do not have the right to ask questions or to make a final address to the committee. However, good practice and the general assumption, reinforced at least in terms of parental expectations, that the governing body as a public authority will operate in an open and fair way indicate strongly that parents should at least be given the opportunity at a hearing to challenge facts and seek clarification. It is also good practice that they should be given the opportunity to have the last word, although the chair can legitimately require the parents not to repeat points that have already been clearly made.

The task that the pupil discipline committee faces is complex and arduous. It is worth looking at one particular Court of Appeal case (which considered the Guidance provided in Circular 10/99, rather than the new Guidance) in some detail, because in it the judges examined the function of the process and defined the role of the committee.

The facts were simple. Three boys were believed to have been involved in the theft of a handbag from the staffroom. The three boys, B (the applicant in the proceedings), D and M were permanently excluded. The governing body discipline committee heard representations against exclusion in each of the cases in turn. Clearly, it had no option as each pupil was entitled to his own hearing. B's case was heard second, after that of D. The committee took into account matters that it had received in D's hearing without making that material available to B's representatives. Furthermore, in the course of investigation D had made a written statement to the headteacher which implicated B but which was not made available to B. That statement was seen by the committee in the course of D's hearing. The committee reinstated D but upheld the decision to permanently exclude B. B appealed to the statutory appeal committee which considered the same material and upheld the exclusion. An application for judicial review failed at first instance but was allowed by the Court of Appeal which concentrated on how the headteacher and particularly the pupil discipline committee approached the matter, and in particular the fact that material had been considered by the committee which had not been disclosed to B or his parents or representatives. In its judgment, the Court of Appeal analysed the respective functions of the headteacher and the governor committee.

A number of points of general principle emerge.

- In considering the question of whether to direct reinstatement, the committee is not simply looking to see if the headteacher has acted reasonably. It has an independent duty to establish the primary facts although its starting point can be the headteacher's findings. As one of the judges said: 'Because [the headteacher] is for practical reasons in the successive positions of investigator, accuser, jury and judge, the governors are there to provide an essential independent check on his judgment'. This is of fundamental importance. What the court is saying is that, ultimately, the decision to exclude is that of the governing body acting by the committee and not that of the headteacher. The committee cannot effectively devolve its responsibility by taking the line that it has a duty to support the headteacher. The principle applies just as much to fixed-period exclusions as it does to permanent ones.

- Any investigation process by the headteacher must be fair, but need not meet the standards required from the police in criminal investigations. However, where what is alleged would constitute a criminal offence, whilst it is not necessary to prove the facts beyond reasonable doubt, it should nevertheless, according to one of the judges, 'be distinctly more probable' than not. In effect, the more serious the allegation, the higher the standard of proof required and it is the task of the pupil discipline committee to consider the evidence in this light. This is reflected in the comments on the 'balance of probabilities' test in the Guidance.

- Physical evidence should, if possible, be retained.

- Natural justice requires that if the committee intends to take any matter in consideration this must be made known to the pupil/parent so that there is an opportunity to comment and answer. This can cause particular difficulties when dealing with a statement where, often to protect the pupil concerned, the author's identity has been withheld. The Court of Appeal has held in a different case that it is appropriate for the governing body and independent panels to consider such statements but that it will affect the weight that attaches to them – and if they are considered, the LEA and school must let the committee or panel know of anything that might qualify or cast doubt upon such a statement. If a committee or panel do decide to take account of an anonymous statement, it must be able to justify it by balancing the fairness and unfairness involved in doing so: the court acknowledged that this is an extremely difficult exercise because whether an anonymous statement is allowed in or not is likely to be unfair either to the alleged victim or excluded pupil. The Court of Appeal in yet another case has also said that panels and committees should be prepared to disregard anonymised statements if they are damaging to the pupil in ways with which the pupil could not be expected to deal without knowing who had made the statement.

- The committee must secure natural justice even if the pupil or parent does not take the point. As one judge put it: 'The governors' duty to ensure fairness is not conditional upon applications or demands more appropriate to adversarial litigation'.

What does this amount to in practical terms?

- The investigation process must be conducted with great care and, as already mentioned, with good records. In most cases, the headteacher will not be a witness to the events that are alleged against the pupil. The first task, therefore, is to understand what is said to have happened and to identify those who are able to provide evidence. The next step is to obtain written statements. Those from adults present no particular difficulty. They should be timed and dated and should set out the facts in a chronological sequence. The statements should include such background as is necessary to provide a context but should concentrate on the facts. Where the adult's evidence is based on what others have said, this must be made explicit and the identity of those others should be stated. It is for the headteacher subsequently to decide the extent, if at all, that anonymity is to be preserved. Statements from pupils should be taken by the headteacher in person, where practicable, or by senior members of staff. Where more than one pupil is involved, steps should be taken wherever possible to take statements in a way that prevents collusion. It is good practice to get the pupil to start by making a written statement and for questions to be confined to clarifying points. Where a statement is based on question and answer it should be recorded as such. The pupil should be given an opportunity to read the statement, make corrections and sign it. It should then be countersigned by the person taking the statement.

- Having obtained the statements, the headteacher must evaluate them, decide what is clearly proved and what is speculation, and come to a conclusion as to what actually happened. The next step is to decide the appropriate response to the established facts, taking the Guidance into account. Assuming the decision is to exclude, the headteacher then has to consider the length of the exclusion. If the exclusion is a response to a 'one-off' incident, or if the facts are complex and need time for consideration or further investigation, it is good practice to exclude initially for a fixed period (perhaps three or five school days) and then to consider whether permanent exclusion is warranted. Although it is not essential, it is good practice to make it clear in the letter advising of the fixed-period exclusion that permanent exclusion is under consideration.

- Headteachers need to make a full presentation to the committee. The hearing is not an appeal against a decision but a review of that decision and, critically, the committee has an independent investigative role. In effect, the headteacher acts as a prosecutor and the case needs to be prepared carefully. The headteacher must consider what has to be proved and what evidence needs to be presented to reach the necessary level of proof. The Guidance indicates that it is usual to hear from those directly involved – possibly including the victim and the investigating teacher. It is normal for the evidence of pupil witnesses to be provided by written statement. A recent case emphasised that there is nothing to stop adult witnesses attending – and if they failed to, the panel could draw whatever conclusion seemed sensible. Schools should not have a policy about the attendance of teachers; each case should be judged individually.

- The committee will need to consider all the facts to form a proper view as to whether the headteacher's view of what happened is supported by the evidence and to be sure that it was properly collected. This is particularly important where there may be room for a challenge to the correct identification of those involved, a dispute as to the exact sequence of events, allegations as to whether the excluded pupil or the alleged victim was in fact the instigator or, as in the case mentioned above, questions as to the degree of responsibility of each of those involved in an incident involving more than one alleged perpetrator.

- The committee must consider such issues even if they are not specifically raised by the representations that are made. Hearsay evidence and evidence in the form of written statements are acceptable and it may be reasonable, subject to the observations made above, for the headteacher to maintain the anonymity of the witnesses in order to protect them. However, copies of the statements must be supplied to the excluded pupil or parent. Inevitably, that may lead to the identity of the witness being evident to the excluded pupil. This creates a dilemma for both headteacher and committee. Presenting the evidence may put the witnesses at risk of possible reprisals, but not presenting it may mean that there is no cogent evidence on which the committee can rely and may make it inevitable that the committee feels constrained to direct reinstatement. There is no escape from the rigour of the evidential requirement and this encapsulates the conflicts inherent in the exclusion process.

- The committee will need to be alert to the possibility of collusion between witnesses and of ideas being put into their heads. Where identification is an issue, the committee will need to be sure that anyone making a positive identification has not been prompted or steered towards a particular person. A case has indicated that where identification is an issue, the committee (and for that matter the appeal panel where relevant) should hear oral evidence from the person making the identification so that the strength of the evidence can be established.

- Only once satisfied as to the facts should the committee consider whether or not exclusion is the appropriate response by balancing the interests of the excluded pupil against those of the rest of the school community. At that point, it has to consider whether the Guidance has been complied with, and an important part of the headteacher's presentation to the committee will be to demonstrate that it was taken properly into account and that the decision to exclude, whether fixed-period or permanent, was consonant with the Guidance. Whilst, as mentioned above, independent appeal panels are required not to direct reinstatement simply because of a failure to comply with any procedural requirement, the Guidance does emphasise that procedural issues will be relevant if the process was so flawed that important factors were not considered or justice was clearly not done – although if justice was not done reinstatement is likely to follow anyway.

The Guidance does not deal with evidential issues in the context of the governing body review. However, it does deal with this in relation to appeal hearings and there is no good reason why a governing body should adopt a different approach. The Guidance says:

> '113.To reach a decision, the panel will generally need to hear from those directly or indirectly involved. The governing body may wish to call witnesses who saw the incident that gave rise to the exclusion. These may include any alleged victim or any teacher other than the headteacher who investigated the incident and interviewed pupils. A teacher may be accompanied by a friend or representative.
>
> 114.In the case of witnesses who are pupils of the school, it will normally be more appropriate for the panel to rely on written statements. Pupils may appear as witnesses if they do so voluntarily and with their parent's consent. Panels should be sensitive to the needs of child witnesses to ensure that the child's view is properly heard.
>
> 115. All written witness statements must be attributed and signed and dated, unless the school has good reason to wish to protect the anonymity of pupils, in which case they should at least be dated. The general principle remains that an accused person is entitled to know the substance and the source of the accusation. The panel must consider what weight to attach to written statements, whether made by adults or pupils, as against oral evidence. They should bear in mind that a written statement may not encompass all the relevant issues, nor can the author be interrogated.'

As will be seen, this is an encapsulation of the decisions of the courts on this difficult area and governing bodies as well as appeal panels should follow this advice. Furthermore, the headteacher needs to be aware of it not just in deciding what material to put before the governing body but, at times, also in relation to the initial decision to exclude – in essence, 'will the evidence stand up in court'.

Difficult problems arise where the offender is subject to potential criminal charges arising out of the incident for which exclusion is being considered. Part 6 of the Guidance seeks to address the problems this presents. In essence it states that the fact of a criminal investigation or proceedings alone is enough to justify a headteacher in deciding upon, and the committee in upholding, an exclusion. It then suggests that it may be appropriate for the independent appeal panel to use its power to adjourn pending the outcome of the investigation or proceedings. This does raise problems of its own, not least of which are the delay and the consequences of that delay that are inherent in dealing with the situation in this way. In particular this does place the excluded pupil at a significant disadvantage: the fact that the action of the headteacher and committee in excluding the pupil is justified means that the pupil is treated as being guilty without any airing of the case at all – this could be particularly difficult in a case of alleged assault including sexual assault where it may well be one person's word against another's. The pupil concerned will remain excluded pending the outcome of the hearing, recollections may dim with the passage of time and a new status quo may have been established in particular so far as that pupil's education is concerned that may make the panel hearing increasingly irrelevant to the pupil. Surprisingly, the Guidance states that the panel 'should have regard' to information about concluded criminal proceedings, but notes that a pupil that has been acquitted by a court may still be guilty. This is in the sense that the pupil may be responsible for the conduct concerned but, because of differences in the evidential standard required in a criminal court or because of a legal technicality, was acquitted. Although it will be a brave panel that fails to reinstate if practical a pupil who is acquitted in these circumstances, this does perhaps eloquently demonstrate the extent to which the balance of influence within the exclusions process has swung away from the excluded pupil and back towards the school.

If the governing body decides not to direct reinstatement, it must inform all concerned. Where the exclusion is a permanent one, it must also give written reasons for the decision, information about the right of appeal and the time-limit (15 school days) for lodging an appeal, identify the person to whom the notice should be given and indicate that the notice must contain the grounds of the decision. The pro forma letters included with the Guidance are useful for this purpose. The decision letter need not go into great detail but must be clear and there must be enough to show clearly the basis on which the decision was reached. It should, therefore, briefly set out the facts on which the pupil discipline committee based its decision, and should indicate why in those circumstances permanent exclusion was considered justified.

RIGHT OF APPEAL

There is only a right of appeal in relation to fixed-period exclusions if it is alleged that a school has discriminated against a disabled pupil by excluding, in which case the appeal lies to the Special Educational Needs and Disability Tribunal (SENDIST). Parents have the right to appeal to an independent appeal panel against refusal by the governing body to direct reinstatement after a permanent exclusion in all cases, and all such cases (including those that allege disability discrimination) will be considered by the independent appeal panel, not SENDIST. The decision of an appeal panel is binding on the governing body.

THE APPEAL PANEL

Appeal panels consist of three or five members. The members of an exclusion appeal panel are appointed by the LEA for all schools. It must be made up of one lay member (who will chair the meeting), one person (or two people for a five-member panel) who is, or who has been within the previous five years, a headteacher of a maintained school and one person (or two people for a five-member panel) who has been a governor for 12 months in the preceding six years and is not a teacher or a headteacher and has not been such within the preceding five years. A lay member qualifies for membership if he or she has no experience in school management or educational provision (other than as a governor or voluntarily) – suggesting that the panel could well be chaired by a governor. If possible, the governor and headteacher panel members should have experience of the phase (primary or secondary) of education concerned and the lay member should have the additional skills necessary to chair the hearing. It is the obligation of the LEA to ensure that all panel members and the clerk are appropriately trained.

No member of the LEA or of the governing body of the school or the current headteacher of the school (or a previous headteacher of the school within the preceding five years) or any employee of the LEA (other than a person employed as a headteacher) may be a member of an appeal panel. Also disqualified is anyone who has or has, at any time, had a connection with:

- the LEA;
- the school;
- anyone employed by the LEA (except, again, as a headteacher);
- the pupil involved;
- the incident leading to the exclusion,

of a kind which might reasonably be taken to raise doubts as to that person's ability to act impartially. Note that it is the *appearance* of possible bias that matters, not whether or not there would be *actual* bias.

There must be at least one member from each category. If a panel of five has begun to hear the appeal and any member dies or is unable through illness to continue, the panel can continue as long as the number of members does not fall below three and there is still at least one member from each category.

The LEA has a duty to advertise for lay members and must indemnify panel members against reasonable legal costs reasonably incurred in connection with any decision or action taken in good faith.

The LEA must take reasonable steps to find out what times would be convenient for all those who have the right to attend the hearing, although the hearing date must still be within 15 school days after the appeal is lodged. If a mutually convenient date cannot be found, the LEA should be asked to arrange for the hearing to commence, if necessary in the absence of one or more of the parties, and to be adjourned immediately so that the statutory requirement is met.

There are explicit rights for representation at the hearing. The appellant may attend and make representations to the appeal panel and may be represented or accompanied by a friend. The Guidance says that the excluded child, if under 18, should be allowed to attend and address the panel if the parent agrees. An excluded person over the age of 18 is the appellant and has the right to attend as such. The headteacher may make written representations and also has a right to attend and make oral representations, although there is no right for the headteacher to be represented by another person. The LEA and the governing body may make written representations, and an officer from the LEA and a governor nominated by the governing body may attend and make oral representations and both may be represented. This means that the headteacher can have a distinctive voice at the hearing and is not necessarily constrained by what the governing body chooses to say or argue.

The Panel's Approach to the Case

An appeal panel hearing an exclusion appeal has to consider the case in two stages. The first consideration is whether or not the facts are proved and the second is whether or not a permanent exclusion was warranted. There is no statutory control on the decision-making process but Departmental Guidance as to when permanent exclusion is justified is as relevant for appeal panels as it is for headteachers and governors. No limit is placed on the powers of the appeal panel and any decision is binding. In particular, the panel has the power to direct reinstatement either immediately or at a subsequent date or can decide, because of exceptional circumstances or other reasons that make it impractical, not to direct the reinstatement of a pupil, although otherwise it would have done so. In deciding whether exceptional circumstances such as this do exist, the panel should consider representations from the governing body, headteacher and parent.

The general principles of natural justice will apply to all appeal panel hearings, and the panel is subject to the jurisdiction of the Council on Tribunals and may be subject to judicial review. All documents that the panel sees must also be supplied to the parties. The Guidance contains detail on the practice both before and at the appeal. It is noteworthy that, in contrast to Guidance in relation to admissions appeals, there is no suggestion that legal representation would be out of place. Indeed, the regulations and Guidance expressly refer to the entitlement for the parent, governing body and LEA to be represented and this is a common event. Teachers who are required to attend as witnesses may be accompanied by a friend or representative although almost certainly a panel would interpret this as referring to union rather than legal representation. Oddly, the same right is not given to non-teacher members of the school staff although with the development of support staff involvement under the Working Time Agreement there must be an increased likelihood that support staff may be witnesses of incidents both in and out of the classroom.

An appeal is a rehearing of the case presented to the committee of the governing body. Appeals can be combined if they are connected and no-one objects. The panel has effectively the same task, in that it first has to consider whether the evidence supports the facts and, if so, it then has to consider whether permanent exclusion was an appropriate response. The hearing will be in private, although a member of the Council on Tribunals has a statutory right to attend and the panel may allow a representative of the LEA to attend as an observer. The Guidance specifies that the hearing should not be at the school and that the appeal panel should do everything possible to establish an atmosphere of informality; this has been emphasised in a recent case which says that details such a room layout are important in order to try to ensure that appellants do not feel everyone else in the room is ranged against them. That case also emphasises the need for the arrangements before the hearing itself to be well organised (which would include, for instance, consideration of the need to call witnesses) in order to avoid adjournments. This is particularly true now given the indication in the Guidance that the clerk should establish whether the alleged victim wishes 'to be given a voice' at the hearing. The clerk should circulate written evidence five days before the hearing including the statement of decision by the governing body and the notice of appeal together with the written representations of the head, governing body and LEA. The school should expect to pass to the clerk all the documentation upon which it based its own decision including statements of witnesses. Even if the pupil is reinstated the fact of the exclusion remains on the pupil record. The governing body must, however, allow the parental appeal statement to be attached to the record if the parents request it. This demonstrates that the purpose of the appeal is simply to decide whether the exclusion should be upheld or not; it is not a forum to clear the pupil's name.

In common with the deregulation of powers to governing bodies and their committees, the panel is largely free to regulate its own procedures. It is likely (and advisable) that they follow the old model which will normally be that, at first, the school presents its case for upholding the exclusion. Unlike the normal position in appeal processes, the onus is not on the pupil or parents to show that the decision to exclude was wrong. The school has to justify its action and it is important that the school presents its case competently. This will involve establishing the facts, and witnesses should be called or their statements produced. The parents have the right to question the school's representative and the witnesses, after which the parents will bring their own evidence and present their arguments (and the parents' own case can be questioned by the other parties). It is advisable that parents are always given the last word before the panel makes its decision. That decision will be taken in the absence of the parties, but the panel's legal adviser will stay with the panel to keep a record and advise on issues of law.

As is the case with the governing body committee, the panel must be pro-active in establishing the facts. If the evidence produced by the school is not sufficient, the panel may ask for further material to be presented. New evidence can be introduced, although new reasons to justify the exclusion cannot. In one case, involving a CTC (CTCs are not bound by the procedures that apply to other maintained schools), the court directed a rehearing on the grounds of unfairness when the appeal panel failed to consider witness statements but instead relied on a summary of them produced by the headteacher. This put the parents and the panel at a disadvantage. The school should have produced the witness statements and the parents would have seen more clearly just what was being alleged. The comments made earlier about identification apply equally to the appeal panel.

The clerk should keep minutes of the proceedings. The decision itself must be given in writing and arrive by the end of the second working day after the hearing. It must state the reasons, and again the Guidance provides a pro forma letter for this purpose. The appeal panel does not have to give elaborate reasons but the decision letter does have to explain, however briefly, why the pupil was excluded and why the exclusion was upheld. Indeed, even if the appeal is allowed, the panel should give its reasons. It is not beyond possibility that the school, either through the governing body or through the headteacher, might wish to challenge the hearing in court and an inadequate decision letter would be grounds for seeking to set the decision aside. In one case, the appeal panel was allowed to produce supplementary evidence to the court to establish that the issues had been properly considered and that there were proper reasons behind the decision although these were not clear from the decision letter. The courts are, however, very aware of the possibility of an *ex post facto* rationalisation and will need to be satisfied that what is said at the time of the court hearing corresponds to what was said and thought at the time of the appeal.

WHAT IS REINSTATEMENT?

Great heat has been generated by the actions of appeal panels directing reinstatement in cases where there were strongly held views within the school that the pupil concerned posed significant risk to pupils or to staff. It is hoped that the heat will have been taken out of this argument by the introduction of the panel's new power, discussed above, not to direct reinstatement in circumstances where otherwise it would have, because of exceptional circumstances. It might, incidentally, have been thought that where this power is exercised, the excluding school would not have lost funding, because the permanent exclusion had been overturned. However, as the Guidance makes clear, for funding purposes the regulations will treat that child as having been permanently excluded. One can see the logic.

In a number of cases, teachers' unions threatened industrial action if a pupil was reinstated, thus placing the headteacher and the governing body in an impossible situation which is now less likely to be repeated. Clearly the pupil had to be readmitted to the school because the appeal panel decision is binding. However, reinstatement that could have had the effect of potentially closing the school was not a palatable outcome. The solution, of arranging to teach the pupil in a greater or lesser degree of isolation and in one instance utilising some off-site teaching in a PRU, led to court action on behalf of the pupil claiming that this was not reinstatement and that reinstatement meant a full return to the classroom and full access to the curriculum. The position, derived from a decision of the House of Lords, and via some rather tortuous logic, is that reinstatement means, in effect, restoration to the school roll and that it was a matter for the governing body, acting through the headteacher, to decide on the practicalities. The governing body was entitled to take strongly and sincerely held views of staff into account and was not required to enter into a confrontation that could have a seriously detrimental effect on the rest of the school community. In another related case, the House of Lords decided that a dispute of this sort between the teaching staff and school did amount to a trade dispute meaning that the teaching staff and union were protected by the immunities conferred on them by the relevant industrial relations legislation and so the teaching staff could not be compelled to teach the pupil within a classroom context. Whilst these decisions are welcome from the school perspective, they may prove under the current exclusions regime to be less relevant than before and must not be regarded as an open-ended charter for using the threat of industrial action as a means of dealing with every reinstatement with which teachers disagree. The governing body does have to exercise its discretion in a reasonable way and will also be concerned at the budget implications of individual arrangements. Decisions will be closely scrutinised by the courts and the reasons for not reintegrating fully into the classroom must be compelling ones.

THE FUTURE

Exclusions issues are bound to remain a focus for departmental attention, particularly given the inevitable tensions that lie between them and a successful attempt at pursuing a policy of social inclusion. One area that has received a lot of criticism but little attention is the independent appeal panel system itself. The Council on Tribunals has produced a lengthy report highlighting the inadequacies it sees in both the current exclusions appeal system and also admissions appeals. It suggests that it would be appropriate to bring all exclusions appeals within the remit of SENDIST. It will be interesting to see whether there is a political will to commit the substantial resources that would be required to make these changes happen.

RELEVANT GUIDANCE

Bullying

DfES Non-Statutory Guidance 64/2000, 'Bullying – Don't Suffer in Silence – An Anti-Bullying Pack for Schools'.

Restraint of Pupils

Circular 10/98, 'Section 550A of the Education Act 1996: The Use of Force to Control or Restrain Pupils'.

Home–School Agreements

DfES Guidance, 'Home–School Agreements – Guidance for Schools' (November 1998).

Pupil Behaviour and Exclusion

Circular 10/99, 'Social Inclusion – Pupil Support'.

Circular 11/99, 'Social Inclusion: the LEA Role in Pupil Support'.

'Improving Behaviour and Attendance: Guidance on Exclusion from Schools and Pupil Referral Units', DfES/0345/2004.

'Guidance on the Education-related Provisions of the Anti-social Behaviour Act 2003', DfES/0345/2004.

'Drugs: Guidance for Schools', DfES/0092/2004.

'Raising the Achievement of Gypsy Traveller Pupils – A Guide to Good Practice', DfES/0443/2003.

Chapter 9

STAFF

INTRODUCTION

Staffing costs can account for 80–85 per cent of a school's budget. It is, therefore, the most financially sensitive area, and one where a mistake can be very costly. Schools have some budget protection against error if the school has acted reasonably and in accordance with procedures but, even if there are no material financial implications, schools will want to act correctly in dealing with their staff. The law is complex and any summary is bound to over-simplify. Schools should, therefore, take proper professional advice in all areas relating to staffing and human resources before starting any process that may affect individual employment terms.

THE RELATIONSHIP BETWEEN EMPLOYER AND EMPLOYEE

Both teaching and non-teaching staff in community and VC schools are technically employed by the LEA, but the employer's functions are almost totally delegated to the governing body of those schools unless the school does not have a delegated budget. LEAs retain full employer functions (subject to the obligation to consult with the governing body on a number of aspects) for schools that do not have delegated responsibility; however, since these now will be restricted to nursery schools and those few schools which do not have a delegated budget or whose delegated budget has been withdrawn, we will not consider such cases further. Staff in VA and foundation schools are employed by the governing body. Generally, although there are differences of detail, the rights, obligations and procedures in relation to staff are very similar for all types of maintained school, and the rest of this chapter should be taken as applicable to all schools unless otherwise indicated.

Employment Protection

In addition to specific legislation relating to schools, staff employed in schools are subject to and have the full protection of the general employment legislation. Thus, they are entitled:

- to employment protection, including the right not to be unfairly dismissed and not to be made unfairly redundant. The right not to be unfairly dismissed arises after one year's continuous employment, but employment at a previous school may rank for continuity if the previous school was within the same LEA. Fixed-term contracts can be taken outside the scope of employment protection if certain procedures are followed, but this does not seem to be a common practice in schools. A series of fixed-term contracts may together amount to continuous employment and create employment protection if there are no material gaps between the periods of employment. Normal school holidays do not count as gaps for this purpose, so that a succession of separate contracts, each for a school term or school year, will be treated as continuous employment. Thus, employment continuing beyond one academic year will attract employment protection. Employment under a fixed-period contract, or a series of fixed-period contracts, that continues for three school terms will effectively give employment protection;

- not to be discriminated against on racial, disability or sexual grounds;

- to equal opportunities;

- to belong to a trade union;

- to maternity rights.

These rights apply to all employees. However, a sharp distinction has to be drawn between non-teaching and teaching staff when their detailed conditions of service are considered.

Conditions of Service for Non-teaching Staff

Non-teaching staff are in a similar position to employees in any other employment, although in community and VC schools they will be employed on the relevant LEA conditions of service for their grade. VA and foundation schools are free to employ non-teaching staff on whatever terms and conditions they wish to offer and the individual employee is willing to accept, subject only to the equal opportunity and non-discrimination legislation. However, many such schools will also employ on LEA conditions so far as these can apply. Any staff member of a former grant-maintained school employed under such conditions before the school acquired grant-maintained status will continue to be so employed even if the school, as a VA or foundation school, decides that future appointments will be on a different basis. Apart from the screening process that operates on appointment to ensure that there are no grounds that exclude the employee from working in the proximity of children, there is no special law relating to non-teaching staff. They will, though, generally be subject to the same disciplinary procedures as teachers.

Conditions of Service for Teachers

Teachers are in a different position and are subject to special rules. First, subject to minor exceptions for temporary staff or staff from overseas, everyone who is appointed to a teaching post in a maintained school must hold a teaching qualification, either as a graduate teacher with a recognised teaching degree or certificate, or as a registered teacher. Secondly, the teaching profession is possibly unique in the degree of regulation that is imposed on individual employees and the lack of freedom to negotiate other terms. Teachers' conditions of service and rates of pay are very largely prescribed by the Secretary of State who, each year, after consultation with the teachers' review body, determines pay and conditions and publishes these in the Teachers' Pay and Conditions Document (TPCD). This sets out the pay scales and the determining factors to be applied in deciding the point on the scale at which any given teacher in a particular post will start. It also sets out in significant detail the conditions of employment, specifying the directed time of 1265 hours per year that a teacher must be available to work under the direction of the headteacher, and the duties that are to be performed both within and outside the directed time. The TPCD is invariably accompanied each year by a related Circular expanding on its provisions and giving Guidance on its application. Much of the content of the TPCD and the related guidance will not vary from year to year, but its republication on an annual basis means that reference need be made to only one set of documents. The National Workload Agreement has led to significant changes being made to TPCD which are being introduced in stages to September 2005.

The unions and government entered into a lengthy negotiation process to improve working conditions for teachers, from which the NUT withdrew. The result of that negotiation was the National Workload Agreement, which contains many laudable aspirations even though much of the language is imprecise. Quite what the practical impact of the agreement will be remains to be seen, particularly since much of the detailed application is effectively left to the discretion of the school concerned. The National Workload Agreement has been translated into changes in TPCD, supported by quite lengthy Guidance. The most significant changes are:

- the transfer to appropriate support staff of a number of clerical and administrative tasks that teachers should not be routinely required to undertake. Although Teachers' Pay and Conditions Document (TPCD) includes a list of 21 tasks that fall into this category, the list is explicitly not exhaustive: any tasks that do not require the professional skills or judgment of a teacher should be included. The Guidance emphasises that the purpose of this change is to raise standards and tackle workload – accordingly, teachers should not be given a choice as to whether or not they continue undertaking administrative tasks;

- headteachers will have to have regard to the need for teachers to have a reasonable work/life balance, and governing bodies must consider this in relation to headteachers. Whilst the fundamental intention here is clear, because the language is not specific and not defined by reference to hours worked, the practical impact (and enforceability) particularly on the leadership group, advanced skills teachers (ASTs) and fast-track teachers is not clear. This will create particular problems for governing bodies when seeking to ensure that a headteacher has an appropriate workload because they do not control the workload and should not be involved in day-to-day detail. The Workforce Remodelling Guide for Governors produced in February 2004 (not to be confused with the somewhat similarly titled Guidance issued the previous September) gives Guidance to governing bodies particularly in relation to the headteacher. It says that the governing body will need to:

'consider measures to ensure that the headteacher's workload is kept at a reasonable level. This may lead to a review of some of the governing body's own practices with relation to the headteacher's workload. It could involve consideration of a number of different issues around distributed leadership, meetings and processes.'

- the Guide then gives some examples which governors might wish to consider such as conducting an audit of meetings, discussions with the headteacher on timing, time-limited meetings and a limit on the number of meetings per term. These steps would, of course, also significantly improve the work/life balance for governors! Further suggestions are a review of committee structure to produce a more streamlined arrangement and looking at areas of responsibility that a headteacher could delegate to senior staff.

Headteachers will be responsible for implementing this change for other teachers including those within the leadership group, ASTs and fast-track teachers. The hours that members of the leadership group, ASTs and fast-track teachers work are simply required to be 'reasonable'. Class teachers are now contractually obliged to work *reasonable* additional hours above the annual 1265 – what 'reasonable' means here is unclear too when balanced against the need to have a 'reasonable' work/life balance. The Guidance suggests various factors could facilitate this change including considering non-contractual provisions such as the conduct and frequency of meetings, the use of local advisers and the department's avowed intention to reduce unnecessary red tape.

The Governors' Guide mentioned above sets out a selection of questions that governing bodies might wish to pose to the headteacher to monitor progress on remodelling. Some of the questions are no longer relevant (assuming that earlier stages of the remodelling were implemented on time which is, perhaps, a rather large assumption) but others are of a more general and ongoing nature such as:-

- How is the remodelling process progressing in the school?

-   How has time been allocated within school sessions to all teachers with leadership and management responsibility?

-   What provision is there for training, particularly for support staff?

-   How are the job descriptions for support staff being reviewed to take into account changing roles? Is appropriate consultation being carried out? And has account been taken of pay and grading implications?

-   What consultation has taken place with unions and staff over changes?

-   What actions have been taken to ensure a reasonable work/life balance?

-   Have all the administrative and clerical tasks been removed and transferred from teachers?

- all teachers should have a reasonable allocation of time to support their leadership and management responsibilities within school sessions. This is in addition to the provisions on work/life balance and guaranteed planning, preparation and assessment ('PPA') time being introduced in 2005, and is another imprecise commitment. The Guidance accepts that it will not be easy by saying 'it is difficult to identify a formula for the amount of time which might be appropriate for each responsibility. This is a matter for the school', and is likely to prove a particular challenge for smaller primary schools. In such schools the Guidance requires them to identify an initial allocation of time and plan to increase it to September 2005;

- from 1 September 2004, revised arrangements have limited the amount of cover an individual teacher can be required to carry out. The initial limit is 38 hours (which cannot encroach on PPA time) which the headteacher must share out fairly to all teachers within the school, including the headteacher. The headteacher should also seek to achieve an even spread of cover throughout each term and only use teacher cover as a last resort, when other alternatives have been exhausted. This is a major change in the culture and will present significant management challenges, not least where funding is constrained. It is worth setting out the Guidance on this extensively:

'COVER

Purpose of the provisions

46. Cover for absence is not an effective use of the time of teachers at a school. In the past, many teachers have borne a heavy burden of cover for absent colleagues, but this should be increasingly unusual. Schools should be providing downward pressure on cover, before and after the introduction of the contractual change, to achieve the objective in the National Agreement that teachers at a school should only rarely cover for absent colleagues.

Definition of absence

47. Absence occurs when the teacher normally responsible for teaching a particular class is absent from the classroom during the time they have been timetabled to teach. The absence could be for a variety of reasons, including internal and external activities as well as sickness. It could be short- or long-term. All absence needs to be carefully managed to minimise the impact on teaching and learning for the pupil.

48. From 1 September 2004, the existing provisions on cover will be removed and two new contractual changes will come into effect:

- a limit on the amount of cover that can be provided by an individual teacher; and

- an amended duty for headteachers to ensure that cover for absent teachers is shared equitably among all teachers in the school (including the headteacher), taking account of their teaching and other duties and of the desirability of not using a teacher at the school until all other reasonable means of providing cover have been exhausted.

...

Reducing the burden of cover

52. From 1 September 2004, each individual teacher will have a 38-hour limit on the amount of cover he/she can be required to do in each academic year. This limit must not be exceeded. No weekly or termly limit within the 38 hours is identified within the contractual limit. However, headteachers should seek to ensure, as far as practicable, an even spread of cover throughout each term.

53. All cover for absence undertaken by teachers at a school counts towards the limit. The Document requires cover to be allocated on an equitable basis. Where schools designate on the timetable non-contact periods specifically for cover these must count towards the 38 hour limit on the occasions when they are used. Leadership and management time can also be used for cover but should not be used disproportionately. The time used counts against the limit.

54. The guaranteed PPA time of teachers at a school will form part of the legal conditions of employment from September 2005 and cannot be used for cover.

Gained time

56. During the academic year, particularly in the summer term, teachers who take examination classes/groups are often released from some of their timetabled teaching commitments as a result of pupils being on study or examination leave. Such time is known as gained time.

57. There are activities directly relevant to teaching and learning for which it would be appropriate and desirable to use gained time and which it would be reasonable for a headteacher to direct teachers to undertake. An agreed list of these activities is listed below:

- Developing/revising departmental/subject curriculum materials, schemes of work, lesson plans and policies in preparation for the new academic year. This may include identifying appropriate materials for use by supply staff and/or cover supervisors;

- Assisting colleagues in appropriate, planned team teaching activities;

- Taking groups of pupils to provide additional learning support;

- Supporting selected pupils with coursework;

- Undertaking planned activities with pupils transferring between year groups or from primary schools;

- Where the school has a policy for all staff to release them for CPD during school sessions, gained time may be used for such activities.

58. If teachers are directed to cover during gained time, it must count towards the 38-hour limit.'

It will be important to maintain a record of cover to ensure that the limits are adhered to. Also, schools that do not at present require staff to cover up to 38 hours per year may not increase the cover load. The Guidance also indicates possible strategies for managing the cover situation. It says that the headteacher should seek to achieve an even spread of cover throughout each term and only use teacher cover as a last resort, when other alternatives have been exhausted. The suggested alternatives include supply teachers, higher-level teaching assistants, cover supervisors, 'floating' teachers and, only then, teachers employed by the school within their contractual limit of 38 hours.

A distinction is drawn between 'cover', which involves teaching by a qualified teacher, and 'cover supervision'. Again, it is worth setting out the Guidance on this:

'**72.** Cover for short-term absences may be provided by persons who are not qualified teachers. To the extent that, during the period of cover, such persons are involved in specified work, they should operate subject to the regulations made under **section 133 of the 2002 Act** and accompanying guidance. Many schools currently employ such staff on a casual as required basis. In future, a permanent arrangement is likely to be more manageable and effective.

73. Those providing cover supervision may be existing members of staff whose job description has been reviewed in accordance with the first joint guidance note issued by the Workforce Agreement Monitoring Group (April 2003) or they may be new staff appointed on contracts which have a defined range of appropriate administrative or support tasks, but which include cover as one of their key functions.

74. The headteacher will need to ensure that any persons used in this way have been appropriately trained, particularly in pupil behaviour management. Such training is essential if those responsible for cover supervision are to make a real contribution to reducing the burdens on teachers.

75. Cover supervision is particularly valid where work has been set, or where pupils are able to undertake effective self-directed learning, for example within an ICT Learning Centre in a school. Strategies should be devised to ensure that the arrangements for providing appropriate work for pupils who are being supervised do not place excessive additional burdens of planning, preparation and assessment on teachers. This could include developing banks of appropriate material and/or attaching a cover supervisor to a year band, department or faculty to enable them to, for example, support the teachers in administrative tasks and to be involved in the planning and preparation of cover when necessary.'

• From 1 September 2005, all teachers will have guaranteed PPA time and headteachers will have dedicated headship time in addition to PPA time. The detail relating to dedicated headship time is currently short on detail, but further Guidance is promised. PPA time should be set at a minimum of 10 per cent of a teacher's timetabled teaching time, should take place during the school timetable and should be allocated in blocks of at least 30 minutes. The Guidance suggests that this time will be found from a number of sources – the use of higher-level teaching assistants, a reduction in teaching time, changes in the use of existing non-contact time and the redistribution of time made available by the reallocation of tasks to support staff. Managing this change within existing budgets will prove a real challenge to headteachers. In addition, teachers will no longer be required routinely to invigilate external examinations, although they may be required to conduct practical and oral examinations in their own subject area and be present at the start and end of an exam (and available through it) to ensure its efficient running and deal with an emergency that might require the teacher's professional judgment. Teachers may also be required to supervise internal examinations and tests where they take place during their normal timetabled teaching time.

- In addition, headteachers will need to ensure that except in exceptional circumstances a teacher is assigned in the school timetable to every class or group of pupils in core and foundation subjects and RE.

The Guidance emphasises the need to plan for these changes, working towards them as far as possible in advance of their statutory introduction.

Support Staff in the Classroom

A major aspect of the National Workload Agreement is the enabling of support staff, i.e. those staff without a teacher qualification or equivalent, to work directly with pupils in the classroom. Regulations made under the Education Act 2002 now define 'specified work' as:

'a. planning and preparing lessons and courses for pupils;

b. delivering lessons to pupils. This includes delivery via distance learning or computer aided techniques;

c. assessing the development, progress and attainment of pupils; and

d. reporting on the development, progress and attainment of pupils.

This is work that can only be carried out by support staff if a number of conditions are met:

'i. the support staff member must carry out the 'specified work' in order to assist or support the work of a qualified teacher in the school;

ii. the support staff member must be subject to the direction and supervision of a qualified teacher in accordance with arrangements made by the headteacher of the school; and

iii. the headteacher must be satisfied that the support staff member has the skills, expertise and experience required to carry out the "specified work".'

DfES has published a planning, preparation and assessment resource pack intended to help schools implement phase three of the National Workload Agreement. This can be downloaded at http://www.teachernet.gov.uk/wholeschool/remodelling. Important guidance has also been issued regarding the new category of support staff known as Higher Level Teaching Assistants (HLTA) who are expected to take on a major role in relieving the burden on teachers.

Schools in an Education Action Zone (EAZ) may be exempted by the Secretary of State from the conditions in the TPCD and will then be free to establish their own pay and conditions. To the extent that the governing body does not override the TPCD conditions they will remain applicable. With this exception, the TPCD conditions apply to all maintained schools.

General Teaching Council

All qualified teachers working in maintained schools must be registered with the General Teaching Council. When making appointments to teaching posts (including the appointment of supply teachers), LEAs and schools must ensure that the teacher is registered. The Council will deal with the award of Qualified Teacher Status and will also exercise disciplinary powers (including the power to remove registration) in all cases, except those involving the safety and welfare of children, which will continue to be dealt with by the Secretary of State.

APPOINTMENT

The process of appointment of staff is very largely in the hands of the school, whatever type of school it may be. Different types of school have greater or less formality but there is no specified process for drawing up advertisements, preparing job descriptions, short-listing or interviewing candidates. There is, however, recognised good practice which applies to all schools, and which will be dealt with in detail later in this chapter. The governing body's responsibility in terms both of appointment and dismissal can be delegated to the headteacher, one or more governors or one or more governors and the headteacher.

Appointment of Headteachers and Deputy Headteachers

All schools have to follow the same procedure for the appointment of a headteacher or a deputy headteacher. There are special rules relating to the appointment of a headteacher of a voluntary aided Roman Catholic school where the trustees of the foundation body are also trustees of a Roman Catholic religious order.

The governing body has responsibility for the appointment and is required:

- to notify the LEA of the vacancy;

- to advertise the vacancy nationally. There is no prescribed form of advertisement and no prescribed journal in which vacancies must be advertised, but the great majority of advertisements will go into the *Times Educational Supplement* and sometimes elsewhere. The cost of advertising has to be met from the school's budget;

- to convene a selection panel of at least three governors to consider the applications, conduct interviews and make a recommendation to the governing body. The selection panel must notify the LEA of the candidates selected, which gives the LEA the right to make representations (which the panel must consider) to the governing body in the event it considers a candidate to be unsuitable. The selection panel has no power of appointment, but can recommend that no appointment be made. Equally, the governing body can decline to appoint despite the fact that the panel has recommended a candidate. In either case, the process will be repeated from whatever point the governing body feels to be appropriate. Thus, it will not be necessary to re-advertise if it is merely proposed to re-interview the existing candidates.

Although it is mandatory that the decision to appoint has to be made by the full governing body – it is one of the functions that cannot be delegated – the selection panel procedure is also mandatory unless the governing body has good reason not to advertise and conduct the selection process. The Guidance provided by the DfES seeks to limit the circumstances that would be considered to amount to good reason. They include circumstances flowing from a school reorganisation scheme, school federations and collaborations and schools which have headteachers of departments. The effect is that the ultimate decision is based on material that those governors not on the selection panel receive at second hand. The governing body will be given information about the candidate who is recommended for appointment but it will probably not have the same detail for the other interviewed candidates. Given the nature of the laid-down procedure, it is right that the full governing body should not have that further detail so that it is not tempted to make a detailed comparison between candidates that it has not seen. The effect, inevitably, is that the governing body's decision cannot be a properly and fully informed one. It may seem surprising that the full governing body is barred from full involvement in one of the most important decisions that it will be called upon to make, but a process that involved the entire governing body would be cumbersome and hard to administer fairly and the present process has been in place for too long for anyone to argue convincingly for change.

One difficulty that the process has to deal with is that strictly, all governors involved in the process should, out of fairness to the candidates, be involved throughout and not miss any part of that process. This, in practice, means that anyone who misses a material stage of the process ought not to take any further part in it. Breaching this guiding principle may give an unsuccessful candidate opportunity to challenge the process on the grounds of discrimination, failure to observe equal opportunities policies, and unfairness.

One way to increase governor involvement is for all governors to have the opportunity to see details of those applicants being considered at the long-listing or short-listing stage, and for the selection panel to consult with governors before that listing takes place. The actual decision on who to select for interview must be made by the selection panel alone and the panel ought not to fetter its discretion by, for example, acting on the basis of votes cast by governors who are not members of the panel.

The appointment is made by the governing body in VA and foundation schools. The LEA must appoint the person nominated by the governing body of a community or VC school unless the nominated person lacks qualification or is not a fit or proper person.

In community and VC schools, the LEA is entitled to be represented at all meetings of the governing body or selection panel that is considering the appointment or the process leading to appointment. The LEA is under a duty to advise the governors and the selection panel on the appointment, and its advice must be considered by the governors, although it does not have to be followed. A VC school can, if it wishes, grant similar rights to its foundation body. In VA and foundation schools, neither the LEA nor the foundation body has such a right or duty unless the school has granted advisory rights, although the Guidance from DfES states that if the LEA is granted advisory rights, the foundation body should too. The headteacher is entitled to attend and offer advice at all meetings of a panel that deal with the appointment of any member of staff. Note, however, that a teacher governor may have an interest that disqualifies that person from membership of the panel or indeed from voting on an eventual appointment. This would obviously be so if the governor were a candidate for appointment. It would also arise less directly if, for example, the governor in question could be a candidate for a post vacated by a successful internal applicant.

Other Staff Appointments

In all schools with a delegated budget, the appointment of staff (both teaching and non-teaching) is in the hands of the governing body. There is now no distinction of substance between the different categories of schools. Temporary appointments for up to four months, or those which the governing body believe will not last more than four months, are not subject to formality. For other teacher appointments, the governing body must simply draw up a specification for the post in consultation with the headteacher and send a copy to the LEA. Beyond that, it is for the governing body to determine its own practice, although good practice would suggest a process not dissimilar to that adopted for headteachers and deputies and the Guidance from the DfES is quite helpful particularly when dealing with the equal pay issues raised when engaging support staff in community and VC schools where the LEA remains the employer.

As with the appointment of headteachers and deputy headteachers, the LEA can refuse to appoint the nominated person to a community or VC school on qualification grounds only.

In community and VC schools, a representative of the LEA is entitled to attend all proceedings (including interviews) of the governing body or any committee or individual to whom responsibility for staff appointment is delegated for the purpose of giving advice. In VA and foundation schools, a representative of the LEA may attend if advisory rights have been granted. The Secretary of State has a reserve power to direct that the LEA should be given advisory rights. Where the LEA does advise, the body or person making the appointment must 'consider' that advice.

As touched on above, the headteacher has similar rights to an LEA representative in appointments decisions.

Advertising and Interviewing

There is no prescribed procedure for advertising posts or conducting interviews. There will usually be a job description and frequently also a person specification to ensure that the candidate who most closely meets the particular needs of the school is identified. Care must be taken to avoid discrimination, actual or perceived. Some appointing bodies remove names, ages and other details that might give rise to discrimination from the papers passed to governors but this practice goes further than is legally necessary. It is, however, good practice to keep detailed records of the selection process.

It is sensible to consider all applications against a set of predetermined criteria (which themselves will have influenced the job description and any person description) and to have a degree of structure and some common questions to be asked at interview. It is neither possible nor necessary for every candidate to be asked the same questions – apart from anything else, supplementary questions will be needed to draw out candidates – but all candidates should be questioned in the same way on the issues and the requirements that have been identified for the job and the appointee. The way in which the information is then assessed in making a final decision will vary, but should again be systematic and should be recorded so that the decision can be supported. Failure to do this can mean that an unmeritorious claim, for example of discrimination, may succeed because the evidence is not available months later to refute it.

List 99 and the Criminal Records Bureau

It should be a matter of routine that a check is made against DfES List 99 and enhanced disclosures are obtained from the Criminal Records Bureau, which records the names of people who are barred from teaching or working with or in proximity to children, before the appointment is confirmed. The checks can take time and if the appointee has to take up the post before the results comes through, it must be made clear that it is still outstanding. The appointee must be told, in writing, that the appointment remains conditional on the outcome. The appointee must not be able to assume (even by implication) that the checks have been completed if that is not the case.

Newly Qualified Teachers

With limited exceptions, newly qualified teachers are required to complete an induction period in a maintained school (other than one that is subject to special measures unless HMCI has certified otherwise) or certain independent schools that teach the relevant areas of the National Curriculum. The induction period for a full-time teacher is normally one year but it will be proportionately longer for a part-time person. It is the responsibility of the employing school to provide appropriate monitoring and support, which can be provided externally if the resources of the school are not sufficient. The teacher is entitled to a teaching timetable reduced to 90 per cent of the normal load. The school must keep records in prescribed form to show that the induction requirements have been met. At the end of the period, there is a final assessment and the teacher has a right of appeal in the event of failure. The induction period can be extended by the school to allow for extended sickness and a teacher on maternity leave is entitled to have the period extended. The period may also be extended by the body responsible for deciding whether or not the teacher has reached the necessary standard. That body will be the LEA for teachers in maintained schools. The period may also be extended on appeal.

Governing bodies appointing a newly qualified teacher must take account of the responsibilities that the induction requirements place on the school and must be satisfied that the school can meet them before making the appointment. Governing bodies would be well advised to ask the headteacher to confirm this in writing or to provide full details of the induction arrangements that apply generally in the school and to indicate how they would be applied in the particular case. Where the appointment is delegated to the headteacher, he or she should make a note of how induction will be dealt with and that should be kept with the papers relating to the appointment.

CONTRACTS AND CONDITIONS OF SERVICE

There is no specific law governing the terms of contracts of people employed to work in schools. The general law applies (although the TPCD adds specific terms for teaching staff), and staff have to be given written particulars of the terms of the employment contract either by way of a formal contract, or an appointment letter setting out the details required by law, or by a statement of terms. The matters that statute requires to be included are:

- the date of commencement of employment and whether the employment represents a continuation of previous employment. If it does, then the commencement date of continuous employment must be stated;

- the nature of the job. The statutory requirement does not go as far as a detailed job description, but the particulars must identify the post in general terms, and any specific areas of responsibility should be referred to. If there is a detailed job description, it is good practice to include it in the contract or appointment letter to avoid potential dispute later;

- the place of work, which will normally be the school. Under the TPCD, teachers may be required by the headteacher to work elsewhere, which covers school visits or games away from the school site;

- the hours of work. For teachers, there will normally be a reference to the TPCD which governs when teachers must work. This raises a number of issues:

    - full-time teachers (other than members of the leadership group, ASTs and fast-track teachers) are required to work 195 days a year, which the employer (or the headteacher if the power is delegated) will determine. Of these days, 190 are to be days when pupils are in school, and the other five days are training days;

–   full-time teachers are required to work 1265 hours a year within those 195 days under the direction of the headteacher ('directed time'), and schools will normally have a 1265-hour 'budget' indicating how that time is to be divided, i.e. between class teaching, meetings (including parents' evenings), in-service training (INSET) and other non-contact time. Part-time teachers will be obliged to work the due proportion of 195 days and 1265 hours' directed time, although this should be specified in the contract. Part-time teachers will be obliged to attend INSET only if the training falls on days when they would normally be teaching. It is no longer possible to specify that part-time teachers be required to attend meetings or INSET days on days or at times when they do not normally work, because this would breach the principle that conditions of employment for part-time employees must be the same as for full-time staff. Additional payments can be made to full-time teachers, including unqualified, licensed and overseas trained teachers, and to part-time teachers, deputy headteachers and assistant headteachers who undertake voluntary INSET at weekends or during school holidays. For full-time teachers, payments may be made only for INSET undertaken outside the 195 days of directed time so no payment can be made for after-hours INSET. Headteachers, advanced skills teachers and fast-track teachers are not eligible for payments but deputy headteachers and assistant headteachers may receive payments for INSET undertaken on a Saturday or Sunday or during school holidays;

–   the TPCD makes it clear that lesson preparation, report writing and marking all fall outside directed time although as noted above, guaranteed planning, preparation and assessment time within directed time must be implemented by September 2005 and so further changes to TPCD are expected. Teachers are required as part of their conditions of service to devote whatever reasonable time is necessary for the effective discharge of professional duties. It still remains to be seen how this requirement interacts with the introduction into general employment law of the European Council Directive on working time and the work/life balance of the National Workload Agreement. Teachers do not fall within the specific exemptions that apply, for example, to doctors in training or those engaged in sea fishing;

- teachers cannot be required to undertake lunchtime supervision and are entitled to a reasonable midday break, either between school sessions or between noon and 2 pm. Headteachers and deputy headteachers have no specified hours or days of work, but are entitled to a midday break. Headteachers must ensure that someone is in charge during their own break;

- the TPCD specifies the extent to which teachers may be required to cover for absent colleagues. Initially individual teachers will be limited to being required to provide 38 hours' cover per year, although this is subject to assessment and review. The Workforce Agreement Monitoring Group, comprising unions (other than the NUT), employers and government has produced Guidance on strategies for dealing with cover situations, including cover supervision, described as cover when no active teaching is taking place. Because this does not involve work that is required to be carried out by a qualified teacher, periods of cover supervision can be allocated to support staff. This Guidance, and other strategies being developed, puts flesh on the bones of the Workload Agreement;

- headteachers and deputy headteachers have their own specified professional duties. There are now 23 specified duties for the headteacher, which represents an increase since the last edition of this book – despite the purported drive to deregulate and reduce red tape. They include a duty to report to the chair of governors annually on the professional development of teachers and to advise the governing body on the adoption of effective procedures to deal with incompetent teachers. Deputy headteachers have the same duties as a classroom teacher (but without the limit on working time) and are required to play a major role under the direction of the headteacher in formulating the aims and objectives of the school, to undertake major responsibilities delegated by the headteacher (including assisting the headteacher with threshold assessments), and to deputise as necessary for the headteacher. Assistant headteachers have the same duties as deputy headteachers other than the responsibility to deputise for the headteacher;

– advanced skills teachers have their own specified additional duties including training and participating in the induction and mentoring of newly qualified teachers and are expected to spend 20 per cent of their time undertaking 'outreach' work by carrying out those duties with or for the benefit of teachers from other schools;

– fast-track teachers are subject to the fast-track scheme which was introduced in England with effect from 1 September 2001. It offers extra financial, training and development support to those who are prepared to make an additional commitment to their professional development and who pass a national selection procedure, although their duties are defined by reference to those of a teacher other than a headteacher. A bursary is paid and fast-track teachers who are appointed as newly qualified teachers receive an additional scale point, called a fast-track point. Fast-track teachers are not subject to the working-time limits that apply to classroom teachers generally;

• hours and days of work for non-teaching staff should be specified. If, as is usual, non-teaching staff are expected to work on days other than the 195 days when teachers will work, this should be stated;

• the amount of salary and when it is to be paid. For teaching staff, the commencing spine point will be identified. For non-teaching staff, the starting salary and basis of review, or the relevant grade and starting point, should be stated;

• what notice each party to the contract has to give. By law, the school as employer has to give a minimum of one week's notice for every complete year of employment, with a maximum of 12 weeks' notice. The employee has to give a minimum of one week's notice irrespective of the length of the employment. In practice, these statutory terms are varied and the contractual notice must be specified. Employment of teaching staff will normally terminate by notice (from either side), terminating at a term end, conventionally 31 December, 30 April and 31 August. Teachers other than headteachers are usually required to give a clear half term's notice (the deadline in the summer term is 31 May irrespective of half-term dates), while headteachers have to give a full term's notice. The employment of non-teaching staff can end at any time, subject to proper notice in accordance with the negotiated conditions;

- holiday entitlement must be specified for non-teaching staff. Teachers are in an anomalous position in that they have no specific entitlement to holidays. Instead, the TPCD specifies the extent to which they must be available for work and, by implication, other time can be spent as the teacher wishes;

- sick-pay entitlement, which will normally be determined by the relevant collective agreement governing the employment;

- pension arrangements and entitlement;

- any collective agreements governing the employment;

- details of grievance and discipline procedures.

Working-time Regulations

There are restrictions on permitted hours of work for many employees as well as provisions requiring that minimum holidays be taken. In general, employees are subject to the following limits:

- 48 hours each week averaged over a 17-week period, unless a voluntary written agreement has been reached;

- a minimum uninterrupted daily rest break of 20 minutes if the working day is longer than six hours;

- a minimum uninterrupted daily rest period of 11 consecutive hours in any 24-hour period worked;

- a minimum weekly rest period of 24 hours, which may be averaged as two 24-hour periods in 14 days;

- a minimum of four weeks' paid annual leave once the employee has been employed for 13 consecutive weeks.

Some categories of employees are specifically excluded. Others are excluded because they do not work under direction and have control over when they do their work. Ironically, because the underlying intention of the regulations is obviously to protect workers from overload, teachers probably come into this latter category. Their statutory working time is prescribed by the TPCD, which is well within the limits of the working-time legislation, and it is up to them how much time they spend on their other duties. Headteachers, deputy headteachers, assistant headteachers and advanced skills teachers, who are excluded from the specification of 1265 hours a year in the TPCD, would, on this reading, fall outside the scope of the working-time regulations because they have no prescribed hours and control their work. Further, the existence of long holiday periods away from the workplace would probably make it unlikely that the hours worked on average over a full year would exceed the statutory maximum. Nevertheless, Circular 12/99, which is the 1999 TPCD Circular, considers that all teachers are covered by the working-time regulations. The Circular does not comment on the interrelationship of the working-time regulations and the TPCD requirement to work such time over and above 1265 hours as may be required to discharge professional duties, nor does it make any suggestions as to how records should be kept of time spent working away from the school. The working-time regulations draw no distinction between time spent working at the workplace and time spent working at home or elsewhere.

Non-teaching staff do fall within the scope of the regulations but working conditions in school, coupled with the normal holiday entitlement, even for those who are employed full-time and not on a term-time basis, will normally ensure that the maximum is not exceeded. None the less, there is an obligation on employers to keep records of their employees' working time and holidays. Where employees receive paid overtime, payroll records will contain the necessary information. In other cases, schools need a system in place for recording time at work. There are criminal sanctions for failure to keep records and comply with the regulations.

The Form of the Employment Contract

Many people believe that no contract exists until something is put in writing. This is not correct. It is good practice to have a formal written contract of employment which covers all the terms that statute requires and any others that are relevant to the school or the post. However, a legally binding contract comes into existence as soon as the job is offered and the candidate accepts it: this will usually be before any written contract is available for signature. It is, therefore, essential to establish all the relevant terms of the contract at the time of making the appointment. This can be done in one of three ways:

- by supplying the candidate with a draft employment contract before interview;

- by negotiating the details before making the firm offer;

- by offering the post subject to the normal terms and conditions of the school or the LEA, which preferably should be available to each candidate prior to interview.

The first method is the most specific, but often the detailed terms will vary according to the particular person appointed and, in any event, this solution produces a great deal of potentially unnecessary paperwork if there is more than one candidate. The second method can lead to delay and uncertainty because the candidate has an opportunity to negotiate, knowing that the job is on offer. The third way is the most practical and effective, but it does depend on the job description being sufficiently specific to encompass all the work that the appointee will be expected to do and wide enough to give the school any flexibility that it needs. This is more important for non-teaching staff because the TPCD contains a wide definition of teachers' duties which will apply in any case, but it is good practice to have a properly considered job description for all appointments. To avoid reinventing the wheel each time a post becomes vacant, it is sensible to maintain a portfolio of job descriptions, regularly reviewed and updated for all permanent posts in the school, including non-teaching ones.

The essence is that both the school and the staff member should have a clear description of the job to be performed, the extent of responsibility, the degree of delegated authority if that is relevant, and the line management structure. Issues of reporting and of confidentiality can also usefully be covered in the job description.

Compliance with School Policies

Any statement of employment terms should include a requirement to comply with all school policies as they apply from time to time. This will ensure that, as a matter of contractual obligation, everyone in the school is bound by those policies and cannot object to new ones or to changes on the grounds that they constitute a variation of terms of employment. Obvious examples are staff discipline and grievance policies and procedures which, in any event, have to be identified in the written particulars of employment. Others that may be relevant are equal opportunities, race relations and sex equality policies and the school's pay policy.

Collective Negotiations

School employment contracts will also incorporate any collective negotiating terms that apply. This will vary according to the type of school. Community schools, where the employer is the LEA and the school acts under delegated authority, will incorporate all the local authority collective bargaining procedures, and terms so negotiated will automatically form part of the individual's contract. VA and foundation schools are in a different position because the school is the employer and has a choice (perhaps at times more apparent than real) of opting out of LEA-negotiated terms; since the advent of the TPCD, this is relevant mainly in relation to fringe benefits such as sick pay and in relation to non-teaching staff. Almost universally, though, teachers' employment will be subject to the collective terms known as the Burgundy Book which, in the absence of specific provision to the contrary, will be implied as part of the conditions of service of every teacher employed by a school or LEA. Attempts to negotiate away from these terms would, no doubt, be strenuously resisted.

Employment contracts for VA and foundation schools need to be explicit as to whether LEA-negotiated terms will apply. Before making that decision, a number of points have to be considered.

- Is the school willing to be bound by decisions reached after negotiations to which it cannot be a direct party and over which it has no effective influence?

- Are the terms that are collectively negotiated applicable to the school and workable in the management structure of the school?

- What would be the effect on morale and recruitment if the school decided not to accept collective bargaining?

- Does the school wish to have the freedom to negotiate individual terms with each new employee or is that seen as divisive and cumbersome?

Foundation schools must remember that the terms of employment of any member of staff who was employed at the school while it was a county school and who has continued in employment remain unchanged until agreed otherwise. Any decision, therefore, not to be bound by collective negotiation will not apply to those employees unless they consent. The specific question of how a foundation school applies terms that relate to specific LEA procedures, such as those dealing with staff discipline or grievance, has not yet been dealt with by the courts and one hopes that with the passage of time such schools will have adopted their own appropriate procedures. There can be unexpected implications. For example, some LEAs have a practice of making pension enhancements on early retirement which have been ratified as policy. Even if the payments were described as *ex gratia*, employees may be able to argue that this is a contractual entitlement that continues to bind the foundation school. This would apply even if the school was unaware of the practice and even if the school subsequently adopted a different policy, unless the employee could be shown to have accepted the change.

PAY POLICY

The detailed conditions in the TPCD relating to teachers' pay (dealt with below) involve a significant exercise of discretion by the governing body. Similarly, although there are no comparable laid-down conditions for non-teaching staff, the governing body will have to make decisions relating to their pay. To ensure that discretion is not exercised in an irrational or capricious manner, schools should have pay policies adopted by the governing body which will set out the basis on which discretion will be exercised. As always, there is a potential conflict between the value of maintaining a flexible position, so that the pay policy does not prevent the school from coping sensibly with unusual circumstances, and a clear objective basis which has the merit of transparent fairness, but which could act as a straitjacket. Within the limits of the pay policy and the TPCD, teachers will negotiate their individual position when taking up a new appointment. The entry point on the spine is an essential contractual term and should always be settled before a formal offer of appointment is made. Similarly, non-teaching staff will negotiate their starting position as part of the appointment process.

The pay policy should:

- be drawn up by the governing body in consultation with the staff of the school. At the same time, the school will usually also consult unions under the established representative procedures. The detailed work will be done by a committee and it is now possible to give a committee delegated powers to formally adopt the policy;

- determine where the decisions are to be taken. This will usually, for effective management, be at governor committee level and a pay committee should be established. Because this involves the exercise of delegated power, the terms of the delegation and any limitation on it must be clearly defined. In particular, the policy should specify the extent to which the committee is empowered to take decisions, and which (if any) decisions are reserved to the governing body. Many schools will feel it appropriate that decisions on the level of the headteacher's pay (and possibly that of deputies) should be made only by the full governing body in which case those responsible for setting objectives and carrying out the detailed review referred to below will make recommendations to the governing body (possibly with an imprimatur from the pay committee);

- include provisions for dealing with complaints. This in itself predicates that decisions be taken in the main at committee level so that a number of governors can remain unaffected by the decision-making process and so may form an effective and impartial appeal committee;

- set out the principles on which pay decisions are to be made, both on first appointment and on review, and establish a pattern of annual review, in time for decisions to take effect on 1 September each year. The way in which the school approaches the review of pay for headteachers and deputies is prescribed by the TPCD, but the policy will specify how the school will apply the flexibility inherent in the points structure for other teachers. This will reflect the needs and circumstances of the school and should be related to the school development plan;

- emphasise the need for the policy and its application in all respects to comply with legislation and school policies on race relations, sex discrimination, disability discrimination and equal opportunities.

Leadership Group Pay

The Leadership Group (headteachers and deputy and assistant headteachers) has its own pay scale called the Leadership Group Spine. The point of entry has to be established on appointment. This will usually reflect all the criteria (discussed below) that apply on annual review other than performance standards, although track record can properly be considered in setting a starting salary.

Schools are grouped according to size, and the pay for headteachers is on a spine point within the band specified for the group into which the school falls. The group is determined by applying an age-weighted pupil number formula (modified for headteachers of special schools) and the governing body then has to determine the individual school range (ISR) within the group. Each group has a range of spine points and the headteacher must be placed on a seven-point scale within that range to be determined by the governing body. In setting the ISR, the governing body needs to consider the circumstances of the school, the extent of any recruitment difficulties and local pay benchmarking data.

The governing body may determine a higher ISR than the group position indicates (but not one that would take the school more than two groups higher) in exceptional circumstances specified as:

- where a school is subject to formal warning, has serious weaknesses or is subject to special measures and needs to appoint a new headteacher to turn it around;

- where the headship is vacant and the governing body decides that an ISR within the school's group would not attract a suitable candidate.

The governing body should formally record and minute its decision on the school's ISR together with the rationale for the decision. It will need input from the headteacher but the governing body must be seen to be taking the decision independently.

The pay of deputy and assistant headteachers is determined by the governing body, which fixes a Leadership Group Range for each deputy and assistant. Each range must cover five points on the Leadership Group Spine.

Members of the Leadership Group are entitled each year to be notified of their position on the spine, the basis on which this has been determined and how future reviews will be dealt with. The governing body may move Leadership Group members up the Leadership Group Spine within their ISRs or ranges by a point on

1 September in any year, but only if there has been a performance review in the light of their objectives (i.e. school leadership and management and pupil progress) and they have demonstrated a sustained high quality of performance against the totality of their responsibilities and not just their statutory objectives. In the case of headteachers, such reviews require the involvement of an external advisor and any subsequent pay decision will be back-dated to 1 September.

If performance criteria are not established, no increase may be given. However, the governing body is under a statutory duty to agree performance objectives for headteachers and should do so in the autumn term each year when the necessary data is available. It is no longer an option for a governing body (or headteacher) to decide to forgo the task and waive any possibility of a movement in pay. The review must be conducted with reference to the quality of the headteacher's leadership and management and the progress made by pupils. These must be considered in the context of the school improvement plan. Governing bodies will normally delegate to the headteacher the comparable duty to agree performance objectives with the other members of the Leadership Group. If agreement is not possible, the governing body may set the performance objectives, although the headteacher may submit written reasons for not agreeing to them. Deputy and assistant headteachers will agree (or have imposed) performance objectives in the same way. The TPCD Circular says that the criterion for increase should become progressively more challenging as the Leadership Group member gains experience and moves up the range.

There is no incremental entitlement for members of the Leadership Group, so any increase beyond that provided in the annual pay settlement requires movement to a different spine point. In relation to the headteacher that will require a governing body decision. The power to move other members of the Leadership Group can be delegated to the headteacher, but if the governing body retains this decision it is axiomatic that any governor (including the headteacher) affected by the decision must not participate in it. Teacher governors are not, however, barred from membership of the relevant committee or from voting on the issue unless they are personally affected: the fact that the pay of Leadership Group members has an impact on the school's budget and therefore on the money available for other salaries which may in turn indirectly affect the governor in question is not relevant. The headteacher (whether a governor or not) is entitled to attend the relevant committee meeting where pay is being discussed but, following the normal rule, must withdraw during the discussion. The committee may invite the headteacher to comment before the discussion starts.

Advanced Skills Teachers' Pay

The rationale of the advanced skills teacher (AST) is to provide a new career path for teachers of high ability who do not wish to take the usual management-oriented route towards headship. There is a national assessment procedure and only teachers who pass it may be appointed to an AST post. An AST is predominately a classroom teacher but has a number of additional statutory professional duties designed to promote best practice among teacher colleagues in their own and other schools.

The working-time provisions, i.e. 1265 hours, do not apply, which is just as well given the substantial extra load that an AST is to bear. This may, however, create an anomalous position for headteachers of department and other senior staff in the same school who could be carrying a similar or even greater workload and yet be theoretically within 1265 hours. There is a separate pay spine for ASTs and the governing body selects the appropriate pay range. Annual performance criteria must be agreed with the AST, and performance must be reviewed annually against those criteria. Any progression up the spine is dependent on the outcome of a performance review. The initial positioning on the spine should take account of the pay of the Leadership Group, so that an appropriate differential is maintained, and should also be reviewed in the light of the new post-threshold salaries.

Teachers' Pay

Pay for other teaching staff is governed by the TPCD, which lays down rates of pay and increments by establishing a scale, with the point on the scale determining the salary to be paid. The TPCD sets out certain conditions relating to the operation of the scale and establishes incentive allowances. Certain positioning is mandatory, for example positioning based on specific qualification, so that the teacher will have a guaranteed minimum entitlement. An appointment may be made at a higher scale point than the teacher's basic entitlement, to reflect age, non-teaching experience and/or recruitment and retention difficulties. There are also discretionary powers for governing bodies to reward teachers, either permanently or for limited periods, for particular reasons. These may be used to reward, for example, a limited period of added responsibility.

Schools also have a discretion, when employing teachers who are not formally qualified as such but who have come into teaching through the graduate and registered teacher programme (GRTP), to pay at the rate applicable either to qualified teachers or that applicable to unqualified ones.

The effect of this is that an individual teacher's pay will be determined by several factors.

(1) Length of Service as a Teacher

A teacher 'earns' one point for every school year in which the teacher has been employed for at least 26 weeks on aggregate. This includes employment in a Ministry of Defence school or in an EAZ forum. Holiday periods and other authorised absences including maternity and parental leave count as employment for this purpose. A maximum of six points are available, so that a teacher will reach the top of the 'experience' scale after six years' teaching. There are special rules governing the positioning on the scale of a teacher who returns to teaching after a career break. Points for non-teaching experience can be awarded. An 'experience' point may be withheld if the previous year's performance has been unsatisfactory, but the governing body must take advice from the headteacher first and the teacher must be notified in writing before the end of the current school year and before any determination is made.

(2) Management Allowances

Five points are available for management allowances, although the School Teachers' Review Body (STRB) has discouraged the award of the fifth management point in its recommendations. Whereas experience and qualification points are specific to the teacher, management allowances are normally allocated to particular posts, reflecting the principle that the points are awarded for responsibilities beyond those common to the majority of teachers. The assessment of points for management allowances should be linked to a clearly defined job description. As from 1 April 2004, all new management allowances were to be fixed term for not more than one year, although they are renewable. Management allowances that existed at 1 April 2004 will continue on the terms on which they were granted. Further changes are likely with a new framework and Guidance for management allowances promised, perhaps for 1 April 2005. The Guidance on this stresses the need not to give assurances or guarantees about the future of any particular management allowance, whether in relation to the post or the person holding it and indeed the likelihood is that, following discussions between Government, employers and the majority of teaching unions, management allowances will disappear and be replaced by a new pay structure for 'excellent teachers'.

(3) Recruitment and Retention Allowances

No new recruitment or retention allowances can be awarded after 1 April 2004. Existing ones awarded on a fixed-term basis will continue until, at the latest, 31 March 2007. The allowances have been replaced by recruitment and retention incentives and benefits which can only be given on a fixed-term basis for up to three years, for recruitment of new teachers and retention of existing ones. The incentives and benefits will not necessarily be straight salary. They may be, for example, a lump sum payment, or assistance with travel or housing costs. Schools will need to consider what, if any, replacement incentives should be offered to those teachers previously on non-fixed term allowances (which will include permanent allowances) which will have come to an end.

(4) Special Educational Needs Allowances

Teachers in special schools, teachers of children who are hearing impaired or visually impaired, and teachers appointed to SEN units in mainstream schools are entitled to SEN Allowance 1. Governing bodies have a discretion to award SEN Allowance 2. They may in certain circumstances use their discretion to award SEN Allowance 1 to mainstream teachers who have significant contact with SEN pupils, whether statemented or not, above and beyond that normally expected of a teacher.

(5) London Allowances

Teachers working in schools in the London area receive additional remuneration. There are separate pay scales for such teachers according to whether the school is in the Inner London area, Outer London area or the Fringe area.

(6) Upper Pay Scale

There are five allowances for teachers who have passed through the performance threshold. Teachers are eligible to move to successive allowances annually based on their performance reviews and their overall performance in post over the previous two years. Movement up the spine can only happen if there has been a performance review and the achievements and contribution of the teacher concerned have been substantial and sustained. However, this is likely to change following agreement between government and the unions. The School Teachers' Review Body has recommended that the third point on the Upper Pay Scale should be the highest and that a new scheme with two scale points for excellent teachers would be introduced to provide further reward for excellent teachers for their work in the classroom and supporting colleagues within their school. The Government proposal was that this should take effect in September 2006 but STRB has doubts about this and suggests September 2007. This is now likely to be introduced alongside the changes mentioned above in relation to management allowances. There will be serious implications for many senior staff who currently hold management allowances and who may find themselves facing pay cuts once safeguarding ceases.

(7) Fast Track

The Fast Track programme was introduced from September 2001 to recruit and develop top quality graduates and serving teachers. Teachers appointed to the programme are rewarded with accelerated promotion through the pay scale. They are expected to earn double spine jumps for excellent performance each year.

Teachers' Annual Review

There must be an assessment of a teacher's points allocation each year, and each teacher must be given a formal statement of salary and how it has been arrived at. Because the fundamental salary of a teacher is governed by matters over which there is no discretion, the assessment will consist of confirmation of the basic scale position and a review of any discretionary allowances that the teacher may hold or which the committee is considering awarding in order to produce the required written statement. Those decisions must be consistent with the pay policy and with the school development plan. They must also be consistent with the Nolan principles of public life: objectivity, openness and accountability.

Safeguarding

Teachers who lose their posts as a result of closure or reorganisation of a school following a significant change of character, but who continue to be employed by the same authority, have their previous salaries safeguarded. There may also be safeguarding in other circumstances, such as a major senior management reorganisation. In this case, the safeguarding is discretionary, but discretion is to be used reasonably in favour of the teacher. All points are safeguarded other than temporary ones: excellence points and recruitment and retention points (assuming they continue under the revised arrangements from 1 April 2004), however, will only continue until they would have next been due for review. It may well be that safeguarding in the future will be limited to three years.

Unqualified Teachers

There is a separate 10-point pay scale for unqualified teachers. There is discretion to pay additional allowances if it is felt that payment in accordance with the scale would not provide adequate remuneration having regard to the teacher's responsibilities or to any qualifications or experience relevant to any specialised form of teaching.

Non-teaching Staff

Pay for non-teaching staff is a matter for direct negotiation between school and employee, although generally schools, including VA and foundation schools, will follow LEA and local authority gradings and pay scales. These are generally negotiated nationally, although there may well be locally negotiated variations. Provided that the school complies with equal opportunities policies and does not discriminate between women and men by paying differently for the same or equivalent jobs, there are no prescribed rates of pay and no requirement for annual review. It is, however, good practice for the school's pay policy to embrace non-teaching staff and to lay down a basis for annual review with appropriate criteria.

Supply Staff

Supply staff, i.e. teachers who are engaged on a short-term basis to cover temporary needs but who do not hold a teaching contract with the school, should normally have qualified teacher status unless they are:

- licensed teachers or authorised under the Overseas Trained Teacher scheme;
- employed as a suitably qualified instructor where no qualified, licensed or authorised teacher is available;

- teachers who hold a teaching qualification recognised by an overseas authority that is itself recognised by the DfES.

The employment status of supply teachers depends on who employs them. Teachers drawn from a pool maintained by the LEA are in all respects employees of the LEA. Teachers engaged directly by the school are employees of the school and, as such, the school is responsible for deduction of tax (PAYE) and National Insurance (NI) unless a particular teacher is registered as self-employed. Schools should check any claim to self-employed status to avoid the risk of a claim for employee's NI contribution and, possibly, PAYE, which inevitably would come well after the particular engagement had ended. Teachers supplied by an agency are not employed by the school, and the school is not concerned with either PAYE or NI.

Supply teachers are subject to the same controls as other teachers. Accordingly, schools must in every case check:

- identity and qualifications;
- List 99, which is a list maintained by the DfES of persons who may not be employed to work with, or in close proximity to, children, and the Criminal Records Bureau;
- whether a work permit is needed and has been obtained;
- criminal records.

Where the teacher is supplied by an agency, it is not necessary for the school to make the checks, but the school should know in advance what checks the particular agency carries out, be satisfied that these are sufficient, and obtain formal confirmation in every case that the checks have in fact been carried out.

PERFORMANCE, EXPECTATIONS AND STANDARDS

Non-teaching Staff

There is no formal requirement that non-teaching staff be appraised, although many schools will have appraisal procedures for all staff, as do many other employers. The question of whether non-teaching staff meet expectations and required standards is a matter of interpretation of the contractual terms and, particularly, the job description.

Teacher Performance

Performance management replaced appraisal for teachers from September 2000. Performance management is intended to help schools improve through support and improvement of teachers' work. It enables teachers and their team leader to agree and review priorities and objectives within the overall framework of the school's development plan. The DfES has produced Guidance on performance management, which supplements the DfES publication 'Performance Management in Schools' that was sent to all schools with the model performance management policy referred to below.

The Guidance says that:

> 'Performance management means a shared commitment to high performance. It works best when it is an integral part of the school's culture; it is seen to be fair and open; understood by everyone and based on a shared commitment to supporting continuous improvement and recognising success.'

This Guidance has been supplemented by a Support Guide for governors and headteachers (DfES reference 0533/2003) together with two videos (0569 and 0534) and a workbook (0535).

The process starts with a performance management policy which the governing body is required under the Terms of Reference regulations to establish. The governing body may (and in practical terms should) direct the headteacher to formulate the policy for consideration, although both would be well advised substantially to follow the model policy produced by the DfES, which has the backing of the main teaching unions. The governing body's role is a strategic one. Having set or agreed the policy its responsibility is to review it regularly and monitor its implementation. It has no role in gathering evidence or making judgements about individual teachers. To quote the Guidance:

> 'Governing bodies need to satisfy themselves that –
>
> - the activities and procedures are happening as described in the policy;
> - the process ensures equality of opportunity;
> - the impact on teaching and learning is positive;
> - the necessary resources are identified to support the training and developmental needs of staff.
>
> Future OFSTED inspections will include an assessment of how effectively schools are using performance management.'

The Headteacher

The governing body has a specific role in relation to the headteacher. It has a duty to review the headteacher's performance with the help of an external advisor. The governing body determines the exact timing of the headteacher's performance review cycle and appoints two or three governors to carry out the review. Staff governors may not be involved, neither in decisions about how to review the headteacher's performance nor in the review itself.

The external advisor, who is funded for eight hours per year of which about four should be in school, should provide high-quality and focused advice to the governors involved in the review on the setting of performance objectives and assessing the extent to which they have been achieved. The external advisor will attend meetings at which the objectives and their achievement are discussed with the headteacher.

The governors appointed to carry out the headteacher's performance review should:

- recognise and praise the headteacher's/school's achievements;
- review, discuss and confirm the headteacher's essential tasks, standards and objectives and the extent to which they have been met;
- confirm action and any changes agreed in any informal in-year discussions;
- identify areas for personal development and training;
- agree new objectives.

Guidance 59/2000 goes into detail on the process.

The headteacher's review statement or self-review may not be disclosed to any other teacher or member of staff. Only two copies of the performance review statement should be made, one for the chair of the governing body and one for the headteacher. However, a further copy can be provided on request for the governors responsible for decisions in relation to pay and they should take it into account when making such decisions. The chair of governors must provide a summary of the headteacher's review statement, to the Chief Education Inspector (CEO) on request or to an education adviser designated by the CEO. The chair must also provide any review officer or new reviewer with a copy of the previous review statement together with the objectives relating to that statement. The training and development annex should be sent by the chair of governors to the person responsible for training and development in the school.

If the headteacher has a complaint about the review statement, it should be referred to the chair of governors or, if the chair of governors has been involved in the review, to another designated governor or governors. The reviewing governor may uphold the statement, amend it or direct a fresh review by other governors. If the headteacher considers that the complaint has still not been dealt with satisfactorily, it should be dealt with under the school's grievance procedure.

Other Teachers

The headteacher implements the performance management policy for the rest of the school and either acts as the reviewer or delegates the task to the teacher's team leader. The process is similar and complaints go to the headteacher, where the team leader is the reviewer, or to the chair of governors.

The significant feature of the performance management system, compared with the appraisal system that it replaced, is the explicit link to pay. Information from performance review can be used to inform decisions about:

- the award of pay points for outstanding performance up to the threshold;
- movement across the threshold;
- movement up the upper pay spine.

Competency and Capability

It is an implied term of any employment contract that the employee will reach a reasonable level of competence in carrying out the work specified, and failure to achieve that standard is a breach of contract. The key issues are identifying the lack of competence and acting fairly in dealing with it. This will normally involve giving the employee an opportunity to improve, together with appropriate support and counselling. This in turn requires that the employer has a procedure for dealing with capability. Although capability in schools tends to be focused on teachers, the principles apply equally to all staff and there is no reason why the same, or a similar, procedure should not apply to non-teaching staff.

Performance review, which forms part of the performance management system, does not form part of the disciplinary or dismissal procedures, but where information from the review gives rise to concerns about the capability of a teacher it may lead to a competence investigation. Concerns about competence arise in many other contexts, such as from parental or pupil complaints or from normal monitoring. Whilst, ultimately, failure to meet acceptable standards may be a disciplinary matter to be dealt with under the discipline procedure, this will normally arise only where the failure is seen to be gross and of a kind that will not be remedied (or has not previously been remedied) by support, training and counselling. Except in most exceptional circumstances, disciplinary action or instigation of dismissal proceedings will not arise until the school's capability procedure has been followed through. The DfES has published a model capability procedure (DfES reference 0125/2000) which, statutorily, schools must 'have regard to'. This, as the policy itself explicitly states, means that schools must either adopt the policy as it stands or adopt a policy has substantially the same effect. It follows closely the recommendations of a working party set up in 1997 which produced an outline capability procedure. In truth, the procedure itself is not very illuminating because it avoids any specific examples of what may be regarded as lack of capability. It sets the framework for action, and its significance lies in the time-scale that it advocates, with its expectation that the improvement that is identified comes about in a maximum of two terms. In extreme cases, where the education of pupils is jeopardised, the improvement may be required within four weeks. The procedure is of great potential value in dealing with the frequent situation that a capability investigation leads to absences, often prolonged, for ill-health: it is clear from the procedure that such absences must not allow the process to become stalled, which may seem to be (and in some cases may be) hard on the teacher, but is of great assistance to a hard-pressed headteacher and governing body. Ultimately, the school must act fairly, otherwise any dismissal may be challenged as unfair in the employment tribunal, but it is difficult to envisage the tribunal holding that a school that had acted in accordance with the model procedure had been unfair. Having said this, there is much to be said for having a capability procedure with a sharper focus and more evident teeth. Ideally, a school should have a procedure that is accepted as fair because the context in which it is applied is genuinely seen as a supportive one. A capability process should be designed to secure improvement and avoid formal disciplinary action or dismissal. Too often, implementation of the capability procedure comes at a very late stage, when the situation is beyond redemption. Early intervention within the context of the formal procedure, even if it does not go beyond the informal stage, can lead to a swifter resolution with a greater chance of saving the teacher's job and, very likely, career.

Regulations used to provide a number of criteria that teachers had to meet, namely, that teachers should:

- have the health and well-being necessary for their specific teaching responsibilities and associated duties;

- be able to communicate effectively;

- possess sound judgement and insight;

- remain alert at all times;

- be able to respond to pupils' needs rapidly;

- be able to manage classes;

- not constitute a risk to the health and safety of those in their care.

Although, apart from health (dealt with below), these do not now have legislative force, they represent a good guide to assessing capability. A consistent failure to meet one or more of the criteria in a material way would justify the invocation of the capability process.

Training

Training, of both teaching and non-teaching staff, is now widely seen as an essential function of the employer. How it is done is a matter for each school but funding is included in the School Development Grant which replaced the previously earmarked funding through the Standards Fund. Under the TPCD, five of the 195 days that teaching staff are required to work in a year are allocated for INSET and are usually used for whole-school or departmental training sessions in school. Additionally, teachers will follow INSET courses on an individual basis either voluntarily or as part of their directed time under the TPCD. Schools are free to add to their funding from their ordinary budget for INSET purposes and can pay teachers (other than headteachers) additionally for INSET sessions that fall outside directed time, i.e. outside 195 days or 1265 hours. The DfES recommends that this money comes from the supply teaching budget.

Sickness

Sickness presents short-term and long-term problems. The former frequently turns into the latter and a key issue for schools is the effective management of short-term absences. In May 2000, the then Secretary of State wrote to all headteachers asking for support in developing improved procedures for managing sickness absence. This was accompanied by a checklist for managing absence which emphasised the need to keep on top of all absences whilst always treating sickness sensitively, flexibly and confidentially. The key feature was advice to investigate more closely if someone has a pattern of short-term absences or has frequent or long-term absences that throw doubt on the teacher's prospects of returning to regular work. One reason (although not one made explicit in this Guidance) for monitoring the position from the outset and acting swiftly is that the longer absences of this kind are allowed to continue, the harder it becomes to deal with the problem in a way that can be seen to be fair. If an employee has had absences over, say, a period of 12 months with nothing being said, the employee will assume that this is acceptable and will feel aggrieved if suddenly the school decides to take drastic action. There is a delicate balance to be achieved, because schools will not want to place unnecessary additional pressure on an employee who is experiencing ill-health, but the employee does have to understand that an entitlement to sick pay does not necessarily mean that no action can be taken in relation to ill-health absence until that entitlement has come to an end.

As noted previously, sick-pay entitlement will depend on the particular terms of the employee's contract and will not normally present problems. Long-term illness, however, can present acute difficulties, particularly if the illness is job related or is thought to be a symptom of lack of competency. In those circumstances, it may be difficult to keep the relevant issues in focus, namely:

- absence on the grounds of illness must be medically justified;

- there is no automatic entitlement to the full contractual period of paid leave if the nature of the illness is such that the employee is not going to be able to resume work as an effective member of staff;

- the overriding concern in respect of a teacher's fitness to teach is the health, education and welfare of the pupils. This is a powerful reason for getting to grips with the problem as soon as it arises. Experience shows that failure to do so merely increases the inevitable pain for all concerned;

- under the Health Regulations, schools should not employ or continue to employ a teacher who does not have or no longer has the health or physical capacity for employment. The school must take the provisions of the Disability Discrimination Act 1995 fully into account in making this assessment. A person with a disability must not be treated less favourably because of the disability than other employees who are not subject to the disability so that, before deciding to dismiss, the school would have to consider whether adaptations to working conditions or terms of employment might make it possible for the employment to continue;

- schools must consider whether a teacher who is ill should be suspended if pupils may be at risk. This would be relevant particularly in cases of mental ill-health;

- unfairness to the employee may lead to a claim for constructive or unfair dismissal.

Due process, as laid down in the Health Regulations, must be followed before a teacher is dismissed on the grounds of ill-health. Good practice suggests that a similar procedure should be adopted for non-teaching staff. As with capability, sickness issues tend to be focused on teachers but the principles apply equally to all staff.

The governing body:

- must give the teacher an opportunity to submit medical evidence and make representations;

- must consider that evidence and any other evidence that it may have received, including material supplied in confidence on the grounds that it is not in the interests of the teacher to see it;

- may require the teacher to submit to medical examination by its nominated medical practitioner. If the teacher fails to attend without good cause, or does not submit medical evidence, the governing body is expressly empowered to reach a conclusion on the basis of whatever information is available to it. The teacher may submit written material to the nominated practitioner and the teacher's own doctor may be present if the teacher requests.

The Secretary of State has the power to bar a teacher on medical (amongst other) grounds but must follow the same procedure.

If a governing body wishes to consider terminating an employment contract on the grounds of ill-health, it must follow the relevant procedure for considering dismissal even though ill-health is not a discipline issue. The specific steps laid down by the Health Regulations will normally have taken place before the actual dismissal process starts.

DISCIPLINE AND GRIEVANCE PROCEDURES AND APPEALS

The power to discipline, including the power to dismiss, effectively lies with the governing body of all schools with delegated budgets. Because those who work in community and VC schools are employed by the LEA, the actual dismissal has to be carried out by the LEA at the requirement of the governing body. If the member of staff is not employed by the LEA to work solely at the school, the LEA must remove that person from the school and relieve the school of its liability to pay the relevant part of the salary. Foundation and VA schools are direct employers of staff and will themselves take the necessary steps to dismiss.

Employees of schools without a delegated budget can be dismissed only by the LEA, which must consult with the governors and must consider any recommendation for dismissal made by the governors. As with all other schools, the headteacher and governing body of a school without a delegated budget can suspend an employee on full pay.

New regulations covering school staffing were introduced in September 2003 and for the first time the governing body can now delegate its power to dismiss to the headteacher, an individual governor, a number of governors or one or more governors and the headteacher. It is up to the governing body to determine how it delegates that power, although the DfES has produced lengthy Guidance. In particular, the Guidance explicitly anticipates that all initial staff appointment (outside the leadership group) and dismissal decisions should be taken by the headteacher, except in exceptional circumstances. This represents a major change which many headteachers will be reluctant to accept. One of the 'exceptional circumstances' which means headteachers do not have to assume this responsibility is if his or her current duties do not include it –

but the expectation is that new headteacher appointments will require the headteacher to deal with appointments and dismissals, and so over the course of time this should become the norm. Governing bodies will have to be prepared to deal with initial dismissal decisions too where other 'exceptional circumstances' apply such as when the headteacher has been closely involved in the process that is leading to dismissal or is the subject of the process him or herself. The practical implication of this is that governing bodies must delegate such responsibilities to a committee different in its composition from the dismissal appeal committee and an appointments panel to step in when required. Each committee should have three members or two if that is impossible, although there should not be fewer dealing with the appeal than dealt with the original dismissal – and the members of both committees must not be contaminated with previous knowledge of the matter. This may mean, for the time being at least, that the old arrangements of having a dismissal committee and a dismissal appeal committee will be mirrored under the new arrangements. Collaborating schools are given the freedom to draw on the resources of all the schools if dealing with staffing issues, although similar requirements apply.

Staff Discipline Procedure

All governing bodies are required to establish disciplinary rules and procedures and to make them known to staff. It is for each school to determine its own detailed procedure, although in practice every LEA will have negotiated procedures with employee representatives which will have to be followed by community schools. VA and foundation schools will devise and set their own procedures, although it is common for foundation schools that were formerly community schools to adopt procedures based on those of their former LEA. This can give rise to difficulties in adapting procedures which work in a multi-layered organisation such as an LEA but which sit less happily in the relatively monolithic structure of an individual school. Any discipline or grievance procedure that is adopted in order to meet the basic rules of natural justice must:

- give the employee adequate notice of the charges that have to be answered, with sufficient particularity to enable the employee to answer the specific allegations;

- give the employee an adequate opportunity to be heard and represented (although not necessarily by a lawyer);

- ensure that the employee sees all documents, etc, that the person or people making the decision see;

- give the employee and the school the opportunity to call evidence and challenge witnesses by questioning them;

- ensure that the person or people making the decision do not discuss the case with or hear argument from the school without the employee being present or represented. If the decision is being made by a panel it may, however, take advice from its clerk although that advice must be limited to advice on matters of law and not on issues of fact. The clerk must not try to influence the decision;

- ensure that the person or people making the decision not only are unbiased but are seen to be unbiased, both in its membership (if appropriate) and conduct. Wherever possible, governors who sit on a disciplinary panel, including any appeal panel, should not have had any prior involvement in the case, but the courts have recognised that there can be circumstances where there may have been degrees of prior discussion at governor level. In those cases, those appointed to sit on panels should be those who have the least degree of involvement.

Who Exercises Discipline Powers?

There used to be important differences in the powers of governing bodies of different types of schools but all schools are now subject to the same procedural requirements. It used also to be the case that governors' dismissal and dismissal appeal proceedings were tightly prescribed by regulation. As a part of the changes devolving power to governing bodies that has informed much of the Education Act 2002, governing bodies are now left very much to their own devices in regulating their own proceedings in this and other areas, although as noted above it is the expectation of the new Guidance that initial decisions about dismissal will be taken by headteachers and logically this should extend to other disciplinary matters too.

Previous detailed procedural requirements relating to schools have now been rendered obsolete by standardised (and very simplistic) procedures that apply from October 2004 to all employment. These procedures will not essentially change the way in which grievance and disciplinary procedures have worked in the past and in practice schools will have much more complex arrangements than the Act requires. To comply with the Act (and non-compliance will constitute automatic unfair dismissal) before making the initial decision to dismiss (unless dismissal is summary without notice or payment in lieu of notice for gross misconduct, it is reasonable for the employer to dismiss before enquiring into the circumstances and the dismissal takes place immediately the employer becomes aware of the relevant conduct), the headteacher or other governing body delegate must give the individual concerned the opportunity to make representations (including, if desired, oral representations) about the action it is proposing to take, and have regard to those representations. Thereafter if a decision is made to dismiss, the governing body concerned must make arrangements to give the individual the opportunity to appeal. The DfES Guidance requires that the appeal be to a panel of (where possible) at least three governors. The regulations on which this Guidance is based only stipulated this until the October 2004 changes and the standardised regime has no specific requirement about the constitution of an appeal body. However, it would always be good practice to follow this Guidance even if it is not a statutory requirement. Staff, and their unions, will expect it.

The headteacher (unless it is the headteacher who is the subject of the dismissal proposal or the headteacher has been delegated the power to determine the issue) has the right to attend and advise at any meeting of governors that considers dismissal of an employee, and a representative of the LEA has the same right in all community and VC schools and in those VA and foundation schools that have granted that degree of advisory rights. This right should not be seen to entitle the headteacher to remain with the committee when it considers its decision. The headteacher would normally be expected to make any representations during the course of the hearing in the presence of the employee so that the employee can deal with those representations. The same applies to the LEA or foundation body representatives.

Every dismissal decision, whether it arises for disciplinary reasons or not and irrespective of whether it relates to a teacher or other member of staff, must be made by the headteacher or other governing body delegate with a right of appeal to the dismissal appeal committee. This can be restrictive. For example, a member of the non-teaching staff may be engaged on a probationary basis and may very quickly prove to be unsatisfactory. To have to go through the dismissal procedure and consequent appeal process is cumbersome and possibly not in the interests of the school even though it is now possible for notice to be given and even for the dismissal to take place even though an appeal may be pending – if the appeal succeeds, the notice or dismissal will be rescinded. The answer is to make such appointments initially for a fixed short term and to renew the employment at the end of the initial term only if performance is satisfactory. If there is still a doubt, a further fixed-term contract can be offered. Care should be taken not to extend such fixed-term contracts to the point where employment protection arises (now after only one year), and schools are advised not to make themselves unnecessary hostages to fortune by making promises or representations about a permanent contract following on automatically from a fixed-term contract.

When does Dismissal take Effect?

Technically, community and VC schools do not dismiss employees. Because the LEA is the employer, only the LEA can effect a dismissal and the court has now decided that this power cannot be delegated to the school by the LEA. Once the school has resolved that a member of staff should be dismissed, it must request the LEA to give effect to that resolution and the LEA must do so within 14 days. That request can be made as soon as the decision to dismiss has been taken. VA and foundation schools, being the employer of staff, will dismiss the employee directly.

Reporting Dismissal of Teachers

Where a teacher is dismissed for misconduct, or the teacher resigns but would otherwise have been dismissed or considered for dismissal, the employer (which will be the LEA for community and VC schools and the governing body for VA and foundation schools) must report the fact to the Secretary of State. The Secretary of State considers whether the case involves the safety or welfare of children. If it does, then the Secretary of State retains the function of considering whether the teacher should be barred, which automatically makes the teacher ineligible for registration with the General Teaching Council. Otherwise, the Secretary of State will pass the papers to the General Teaching Council which will consider the question of continuing registration under its discipline provisions. Guidance about reporting is available on Teachernet.

If a teacher is dismissed on the grounds of incompetence, or the teacher resigns but would otherwise have been dismissed or considered for dismissal, the employer must report the fact to the General Teaching Council which again will consider the question of continuing registration under its discipline provisions.

The obligation to report dismissal or resignation on either ground applies also where the employment is terminated under a compromise agreement referred to below.

Grievance Procedures

There are very simple prescribed requirements for grievance procedures and every school must have a grievance procedure in place. Grievance procedures should be less formal than discipline procedures and should be structured in a way that produces speedy decisions. It is not essential that there should be a right to bring a grievance to governors or a governor committee. It would, however, be difficult to construct a grievance procedure that would cope with a grievance by the headteacher without governor involvement, and there will normally be at least a right of appeal to a governor committee – and the new statutory scheme does require inclusion of a right of appeal.

Any procedure should also meet the basic requirements of natural justice at least in the formal stages, although it is good practice to have a procedure that first attempts to resolve grievances informally. The employee must make the grievance in writing and must inform the employer of the basis of the grievance as a precondition to a hearing. The employee is required to take all reasonable steps to attend the hearing (or 'meeting' as it is described in the statutory procedure). It is good practice to provide that the appeal is not a rehearing but is restricted to a review of the material first considered. If this is not done, the appeal body may be faced with voluminous 'new' evidence as the parties seek to counter what was said at the original hearing.

An important change in relation to grievance procedures is that an employee does not now have the option of going straight to the Employment Tribunal in relation to a complaint that could have been the subject of a grievance process. The grievance procedure must be followed and then a 'cooling-off' period of 28 days must elapse in an attempt to secure a resolution. This will be of particular use in pay and discrimination complaints

MATERNITY LEAVE AND PATERNITY LEAVE

All female staff (regardless of the length of their employment) are entitled to ordinary maternity leave, which is a period of 26 weeks. To qualify for this right, the employee must notify the school by at least the end of the 15th week before the expected week of childbirth ('EWC') of: (i) the fact of the pregnancy, (ii) the EWC, and (iii) the date on which she intends the ordinary maternity leave period to start – not earlier than 11 weeks before the EWC. The school may request that the employee produces for inspection a certificate from a registered medical practitioner or midwife asserting the expected week of childbirth. The employee may change the start date by giving 28 days' notice, unless it is not practicable to give that length of notice.

All employees who have been continuously employed for a period of 26 weeks at the beginning of the 14th week before the EWC are entitled to additional maternity leave. Additional maternity leave is for a period of 26 weeks.

An employee who takes maternity leave is entitled to return to work afterwards. If she intends to return at the end of her maternity leave, no notice need be given. If she wishes to return sooner, then she must give 28 days' notice of the intended return date. If she does not intend to return, she must give whatever notice is appropriate under the terms of her contract. An employee who is entitled to additional maternity leave can extend it by up to four weeks in certain circumstances, including illness.

The employer must take the employee back into the same job after normal maternity leave unless a redundancy situation has arisen. The same applies after additional maternity leave except that, in addition, if there is some reason why it is not reasonably practicable for her to return to the same job the employer may offer an alternative job. The job offered must, however, be of a similar nature and must be work that the employee is capable of doing at the same place of work. If the employee refuses to accept such an alternative job, the employer need not take the employee back and the dismissal would not be an unfair one. However, great care must be taken to ensure that any offer of a different post does not infringe equal opportunities and sex discrimination legislation.

If the terms of employment in any particular case give more beneficial terms than the statutory scheme then the contract terms prevail. This will be the case for all teachers with at least one year's continuous service on with one or more LEAs (which would include VA and foundation schools) on terms that incorporate the Burgundy Book. They will be entitled to more than the statutory maternity pay. The amount will depend on the length of service.

Fathers who have been employed for at least 26 weeks have the right to two weeks' paid paternity leave, although collectively negotiated terms may enhance this. The leave must be taken within 56 days of the birth or 56 days after the first day of the EWC if that is later – catering for the premature baby. The father can only take complete weeks – one week or two weeks.

All employees (whether male or female) who have been continuously employed for one year and who have responsibility for a child born or adopted after 15 December 1999 are entitled to unpaid parental leave (not to be confused with the paternity leave mentioned in the previous paragraph) of up to 13 weeks in total and no more than four weeks in any 12 months until the child reaches the age of five (except in certain circumstances relating to disabled or adopted children where the upper age is 18). The conditions that have to be satisfied in order to take parental leave are:

- the employee must give at least 21 days' written notice of the wish to take leave and must state the amount of leave to be taken;
- the employee must supply whatever evidence the school reasonably requires to establish entitlement to parental leave.

Except where the parental leave is to be taken to coincide with the anticipated birth of the child or the date of placement of an adopted child, the school may request that the leave be postponed if it considers that the operation of the school would be unreasonably disrupted. In those circumstances the employee must be given at least the equivalent amount of leave within six months at a time to be specified by the school but after consultation with the employee. To take advantage of this right of postponement, the school must notify the employee in writing within seven days of receiving the notice requesting parental leave.

Discrimination against any employee that can be identified with pregnancy or the possibility of pregnancy is unlawful and may give rise to a claim of unfair dismissal. This is dealt with in more detail later in this chapter.

Broadly similar leave and pay provisions arrangements apply now to adoptive parents.

UNION REPRESENTATION AND PUBLIC DUTIES

Unions do not have an automatic right of representation in a school, although collective agreements that apply to or that are adopted by a school may give such a right. However, employees do have a right to belong to a union, and that right may not be interfered with.

Employees are also entitled to reasonable paid time off for trade union activities if:

- the employee is an official of a recognised union; and

- the time off is taken for training or to carry out negotiations relating to the employer or a trade dispute with the employer. In this context, the employer of staff in community and VC schools is the LEA and not the school.

Employees are entitled to unpaid time off to participate in union activities short of industrial action.

UNPAID LEAVE

Employees are entitled to reasonable unpaid time off for certain public duties, which include acting as a governor of a school. An employee who is called for jury service or who is subpoenaed to give evidence in court must be given time off. It is often possible for the employer to arrange for jury service to be deferred if it comes at a particularly inconvenient time by writing a moderate and reasoned letter to the jury summonsing officer at the court.

UNFAIR DISMISSAL

Employees who have been continuously employed (whether with one employer or a series of employers) for one year have employment protection which confers the right not to be dismissed unfairly. Unfair dismissal claims go to an employment tribunal which has the power to award damages and in certain circumstances has the power to direct reinstatement. Dismissal can include failure to renew a fixed-term contract and constructive dismissal. Constructive dismissal is conduct by the employer that makes the employee's position untenable to the extent that the employee cannot reasonably be expected to continue in the employment.

Compromise Agreements

Whenever an employee who has employment protection ceases to be employed, there is a prospect of a claim for unfair dismissal being made. This applies even if the employment is terminated by agreement, unless a compromise agreement is entered into, and it is quite common for such a claim to be brought even when the school believed that the parting of the ways was amicable and reasonable. To prevent the possibility of claims, schools should always insist on the employee entering into a compromise agreement whenever employment ends otherwise than by the unprovoked resignation of the employee. A compromise agreement is a formal agreement recording the terms on which the employment is to be ended. The agreement contains an express waiver of all employment protection claims and the agreement has to be signed by a lawyer or suitably qualified trade union official who will certify that the employee understands that the employment protection rights and the right to bring an employment tribunal claim have been given up. The employer will pay the employee's reasonable costs in taking legal advice.

Grounds for Unfair Dismissal

If challenged, the employer has to demonstrate that the dismissal was not unfair. The dismissal must be based on one of the following grounds.

(1) Lack of Capability or Qualification for the Job

Incompetence will certainly be a justified ground for dismissal, if proved, but schools will normally try to solve the problem through a competency procedure rather than a disciplinary one unless the incompetence is such that it can be described as gross misconduct. Failure to show the required improvement identified in competency proceedings may well then become a disciplinary matter.

Ill-health which prevents the employee from working will come within this heading but the employer will have to show that the illness or degree of absence goes beyond what the school can reasonably be expected to accept. Agreed levels of sick pay will often be indicators on this, and terms of employment, particularly of non-teaching staff, may have specific provision entitling the employer to end the employment after a given period of continuous or aggregate absence.

(2) Unacceptable Conduct

This covers all aspects of behaviour in school and can include actions outside school if relevant to the employment or to the reputation of the school. However, conduct that the school finds unacceptable may not justify dismissal if that would breach equal opportunities or sex discrimination legislation. Specifically, a dismissal on the grounds of pregnancy will be held to be unfair even in denominational schools that would regard, for example, the pregnancy of an unmarried person as contrary to the ethos of the school. Even an express term of employment stipulating the school's right to dismiss in such circumstances is unlikely to be effective. The mere fact that the dismissal occurs because the employee is pregnant will put the school in the wrong: the motive behind the dismissal has been held to be irrelevant although the surrounding circumstances and the conduct of the employee may have a bearing on the level of compensation that is awarded. The test is whether or not a man would be dismissed in similar circumstances and *ex hypothesi* this cannot be so where pregnancy is involved. On the other hand, dismissal of an employee on the grounds of an inappropriate relationship that has adversely affected the reputation of the school might be justifiable, provided that the school can show that the decision was taken on grounds that did not involve a discrimination between men and women. Cases of this kind will depend on their particular facts, and legal advice should always be taken before starting the disciplinary process.

(3) Redundancy

A redundancy must be fair otherwise the employee will have a claim. Redundancy can arise in a number of situations:

- cessation of the business in which the employee is employed. This would happen when a school closes;

- the business moves to a new location, i.e. the school moves to a new site;

- the requirements for the work in question have ceased or diminished. This is the normal situation that gives rise to redundancy in schools. Because it is necessary to show that the job is to disappear, the redundancy process must start with an assessment of the school's needs, teaching or non-teaching, and only then consider individuals. Procedures for teacher redundancies will normally, therefore, take curriculum needs as the starting point;

- if a fixed-term contract is not renewed, the employee is deemed to have been dismissed for the purposes of employment protection. This may raise a presumption of redundancy (which could be an unfair redundancy) if the post is not refilled. If it is refilled, then the non-renewal may be treated as an unfair dismissal.

An employee faced with redundancy who is offered reasonable alternative employment and refuses it will not be entitled to redundancy pay and the dismissal will not be unfair. Note that this is limited to redundancy: it is not possible to require an employee to take up other work unless the terms of employment permit it.

(4) Circumstances Making it Impossible to Continue the Employment Without the Employer being in Breach of the Law

An obvious case in relation to schools would be if a person became prohibited from working with or in proximity to children.

(5) Other Grounds

There may be some other substantial reason justifying dismissal.

Claims for Unfair Dismissal

Employment tribunal claims are expensive in terms of potential compensation, the cost of representation and the management time that will be required to defend a claim properly. A VA or foundation school, as the employer, will normally have to meet the full cost. Community schools are in a more protected position in that the LEA as employer has to deal with the tribunal case and meet any compensation. The LEA can, however, recharge all or part of the cost to the school if it considers that the school has acted unreasonably. Prudence, therefore, suggests that schools should terminate employment only after taking proper advice from the LEA or the school's personnel advisers and lawyers.

Unfair dismissal claims will almost always present difficult questions of fact and degree. They can arise in one of three ways:

- a dismissal that arose after correct procedures were followed but which, on the facts, was not justified. If there has been a fair and impartial investigation, discipline hearing and appeal, an employment tribunal will be relatively unwilling to find a dismissal to be unfair unless it was also discriminatory. This will arise less often in dismissal cases than on appointment, but it can arise on redundancy, where schools have to be careful to ensure that their redundancy criteria are not unwittingly discriminatory. For example, a decision that part-time employees should be made redundant in preference to full-time employees may be defensible in management terms, but may be discriminatory because more women than men work part time;

- a dismissal preceded by incorrect procedures. This will always be held to be unfair even if the facts fully justified the dismissal unless the procedural defect consisted of a failure to take a step that would in any event have been futile. Every employee is entitled to due process;

- a dismissal that the law declares to be inherently unfair. 'Whistleblowing', dealt with below, is one example.

REDUNDANCY PROCEDURES

Redundancies have been relatively common in recent years and are a nightmare for schools. This is partly because the process is inherently painful and partly because of the combination of the timing of the budget process, the start of the financial year and the limitations on the giving of notice.

Timing and Time Constraints

Schools may know at the beginning of the calendar year that redundancies are possible but will not know for sure until shortly before 1 April (the start of the financial year) whether and to what extent they are necessary. It is not possible to start the formal redundancy process until specific requirements are known. The earliest that any saving can be made is 1 September because any notice (at least in respect of teaching staff) cannot expire until then. That requires that notice be given by 31 May, giving only about two months in which to carry through all the procedures. This may be difficult to achieve unless redundancies can be achieved by negotiation and agreement, so that any compulsory redundancy will frequently not take effect before 31 December. A redundancy taking effect in September will save seven-twelfths of an annual salary in the financial year in which the saving has to be made: one that takes effect in January will save only three-twelfths. Because schools are required to balance their budget year by year and are not allowed to budget for a deficit, this means that the level of redundancy has to be greater than would be necessary if the school was able to take account of projected savings in the following financial year. Schools with accumulated reserves can use these to cushion the effect of redundancy with a view to recouping in the next year, but this will not help a school with reducing rolls, since the effect of roll reductions is cumulative as the smaller year sizes work their way through the school.

The Formal Process

Once a school in its budget setting has decided that redundancies are necessary, it has to go through formal procedures. Community and VC schools will normally have adopted a procedure negotiated by the LEA with the unions. VA and VC schools should adopt a procedure that is workable within the resources available, bearing in mind that sufficient governors must be excluded from the process of selection for redundancy to allow for rights of appeal.

The principles behind making redundancies in schools are the same as elsewhere and can be summarised as follows:

- establish a policy;

- ensure that any criteria are objective ones;

- consult before making decisions. There may be a statutory requirement to consult with unions if there are to be many redundancies. That may not often happen to schools, but negotiated procedures will normally require consultation before specific posts are declared redundant irrespective of numbers. Union negotiators will often, quite properly and in the interests of their members, probe the reasons for proposed redundancies in great detail and at great length. They will use all means to avoid, or at least postpone, the operation of a redundancy, and schools should keep in mind that a duty to consult is just that and not a duty to reach agreement. Consultation is not just with union representatives but with the staff generally. One objective of negotiation is to see if redundancy can be avoided by redeployment, early retirement or natural wastage;

- be sure that there is a true redundancy, i.e. that there is no longer a need for the job in question. Removing a person in order to employ someone else who is cheaper, perhaps because of age or level of qualification, will rarely be sustainable as a redundancy;

- consider who has statutory protection. Generally speaking, only those who have been employed for two years or more will be entitled to redundancy pay or compensation for unfair selection for redundancy, and that may be a relevant consideration. This ties in also with the principle of 'last in, first out' discussed below;

- be fair and be dispassionate. Think of jobs, not people, when making a decision as to where a redundancy should fall.

Identifying the Redundant Staff

Redundancy procedures go through three stages:

- a decision that redundancy is necessary. This will normally be a governor decision following the setting of a budget where it is decided that savings cannot be made elsewhere;

- a decision as to where the redundancy is to fall. This, in terms of teaching staff, will involve an examination of the curriculum to see where there is over-provision or where least damage will be caused by a reduction in provision. At the same time as considering teacher redundancies, the possibility of a reduction in non-teaching staff will probably be investigated. The principle is the same, namely that functions and needs have to be considered rather than individuals. The identification of a post as redundant has to be an objective one and has to be seen to have been arrived at objectively;

- the identification of the individual to be made redundant. Redundancy procedures should have clear criteria for this and they should be objective where practicable. It is very common to operate a 'last in, first out' rule which has the merit of being clear and objective. It does, however, have the disadvantage that a young and promising teacher may be made redundant when a wider consideration would suggest that the school would benefit from a more senior person leaving. Schools that wish to avoid this will need a procedure that allows for a management assessment of staff within a particular curriculum area. This is fraught with difficulty. It is not easy to establish objective criteria for selection, and an unfair selection for redundancy is an unfair dismissal. Schools should not try to use redundancy as a means of dismissing staff who are considered ineffective. Competency procedures should be invoked in such cases. This applies to non-teaching staff just as to teachers.

Giving the Redundancy Notice

Once a person has been identified as redundant, notice has to be given. In the case of community and VC schools, it will be given by the LEA at the request of the school when the procedures, including any appeal to governors, are complete. In the case of VA and foundation schools, notice will be given by or on behalf of the governors. The decision will be taken by the person delegated with the responsibility as with any dismissal. There is a right of appeal against such a decision to a committee of at least three governors, and the decision cannot be implemented until the appeal has been heard or (if no appeal is lodged) the time for appealing has expired. This needs to be kept in mind in calculating a timetable based on a date for the giving of notice. It is easy for schools to find themselves short of time with the result that the effective termination date is a term later than anticipated. This can have serious budget implications, as indicated earlier.

WHISTLEBLOWING

Under the Public Interest Disclosure Act 1998, employees who report malpractice or unlawful activities at work are now protected from disciplinary sanctions taken as a result of that reporting. To be protected, the report must (in general terms):

- show an action (or an anticipated action) which is (or may be) a criminal offence, failure to comply with legal obligations, a miscarriage of justice, a danger to an individual's health or safety or prejudicial to the environment;

- be as a result of a reasonable belief that what is reported did happen;

- be made in good faith;

- be made to the employer, the reporting person's lawyer (in which case the requirement of good faith does not apply) or to a number of other people holding public office specified in regulations.

An employee who is dismissed as a result of a report that is protected by the public disclosure legislation will be entitled to enhanced compensation.

TRANSFER OF UNDERTAKINGS

When a business changes hands, there is said to be a transfer of an undertaking. The Transfer of Undertakings (Protection of Employment) Regulations 1981 (TUPE) provide, very broadly, that when a business is transferred the new owner of the business has to honour all existing employment contracts and the employees have continuity of employment. Schools will not normally be affected by this, but areas that could be affected are cleaning and school meals. A school taking over a cleaning or meals service from an LEA or an outside contractor will be treated as having taken over a continuing business and having become liable for the existing employees. If the school refuses to take on an employee, that person will have a claim for unfair dismissal, subject to having been employed for one year. It is also not possible to avoid the problem by insisting on the original employer giving notice, but it is permitted for a contract to require that the original employer keeps the new employer indemnified against the cost of claims if the new employer decides to dismiss some or all of the old staff. This is good protection for a school taking over a contract, but if the school is handing over to an outside contractor, the boot will be on the other foot and schools must look carefully at the small print of any such contract.

RELEVANT GUIDANCE

Teachers' Qualifications

Extending Fitness and Qualifications and Barring Checks to Agency Teachers and Volunteers (DfES, July 1998).

Circular 4/98, 'Requirements for Courses of Initial Teacher Training'.

Circular 5/99, 'The Induction Period for Newly Qualified Teachers'.

Teachers' Pay and Conditions

'School Teachers' Pay and Conditions of Employment' (Guidance issued annually).

Disability Discrimination

Circular 3/97, 'What the Disability Discrimination Act 1995 Means for Schools and Local Education Authorities'.

Performance Management

DfES Guidance 59/2000, 'Performance Management: Guidance for Governors'.

DfES Guidance 0051/2000, 'Performance Management in Schools'.

Redundancy Payments and Premature Retirement

Circular 7/89, 'The Teachers (Compensation for Redundancy and Premature Retirement) Regulations 1989'.

Supply Teachers

Circular 7/96, 'The Use of Supply Teachers'.

Sickness

Circular 4/99, 'Physical and Mental Fitness to Teach of Teachers and of Entrants to Initial Teacher Training'.

Procedures

School Staffing (England) Regulations 2003 and DfES staffing guidance.

National Workload Agreement

DfES Guidance: Resource Pack dealing with the implementation of the National Workload Agreement including statutory Guidance accompanying the Section 133 Regulations issued under the Education Act 2002 and Guidance For Schools On Higher Level Teaching Assistant Roles For School Support Staff.

Information Pack for Governors on Workforce Remodelling.

Chapter 10

MANAGING THE BUDGET

*Governing bodies' financial responsibilities – Budgeting – Borrowing – Charging
– Taxation – Relevant guidance*

GOVERNING BODIES' FINANCIAL RESPONSIBILITIES

Governing bodies of all maintained schools with delegated budgets
have a statutory responsibility to oversee the financial management
of their schools. Their main responsibilities include:

- fixing the school's budget (in accordance with the SIP and
  statutory curriculum requirements);

- keeping accurate records;

- providing regular accounts/returns of income and expenditure for
  the relevant authorities;

- complying with any competitive tendering requirements;

- accounting for any earmarked expenditure which may have
  been delegated;

- exercising appropriate monitoring and control, and not
  planning to overspend.

They may choose to delegate various aspects of the practical
implementation of their policy decisions to formally constituted
committees and/or to the headteacher concerned, but must retain
the residual responsibility.

It is worth noting that governors are expected to carry out their
responsibilities in good faith. As they are a corporate entity, if they
do this they will not incur any personal liability in the exercise of
their power to spend the school's delegated budget as they see fit.
They may also be reassured to know that, whilst fraudulent acts
would always be regarded as a breach of good faith, failure to
observe all the requirements of a scheme or to abide by any advice
the LEA may have given in respect of financial management would
not.

Accountability

Governing bodies are obliged to comply with the financial regulations (and the notes of advice and Guidance that stem from them) specified in their authority's local management scheme and the standing orders of the local council.

All schools are expected to produce their accounts on request for audit purposes and to ensure that they exercise a proper stewardship of the public funds under their control. Schools are audited internally by their authority, but will also have to submit their accounts periodically to the additional scrutiny of external auditors, appointed by the Audit Commission for LEAs generally. The specific remit of the external auditors is to ensure that financial transactions involving public money are carried out, both by schools and by authorities, with due regard for probity and legality, and that appropriate consideration has been given to securing value for money. Under the new arrangements, a school may also appoint its own external auditors to certify its accounts, but it would have to pay for the costs of this service from its delegated budget.

Governing bodies should give their formal imprimatur to any unofficial or private fund before it is opened and should monitor the operation of any such fund once it has been started to ensure that it satisfies the requirements of HM Customs and Excise, the Inland Revenue, and the Charity Commissioners. Voluntary and Foundation schools may, moreover, be under a duty to arrange for such funds to be properly audited in order to meet charity law requirement. Schools are required to include private funds in their statutory return to the LEA but, at least at the moment, the DfES view on private funds is that the LEA should not seek to audit the funds or to have access to the accounts of the fund. The LEA should only intervene if any audit certificate required under the LEA financial scheme is not provided.

Schools are also liable to an inspection of their efficiency, as far as the management of the resources allocated to them is concerned, under the arrangements outlined in the *Framework for the Inspection of Schools*. The inspectors' basic premise is that:

> 'schools are accountable for balancing costs (in terms of economy and efficiency) and effectiveness (in terms of their performance and the quality of what they provide) as required by the best value framework.'

To achieve this, schools need to demonstrate that they apply best value principles in arriving at decisions about all their activities, especially how the financial resources delegated to them are managed. The best value framework covers four principles: compare, challenge, consult, compete. Examples of the ways in which these principles apply to schools can be found in the *Handbook for Inspection of Schools*.

Standards of Financial Administration

General advice on financial control and monitoring is provided for all schools in the important joint Audit Commission/OFSTED publication *Keeping Your Balance* and in the detailed budgetary requirements to be found in all authorities' schemes of financial delegation, and in any explanatory Guidance that may thereby have been issued.

Keeping Your Balance outlines the key standards of financial administration under 12 different headings and contains a very useful checklist for each of these headings in its appendix. A summary of these standards is reproduced below for ease of access (and some are dealt with in greater detail subsequently), but the reader is urged to delve further and to become acquainted with the full text.

(1) The responsibilities of the governing body, its committees, the headteacher and the staff should be clearly defined and limits of delegated authority established.

(2) The budget should reflect the school's prioritised educational objectives, should seek to achieve value for money and should be subject to regular, effective monitoring.

(3) The school should establish sound internal financial controls to ensure the reliability and accuracy of its financial transactions.

(4) The school should be adequately insured against exposure to risks.

(5) If the school uses computers for administrative purposes, it should be registered under the Data Protection Act 1998. All data should be protected against loss.

(6) The school should ensure that purchasing arrangements achieve the best value for money.

(7) There should be efficient procedures for the administration of personnel matters, including the payroll where this applies.

(8) Stocks, stores and other assets should be recorded, and adequately safeguarded against loss or theft.

(9)   All income due to the school should be identified and all collections should be receipted, recorded and banked promptly.

(10)   The school should properly control the operation of bank accounts and reconcile bank balances with the accounting records.

(11)   The school should control the use of petty cash.

(12)   School voluntary funds should be administered as rigorously as public funds.

Role Definition

Governors should ensure that every member of staff involved in the financial management of the school is issued with a precise definition of his or her fundamental responsibilities and a clear job description. This will not only avert duplication (or inadvertent omissions), but will establish a proper framework of accountability within the overall organisation of the school. If key people are absent, moreover, it is far easier to pick up the reins and to carry out their functions against such a background. Care, however, should be taken not to place too heavy a dependence on a single individual's technical knowledge, skills and expertise, both to foster succession planning and to avoid problems following a serious illness or departure, by making provision for some form of shadow structure (i.e. whereby members of staff are familiar with a colleague's responsibilities and may even undertake them for short periods of time).

The terms of reference of governors' committees should also be defined. Their specific responsibilities, for example, and delegated powers of decision-making should be clearly spelled out and formally recorded in the minutes of the meeting at which they were determined, both as a protection for the individual governors concerned and to remove the possibility of any future misunderstanding (and of any souring of relationships that might ensue as a result). The same principle holds good in the case of executive powers which may be delegated to the headteacher to facilitate day-to-day running of the school. The authority for switching expenditure from one budget heading to another ('virement') for both the finance committee and the headteacher should also be clearly set out (indeed, under Fair Funding, LEAs usually require formal notice to be given of any deviations from financial information previously presented to them).

Internal Controls

Properly documented procedures covering all aspects of a school's financial *modus operandi* should be readily available and should be the subject of regular review. Strict adherence to the procedures (conveniently brought together in a financial manual) should be demanded and staff to whom they apply should be carefully monitored to safeguard the school's assets and to reduce the risk of error or fraud.

Segregation of duties is an extremely important dimension of procedure and control. The essential principle behind this is that the same person should not be able to initiate, record and process a complete transaction; if at least two people are involved, one is in a position to check on the work of the other. Any system, of course, is capable of subversion, but if duties are appropriately segregated, any transgression or illegality would require collusion.

The main functions which should be segregated (and it is acknowledged that not all schools may be in a position to do this) are:

- authorisation;
- execution;
- recording.

For example, a budget-holder (a head of department) authorises a purchase order, which is placed by the finance officer with the external supplier and a copy of the order retained. When the goods arrive, they are checked by an appropriate designated member of staff and the invoice is passed for payment; the cheque for payment is prepared by the finance officer and signed by one of the official signatories. In this instance, the finance officer has executed and recorded the order, the goods have been checked by someone other than the person who authorised it and another party has executed payment. Where difficulties arise, e.g. in the case of small schools or departments that consist of only one person, all reasonable precautions should still be taken (although other measures of control will assume greater importance).

Particular care should be exercised in the following areas.

(1)   Payroll

Where this is administered by a bureau or an LEA on behalf of a school, the final responsibility for accurate returns remains with the governing body. Payments should be made only:

- to *bona fide* employees;
- in accordance with the relevant pay-scales and conditions of employment;
- for services rendered.

Deductions, e.g. for income tax, NI and superannuation (which are statutory responsibilities), should be properly processed and the requisite forms, e.g. TR17A, P9D/P11D, P35, P14/P60, returned by the due dates. Alterations to payroll, for example an increase in a teacher's salary following the award of an additional responsibility point, must be authorised by a different person from the one who has prepared the alteration and never by the recipient of the award. Such alterations are normally effected by the headteacher on behalf of the governors, but any adjustments to the headteacher's own pay must be authorised by, for example, the chair of governors or the chair of the finance committee. When processing payments to individuals who purport to be a company or a sole trader (i.e. a person who should not be treated as an employee), schools are authorised to pay invoices by cheque (usually in the name of the company). They can be reasonably sure of this being *bona fide* when:

- the contractor supplies his own materials, transport and equipment;
- the contractor has organised his own public liability insurance;
- the invoice presented gives the appropriate details of the organisation in question (including the VAT number, if this is applicable), itemising the work carried out and the charge being levied.

It should be noted that in this context only the labour costs are liable to income tax/NI deductions. Otherwise, all payments to individuals in their own names should be made through the usual payroll channels, except in the case of external training providers or peripatetic music teachers, who can be regarded as self-employed if they so wish and, therefore, may be paid gross, without any deductions, by cheque.

(2) Banking

Where a school has its own cheque-book, limits should be imposed on the number of authorised signatories (four would normally suffice) and the maximum amount payable on a single transaction. A proper balance, however, needs to be maintained between operational efficiency and financial security, and the model outlined below might be regarded as a reasonable compromise for practical purposes:

- up to £100: one signatory;

- £100 to £5000: two signatories;

- £5000 and over: two signatories, one of whom must be the chair of governors or the chair of the finance committee.

Blank cheques should not be signed under any circumstances. Specimen signatures should be registered on the appropriate forms and lodged with the bank. The governing body should also instruct the bank that the school cannot be overdrawn. Statements should be obtained monthly and reconciled with the school's own records. Any discrepancies should be investigated promptly (and reported to the governing body if they are more than clerical errors). Cheque-books and paying-in books should be ordered by post and kept securely in a locked cabinet when not in use. Banking arrangements should be reviewed regularly, e.g. at two-year intervals, or at times specified in the LEA's scheme of financial delegation.

It will usually be financially advantageous for schools to bank with the LEA's nominated/contracted bankers. If a governing body opts to use a different (but approved) bank or building society and has its budget share paid into this account (e.g. in 12 monthly instalments), the school should expect to have to compensate the authority for the loss of interest it has incurred as a result (for the early release of the funds in question).

(3) Cash

Pre-numbered, sequential receipts should be used for miscellaneous cash income, which can be reconciled independently with the actual sums collected, and detailed accounts should be kept by those responsible, e.g. for school trips. This, however, will pose problems for schools when very small amounts are brought in, e.g. for charity. The same person should not be responsible for the collection and recording of money received and any payments against such income should be authorised and processed by a third party. The encashment of personal cheques either on the school accounts or from petty cash should be prohibited. Cash income, not exceeding the limit prescribed by the school's insurers, should be stored securely in the safe (and not in offices around the school, as this will give rise to a personal liability in the event of losses) and banked promptly. In regard to petty cash:

- payments should be made only on the production of the appropriate receipts, vouchers etc;

- full records of authorised payments should be kept and regular reconciliations (and spot checks) undertaken;

- payments should be restricted to duly authorised and relatively minor items which can be accommodated within a budget-holder's existing balance;

- the amount kept on the premises should be small, but compatible with operational needs for ready access.

(4)   *Other Internal Controls*

Many additional controls are usually operative in schools. When the governing body sets its budget for a given year, it is aware of both the major areas of expenditure and the breakdown of these areas into their various components or sub-headings, and exercises its control at the outset. Budget-holders appreciate that they are only authorised to spend within prescribed limits and it is a relatively easy matter to ensure that they keep within the bounds specified. Any provisional order, for example, can be checked as a commitment against an existing balance in the finance office and should only be allowed to go ahead if sufficient funds are available to cover it (unauthorised telephone orders should not be permitted). Budget-holders, moreover, are normally required to submit details of their expenditure needs in advance so that relative priorities (in keeping with the school development plan) can be suitably assessed when the budget is being set. Orders can, therefore, be checked against the items of expenditure that have been sanctioned and spot checks carried out periodically on, for example, departmental inventories. This would be particularly appropriate in the case of error-prone or high-value items. Furthermore, a clear 'audit trail' should be discernible for every transaction (e.g. it should be possible to trace a copy order via the invoice, the delivery note and the record of expenditure in the accounts, through to payment by a cheque, and vice versa).

Security

On a macro-level, school security will depend on, for example, whether schools have a resident caretaker or not, the vulnerability of the site, the prevailing incidence of vandalism and where they are located. Schools can face enormous difficulties in respect of the security of their premises and the ease with which intruders can gain access, but they have a duty to take all reasonable precautions.

On a lesser scale, schools are under a duty to look after goods and other items which have been purchased with public money and to safeguard their assets generally. All staff should be encouraged to be security conscious as a matter of course, and systematic risk assessments should be undertaken annually. Governors, moreover, should ensure that a number of specific danger-spots (in addition to those already mentioned under other headings) are properly covered. For example:

- all attractive and portable items should be clearly and indelibly marked with a customised brand (and a note taken of their make, model and serial number) and securely locked away (preferably in an alarmed area) when not in use;

- a central register should be compiled for all assets, including details of the purchase price, date of purchase and location, and this should be regularly updated to take account of new purchases. Most schools are likely to start with a considerable backlog of unrecorded items and will not relish the prospect of undertaking such a mammoth task, but it must be done and senior staff should carry out physical checks of, for example, departments' assets against their inventories or stockbooks from time to time. It is essential for such 'local' records to be kept until all the relevant information is known to have been transferred to the central assets register. Software packages, thankfully, are now available which will automatically process items entered at the ordering or commitment stage onto the central register, once it is confirmed that the goods have arrived. In the case of fixed assets, it might be sensible to record on a fixed assets register details of all such purchases, including the date of acquisition, serial number, cost, depreciation and location. Schools are at liberty to determine the value at which an item should be regarded as a fixed asset (a figure of £250–£500 would not be unreasonable), except where the value has been specified in their LEA's scheme of delegation;

- a register of pecuniary interests should be drawn up to reduce the scope for 'insider dealing' and self-aggrandisement on the part of those in a position of trust. This should cover all governors and members of staff who have financial responsibilities. Where governors or staff are present at, for example, a committee meeting, when any matter is being discussed in which they have a vested interest, they should declare that interest and offer to withdraw from the meeting for the duration of that discussion. If they are allowed to stay, they should not vote or participate in any decisions that may be made;

- when it is impossible for goods to be properly examined on receipt, the person who accepts delivery, e.g. the caretaker, should sign to that effect on the delivery note (e.g. 'unseen' or 'unchecked/ unopened');

- a list of all key-holders should be maintained and any losses reported immediately to the headteacher. Staff who leave the school must hand over all the keys in their possession on their last day of work;

- all authorised users of a school's computer system should be given instructions on how to access workstations and should be assigned individual passwords. These passwords must be regarded as strictly confidential and must not be revealed to another person (thereby permitting 'illicit' access to the system). Passwords should be changed regularly (at least every six months). Backup disks should be made on a daily basis and stored securely in different locations; if three copies are produced, one of these should be kept off-site. Schools should ensure that they are registered under the Data Protection Act 1998 and should comply with the data protection principles;

- clear procedures should be established for the disposal of assets. The Secretary of State has stipulated that schools should be able to retain the amounts raised from the sale of assets, except where they were bought with non-delegated funds (in which case it would be a matter for the LEA to determine) or the asset in question is land or buildings (which constitute part of the school premises) and are owned by the LEA;

- the LEA's financial delegation provisions should also be applied in respect of:

- *ex-gratia* payments;
- the writing-off of losses (including bad debts);
- gifts; and
- the governors' allowance scheme.

Schools must, similarly, abide by their authority's financial regulations and/or any conditions laid down by their trustees in respect of capital-related items. They should, moreover, have a clear policy on bad debts and the extent to which these will be pursued above or below a certain limit. For example, a school with a bad debt of £200 could decide to drop the matter, after sending out several reminders, on the grounds that it was not cost effective to take any legal action to recover the amount in question. In regard to lettings, it is advisable to require new hirers to pay for the use of the facilities in advance to reduce such risks; when their *bona fide* nature has been established, a different approach may be adopted. In respect of the writing-off of losses, the governing body should specify the limit above which its official approval is needed. The headteacher should authorise any write-offs below this level, and adjust the central assets register or budget-holders' inventories accordingly. In addition:

- when members of staff, for perfectly legitimate reasons, take expensive items of equipment off-site, they should make sure that the items are insured and record the details formally in a book kept for this purpose. They should also sign the book when the items are returned;

- excessive, over-generous entertaining, for whatever reason, should be avoided as an unnecessary drain on public funds;

- care should be taken that a school does not hold too much stock (e.g. exercise books) that is not required for immediate use, thereby tying up resources which could be beneficially deployed elsewhere (or earning interest);

- all the usual risks in regard to personnel and assets should be properly covered by insurance. Schools should also consider whether it is worth paying additional premiums to insure items or risks that are not normally included in, for example, their LEA's policies.

BUDGETING

A budget is merely a costing of what a school wants to achieve – a tool for implementing its educational aims and priorities, as depicted in its school development plan (in the context of a longer-term three-year or five-year strategic plan). The concept of strategic planning often meets with some resistance in schools, because of the volatile nature of their year-on-year funding and on account of frequent shifts in central government policy, but most will, in any case, have a sound appreciation of prospective developments, even if these are not formally recorded in a single document. It is, however, good practice to undertake a thorough assessment of the future impact of certain trends on a school's financial position from time to time, and, if they are deemed significant, to incorporate any preparatory action plans that may have been formed into the SDP. For example:

- *Curriculum*. The introduction of new courses or alterations to the balance of the curriculum has cost implications for schools, particularly in terms of staffing and the management of human resources. (Have these been quantified? Where are the necessary savings going to come from? How will staff with a reduced teaching load be deployed?)

- *Pupil numbers*. The importance of pupil numbers cannot be overestimated, because so much of a school's 'income' is pupil-driven. Demographic patterns in the area of the school (which can be extremely wide in urban districts) and other critical factors should receive careful and regular consideration. Are new intake numbers stable, for instance, and, if they are, will they remain so? Are the school's main feeder primary schools experiencing any difficulties with recruitment (overall or in a given year group)? What percentage of its pupils does the school usually lose at 16+ (in the case of schools for 11- to 18-year-olds)? (Figures for the previous five years should be scrutinised.) Has the impact of competition (e.g. the presence of a flourishing sixth form or FE college in the immediate vicinity) or of the decision of a neighbouring school to become selective been appropriately assessed?

- *Maintenance*. Schools should undertake a survey of the condition of their premises, if they have not already done so, and develop, for example, a five-year rolling programme of essential maintenance, repairs and refurbishment (i.e. those governed by legal obligations) on the basis of clearly established priorities. The suitability survey for the school should form part of the asset management records and should inform that rolling programme.

- *Capital.* The state and suitability of existing accommodation should be the subject of a detailed analysis. If major capital investment is required, owing to a progressive increase in pupil numbers or curricular changes or the poor condition of the buildings, what measures has the school already taken in this direction? Have any avenues of funding other than the traditional ones been explored? For example, does the LEA have a project or needs involving other schools that might be the subject of an LEA PPP or PFI scheme?

- *Major decisions.* These Involve critical changes to the existing character of a school, e.g. the application for technology college status or becoming a fully or partially selective school instead of a comprehensive.

- The cost of Workforce Remodelling also needs to be considered. For example, there may be a need for more administrative staff in schools to pick up tasks formerly done by teachers There may also be areas of work that can be undertaken by support staff which may in the longer term lead to a reduction in the number of teachers that the school needs to employ.

It is obviously of critical importance to synchronise the planning process and the budget cycle. Councils fix their local tax rates at the end of March, and a final draft version of the school's plan and associated budget, suitably costed with alternatives, should have been produced by this time for the governing body's formal ratification and approval. The previous six to nine months should have been used for preparation: for holding internal meetings, involving individual governors, members of the curriculum committee and other interested groups; forming working parties to make recommendations on specific issues; and developing a professional consensus, generally, on the school's priorities, through the usual consultative channels. The initial draft budget should then be discussed in detail at a meeting of the finance committee and fine tuned. An illustration of a possible timetable is as follows:

Year 'X'	Year 'X'/'Y'	Year 'Y'	Year 'Y'
July/Sept	*Dec/Feb*	*Mar/Apr*	*Sept*
planning starts	draft school plan	school plan and budget fixed	school plan implemented
	council estimates	council budget set	

The essential point to note is that planning for a given academic year should start some 12 to 15 months beforehand and that a proper, workable schedule of meetings, etc, needs to be arranged, otherwise individuals and groups will be left to operate in isolation and their particular views or suggestions will not be able to influence the deliberations of others. During the period from July to November, moreover, a school will be engaged in evaluating its out-turn figures for the previous financial year, monitoring progress for the year in question and planning for the following financial and academic years.

Late notification of significant departures from what was anticipated or sudden reductions in funding year-on-year can obviously create serious difficulties; schools have to absorb the effect of such changes in the period from September to March, as they are already committed to the previous academic year's expenditure for the first five months of any financial year and have no scope whatsoever for instant manoeuvring. If schools do not receive details of their final budgets until after the beginning of a financial year (as sometimes happens), best estimates of income and expenditure will have to suffice *pro tem*.

When preparing their budgets, schools should aim to make full use of the historic data available to them and their known spending patterns, as a basis for accurate predictions of likely future expenditure. A unit cost comparison over a number of years would also pay dividends. Equity issues need to be given due consideration at this stage, for example whether all departments or all pupils are receiving a fair share of the school's resources (it should be remembered that governors are obliged to give an account in their annual report to parents of the way in which they have spent SEN funds).

Staffing costs, which account for over 80 per cent of schools' expenditure, warrant particular attention and the effects of incremental drift (teachers who have not reached point 6 on the main pay scale – the maximum allowed for 'qualifications' and 'experience' – cost more in September than they do in July, because of their progression up the scale by one point in the interim), for example, need to be carefully assessed. Any calculation errors in this area are almost irretrievable, because there is such little room for compensatory adjustments elsewhere in the budget. Additional allowances (for management responsibilities) do not have a bearing on incremental drift, except insofar as the cash value of an allowance is different at various points on the scale.

Schools, moreover, should be wary of appointing the maximum number of teachers which their budget will bear in a given year and of using the flexibility at their disposal in regard to discretionary pay awards too liberally, as they are likely to be storing up financial problems for themselves in the future. The previous movement of some governing bodies to reduce their ongoing, permanent commitments in respect of teaching staff, by putting a significant proportion of new appointments on temporary or short-term contracts, has effectively been nullified by the change in the employment protection legislation which means that protection arises after one year's service. Failure to renew a one-year contract will be a potentially unfair dismissal.

On another cautionary note, the assertion that schools will always benefit from the admission of additional pupils cannot be accepted without question. A few extra pupils, distributed evenly amongst different year groups, would certainly represent an increase in income at relatively little cost, but, in the case of a significant influx into a single year, which would necessitate the creation of additional teaching groups, the extra income might be far outweighed by the additional expenditure incurred. Governing bodies need to establish the break-even point on such transactions extremely carefully to avoid unwittingly losing out.

Governing bodies usually include a contingency element in their budgets to cover unforeseen expenditure that may arise during the course of the year and it is prudent to do so. It is impossible to specify an optimum figure and schools must judge for themselves, in the light of their experience and local circumstances, what constitutes a reasonable allocation. Too large an allocation, however, militates against the effective implementation of a school's priorities (and almost treats a prospective emergency as a reality from the outset). A figure in the region of 1 per cent of the budget should normally suffice.

Monitoring

A budget, it should be remembered, is not a one-off activity to be cast in tablets of stone annually, but a set of assumptions, formulated at a given time, which must be monitored carefully and reviewed at frequent intervals as the financial year unfolds. Initial checks (monthly, to coincide with bank statement reconciliations would seem sensible) should be carried out by the headteacher, both to verify the reliability of the data and to discern any unexpected trends. Particular attention should be given to payroll details, and the headteacher should be notified immediately by the finance office of any significant deviations from the 'norm'. Official returns, e.g. of income and expenditure, and cash-flow statements should be rigorously tested for accuracy. Profiled expenditure (i.e. expenditure that is allocated in accordance with seasonal fluctuations rather than uniformly throughout the year, for example examination fees or services such as gas and electricity) of its very nature requires more careful interpretation to ensure that low expenditure at any one time is not taken as indicative of the likely cost over the course of the year. Contracts should be monitored both in respect of expenditure and of standards of service provided.

More formal reviews of predicted expenditure against actual costs should be conducted by the finance committee of the governors (termly, quarterly or twice a term in accordance with individual schools' preferences and circumstances). It is particularly important that substantial variations, particularly in the first few months of a financial year, are investigated promptly and any necessary adjustments made to the budget. Those adjustments must be made so as to secure that the budget does not go into deficit after taking available and uncommitted reserves into account and as a matter of good practice should always be decided, or approved, by the finance committee. The chair of the finance committee should, again as a matter of good practice, meet regularly with the Bursar or finance officer to review budget performance. The headteacher should be part of this process but it should be seen as a way for the governing body to exercise a degree of independent monitoring.

If an adverse trend is confirmed, urgent remedial action will need to be taken, e.g. by reducing the volume or quantity of the particular item (in the event of an unexpected price increase) and/or by transferring money from an underspent budget heading to offset the deficit. The worst-case scenario, with which many schools have had to contend, is a significant reduction in funding, which can only be accommodated by making several members of staff redundant. If this occurs, it is vital that the correct procedures are followed, otherwise schools are in very real danger of incurring a massive deficit or overspend. Again, this will necessarily involve the governing body through, in the first instance, the finance committee.

Perhaps the most important aspect of monitoring (and the budgetary process) is evaluation. This will include an assessment of educational outcomes. Schools are much better placed than before to undertake evaluation in its broadest sense. The *Handbook for the Inspection of Schools*, for example, is an invaluable source of Guidance and advice in this context. Schools would benefit enormously from noting the criteria to which the inspectors have to pay due regard when forming their judgements, and applying the same criteria to themselves across the board as a matter of course (internal inspection).

Value for Money

Governing bodies should establish clear guidelines on how value for money (VFM) is to be secured in their schools and should lay down procedures to be followed scrupulously by all budget-holders. Budget-holders should be expected to demonstrate that they have tested the market and should keep accurate records (including details of the reasons why, for example, a particular supplier was given a contract), especially in the case of expensive transactions.

Strict tendering procedures, for example, should be observed and governing bodies will need to specify:

- the limit above which a tender must be sought for goods or services;
- the minimum number of tenders that must be received (and whether this should be on the basis of open or restricted tenders, i.e. whether all potential suppliers should be canvassed or just a few invited to submit a tender);
- the levels of delegated authority for making decisions.

The table below (provided as an example only) illustrates how these principles might be applied in practice. The suggested values should be kept under review in the light of inflation and the need to keep a balance between sound controls and the avoidance of excessive 'red tape'. In particular, a large school with a substantial budget might well increase the suggested levels overall by a third or more.

Estimated Cost	Procedure
Under £2,000	The budget-holder must undertake market research before proceeding.
Over £2,000 but not more than £6,000	The budget-holder should (where practicable) seek no fewer than three quotations before proceeding.
Over £6,000 but not more than £15,000	Three quotations must be obtained. The budget-holder must seek the approval of the governors' finance committee before proceeding.
Over £15,000	A tender board should be set up.

In preparing a tender, governors should ensure that the initial specifications are suitably precise and detailed (to avoid any scope for misunderstanding or sub-standard service) and that the same specifications are issued to all suppliers. The following items might reasonably be included in an invitation to tender:

- an introduction to the project;
- its scope and objectives;
- the implementation of the project;
- the terms and conditions of tender;
- the form of response required (and the date by which it must be submitted).

To avoid wasting the school's time and resources on fruitless enquiries, the governing body may wish to set a charge for the provision of the relevant documents. The evaluation of tenders should be conducted by the committee or group entrusted with the responsibility of processing the tenders (or by at least two people) against the predetermined criteria. A formal report of the evaluation process, and the basis of the recommendations made or decisions taken (depending on the powers delegated to the committee), should be produced. All the relevant documents should be retained for audit purposes, including the unsuccessful tenders, and the implementation of the project carefully monitored.

The tendering process for major expenditure should normally be handled by the professional consultant advising on the project. It is not a task for governors or for school personnel who are unlikely to have the time or the expertise for it. EC Regulations require that contracts over a specified threshold (approximately £150,000 for services and £3.75m for 'work') must be advertised in the *Official Journal of the European Communities* (OJEC) as part of the requirement that markets be open to the whole of Europe. The professional consultant will advise on this where appropriate and will allow for this process in the project timetable.

On a related tack, LEAs are obliged to include in their schemes an explicit reference to the disapplication of any section of their policies or procedures which would have the effect of requiring schools to:

- do anything that might contravene any of the schemes' provisions, or any statutory requirement, or any EC procurement directive;

- secure the countersignature of an LEA officer for any contract (whether for goods or services) for a value below £50,000 in any one year;

- only choose suppliers from an approved LEA list;

- seek fewer than three tenders for a contract worth more than £5,000 in any given year.

A list of approved suppliers should be drawn up, especially in the case of low-value items, so that precious time (and money) is not wasted on securing VFM on every single small-scale transaction. The list should be appended to a school's financial procedures and available in the finance office for consultation. The list should be reviewed every two to three years. Similarly, a list of suitable contractors, formally approved by the governing body, should be compiled. VFM will automatically be deemed to have been secured if any of those contractors on the list is asked to undertake, for example, relatively minor maintenance repairs, on the premises. This list, too, should be subject to regular review.

Some schools seek to achieve VFM by joining forces with their neighbours to form consortia. They are, consequently, able to buy various goods, services or utilities at a lower rate (because of the discounts negotiated) than would have been available to each of them individually. Generally, schools should be alert to all reasonable opportunities to secure savings so as to be able to demonstrate when audited by the LEA, or indeed by the National

Audit Office, that they have discharged their responsibility to apply delegated funds prudently.

An operating lease or rental agreement might represent good value for money under certain circumstances, particularly if a school does not have sufficient resources at its disposal for a major capital outlay on, for example, a computer network. Service charges are normally incorporated into the monthly repayments and, if new models appear, the school will be able to upgrade its hardware relatively quickly. Finance lease agreements or hire purchase contracts are prohibited and schools need to be sure that any proposed finance method is permitted. Salesmen often do not appreciate the restrictions imposed on schools and advice should be taken if there is any doubt.

BORROWING

Borrowing is not a matter to be taken lightly and it is likely that many schools will be deterred from embarking on such a course of action by the bureaucratic and administrative burdens involved in the application process and because of the unstable and volatile nature of revenue-funding in the current climate. For some, however, it may represent the only means of achieving a vital objective and, as such, would warrant serious consideration. In any case, governing bodies need to be aware that they may borrow monies only with the express written permission and approval of the Secretary of State. The legislation does allow the Secretary of State to delegate approval to the LEA but this has not been implemented. Indeed, the current Guidance from DfES to LEAs on schemes for financing schools requires the LEA to draw attention to governing bodies of the need to obtain consent from the Secretary of State. There are two exceptions to this. The first relates to licensed budget deficits which, although in many ways might be regarded as borrowing, are not treated as such and are to be dealt with by specific provision within the LEA scheme. The second relates to assistance given by a foundation body or trustees for a school which may take the form of borrowing even with an interest charge without the need to get consent. The only proviso is that any interest or other charge made for the facility may not be met out of the delegated budget. By contrast, the Guidance says that schemes may explicitly bar the use of credit cards as these are regarded as borrowing. By contrast, debit cards are permitted as a useful means of facilitating electronic purchases.

The Government is, however, keen to maximise the use of schools' surplus balances by the introduction of loan schemes and LEAs must provide details of how these might operate in their schemes of financial delegation. The precise arrangements will vary between authorities, but the following terms and conditions will normally be specified:

- the maximum period for repayment (e.g. five years);

- the purpose of the advance (usually for a major, durable asset that is likely to produce a long-term benefit for the school);

- the maximum and minimum amounts involved (e.g. not below £20,000 or above £100,000 – this may also be expressed as a percentage of the school's budget share at the time of the application);

- the calculation of the interest payable.

Before granting a loan, an authority will want to be satisfied that the borrower's financial position is secure and that the school is able to meet the projected repayments from its annual income. LEAs will also usually stipulate the percentage of the total schools' balances that may be used for loan purposes in any given financial year.

CHARGING

The charging provisions of the Education Act 1996 apply to all maintained schools, including sixth form colleges and special and nursery schools.

Prohibited Charges

The underlying principle is that education should be free of charge if it takes place wholly or mainly within school hours, i.e. the hours a school is in session, not counting the mid-day break, and that charging is, therefore, illegal unless it comes within certain permitted exceptions. There is a total prohibition on charging for:

- admission to a maintained school;

- the National Curriculum;

- anything required as part of the syllabus for a prescribed public examination, such as GCSE, GNVQ, AVCE, AS and A2 Level;

- examination entry fees, in the case of public examinations for which registered pupils are being prepared at the school. Schools and LEAs can, however, recover examination fees where a pupil fails 'without good reason' to meet the relevant examination requirements. There is no definition of what constitutes good reason, but schools and LEAs must act reasonably. Schools may, however, pass on the costs of private entries or the charges made by examination boards for a re-scrutiny of results to parents (if this has been requested by them);

- religious education;

- the provision of books, equipment (excluding clothing, but including, for example, safety glasses), materials or transport in relation to any activity that cannot itself be charged for. It is, however, lawful to charge for the supply of materials or ingredients, where the parents have expressed in advance a wish to keep the finished product. The costs of travelling to and from home when pupils are on work experience would normally be met by their parents;

- non-residential school trips and visits that take place substantially (50 per cent or more) within school hours. A contribution towards the costs may be requested, but it must be made clear to parents that they are under no obligation to contribute. No pupil may be excluded from such a trip because his or her parents have not contributed. If a particular trip is dependent on voluntary funding and insufficient funds are raised, the trip will have to be cancelled or the school must find the shortfall from its own resources. There is, however, nothing to prevent schools from notifying parents that such trips can only go ahead if sufficient income is generated.

Permissible Charges

Charging is permitted for:

- instrumental music tuition (other than that required by the National Curriculum) individually or in groups of up to four. Vocal/singing tuition, on an individual or a group basis, must, however, be provided free of charge;

- residential school trips (one or more nights away) under certain circumstances. The duration of a trip is divided into half days. A half day is 12 hours from midnight or noon as the case may be. If at least six hours of a half day are spent on a trip, that half day counts as part of the trip. If the number of school sessions missed is less than 50 per cent of the number of half days spent on a trip, the trip is deemed to take place outside school hours and a charge can be made for the full trip. A trip, for example, that starts at noon on Wednesday and finishes at 10 pm on Sunday, i.e. nine half days, including five school sessions, would be regarded as taking place within school hours, but one starting at noon on Thursday and finishing at 10 pm on Sunday, i.e. seven half days, including three school sessions, would not. The board and lodging element of a residential trip may also be charged for, irrespective of whether the trip is deemed to have occurred within school hours or whether the trip is undertaken to fulfil the requirements of the National Curriculum or religious education or part of a prescribed syllabus;

- non-residential school trips, visits and activities where the majority of the time spent on the activity (including travelling time) falls outside school hours. Thus, a charge may be made for an evening theatre visit because it occurs outside school hours. A matinee performance, on the other hand, probably cannot be charged for, because most of the time involved will be within school hours: all a school can do is to request voluntary contributions. It should, however, be remembered that, if an external examination syllabus specifies a visit to a performance of a play, no charge can be levied for the visit, even if the performance takes place in the evening;

- 'optional extras' (activities which by definition take place outside school hours). Participation in such activities is dependent on parental choice. A charge (including board and lodging where relevant) may be made, but it must not exceed the actual cost of provision – and cannot include an element of subsidy for other pupils wishing to participate, but whose parents are unwilling, or unable, to make a contribution;

- the costs of damages, e.g. a broken window or a defaced or lost textbook, for which a pupil has been responsible.

LEAs and governing bodies must adopt a charging policy and keep it under review. This policy must outline the basis on which charges may be made and how they are to be remitted. A policy must provide for charges for board and lodging to be remitted in full for all pupils whose parents are in receipt of income support or family credit, in the case of an activity that relates to the National Curriculum or takes place wholly or mainly within school hours. Other charges may be remitted wholly or partially in line with the policy. Failure to have a charging policy, or having a policy that does not deal appropriately with remission, renders all charging and requests for voluntary contributions unlawful. Furthermore, all requests for voluntary contributions must make the voluntary nature of such contributions absolutely clear and must state that no pupil is to be disadvantaged by the unwillingness or inability of his or her parents to pay. A school's charging policy must also be published in its prospectus.

TAXATION

Value Added Tax

The law surrounding the operation of value added tax (VAT) is extremely complicated, and schools and governing bodies should seek professional advice promptly, if they are in doubt, both to maximise potential tax benefits and to avoid incurring unnecessary expenditure. Stiff financial penalties may be imposed in cases of default or non-compliance, and ignorance of the law, it should be remembered, cannot be used in mitigation or as an excuse for failure to observe legal responsibilities. Several accountancy firms now offer 'consortium' services, whereby they negotiate with HM Customs and Excise on behalf of all participating schools in a group and charge a fee of some 20 per cent on any repayment received in respect of previous purchases on which VAT was incorrectly charged.

VAT is a consumption tax levied on designated goods and supplies, currently at the rate of 17.5 per cent (although some items are zero-rated). Schools are required to charge VAT on taxable supplies if the value of these supplies exceeds the prevailing VAT threshold, (£58,000 in the financial year 2004/2005), and to register formally with HM Customs and Excise (the de-registration threshold is £56,000). Payment of VAT to HM Customs and Excise should be made on a quarterly basis and proper records of sales, supplies and purchases maintained (and kept for a period of six years).

Schools should not consider registration just to be 'on the safe side', if their turnover from all relevant income does not breach the VAT threshold, because of the considerable additional administrative burdens and paperwork entailed, even though they would thereby be able to recover some of the VAT which they have had to pay. They would consequently either have to add VAT to any charges made for a taxable supply – thereby increasing costs to the consumer – or account for VAT out of the charge made and thus suffer a reduction in income. Governing bodies are, however, obliged to monitor their total income from any 'taxable supplies' provided in the previous 12 months and the anticipated total in the following 30 days and should ensure that appropriate procedures and financial controls are in place for regular checks.

Education, however, is an 'exempt' supply, and most schools are unlikely to be required to register for VAT purposes. The exemption also covers supplies that are classified as incidental to a school's supply of education, although closely related to it.

The Scope and Application of VAT

What follows is not intended to serve as an exhaustive list, but to provide broad guidelines on various sources of income derived from the wide range of 'activities' usually offered by schools, although it must be emphasised that concerns on specific issues should be referred to suitable experts in the field.

- *Grants.* Funding received through authorities' delegation schemes is exempt.

- *Sponsorship.* This is not normally subject to VAT, provided that only a small acknowledgement, for example in the programme of a play or in the school magazine, is recorded of the sponsor's contribution. If, however, the sponsor receives some tangible, promotional benefits in return, for example advertising, display of logo, free tickets or access to facilities without charge, then the amount involved is subject to VAT. The same principle applies in the case of cash donations, but where goods or equipment are provided by a VAT-registered donor, the gifts attract VAT, even if there are no strings attached.

- *Catering.* The provision of school meals for pupils is exempt, on the grounds that it is incidental to the supply of education. Care needs to be exercised, however, when a contractor is employed for this purpose: if the contractor acts as 'principal', then the meals are standard-rated and the caterer is liable to pay VAT on the supply; if the contractor is acting as an agent of the school, the meals are not subject to VAT. In this case, however, a management fee is charged for the operation of the meals service which itself attracts VAT – although, if the fee is absorbed in the discount given on the goods purchased on behalf of the school, the VAT is no longer payable. When a school provides meals to, for example, staff, governors, guests or visitors in an area which caters mainly for pupils, and the supplies to such adults cannot be readily identified, it would not normally have to pay VAT on the service. If, however, the same facility is offered in a separate dining room or canteen or at a different price or from a discrete menu, then the supply is subject to VAT. Where taxable foods which do not constitute part of an exempt meal, for example soft drinks, ice-cream or crisps, are sold in a school shop, for instance, or from a vending machine, they are liable to VAT at the standard rate, as are alcoholic drinks (even when served with an exempt meal) and catering supplies at school dances or other similar functions.

- *School trips*. Supervised excursions undertaken for educational purposes, for example field trips which are clearly related to the curriculum, are exempt. All other trips, for example ski trips or a pilgrimage to Lourdes, are standard-rated. It should, however, be noted that when a school is merely acting as an agent for its pupils in its dealings with a travel company, the service provided is not subject to VAT (many LEAs have now introduced specific provisions covering school trips in their LMS schemes). Under the Tour Operators' Margin Scheme, moreover, if a school arranges a holiday for its pupils as 'principal', it is only the profit that is made on the transaction that is liable to VAT. Money that is collected by a school and held on the pupils' behalf (in trust, as it were) does not qualify for VAT.

- *Lettings*. Income from the letting of halls, classrooms etc for an educational activity is exempt from VAT. The hire of facilities, however, particularly sports halls etc, is regarded as a taxable supply, although even this service may be free of VAT if the following conditions apply:

   - the facilities are used for political or religious meetings;

- the facilities are let to the same hirer for a continuous period of use exceeding 24 hours;

- the facilities are let to another school, club or association for a series of 10 or more sessions for the exclusive use of the hirer and: (1) each session involves the same activity in the same place; (2) the interval between sessions is at least one day and not more than 14 days; (3) the series is paid for as a whole (i.e. the income is guaranteed whether or not the facilities are used on a particular occasion) and there is written evidence to that effect.

If a school, moreover, provides a service that is incidental to education, such as catering, to a third party which is supplying VAT-exempt education on its premises, any charges levied are exempt from VAT.

- *One-off events.* VAT exemption is available for one-off fund-raising functions, such as fêtes, jumble sales and bazaars, where the funds are being raised by a charity for the purpose of that charity. It will normally be required that such events:

  - take place within the compass of a single day (or for a single admission fee, if they are spread over a weekend); and

  - are fairly well spaced out over the course of a year; and

  - are part of a regular annual cycle.

- *Gift Aid.* Gift Aid payments to a school, even if they are regular payments from the same donor, do not count for VAT purposes.

- *Materials.* Educational materials (such as pens, ink, exercise books, drawing or art materials, mathematical instruments and materials used in craft lessons) which are sold to pupils in class, at or below cost price, are exempt. The exemption does not extend to the sale of the same items in a school shop.

- *Car-boot sale pitches/market stalls.* The rental from spaces provided for stallholders at car-boot sales is exempt, on the basis of a licence to occupy land which is an exempt supply, on condition that the area occupied is clearly marked out for the duration of the letting and reserved for the hirer's exclusive use. When stallholders can set up their pitch wherever they wish, the standard rate applies.

- *Building work.* New buildings (including extensions) that are to be used solely for educational purposes may be zero-rated (HM Customs and Excise often turn a blind eye to lettings in this context, provided that they do not account for more than 10 per cent of the time that the building in question is available for use) on condition that the school issues a certificate to the contractor before any work on the building begins, stating that it will be used for charitable purposes and should accordingly be zero-rated. If, however, the prime purpose of the building is changed at any time (for up to 10 years) after its construction, the zero-rating may be forfeited, and a retrospective demand made for the additional tax due at the standard rate on the original costs. The zero-rating does not apply to the conversion, reconstruction, alteration or enlargement of an existing building, or to repairs and renovations.

- *Minibus sales.* Where a school has reclaimed VAT on the purchase of a minibus that is capable of carrying 12 or more passengers, it is liable to VAT at the standard rate on the total sale price as a taxable supply if it subsequently decides to sell it.

Income from the following items, in addition to those mentioned in the text, would normally attract VAT at the standard rate:

- school uniforms and sports kit (except where they qualify as children's wear and are zero-rated);

- school photographs (if the sale is for profit);

- advertisements in a school magazine or equivalent publication;

- admission charges for plays, discos and concerts, etc;

- tuck-shop sales or items sold in a school shop (except if the tuck shop is located within the school's dining hall);

- the provision of car-parking at special events;

- games machines and pool or snooker tables;

- telephone charges;

- private photocopying.

It should be noted in this context, that many LEAs are now requiring schools to levy a VAT charge on the activities listed above, even when the schools themselves do not qualify for VAT registration (presumably on the grounds that the LEA as a single entity does qualify and is consequently liable for the payment of VAT).

LEAs are able to reimburse schools which are maintained by them for VAT expenditure incurred on the purchase of educational goods and supplies, if these have been paid for through their general account.

A school will not be able to reclaim VAT on purchases made from private funds, unless the fund itself is registered separately for VAT. The same principle applies to PTA funds. However, if a PTA fund provides a school with money to purchase items that are paid for from its general account, the LEA can recover the VAT element in the normal way, to the benefit of the school and the PTA. The only drawback is that such items then become the property of the LEA. If a school has several private funds at its disposal, it should ensure that they are completely separate entities to avoid the risk of their cumulative income exceeding the VAT threshold.

After such a plethora of detail, it is perhaps worth recapping that the issue of charging VAT on taxable supplies only arises when the £54,000 limit has been exceeded and registration has become necessary. Schools that are not registered need not (and indeed must not) charge VAT on their supplies, except where this is required by the LEA's scheme of financial delegation.

Corporation Tax

Companies are liable to corporation tax on their profits. The term 'company' includes a corporate body and will, therefore, encompass schools and colleges. VA schools, however, are also charities and, as such, will generally be exempt from the provisions of corporation tax, provided that their income is applied purely for charitable purposes, i.e. for the education of their pupils. The exemption has, none the less, to be sanctioned by the Inland Revenue, and it is important for a school to secure the necessary dispensation by making a formal application to the Inland Revenue. (A letter, backed up by documentary evidence as proof of its charitable status and the date of incorporation, together with a copy of the annual accounts, will normally suffice.) An annual return, even if it is a 'nil' return, should also be made – although it is not uncommon for the Inland Revenue to grant a temporary dispensation from the requirement to submit annual returns for a fixed period or until a school's circumstances change. Any such change in circumstances must be reported promptly and a further dispensation sought, in any case, when the initial relief period comes to an end.

An exemption, however, is not all-pervasive in its coverage and only applies to income devoted to charitable purposes. Additional income raised by schools may come under the heading of 'trading activities' (defined as 'any trade, manufacture, adventure or concern in the nature of a trade') and thereby create a corporation tax liability. Schools, when assessing their corporation tax position, should take account of the following issues.

Charitable exemptions

VA, VC and foundation schools (including foundation special schools) are themselves charities. Community schools are not and if they wish to take advantage of charitable status including tax relief they need to form a charitable trust. This is dealt with in more detail in Chapter 15. All charities are exempt from tax in respect of:

- rental income;

- interest received;

- dividends;

- capital gains;

- covenanted income;

- trading income if:

  – the trading is conducted during the course of carrying out the prime purpose of the charity; or

  – the work is mainly undertaken by its beneficiaries;

- concessions such as jumble sales, bazaars, fêtes, firework displays and sporting events come within the purview of trading activities, but an exception may be allowed if:

  – they are not frequent;

  – they are not seen to be in competition with other traders;

  – the public is aware that the profits will go to the charity;

  – the profits are used for charitable purposes.

Problem areas

The main areas of difficulty (i.e. those which might be deemed to constitute trading activities) are likely to be:

- lettings, especially of sports facilities;

- sponsorship;

- advertising;

- tuck shops or school shops (particularly the sale of uniform, sports kit and equipment and confectionery items);

- adult education or evening classes and vacation courses;

- catering/vending machines;

- sales of goods (to staff, pupils, parents and/or the general public);

- hire of equipment (including the school minibus);

- photocopying or reprographic services.

Provided that schools keep within the permissible exemptions and do not make a profit, all should be well, but, even if a tax liability is established, ways in which it might be legitimately reduced should be explored as a matter of course. If, however, their profits are substantial and/or a liability cannot be avoided, schools may wish to consider setting up a separate limited trading company to run the relevant activities. A charitable trust (which would wholly own the trading company) could also be established. The advantage of a trading company is that taxable profits can be donated, under a deed of covenant or by way of Gift Aid, to the school (the parent charity) without having to pay tax at all (for further details, see Chapter 15).

RELEVANT GUIDANCE

Charging for School Activities

Circular 2/89, 'Charging for School Activities'.

Circular 2/94, 'Local Management of Schools', paras 147–151.

Chapter 11

PREMISES

Regulations relating to school premises – Who is responsible? – Delegated capital funding – Health and safety – Liability to visitors – Insurance – Ownership of school premises – Lettings – Building projects – Public private partnerships – Relevant guidance

REGULATIONS RELATING TO SCHOOL PREMISES

Premises are a major concern for all schools. Many schools still face backlogs of maintenance, frequently in buildings that are inadequate for the modern curriculum demands. Furthermore, increased expectations generally mean that standards which may have been acceptable even 25 years ago are now too low. In theory, until relatively recently, all schools had to comply with specific regulations relating to space, design and construction. In practice, as a result of years of underfunding, those regulations were often honoured in the breach and new, far less prescriptive, regulations were introduced in 1996 and modified as from 1999. However, as mentioned below, the DfES has its own parameters for assessing new capital projects and deciding on funding.

The only current school-specific standards relate to the following issues:

- *Washrooms and toilets for pupils and staff.* The facilities provided for pupils must include a number of toilets equal to the aggregate of 10 per cent of the number of pupils under five plus 5 per cent of the rest (rounded to the nearest whole number above). For special schools, the requirement is at least 10 per cent of the number of pupils. The number of washbasins provided by schools where the majority of pupils are 11 or over must be at least two-thirds of the required number of toilets (with a minimum of three). All other schools must have at least as many washbasins as the minimum number of toilets. Staff facilities must be separate from those for pupils, although disabled facilities may be shared, subject to certain safeguards designed to secure privacy.

- *Changing facilities* including showers for all pupils over the age of 11 receiving physical education.

- *A shower, bath or deep sink* for every 40 pupils in the school under the age of five.

- *Accommodation for medical or dental examination and treatment*: this must have a washbasin and be reasonably near a toilet.

- *Staff accommodation* must be provided for every school other than a PRU for work and for social purposes. There are no minimum space requirements but any school with more than 120 pupils and all nursery and special schools must have a separate room for the headteacher. There are no minimum requirements.

- *Ancillary facilities*. These must allow free access in common parts of the building, must provide for storing and drying pupils' outdoor clothing and storing their belongings, and must provide for food preparation and washing-up.

- *Boarding schools*. There are specific requirements for boarding schools setting out minimum sleeping accommodation, and other requirements which are similar, but with different numbers, to those for day schools.

- *Health and safety standards*. There are generalised requirements (including minimum standards) relating to structural safety, escape in case of fire, general health and safety standards, acoustics, lighting, heating, ventilation, water supplies, and drainage.

- *Sports facilities*. Minimum space requirements are laid down for team-game playing fields for schools for pupils of eight and over. A playing field is defined as an outdoor area (not necessarily all grassed) which is suitable for team games and is laid out for that purpose. The minimum space depends on the size of the school and its age range. The grassed area must be such as will sustain the playing of team games on it for seven hours a week during school terms. Where the school has other facilities for team games or swimming, whether in school or off-site, the minimum areas can be less if those facilities existed before 1 February 1999, meet the requirements of the 1996 Regulations, and have not been reduced. New or relocated schools will have to meet the minimum requirements for grassed areas without taking other facilities into account.

WHO IS RESPONSIBLE?

- There are detailed differences in how premises responsibility is dealt with according to the different types of schools. A few general principles apply to all schools managing their own budgets.

- The governing body is responsible for health and safety within the school.

- The governing body is responsible for the general repair and maintenance of the school premises.

- The use of premises outside school hours is under the control of the governing body.

- School premises can be used for community purposes and for non-school events, but the governing body may not use the main school budget to subsidise these.

- The governing body can enter into an agreement (known as a 'transfer of control agreement') with a third party to encourage community use. This, as the name suggests, involves transferring responsibility for the management and maintenance of part of the school premises to a third party as part of a shared-use arrangement. This would not normally apply to the main school premises but might well, for example, apply to a sports hall or swimming pool which could have substantial community use in the evenings and at weekends. A transfer of control agreement could be a crucial element in the development of such facilities on a school site where an investor, whether from the public or private sector, may require a degree of control. Conversely, the school may be willing to provide communal facilities but only if relieved of maintenance and management responsibilities.

- Schools may be required to make their premises available for public meetings to candidates at local and parliamentary elections during non-school times, and the returning officer can require the use of the school for the day of the election itself.

- The governing body must keep any open land under its control free of litter and dog excrement as far as practicable. This only applies to areas that are accessible to pupils. There is a Government Code of Practice on the subject, and schools should be aware of its provisions.

Beyond this, the specific powers and responsibilities depend on the type of school and, to some extent, the specific terms of the LEA's delegated funding.

Community Schools

The LEA:

- owns the school premises and has overall control during school hours;

- has to establish an overall health and safety policy which the school will usually adopt and apply as its own;

- determines and funds capital building projects;

- provides specialist advice on premises issues if schools elect to buy it back;

- insures the premises, although again this may be on a 'buy-back' basis as insurance is to be a delegated item and schools will be free to seek alternative cover;

- retains liability for maintenance of the main structure and fabric of the buildings. There is detailed Guidance from the DfES as to how the responsibility for premises maintenance should be divided between the LEA and the school under the delegated funding regime. Generally speaking, day-to-day repairs and decorations come out of the school's delegated budget share and will be the responsibility of the governing body. Larger items and renewals are dealt with by the LEA;

- may establish general rules about use of school premises outside school hours;

- should be consulted about proposals to allow community use of the premises during school hours and be a party to any agreement.

The governing body decides on the use of the premises subject to the LEA's right to be consulted as mentioned above.

Foundation Schools

Foundation schools have total control of their premises. Capital funding will be through the LEA programme or by the school raising funds from its own resources. The LEA will pay 100 per cent of the approved cost of programmed work but it may agree with the school that it should provide a proportion from its own funds, which may include funds generated by fund-raising or from third parties. Additional funds should also be available from the LEA to meet emergency repairs or maintenance that, through no fault of the school, cannot reasonably be budgeted for.

VA Schools

VA schools have almost total control of their premises although since the school buildings will have been provided by the school's trustees the school's ultimate responsibilities may be governed by the terms of any lease or user agreement. The LEA has a right to require use of the premises on no more than three days in each week for education or other activities promoting the welfare of young people, but only if there is no other accommodation available. This is, on the face of it, a very wide power, but the LEA must use it reasonably.

As with foundation schools, capital projects depend on the availability of funds or inclusion in a building programme. There is no specific allocation for minor works, although there will be a specific minor works programme. Normally, 90 per cent of the approved cost will come from grant, but VA schools have to provide the balance and this will include full liability for any work that the DfES does not regard as necessary. This would apply where the school wishes to build to a standard in excess of that agreed to by the DfES although persistent bargaining has been known to secure agreement to fund work that goes beyond what is generally regarded as the norm. Certain work, relating mainly to premises that were previously the responsibility of the LEA but which were transferred to governing body liability in April 2002, will normally receive 100 per cent grant for approved work carried out within five years of the change. VA schools that have acquired such property – characteristically caretakers' houses – should if they have not already done so commission a condition survey to see whether any claims for 100 per cent grant should be made during the qualifying period.

The governing body liability extends to all building work, including emergency repair and maintenance work that is funded outside the delegated budget.

It is worth noting that funding for capital projects for VA schools are approved and funded by the DfES and not by the LEA. Community, Foundation and VC schools that see no long-term prospect of capital funding from their LEA might want to consider a change of status to VA. This would bring with it a commitment to meet the non-funded elements of capital works and the process will require a demonstration that the school is likely to be able to meet those liabilities. That will be an insurmountable hurdle for many schools but some schools have sought to go down that route and others will follow. Although VA schools are frequently perceived to be denominational, there are many non-denominational VA schools with no specific religious character.

VC Schools

The foundation governors decide how the school is to be used on Sundays. The LEA can require the use of the school on Saturdays for educational or welfare purposes, but otherwise the governing body as a whole decides on Saturday use.

Controlled schools are dealt with in the same way as community schools so far as maintenance, repair, renewals and new construction are concerned.

DELEGATED CAPITAL FUNDING

Capital repair costs are now the subject of delegated funding. This is delegated in accordance with a formula which comprises a fixed sum and a per pupil sum, in each case related to the type of school. VA schools are funded by the DfES direct and on the footing that the governing body will contribute 10 per cent of the cost of governor liability work and that the LEA is funded for that part of the repair liability that is theirs. VA schools also have additional funding to reflect liability for VAT. Other schools are funded via the LEA but the basic rules are essentially the same. They are intended to ensure that (subject to VA school governor liability) all categories of school are treated in the same way. The DfES retains the funding for VA schools and settles cost against claims. LEAs are required to pay the delegated funding in quarterly tranches to the other schools unless a particular school requests otherwise. There are special rules for schools that open in or move into completely new buildings: they are assumed not to need this funding during the first three financial years in the new premises. If a school is to close, it will need to negotiate whether devolved capital funding is to be paid. Schools that are operating under a Private Finance Initiative (PFI) contract will in the first two years be excluded from devolved capital funding and thereafter will receive it at 50% of the folrmulaic rate. They may not use the devolved capital funding to pay the PFI service charge.

Devolved capital funding is for capital expenditure on buildings and, since the start of the 2004/2005 funding year, for investment in ICT equipment. Guidance is issued annually and that issued in March 2004 (which can be found with other funding information and guidance at: http://www.teachernet.gov.uk/management/resources financeandbuilding/funding/) sets out the ways in which devolved capital funding may (or might) be used as follows:

'3.   Devolved formula capital may be used:

- to fund small capital projects;

- to pay for more substantial capital projects through accumulation over periods of up to three years;

- as a contribution to a larger capital project where other funding comes from another source, such as the LEA. This might, for example, include Seed Challenge funded projects (although this funding does not count as "new" money for such a project).

4.   The priority use of Devolved formula capital should be for condition needs of school buildings. Schools should consider potential as well as actual condition needs when considering best use of this funding. Otherwise, schools may use their funding for suitability needs targeted at raising educational standards. Schools can also invest this funding in capital projects which:

- support the school workforce programme – and in particular projects that address the implications of the National Agreement *Raising Standards and Tackling Workload*;

- support the development of a broader, more flexible curriculum for 14-19 year-olds;

- expand successful schools;

- support making school fully inclusive, including measures to improve behaviour and projects for improved facilities for children with Special Educational Needs (SEN).

5. Particular types of investment schools may want to consider include:

- improvements to security, protecting both people and property;

- improvements supporting better delivery of the curriculum, including specialist teaching areas such as science and technology, and interactive white boards;

- support for pupils with behavioural problems;

- accommodating a larger and wider range of support staff; improving accommodation to help teachers make the most effective use of time spent on key activities like planning, preparation and assessment; or providing innovative and flexible spaces for teaching and learning needs;

- the development of community use of facilities and integrating education and other local authority services within the school. This can include investment in such areas as nurseries, childcare facilities, lifelong learning facilities;

- improvements to social, play and recreational areas where these address curriculum or behavioural needs.

- This funding can be used for improvements to school grounds as well as school buildings, with the exception of VA schools where it cannot be used for improvements to school playing fields.'

It should normally be in line with the priorities agreed locally and set out in the LEA's Asset Management Plan.

Devolved capital funding is earmarked for the specific purposes mentioned above. In particular, it may not be used for general maintenance, redecoration or routine repairs, or for the purchase of books, funding of operational leases, hire of temporary accommodation (unless that is an essential but ancillary part of the project) or for any element of maintenance that is included in revenue delegated funding. Schools may, however, utilise funds from other sources to complement the capital funding for eligible projects provided they do not prejudice their need to meet routine repair obligations. Devolved capital funding may be carried forward for up to three years and if it is not then spent it will be clawed back. It is also possible for schools to agree to form a cluster and to pool their devolved capital funding with a view to schools drawing against the pool in a manner that is agreed between them.

Great care must be taken over costing because any shortfall in devolved capital funding will have to be met by the school from its other resources: there is no mechanism for payment of devolved capital funding in addition to the formula allocation. The devolved capital funding has to cover the cost of management of the project and schools are advised to take proper professional advice, either from the LEA or from external consultants as discussed below. DfES Guidance is that the cost of such management, whether from the LEA or otherwise, should not exceed 15 per cent of the total project cost.

HEALTH AND SAFETY

All schools face the same issues on health and safety, and they are issues that face all employers. The school has to be a safe workplace. Given that there is no part of a school that is not open to at least one employee, it follows that the governing body's duty is to secure the safety of the entire school. This duty is highlighted, but not increased, by the parallel duty to pupils and visitors to avoid being negligent.

The duty to provide a safe workplace covers all aspects of the premises and their use, not merely the physical condition of the buildings. There are specific regulations for many areas of activity, for example:

- control of hazardous materials, which is particularly important in science laboratories;

- use of computer screens, including the general work environment, which will affect administrative staff and many teachers. There are specific requirements relating to training of staff, availability of eye tests and the taking of regular breaks from work with the screen;

- food preparation;

- handling of equipment, which will apply to any situation where items have to be moved by hand. These regulations impact on such mundane activities as moving desks, tables, chairs and other furniture, as well as equipment such as photocopiers, computers and laboratory equipment;

- electric installations. These regulations apply to electrical equipment and their maintenance, down to the detail of changing plugs and fuses;

- supervision of construction work. Regulations, commonly referred to as the CDM Regulations, require that the school appoints a planning supervisor, designer and principal contractor with responsibility for health and safety aspects of their respective areas for certain construction projects. These are projects which either:

    – last for more than 30 days; or

    – involve more than 500 person days of work; or

    – involve five or more people on site at any one time; or

    – involve demolition work, regardless of the size of the job.

The school has to make sure that all relevant information about health and safety (including the school's health and safety records) is available, and that adequate resources and time are made available.

Health and safety records have to be maintained and accidents reported. Information on health and safety, including the risk control measures that have to be taken, must be provided in a prescribed form to staff. Most importantly, training has to be given to all those whose work has a health and safety implication: in a school, this will involve everyone to a greater or lesser extent. A record of training given should be kept.

Breach of health and safety requirements is a serious issue, capable of leading to criminal proceedings against individuals, including governors. Prosecutions are rare, due in part to the good sense of the enforcers but mainly to the fact that the duty to provide a safe working environment is a qualified one: it is only required to the extent that is reasonably practicable, which means that resources (or the lack of them) can be taken into account. It should be noted that damaging anything used for safety purposes may be a criminal offence, and that this applies just as much to pupils (at least if over the age of 10) as to adults.

The school must have a health and safety policy, and this must be kept up to date. It must identify and assess the health and safety risks inherent in the running of the school. It must also define responsibilities, show how the policy will be implemented and state how the implementation will be monitored. It will normally provide that the headteacher is the person with overall responsibility for health and safety within the school, at times designated as the 'premises controller'. This is the hot seat because it is this person who is first in the firing line when things go wrong and the most obvious person to prosecute if the situation escalates to that extent. The headteacher therefore has a particular interest in seeing that health and safety issues are properly dealt with and not swept under the carpet.

There will normally be a regular review of the school, possibly by an outside consultant, possibly by the school's insurers, to identify areas that need attention. One of the hardest tasks that a governing body faces is having to prioritise health and safety issues. It is a risk assessment exercise, which is a phrase that sends shivers down the collective spine. Any suggestion that a risk could reasonably be taken by deferring work identified as necessary but not urgently imperative causes understandable concern, particularly where there may be a risk to pupils. None the less, risk assessment is an essential part of the balancing act of identified need against available resource. Governors should take proper professional advice in this area so that their decisions are seen to have been duly considered and reasonable.

A typical review will look at the specific areas where there are regulations to be met and comment on whether the school complies. It will also look in detail at the school in action because most health and safety problems come not from the premises themselves but from how they are used. It will contain a huge list of small or seemingly trivial items, for example (to take just a few):

- doors whose self-closers are not working properly;
- chemicals in the darkroom not kept in secure containers;
- uneven floor surfaces;
- trailing cables that people could trip over;
- too many electric plugs in an adapter socket;
- slipped tiles on the roof.

Schools will normally have a health and safety committee. This will be an internal school committee as distinct from a committee of the governing body because health and safety is largely a management issue. Recognised trade unions are entitled to nominate a member-employee as safety representative on the committee: this is an important mechanism in enabling the unions to protect their members' interests by being involved in discussions and decisions on the subject. Staff are entitled to paid time off to attend training as safety representatives.

Staff have their own obligations. They are required to carry out their duties so as not to put themselves or others at risk. They also have a duty to co-operate with those responsible for health and safety. They must implement health and safety measures and report defects.

Health and safety issues do not confine themselves to premises issues. They also impact on the delivery of the curriculum and on matters relating to the appropriateness of dress for particular activities. The case of the pupil who challenged the right to insist on her wearing a particular form of dress approved as part of the uniform policy for Muslim girls is referred to elsewhere in the context of exclusion from school and human rights but there was an interesting discussion on health and safety issues. These were not determinative of the case but the school had concerns about the nature of the dress, which was a full-length flowing garment. In particular, there were concerns relating to working in laboratories and food technology workshops where there might be burners with naked flames giving rise to a risk that the garment could be ignited or could itself knock the burner over. There were also concerns of a rather different nature in relation to PE, where it was felt that the nature of the garment would make it impossible for the pupil to participate in PE effectively and without danger to health. It should be said that these concerns did not seem to weigh very heavily with the judge and one questions whether they would in themselves have been sufficient to warrant the school banning the form of dress in question. However, the issues are relevant ones to be considered when conducting risk assessments in relation to particular subject areas.

LIABILITY TO VISITORS

Many people visit school premises in the course of a day. The school owes a duty of care to all of them to see that the premises are safe and that they will not come to harm. The duty is to take reasonable care so that if an accident happens but the school was not negligent it will not be liable. This involves two elements:

- *Knowledge.* Did the school know, or should it have known, of the particular defect that led to the accident? If no one knew about it, and no one had been at fault in failing to spot it, then the school will not have liability. If, however, the defect was known to someone who should have reported it but did not do so, then the school may be liable. Equally, if the defect is obvious, such as a trailing electric cable, the school will be treated as having knowledge even though no one had specifically noted it as a danger. Liability to visitors arising from transient conditions, such as icy footpaths, will be tested in the same way as liability to members of the school community.

- *Foreseeability.* Is it reasonable to expect the school, if it knew or should have known of the defect, to have realised that an accident of the particular kind was one that could happen? If so, then, so long as the person injured is a person to whom the school had a duty in the first place, the school will be liable. Again, the test of liability will be similar for lawful visitors as for members of the school community.

Note that, generally, the school will not be liable to those who have no business coming onto the school premises. A burglar who trips over that trailing electric cable and breaks his leg while trying to make off with the school's computers cannot make a claim for damages on the grounds that the accident was foreseeable.

INSURANCE

Schools must, as a matter of basic prudence, carry proper insurance for their premises. There is Guidance from DfES – 'Insurance – A Guide for Schools' – which gives valuable Guidance on all forms of insurance commonly required by schools of all categories and not restricted to premises insurance.

For community schools, insurance of the premises will usually be dealt with by the LEA and other schools may well also buy into the LEA insurance arrangements. The cover will be for the normal buildings risks such as fire, lightning, explosion, subsidence, ground heave, riot or civil commotion, malicious damage, earthquake, storm, tempest, flood, or bursting and overflowing of water pipes, tanks, and other more esoteric headings such as damage caused by an object dropped from (or falling off) an aeroplane. Damage resulting from terrorist activity may well not be covered unless special terrorism cover is bought. The cost of this varies dramatically around the country. In addition, schools need to consider cover for contents: the cost and availability of cover again will vary considerably dependent on the school's theft record and security precautions.

The level of cover has to be sufficient to meet the likely cost if the school had to be completely rebuilt. A margin has to be allowed for demolition costs and professional fees (architects and surveyors) including the cost of getting planning permission. The insurance companies can advise on building costs but these will always be expressed in terms of cost per cubic metre, which is not illuminating if the size of the school is not known in the first place. Schools should take professional advice from competent insurance brokers and surveyors on the appropriate level of cover. However, VA schools are in a special position because, as the DfES Guidance confirms, in determining the level of insurance cover, it is appropriate for VA schools to take into account the fact that necessary work will be grant-aided.

As well as insuring the tangible buildings and contents, the policy must also cover the school's potential liability to third parties. The level of cover needs to be high: the damages awarded to a promising student who becomes a quadriplegic through an accident for which the school is liable will be very substantial, and it would be a double blow for the victim (and, for that matter, the school) if the insurance cover was insufficient to meet the award.

An important element of third-party cover is that the scope may be limited. It will always cover those who come to the school on relevant school business, but it will not necessarily cover third-party activities on school premises. An important aspect of lettings is to be sure that the particular proposed use is covered by insurance, and this is dealt with below. There may be other grey areas that will need to be checked with the insurers or the LEA. What, for instance, is the insurance cover for people attending a car-boot sale organised by the PTA on the school playing fields?

OWNERSHIP OF SCHOOL PREMISES

The LEA will normally own the premises of a community school.

Premises occupied by VA schools will usually belong to the foundation body (other than playing fields which may well belong to the LEA), and the school's use, and entitlement, may be governed by a trust deed or a lease or other regulating document. The rights of the foundation body and the rights of the school may not be clearly defined, and there is no clear law on the extent to which the foundation body is obliged to continue to provide accommodation. The duties of VA trustees towards the school are often not well defined. In one particular case, the foundation body was held by the court to be entitled to require the school to pay a full market rent for the school premises. The case was decided on the interpretation of the particular trust documents and is not to be taken as a precedent for other schools, but it raises two major issues. The first is how the foundation body could reconcile its demands with its presumed duties towards the school, and the second is how the school can be expected to find the rent when its delegated budget cannot make provision for it. In that instance, the dilemma was resolved by the liability for rent being capitalised and being covered by capital grant from DfES and assistance from the LEA. The case has led to stringent controls by the DfES over any new arrangements, e.g. when a new VA school is proposed, to ensure that a similar situation cannot arise.

Foundation schools that were formerly community schools and new foundation schools will either own their own premises with a shared-use agreement for any property (such as playing fields or a sports centre) which was previously used with the LEA or others and which cannot be physically divided, or the premises will be held for the school by the foundation body as described in Chapter 2. The shared property may be retained by the LEA, with the school having rights, or may be transferred to the school's (or foundation's) ownership, with the other interested parties having their rights protected. The premises of foundation schools that are former VA schools remain in their previous ownership unless any part belonged to the LEA, in which case they transfer to the school. Again, there may be shared-use agreements.

Where premises occupied by a foundation or voluntary school are owned by trustees and the trustees (assuming they have the right to do so) give notice to the school terminating its rights of occupation, the Secretary of State has wide powers to impose terms (including compulsory purchase of the land) to secure that the school can either continue in occupation or that any public funds provided in relation to the premises be repaid. The notice must be at least two years and has to be long enough to enable the governing body to discontinue the school if it so decides.

LETTINGS

Most schools now exploit their premises to a greater or lesser extent by making them available to outsiders, and charging for this use. These may be single ventures, such as a wedding reception, or ongoing arrangements, such as a Sunday football side using a pitch every week. In either case, it is important that the rights and obligations of each side are clearly identified and recorded. It is not necessary for solicitors to be asked to draw up a formal agreement, although it would be sensible for the school to develop a standard form for lettings and have that form vetted by solicitors or the LEA's legal department. What is needed is clarity of thought and clarity of expression.

Schools should devise a checklist that ensures that any letting agreement covers the following issues.

- What is the purpose of the letting?

- Who is accepting responsibility? Clearly, the school will always be in the position of landlord, but who is the tenant? If the agreement for the use of the football pitch is with the club and the club does not pay, who do you pursue? The club will almost certainly not exist as a legal entity so you have to choose between suing every member of the club or every member of its committee if you can find out who they are and where they live. The problem does not arise if the school insists that the secretary or treasurer (or any other individual who seems to be responsible) takes personal responsibility, for example by agreeing to guarantee the school against loss from any breach of contract (such agreement must be in writing to be enforceable). The law relating to guarantees is, however, very technical, and a guarantee document should be prepared or approved by a solicitor. The better (and simpler) way is to insist that the individual takes on primary rather than guarantee responsibility, i.e. takes the letting in his or her own name. Bear in mind that responsibility in this context does not just involve payment of the rental: the school may need to make a claim for damage to the building or its contents.

- It should be made clear exactly which part of the school premises can be used. There should always be an express ban on entering any other part. That covers the school if, for example, the adult evening class overspills into a chemistry laboratory and damages expensive equipment set up for the next day's first lesson. The door should, of course, have been locked, but that is another story and the tenant should not have the opportunity to raise the point.

- The date and times of the letting should be specified. Where timing is critical because the caretaker's overtime will be astronomical if the letting overruns, this should be stated and the extra cost made the tenant's responsibility.

- If the agreement covers ongoing lettings, it must either specify for how long it will continue or contain a provision enabling either side to give notice. The notice period should be long enough to allow each side to make proper alternative arrangements. In particular, the tenant must understand that premature cancellation will not stop the liability to pay the rent during the proper notice period.

- How much is to be paid and when is payment to be made? It is obviously best for the school to receive money in advance, particularly in the early stages of the relationship with the tenant. It should go without saying that in setting a rent the school needs to consider the cost it will incur in making the school available. Salaries, heating, lighting, wear and tear, cleaning and administration time are examples of letting expenses.

- The school should consider taking a deposit against damage. It is easier to make a refund if there is no damage than to demand payment after the event when there have been problems and neither side is on the best of terms with the other.

- What, if any, facilities or services will the school provide over and above the mere use of space? If this is clearly set out in the agreement, there is no scope for the actuality not meeting the expectations.

- Who is responsible for insurance? If the school is to insure the event, it must check with its insurers that it will be covered under the ordinary terms of the policy. There may be an additional premium to pay: if the tenant is to pay this, the agreement should say so. If the tenant is to take care of insurance, the school should insist on having the policy details and confirmation (from the insurance company or reputable brokers) that the premium has been paid and that cover is effective. The tenant should not be allowed onto the premises unless that confirmation has been produced beforehand.

The agreement should specify that the tenant will keep the school indemnified against any claims that any participator in the tenant's event may bring against the school unless the claim relates to negligence or other breach of duty by the school. This protects the school to some extent against the possibility that in some way it might be held responsible for the tenant's activities. It is difficult to envisage circumstances in which this would arise, but the law is infinite in its capacity to find new concepts, and a term of this kind is a sensible protective measure.

BUILDING PROJECTS

A major concern for governing bodies of VA and foundation schools is the management of building projects. Community schools do not necessarily have this problem because any new building will be organised by the LEA, although this will not necessarily apply to a project being funded by the school from its delegated New Deal for Schools (NDS) funding. The school has the option of managing such projects itself or passing the responsibility to the LEA.

The key to a successful project is preparation and planning. The first essential is to have a professional team (architect, quantity surveyor, building surveyor, consulting engineer and possibly a project manager) who know one another and who can work well together. The architect is the best person to organise the team so, from the school's point of view, this is the key appointment. The architect needs to be well aware of the special factors that apply to school projects:

- the regulations that specify minimum standards for school accommodation. Although these have been repealed, they still represent good practice and the DfES has its own benchmarks for use when approving projects for grant purposes. In this respect, 'minimum' frequently equates to 'maximum' in terms of what will be funded. Advisers need to be realistic when designing new accommodation unless the school has other resources from its foundation body or fund-raising;

- suitability of the design for educational purposes. The accommodation must be functional and educationally viable, and the architect should be able to make independent judgements on this: the school should not have to double-check the architect's work;

- all space is useable within a school for (almost) all purposes, and requirements change with the passage of time. The architect needs, therefore, as part of the design process to consider possible future adaptations and produce accommodation that is as flexible as the initial brief permits. Ingenuity is a valuable attribute;

- the availability of grants and the formal processes first for obtaining grant approval and then for certifying work and obtaining payment. The school has to pay the contractor whether or not it has obtained grant payments. Delay in submitting claims or delay due to claims being incorrect can be very expensive for the school;

- the fact that approval is likely to come suddenly and with a severe time-constraint for start and completion of the work. There is often very little time to put a scheme together and make a start on site. That is one prime reason for identifying a professional team in advance;

- planning considerations may be important and there may be little time in which to get consent. The architect needs to know the area, be aware of local sensitivities and be able to negotiate with the local planning authority.

The architect will draw up an outline specification with broad costings for grant approval purposes. Schools with ambition will usually have a few potential schemes, of varying sizes, available for submission each year. Once approval is given, a detailed specification is drawn up by the quantity surveyor and put out to tender. The architect will advise on the outcome of the tender and will negotiate further with the contractors if aspects of the tender are not clear.

The architect will prepare the building contract. There may be a temptation to take legal advice on it, but this should be resisted unless the architect specifically asks that a particular aspect be referred to solicitors. Drawing up a proper contract is part of the architect's responsibility, and the school should rely on the architect's advice. Solicitors cannot advise competently on a building contract without going into a great deal of detail about the project which will already be known to the architect and consulting a solicitor would usually not be an effective use of resources.

The architect will supervise the project in all respects, co-ordinating the work of the professional team and certifying each stage. Contractors are usually paid monthly against a certificate showing the value of the work done in the current month. The quantity surveyor values the work that has been done against the original priced specification to ensure that only work that has been done is paid for and that it is paid at the correct rate. A proportion of the certified value will be retained until the end of the defects liability period, usually six months from the date of practical completion. If the school is employing contractors on a self-employed basis, tax must be deducted from payments to them unless the contractor produces an Inland Revenue certificate authorising gross payments. If the school gets this wrong, the Inland Revenue will require the school to pay the tax.

At the end of the job, the architect signs a certificate of practical completion, and the accommodation is handed over to the school. Up to that time, the building site will have been in the hands of the contractor who will have had responsibility for it and for insuring it. It is another of the architect's responsibilities to make sure that the contractor has proper insurance cover. After practical completion, the contractor may be required to deal with defects and, at the end of the defects liability period, assuming no outstanding claims, the retention is paid over.

Although the contractor has responsibility for the working site, the school has to function around it. Health and safety issues become very important, and the school must plan carefully for the disruption and additional hazards that building work presents. The school needs to work closely with the architect on issues such as site security – contractors and their staff will be moving around the school with very little effective supervision and this in itself presents possible hazards to the school. There may be timetabling implications if the work is internal and involves taking some areas of the school out of use. A particular concern will be to ensure that contractor staff do not have access to, or work in proximity with, pupils. If this is unavoidable because of the nature of the project, the contractor must be required to carry out police and the DfES checks against its staff to ensure that none are subject to a barring order or present a risk.

The architect will need to look at the timing and phasing of the work to fit in with school requirements and to make the most of holiday periods. This may not be easy, particularly since the pattern of the building work also has to be geared to the timetable for grant payment. It may be possible to complete the work in three months by working intensively, but if the grant is to be paid over nine months the school will have a problem. The negotiating skills of the architect may produce a faster payment of grant, but if that does not work the school will either have to settle for a longer period of disruption or find the cash from other resources.

Inevitably, it is not possible to do more than give an outline sketch of the process for handling a building project. This topic was dealt with in more detail in an Occasional Paper, Series 4, Number 3 'Capital Building Bids', published by the Grant-Maintained Schools Centre. The advice it contains remains relevant to building contracts generally for all schools, even though grant-maintained status has now been abolished.

PUBLIC PRIVATE PARTNERSHIPS

The severe restriction on public capital expenditure has led to the development of an alternative financing method using the ability of the private sector to raise capital. The Private Finance Initiative (PFI) was renamed, revamped and re-launched in 1997 as the PPP but the name has not gained currency and projects are still generically described as PFI projects. It is a topic which can only be dealt with in outline here although such schemes are potentially significant tools for school building and facilities management, either for individual schools or as part of an LEA grouped project. Thus, PFI will always have to be kept in mind as a possible means of realising projects for which conventional funding is not available, although the complexity and nature of the exercise means that it will only be relevant for large-scale schemes.

The two essential features of any PFI scheme are:

- the ability of the private sector to raise risk capital for projects that provide a sufficient and secure return on investment;

- the conversion of capital cost, usually paid on a once-for-all basis, into a series of revenue payments over a long term.

It is this conversion of capital to revenue that enables schemes to proceed without adding to the Public Sector Borrowing Requirement. Clearly, if the private sector is to be involved, it must be able to earn a profit and there has to be a proper justification for allowing that profit to be earned. In simplistic terms, this is seen as permissible because the private partner takes on a basket of risks, relating to the raising of capital and other relevant risks in relation to the particular project. This is known as risk transfer and is critical to the viability of a scheme. The value to the public sector of being protected against those risks is reflected in the calculations that are made to ascertain whether the particular project represents value for money and compares with the cost that the public sector would have incurred to secure the same result – the public sector comparator (PSC). One consequence of this is that the scheme has to involve more than simply procuring the construction of a new facility. The private partner has to undertake also to provide continuing services on a long-term basis, and the payment for those services is structured as an annual unitary service charge.

Thus, in a project to build a new school, the private partner will undertake to fund, design, build and equip the school and then to provide facilities management and to maintain and equip it for an extended period, say 25 years. This is known as a DFBO scheme (Design, Fund, Build and Operate scheme). The maintenance obligation will extend to the day-to-day management of the premises, including cleaning and caretaking, and the equipment obligation will include replacement and renewals according to the life-cycle of the items supplied. It could, for example, extend to the replacement and upgrading of IT equipment and it may also include providing school meals. It becomes the private partner's responsibility to provide the contracted services at a fixed price which will vary only by reference to inflation and any changes to the level of service that may be agreed. The service charge paid by the school will be for the entire provision of the school facility. This enables the private partner to service and recoup its capital outlay, meets the cost of providing the facilities management and gives a profit to justify the exercise. The school only retains the risks relating to pupil numbers, the provision of education and those specific services that are excluded from the project.

A project such as a sports hall intended to have community use may take a similar shape (although not necessarily designated as a PFI project as many non-PFI projects are now set up with a management structure that is effectively a DFBO scheme), but the private partner will add income from community use of the facilities into the equation. Those income projections will reduce the service charge to the school, and the private partner will take the risk of the income not meeting expectations. Sometimes the risk may be reduced by the school being entitled to a guaranteed minimum income but if a guarantee is given, the private partner will expect a greater share of any surplus. There could be a variety of permutations in a project that has a commercial as well as an educational purpose. It might well be attractive to the school to share some of the income risk in order to share some of the potential profit, but any school looking to act in this entrepreneurial way will have to weigh the risk very carefully. It would, for example, be wrong to jeopardise the delegated budget by leaving the school dependent for its normal operation on a stream of income that might not materialise. Schools with foundation bodies might have access to resources that would enable some risk to be taken, but even in this case the foundation body would have to consider very carefully its own charitable position and the obligations placed on its trustees.

The funding for the service charge will come from a number of different sources. Part will come from the DfES (for VA schools) or LEA (for other schools) representing the element of the service charge that relates to capital expenditure. This effectively converts the capital expenditure, which would have been constrained by the Public Sector Borrowing Requirement, into revenue payments which are not constrained in the same way. A further part will come from the LEA, representing that part of the cost that relates to other capital (in the case of VA schools) and non-capital elements that would be provided by the LEA outside the school's delegated budget. The third part has to be found by the governing body from within its delegated budget and should, if the project has been established with proper cost parameters, represent no more than the amount (including prudent reserves and contingencies for repairs and renewals) that it would have spent in conventional circumstances to procure the services relating to facilities management and equipment replacement, etc. Since schools are rarely in the fortunate position of being able to budget more than minimally for reserves or contingencies, the actual amount that will be taken out of the delegated budget may look high, but against this the school must take into account that a major element of uncertainty is removed from the budget. Further, it will have achieved a major objective and that in itself will have a value. A fourth part, for VA schools (which still have to fund at least 10 per cent of the capital cost) and any other school that agrees to find part of the capital cost from its own resources will come from the governing body or the school's foundation body in addition to what comes from the delegated budget.

The attractions of this approach are, evidently, that the project is made possible and that throughout the period of the contract the school is assured of a proper level of maintenance and equipment. There are, however, difficult areas that have to be addressed.

- The contract is a long-term one, and a governing body will have to be sure that it is in the best interests of the school. Guidance from the DfES confirms that a contract of this kind is within the powers of a governing body provided that this test is met. It is the fundamental question to be answered but the governing body can only reach its conclusion once it has considered all the detail.

- If the scheme is being proposed by the LEA there will be a formal agreement between the governing body and the LEA, under which the governing body will commit itself to making payments (usually by way of deduction from the delegated budget) to the LEA to cover what would be governor liability to provide under conventional arrangements. The governing body will need to look closely at the figures and also at the basis of the deduction. If the LEA proposes a fixed amount each year, the governing body is effectively taking an element of risk over pupil numbers, because pupil numbers play a major part in determining the level of the delegated budget. If numbers drop, the school could be seriously prejudiced. The alternative approach is for the school to agree to pay a percentage of its annual budget, calculated by taking the ratio that the cost of the services being provided under the project bears to the overall budget. This keeps the payments to the LEA in step with the budget and places more risk on the LEA which, many would feel, is better equipped to meet the risk. A prudent governing body will wish to take independent advice on the proposed agreement and the DfES Guidance confirms that this should be done. This will protect governors from any claim that they did not properly consider the matter. The interests of the LEA may not necessarily coincide with those of the school and the LEA cannot advise the governing body impartially. The LEA should meet the cost of such advice. It is as much in the interests of the LEA as of the school that the governing body feels comfortable with the scheme and does not feel that it has been forced into a decision, and there is no justification for requiring that this cost is met from the delegated budget. The school will certainly need legal advice. It may feel that it needs independent financial advice as well but there is likely to be greater resistance from the LEA to meeting the cost. In that event, the school should state formally to the LEA that it enters into the agreement in reliance on the information supplied by the LEA including any financial information.

- The payment commitment means that the school cannot easily reduce its premises costs at times of financial stringency. The classic method of making ends meet by neglecting maintenance is simply not an option. The management issues in those circumstances become quite different, and there is a risk that the school will find itself having to make cuts in curriculum-related areas because it is bound to meet the service charge. The contract will have provision for changes in the service specification which may enable savings to be made, for example by deferring replacement or renewal of equipment, but the private partner will insist that no change may be made that would adversely affect the ability of the partner to keep the buildings up to standard. The governing body must, therefore, be sure that it will have sufficient resources after it has met its part of the service charge to deliver the curriculum.

- A system of monitoring will be needed to ensure that the private partner maintains standards, and the contract will provide for an adjustment of the service charge to reflect any periods when parts of the school are not available for use or to reflect an unsatisfactory level of service, for example poor-quality cleaning or slow attention to necessary repairs. The governing body needs to be confident that the monitoring system is manageable and that the cost (in terms of time as well as money) will not exceed the benefit from the exercise. If monitoring is not carried out rigorously, the school is likely to find that the standard of service declines.

- The governing body will be told whether or not the PFI project meets the financial tests imposed by government. These tests are expressed in terms of value for money and affordability. Both terms are highly technical and do not mean what they appear to mean in colloquial language. Governors should beware of taking them at face value as confirming that the project is manageable from the school perspective. The governing body needs to be more simplistic in its approach. Is it getting the services at a reasonable cost? Is it getting what it needs? Can it afford to meet the contractual payments from its delegated budget? Without an affirmative answer to each of these questions, the governing body should not go ahead, at least without assurances from the LEA, contained in legally binding form, that if the concerns that are identified actually materialise, the LEA will meet the cost.

PFI contracts will only be possible where it can be established that the service charge cost is reasonable and compares favourably with the cost of providing the same end result by conventional means. It is also necessary to show that the contract gives value for money. This will most easily be achieved where the project provides for an ancillary opportunity for the private partner to make profit as, for example, where a school has surplus land which the partner can develop for its own purposes. Another possibility may be for the development of a facility, such as a sports hall, which can have community use and provide the private partner with an opportunity for additional income. One project is for a redevelopment that involves incorporating the school in a larger building which contains commercial elements. There is, after all, nothing necessarily sacrosanct in the idea that a school must exist in a totally self-contained building.

By no means all projects involving capital cost will lend themselves to a project of this kind. The private sector will be interested only in schemes where the risk being undertaken is quantifiable and acceptable. Thus, a new school, or the complete rebuilding of an existing one, may be viable because the private partner has control over the building from the outset and can build in the quality standards necessary to ensure maintenance costs will stay under control. A scheme for renovating existing buildings may be a much harder proposition because the potential for future deterioration may not be easy to assess. This may lead to the private partner taking a very conservative view on the cost of taking on that risk, with the result that the overall service charge may be higher than can be justified in terms of the public sector comparator. Nevertheless, there are an increasing number of schemes involving refurbishment and facilities management for a number of schools within an LEA.

In a sense, PFI is akin to borrowing, with the private partner acting as the lender. However, a school which simply borrows has to secure repayment from its own resources without access to capital grant. PFI unlocks the missing capital element by a sleight of hand that is perhaps too subtle for teachers and lawyers but to which accountants and economists (who, after all, end up as the paymasters) can give their imprimatur.

One word of warning: PFI is frequently described as a partnership between the public and private sector. That is true up to a point, and that point comes when the actual contract is signed. From then on, the private contractor can be expected to implement the contract to its letter, notwithstanding assurances that may have been given during the previous negotiations. Schools must make sure that they know what they require and that these requirements are specified in detail in the contract. There is no room for the doctrine of 'it will be alright on the night'.

RELEVANT GUIDANCE

Standards for School Premises

DfES Guidance 29/2000, 'Standards for School Premises'.

'New Deal for Schools (NDS) Phase 4' (DfES, 2000).

Use of Premises

Circular 15/93, 'The Use of School Premises and the Incorporation of Governing Bodies of LEA-maintained Schools'.

Insurance

'Insurance – a Guide for Schools' – DfES/0256/2003.

PFI/PPP

4ps Schools PFI Procurement Pack obtainable from 4ps 7th Floor, Artillery House, Artillery Row, London SW1P 1RT.

New Deal for Schools

'Guidance on New Deal for Schools (NDS) Devolved Formula, NDS Condition and Seed Challenge Grants' (DfES, July 2001).

Chapter 12

LIABILITY TO PEOPLE

Negligence – Nutritional standards – Welfare – When school is not the answer – Relevant guidance

Schools owe a duty of care to their pupils. This, in legal terms, has two distinct aspects. The first arises in connection with the common-law duty not to be negligent (which itself falls into two categories – negligent provision of education and maintaining safety), and the second relates to the school's welfare responsibilities. Schools also owe a duty of care to their staff to ensure safe conditions of work. Finally, they owe a duty of care to their visitors, which was dealt with in Chapter 11.

NEGLIGENCE

Negligent Provision of Education

It is now firmly established that schools have a responsibility not to be negligent in the provision of education. A child who can demonstrate that the school has been negligent and that the negligence has led to financial loss can recover compensation from the school.

What, though, does 'negligence' mean? It is not a synonym for 'carelessness' but a very specific legal concept which, in an over-simplified nutshell, says that everyone owes a duty to take care in relation to those people who can reasonably be foreseen to be at risk from a failure to take such care. The principle is seen at its most basic in road accident cases: a driver knows that if he causes an accident another road user may be hurt. Therefore, a driver who does not take proper care has to compensate those who are injured as a result. Conversely, if someone is hurt in an accident where no one else is to blame, no damages will be paid. There has to be fault on someone's part, that fault has to cause damage to another person, and that other person has to be someone who can be anticipated as someone who is likely to suffer. Quite clearly, a school pupil comes within that category: there is an evident connection between the actions of the school and the performance of the pupil. Finally, it has to be reasonable that the person hurt should be compensated by the person who caused the injury. After many years of litigation, the House of Lords in the *Phelps* case, (known as this after the name of one of the claimants – law cases are called after the names of the parties and this is an abbreviated form of the full title of the case, which has now come into common parlance in educational law circles) held that it was reasonable for the claimant to recover damages. The contrary view of the Court of Appeal, that it was unreasonable on public policy grounds because it would 'open the floodgates' to claims, was rejected.

With the passage of time, it can be seen that the House of Lords decision was the correct one. The floodgates have not opened. Granted, there have been many claims based on alleged educational negligence but the courts have be diligent in respecting the professional position of schools in recognising the practical constraints that apply. It is not possible to identify any case, at least amongst those that have reached the eminence of formal reporting in the law reports, where the result could be said colloquially to have been unfair to the school.

A good illustration of this arises from the detailed decision in one of the cases considered on an issue of principle in the *Phelps* group of cases that were first considered in 1995. The 1995 decision established that in principle, if the facts supported a finding that there had been education provision that fell short of what the pupil could reasonably expect to receive, the pupil could legally maintain a claim for damages. Subsequently, the courts heard the actual evidence. *Phelps* itself was one of those cases and the court held that the evidence was sufficient. However, *Phelps* was not a case about school provision: the issue was whether the education psychologist employed by the LEA had been negligent. The other relevant case did relate to school provision, specifically negligence on the part of the headteacher, for failing to diagnose the child's dyslexia. The claim was rejected. The judge found as a fact, having looked at the background documentary evidence such as reports and minutes of governors' meetings, that the headteacher was aware of special needs issues (the facts related to a period not very long after the introduction of the statementing process) and the child had been the subject of review because he was not progressing. A key factor was that the child had subsequently moved to another school (an independent one, as it happens, although that does not affect the principle) and that school had also not diagnosed dyslexia despite the involvement of a child psychologist. The judge held that negligence had not been proved so the school was not liable. This illustrates an important aspect of claims by or on behalf of children. The school does not have to prove that it was not negligent. The claimant has the burden of proving negligence and must satisfy the judge that 'on the balance of probabilities' there was negligence. That is a hard task and the approach of the court in this, effectively the first of the line, has been the benchmark for the judges subsequently.

Phelps was also a dyslexia case but was brought against both the school and the LEA. Here, the LEA professional team including a child psychologist were involved. The school acted in accordance with the advice that it received and was held to be entitled to rely on this. It did not have to form its own judgement as to whether the advice was correct and it would not be held negligent if the advice turned out to be wrong. The judge who heard the evidence came to the conclusion that the child psychologist was negligent in her advice. Because she was an employee of the LEA, he held that the LEA was liable as employer and awarded damages on the grounds that the failure to diagnose the dyslexia would, in effect, cause an injury that would lead the claimant to be disadvantaged in the labour market. That established the facts and the subsequent history of the case related to the legal consequences of those facts. The House of Lords, as already mentioned, allowed the claim and it is worth analysing the reasons for this because this is one of the most important cases in educational law. In considering what follows, it is necessary to keep in mind that the case involved an LEA and an LEA employee, not a school and a school employee, but one can and must extrapolate from one to the other. On the specific facts, the House of Lords held that the negligence that the judge had identified at the original trial was such that it was reasonable to hold the psychologist liable to the pupil for the adverse consequences that she suffered from the failure to diagnose and advise properly. The fact that the advice was tendered to the LEA and not to the pupil or parents was irrelevant: it was clear that all concerned, including the parents, would act in consequence of the advice and it was too narrow a view of the concept of duty of care to restrict the scope of the advice as being for the LEA. The judges were clearly influenced by the fact that the parents would not necessarily be expected to take their own independent advice.

The Effect of the House of Lords' Decision

What did *Phelps* actually decide so far as schools are concerned?

- The general principle that liability may attach for negligent advice in the education sector. This would have taken no one by surprise.

- The general proposition, previously stated by the House of Lords, regarding the potential professional liability of teachers was upheld. To quote one of the judges:

'A teacher must exercise due skill and care to respond appropriately to the manifest problems of [an under-performing] child including informing the headteacher or others about the child's problems and carrying out any instructions he is given. If he does not, he will be in breach of the duty he owes the child.'

This goes beyond the case of the child with special educational needs. Without needing to say it, two of the judges were quite explicit that the duty extends to all children. The Court of Appeal had been concerned about the consequences of recognising such a duty because of the likelihood that a flood of cases would follow, but the House of Lords took a much more robust view. One of the judges said:

'I am not persuaded that there are sufficient grounds to exclude these claims even on the grounds of public policy alone. It does not seem to me that there is any wider interest of the law which would require that no remedy in damages be available. I am not persuaded that the recognition of a liability upon employees would lead to a flood of claims, or even vexatious claims, which would overwhelm the school authorities, nor that it would add burdens and distractions to the already intensive life of teachers. On the contrary, it might have the healthy effect of securing that high standards are sought and secured.'

Teachers might with some justice say that they do not need threat of court action to maintain proper professional standards, but the judge clearly saw a relationship between the need to maintain proper levels of professional performance and the availability of a legal remedy if there is a falling short. Here, educators are in no different a position to doctors, architects or, dare it be said, lawyers. Another of the judges, however, did go to some pains to discourage the idea that there is a separate category of institutional negligence in which liability may arise for a general failure without specified, quantifiable mistakes being identified, stating:

'This is not to open the door to claims based on poor quality of teaching. It is one thing for the law to provide a remedy in damages when there is manifest incompetence or negligence comprising specific, identifiable mistakes. It would be an altogether different matter to countenance claims of a more general nature, to the effect that the child did not receive an adequate education at the school, or that a particular teacher did not teach properly. Proof of under-performance by a child is not by itself evidence of negligent teaching.'

He went on to identify various factors that may lead to under-performance, such as emotional stress, the home environment, the personal relationship between child and teacher and differing teaching styles.

'The list of factors could continue. Suffice to say, the existence of a duty of care owed by teachers to their pupils should not be regarded as furnishing a basis on which generalised "educational malpractice" claims can be mounted.'

In other words, a claim must show specific acts of negligence by identified people leading directly to loss.

- The evidence at trial will be critical. It will remain difficult initially to establish negligence and then to show the link between the negligence and the loss that is claimed. Without some proof of damage, no claim can succeed. The damage must also be attributable to the negligent act. In the specific field of education, a pupil whose special educational needs are, through negligence, not diagnosed will not necessarily be entitled to damages for a lower earning capacity. There would need to be clear evidence that a proper diagnosis and effective implementation of whatever that diagnosis would have indicated would have led to higher earnings than is or might be the case.

- All staff need to be aware of the importance of early diagnosis of special educational needs and of the need to communicate with colleagues. Headteachers need to emphasise the statutory duties on staff (including themselves!) and on the governing body in relation to the identification of special educational needs and be able to demonstrate that this was done.

- Schools should seek external professional Guidance at the earliest opportunity. One important aspect of the *Phelps* case is that the claim against the school was dismissed, broadly on the grounds that the school had done all that it reasonably could be expected to do by seeking advice and acting on it. The fact that the advice was wrong did not affect the school, which was held to be entitled to rely on it.

- The case is not limited to failure to deal properly with learning difficulties. The principles enunciated will apply equally to a gifted child whose needs are insufficiently recognised and/or met. It is hard to see the duty to nurture talent as essentially different from the duty to help those who are disadvantaged.

- It is important that parents are not lulled into a false sense of security where the school knows that the pupil has a learning difficulty. This is particularly true when dealing with written reports on the pupil. There is an understandable wish not to undermine confidence by what is written in such reports but there is also a danger that the coded messages used by teachers to suggest that all is not well without explicitly stating it can be misunderstood. Those reports may be used as evidence that the school had not diagnosed the problem, whereas the truth was that the school was aware of it but was trying to apply strategies that would deal with the problem without causing concern to pupil or parent. Generally, schools should make sure that there is no room for doubt: in particular, if a pupil is placed on the SEN register the parents should be told, and they should be told what the problem is and how it is proposed to address it.

- It is essential that good records are kept and can be found when they are needed, possibly many years after the pupil has left school. The difficulty for primary schools, where records will pass to the secondary school and, indeed, for any school when the pupil moves to another educational establishment, is obvious and insurmountable, short of keeping copies of everything. Record keeping is dealt with in more detail in Chapter 16. Good record keeping will enable the school to demonstrate that it did do all it could reasonably have been expected to do. The fact that the child did not respond, or that the action taken is shown in hindsight not to have been the best option, will not in itself give rise to a successful claim if the steps taken were ones that would be accepted as appropriate within the teaching profession. However, it would be good practice to record the reasons for choice where choice exists.

One word of warning on the subject of records: for highly technical reasons related to how litigation is conducted, there will often be 'fishing' expeditions in the form of a request for records. The purpose of this is to see whether evidence can be found on which to base a claim. Any request for copies of records, particularly if the pupil has left the school some time previously, should be treated with caution, bearing in mind that a request by a parent may well have been instigated by a lawyer who is staying in the background. Parents and pupils have certain statutory rights in relation to records, so disclosure may be necessary, but advice should be sought first. If there are grounds for believing that a claim may be made it would be sensible to refer the matter to the LEA or to the school's insurers at the outset for Guidance.

- The case adds to the reasons why it is important that teachers' performance be properly monitored and that the capability procedure is used effectively. All schools are now required to have a capability procedure in place. The best way to avoid claims is to ensure a teaching staff that is competent and aware.

- The well-run school has nothing to fear from the judgment. Meeting current requirements of good practice will ensure that, even if the school has children who, for whatever reason, do not thrive, there will be no scope for negligence claims. Failure may suggest that there has been negligence but it is not in itself evidence of negligence.

It is worth keeping in mind that teachers and other professionals involved in education do not have an obligation to do the impossible but only to work in a competent and reasonable manner and to meet the standards that may reasonably be expected from someone of that qualification and standing. A court will need cogent evidence before it is likely to make a finding of negligence, and the hurdles that a pupil must overcome to bring a successful damages claim will be great. It is difficult to see many cases succeeding. It is, however, important that schools protect themselves against this risk, not merely by being careful, but by being able to demonstrate that due care was taken. This emphasises the importance of having good procedures in place, complying where applicable with statutory requirements or the recommendations of the SEN Code of Practice. Schools must know their pupils and must be responsive to their needs and their parents' concerns, difficult though that may be in large classes and where staff are under pressure.

This is not to say that schools can be careless. A clear case of negligence will be punished, either by an award of damages or, more likely, by the insurance company settling because of the financial risk of fighting to a hearing, and schools will have to learn to live with a degree of uncertainty. Schools do, therefore, need to be aware of this element of potential liability when planning the delivery of the curriculum and the organisation of the school, but should not be excessively concerned. Generally speaking, if the school acts reasonably in the deployment of the resources available to it, one would expect the courts to recognise this and to judge the school by what was possible rather than by some absolute or abstract standard.

Negligence Relating to Pupils and Safety

The other, and perhaps more familiar, aspect of negligence is in relation to the duty to secure the physical safety of pupils and staff. This duty arises in many different ways, and some of these issues of pupil safety are considered below.

(1) The Condition of the School Premises

School premises must not endanger pupils or staff nor, for that matter, other visitors to the school.

The school must be properly equipped to deal with safety aspects such as means of escape in case of fire. Fire-fighting equipment must be maintained in proper order, and the school must have a proper fire-drill procedure which must be tested regularly. It is common for the headteacher's report to the governing body to report on fire-drills and to state the time taken to evacuate the school.

Routine maintenance must cover such matters as the state of the gas, water and electricity services, although frequently lack of resources will make it difficult to do more than meet the most obvious and pressing needs.

(2) Safety in the Classroom and on the Playing Field

Lessons must be conducted in a safe manner, particularly those that are inherently dangerous such as PE and games, some science activities and some technology subjects. Risks have to be assessed and guarded against as part of the school's health and safety policy, and staff have to be vigilant to see that no injury arises. There is a particular responsibility in the supervision of contact sports to see that the players are evenly matched in terms of physique and strength. Gym and laboratory apparatus and all electrical and mechanical equipment (down to the last electric kettle in the staff room) must be checked regularly, and the result of the inspection noted. Each item should be tagged and marked with the date of inspection. Health and safety issues are dealt with in more detail in Chapter 11. There is a particular obligation for schools to ensure that those in charge of potentially dangerous activities are suitably trained and qualified. For example, a sports referee has a legal duty to apply the laws of the game competently, because one of the purposes of rules in any sport is to protect participants from injury. This places a legal duty of care on the referee. A case in which a rugby referee was held to be liable for injuries sustained by a player highlights the point. Because certain of the laws, in this case the scrummage laws, are there for the protection of the players, and injury is foreseeable if those laws are not applied, the referee was held to have a duty not to be negligent in enforcing them. If, as the Court of Appeal held in this particular case, the referee fell below the standard of a reasonably competent referee and, as a result, a player was injured, the referee had to pay damages for those injuries. This was not a school case but, if anything, the duty on teachers is higher because of the vulnerability of children. The risk is obviously greater in some activities than in others, but the general rule should be that teachers should only be allowed to run a games session if they are clearly competent by virtue of qualifications or established experience to do so.

Safety is not merely a matter of ensuring that there is no physical danger. All aspects of health and safety are relevant so that, for example, when pupils are out-of-doors for long periods (a sports day is an obvious instance) those in charge need to consider such matters as over-exposure to the sun and the availability of sufficient drinks to prevent dehydration.

(3) First Aid and Other Medical Issues

First-aid facilities must be available. Schools should aim to have at least one qualified first-aider available at all times. This can cause great difficulty because the requirement for constant cover means that at least two qualified people are needed. Furthermore, if the first-aider is a teacher there may be difficulty in reconciling the needs of an injured person with the requirement not to leave a class without a teacher in charge. Small schools, with few non-teaching staff, will have a particular problem.

Pupils who need off-site medical attention must not be left without an appropriate adult in charge. Most schools faced with the need for a pupil to go to hospital will want an adult to accompany the child and will wait until a parent or other responsible person arrives. The legal responsibility does not go that far; it may be discharged by placing the child in the care of the hospital or indeed that of an ambulance crew. Ambulance crews may be reluctant to take a child without a member of staff, and this is understandable given that there is always a risk of allegations of improper behaviour which the crew may find difficult to refute. Schools will usually respect this, but there may be times when no member of staff is available to accompany the pupil. In those circumstances, the ambulance crew should be pressed to take the child unaccompanied: that, ultimately, is their legal duty.

Frequently, pupils need medication, either as a result of an incident in school or because of a pre-existing condition. Schools need to have a clear policy about the administration of medicine. Whilst the needs of the child must be met, the school has to ensure that it does not attempt to make medical decisions without proper qualifications. No particular problem should arise over the administration of medicine such as an antibiotic prescribed by a doctor for a specific illness. Greater difficulty arises where a child is on constant medication. Parents will want to ensure that the child receives the medication regularly and punctually. There is Guidance from the DfES, but this does not grapple with the central issue of whether or not a parent has the right to insist on the school making arrangements to administer medicine. Teachers cannot be required to do so, although they may volunteer. A welfare assistant or the school nurse may be required to administer medicine if this is within that person's experience and expertise and this function is covered by the job description. If a school does accept responsibility, then it must set up a system that will work, including cover for when the designated person is absent. Failure to do so may expose the school to a negligence claim. Because of the risk attached to such failure, both to the child and to the school, schools may well decline to take on the task and may insist that the parent makes whatever arrangements are needed. In response, the parent may argue that the school does have a duty as it is *in loco parentis*. Whether the *in loco parentis* rule goes this far is something that has not been considered by the courts. However, as mentioned below, there may be doubt as to whether the rule has any application in the maintained school context.

There is a comprehensive good practice guide issued jointly by the DfES and the Department of Health covering the whole issue. A school that uses the guide and adopts the systems that it advocates will be well protected against claims if, despite the school's best endeavours, something goes wrong.

If there is an emergency, anything that cannot be dealt with by a nurse or first-aider within the limits of their experience and qualifications should be referred to a doctor or hospital.

As always record keeping is vital. The school must keep a record of any injuries or medical incidents in case questions arise about the treatment given or the action taken. The school also needs to maintain records on each pupil with details of any known medical conditions, allergies and any other information that may be relevant to treatment. Those records need to be immediately accessible and up to date. All those who may potentially deal with a medical emergency must know where the records are kept and be aware of the need to consult them. The good practice guide referred to above has a comprehensive set of forms and records designed to be photocopied.

Schools frequently act as hosts for health inspectors, dental checks and immunisations organised by the local Health Authority. Apart from the organisation aspects, schools need to keep in mind that parents will view the school as having a responsibility even if none exists. It is, therefore, good practice for the school to deal with notification to parents and to be satisfied that any necessary parental consent has been given.

(4) Supervision

Children must be properly supervised during the school day while on the school premises. Key times, clearly, are lesson changes and breaktimes when there is large-scale movement around the school and accidents can easily happen. The school must have a system of supervision which takes into account the fact that teachers cannot be required to supervise at lunchtime. This responsibility rests with the headteacher and, in all too many instances, hard-pressed headteachers and deputies spend their lunch periods patrolling the school, inside and out. The standard of care is high but is not an absolute one. A school that takes all proper and reasonable steps to ensure safety will not be liable. In one case, a primary school was held not to be liable when a child ran out of school during the lunch break and was injured by a car. The judge recognised the need to strike a balance between maintaining security and turning the school into a fortress (his phrase) and said that no school could ensure that accidents would never happen. In this case, the judge took the fact that there had only been one similar incident six years earlier as evidence that all proper and reasonable steps had been taken. The claim against the school failed. A later case involved injury to a child on a short pathway leading from the school building to the school gates as the children were leaving school at the end of the school day. The claimant was hurt when hit by an anorak being swung by another child. The judge held that the school was not required to have an adult on duty supervising that movement. Interestingly, the evidence showed that two adults were normally on duty in this area during the lunch break. The judge felt that different considerations applied at the end of the day when the children would only be on the path for a short period.

These cases will give schools comfort, but they cannot afford to be complacent: different facts may lead to a different conclusion, and the fact that there have been no previous accidents will not necessarily mean that the school is not negligent. This is illustrated by a third case, where a school was held liable for injuries to a young pupil in a road accident because the child had left the school premises during school time and the school was not able to show that it had taken precautions to ensure that children could not get out. Critically, there was doubt as to whether a particular gate was normally kept closed. The Court of Appeal held that the combination of the child being in the wrong place at the wrong time and the fact of the accident having taken place gave rise to an assumption of negligence which the school then had to rebut to avoid liability. In the particular case, the school could not do this and was held liable.

Classroom supervision is equally relevant. The school may be held liable for injuries sustained as a result of poor classroom discipline if the teacher concerned has not exercised reasonable skill in keeping the class under control or, indeed, if the class is left unsupervised. This is one reason (of many) why teachers who have difficulty maintaining good order need to be monitored, counselled and ultimately disciplined.

(5) *Responsibility for Pupils Before the School Day Begins*

Children frequently arrive at school well before the start of the school day. The school has no formal responsibility to supervise them, but the circumstances may well mean that some steps should be taken to protect them from particular dangers. For example, if children are allowed into the school buildings, it should be impossible for them to get into the dangerous areas such as laboratories. The playground presents its own problems; the school is not liable for accidents that happen in the course of ordinary play, but if the children are known to take part in obviously dangerous activities it might be necessary for the school to arrange some supervision. The condition of the playground in bad weather can also bring potential liability for accidents. It is true that some years ago a claim by a 14-year-old for damages for injuries that arose from sliding (deliberately) on an icy playground was rejected, but that was in possibly more robust times and the decision might go the other way now. Certainly, if there are snowfalls the school must take reasonable steps to clear a way into school so that all visitors (not merely the children) can have safe access.

A recent case illustrates the current approach. A Year 9 pupil was struck in the eye by a football about five minutes before school started. There was no supervision in the playground even though it was normal for between 30 and 40 members of staff to be in the staff room 15 minutes before the start of school. The headteacher said in evidence that in his experience of other schools it was not normal to supervise the playground before school began and this was backed up by evidence from other staff. However, this was not the first accident involving a football in the playground. Only two months previously there had been an incident which led to a direction being given that leather footballs and basketballs were banned in the playground. Despite this, the records showed that subsequently there had been no less than eight further accidents, happily only minor. There was no evidence that any action had been taken to enforce the ban. The judge discussed the question of the duty to supervise and it is worth quoting at length:

'In my judgment, a school owes to all pupils who are lawfully on its premises the general duty to take such measures to care for their health and safety as are reasonable in all the circumstances. It is neither just nor reasonable to say that a school owes no duty of care at all to pupils who are at school before or after school hours ... It is inevitable and entirely reasonable that pupils will wish to arrive at school some time before school hours. In the present case, the claimant arrived at the school at about 8.30 am. That is typical of what happens in schools up and down the country. The real issue is what is the **scope** of the duty of care owed to pupils who are on school premises before and after school hours. It may be that it is not reasonable to expect a school to do as much to protect its pupils from injury outside school hours as during school hours. All will depend on the circumstances. The longer the period before the start of school hours, the more difficult it may be for a pupil who is injured to say that there was a breach of duty of care in failing to supervise. Moreover, it may be unreasonable to expect constant supervision during the pre-school period, but entirely reasonable to require constant supervision during the break periods. ... But the governing principle is that the school is required to do what is reasonable in all the circumstances.'

After reviewing the particular facts, the judge came to the conclusion that the accident had occurred because the school had failed to enforce the ban. Again, it is worth quoting from the judgment:

> 'I am conscious of the ever increasing pressures piling on the teaching profession. As Lord Slynn pointed out in *Phelps v Hillingdon Borough Council* ... "the professionalism, dedication and standards of those engaged in the provision of educational services are such that cases of liability for negligence will be exceptional". But the law expects of schools no more than that they show such care towards their pupils as is reasonable in all the circumstances. It is important to emphasise that the claimant in the present case was not playing football; he was merely a bystander in a crowded playground where a number of games were being played, and he was behaving entirely reasonably in being where he was and doing what he was doing. The school appreciated that full size leather footballs were dangerous and that the ban on their use was being flouted daily. The attempts to enforce the ban during school breaks were desultory, and during the pre-school period, non-existent. This was a well-behaved school. If the pupils had understood that the school was serious about enforcing the ban, they would have complied with it. To require the school to make spot checks during the pre-school period (at any rate during the period shortly before registration started at 8.45 am) was not unduly onerous. There were 30–40 members of staff in the staff room during that period.'

In one sense, the school might have regarded itself as unlucky because had there not been a policy it might not have been held to be negligent for failing to enforce it. However, there was a clear pattern of accidents over a very short period and common sense (which very often is what the law of negligence equates to) says that something should have been done.

On the other hand, another case brought much relief. It related to an out-of-school activity rather than an event before the start of the school day but the essential issues are the same. In that case, a five-year-old boy was injured on a swing. The facts are worth quoting in some detail:

> 'The claimant, aged 5 at the time of the incident, was a pupil at ... Primary School, for which the [LEA] was responsible. In July 1997, a sports day was organised by the school for some 25 pupils on a playing field, to which access was obtained via a wicket gate. The distance from the gate to the place where the sports events took place was 50 yards. Approximately 20 yards from the gate were some swings. Around 20 of the children taking part in the sports day were accompanied by a parent. The claimant's mother attended with him and sat on a seat between the gate and the swings. She remained

there throughout her stay, which commenced at 11.30 am. At no point did she approach the teachers. At 12.30 pm the claimant joined his mother for a picnic. The claimant's mother did not allow him to play on the swings. The sports events were scheduled to resume at 1.15 pm with kwik cricket, which did not involve the claimant. At about 1.25 pm the claimant's mother decided to leave to do some shopping. She did not return the claimant to the teachers but instead pointed to them some distance away and told the claimant to go and rejoin them, saying something like: "they will tell you what to do". She watched him set off towards them and then turned and left through the gate. The claimant went over to the swings, climbed onto one and played at being "Superman", jumping off. He broke his arm in the process.'

The judge who first heard the case held that, although he did not consider there was a specific failure of supervision, the school (and therefore the LEA) was liable for failing to immobilise the swing and damages were awarded. On appeal, the decision was overturned. Again, a quotation from the judgment:

'First of all, this was a properly supervised event. That is clear on the facts and on the judge's conclusions. As to warnings, any further warnings would have made no difference and I add that it seems slightly unreal to me to suggest that there was a legal duty to warn the claimant's mother that there might be a danger in unsupervised playing on the swings. **Even actions in tort must keep in mind an air of reality and common sense point** [author's emphasis].

The second point on which I would focus is this. The correctness of the judgment hinges on the conclusion that there was a duty to "immobilise" the swings. I do not think that it would be reasonable to impose any such legal duty on the school. Of course, after the event one can think of all sorts of things that might be done to prevent accidents which have happened. But the question here is not whether the school might have done it or whether after the event it becomes apparent that the school should have done it, but whether at the time there was a duty to do so. I do not think there was. The school had a good plan for dealing with the swings. There were some 25 children and lots of teachers or helpers. Those who were taking part in the activities at the time were under the close supervision of those teachers or helpers. No one other than Ryan, it seems, played on the swings at all. While Ryan was with his mother he too did not play on the swings. I can find no breach of duty in the school not going further and immobilising the swings. Playing fields cannot be made free of all hazard. The mere fact that the school had diagnosed a possible or potential hazard did not mean it was duty bound to take the step of immobilising the swings.

Balancing the element of risk with the plan that the school had made, I cannot conclude that it was in breach of duty. I would not expect a prudent parent organising a sporting event on such a field to have immobilised the swings, any more than if there had been a tree on the field, the school or a prudent parent would have been duty bound to rope that off too.

Thirdly, as to the position of Ryan's mother. ... I accept that, so far as the school was concerned, it remained responsible over the whole day. But ... the school discharged its obligation to Ryan when it delivered him to his mother. While he remained with his mother it is plain that the school would not be in breach of any duty of care owed to him. I do not accept that he was ever re-delivered, so to speak, to the school at any time before the accident happened. Accordingly ... that must be an end to the matter. Ryan had remained with his mother, she then left, she did not return him to the teachers, the accident happened, as I have already indicated, before he was re-delivered. In the circumstances, for this reason as well, either there was no breach of any duty owed by the school or such breach was not causative.'

The judge clearly took the view that this was simply an accident and that fault could not be attributed to anyone, except perhaps Ryan who mistakenly thought that as Superman he was immune from harm – perhaps an action against the creator of Superman would have stood as good a chance of success. More significantly, the judge clearly had in mind that a finding of liability in circumstances such as this would have greatly increased the responsibilities on schools, greatly increased the cost of insurance and potentially greatly restricted the likelihood of events of this kind being organised in the future.

(6) Responsibility for Pupils After the School Day Ends

If children are permitted to stay in school after the end of the school day, the school retains responsibility for them, even if they are taking part in 'unofficial' activities organised by individual members of staff or by the pupils themselves. Schools, therefore, need to have procedures in place for such activities to be supervised and for records to be kept of those on site after hours – these would be important if, for example, there was a fire and the school had to be evacuated.

Security and Access to the School

Security is now a major issue for schools. Schools should have clear and workable security procedures which will enable them to control access so as to minimise the risk of unwelcome intruders. It is probably impossible to make a school totally secure, particularly where the school site consists of several separate buildings, but there are many steps that can be taken to reduce exposure.

Within the School Precincts

No one is automatically entitled to come onto school premises – not even governors. The premises of community schools are under the control of the LEA during school hours, and those of VC, VA and foundation schools are under the ultimate control of the governing body. In each case, the immediate day-to-day control would normally be delegated to the headteacher. Such delegation gives the headteacher the power to refuse entry and to insist that an unwelcome person leaves. The legal backup is now to be found in section 547 of the Education Act 1996, which makes it a criminal offence for anyone to cause a nuisance or disturbance to the annoyance of those who lawfully use school premises, including playgrounds and playing fields. The police have the power to remove anyone who is reasonably suspected of committing an offence under the section. That power can also be exercised by anyone authorised to do so by the governing body. Accordingly, every governing body should formally resolve that the headteacher (including any person acting as headteacher) should have that authority. Reasonable force can be used but, again, there should be guidelines that make it clear that a person exercising this power should not do so at personal risk. There is, however, a hidden trap in the exercise of these powers: the right to remove anyone depends on there being reasonable grounds for suspecting that an offence has been committed. If those grounds do not exist, the person ejected may have a claim against the school. It is, therefore, sensible for the police to be called wherever possible.

There is other legislation relevant to school security and, for that matter, school discipline. One such statute is the Public Order Act 1986 relating to threatening, offensive or abusive behaviour. Another is the Offensive Weapons Act 1996, which made it a criminal offence to carry a knife or other offensive weapon on school premises. Folding pocket knives with a blade no longer than three inches and knives carried as religious symbols are still legal. The police have the power to search and arrest if they have reasonable grounds to suspect that an offence under the Act has been committed. Finally, the Protection from Harassment Act 1997 makes it a criminal offence to pursue a course of conduct that amounts to harassment or makes someone fear violence. Single incidents will not amount to a course of conduct but the Act could be relevant in dealing with repeated threats, perhaps from disgruntled parents, or even repeated bullying of, or by, pupils or staff.

In addition to criminal procedures, civil action can be taken through the courts for an injunction to prevent a named person from coming onto school premises. That, though, involves cost and time: the injunction can be obtained quickly but it will need a lot of energy that is perhaps better applied to running the school. Less drastic remedies should be tried first. Schools have the power to ban individuals from coming onto school premises or to impose conditions on entry. One advantage of this is that it extends beyond the most obvious areas of security threat to instances of unacceptable behaviour which may not be a breach of the law, e.g. it may be used for rudeness or other forms of conduct that do not fit with the school's reasonable expectations. The threat may be enough to resolve the problem and if it does not, then the injunction route is still open and can be used even for conduct short of assault if the school has behaved reasonably. There are some simple rules to follow:

- the ban should be imposed by the headteacher. No one else should be given authority to take such action;

- the offender must be told, in writing, that the headteacher is considering revoking the implied permission that parents (assuming that the offender is a parent, although the same rule applies to any unwelcome visitor) have to come onto the school premises and brief reasons must be given;

- if the headteacher is prepared to allow some degree of access but subject to conditions, they should be listed and should be easily complied with. It is better to impose a total ban than to try to enforce unworkable conditions;

- the headteacher needs to avoid over-reaction and to make sure that the ban will not cause unreasonable child-care problems. This is particularly important where young children need to be collected from and delivered to the school;

- unless matters are very urgent, the offender should be given an opportunity to give reasons why the ban should not be imposed. To avoid further confrontation it is possible to ask for those reasons to be given in writing or via a third party. Only a brief time need be given for response – two clear school days would probably be enough;

- the headteacher should consider any comments that are received and make a calm decision, which should then be confirmed in writing.

Many LEAs will have standard-form letters to use in this situation. However, LEAs are often reluctant to see this power used and sometimes headteachers may need to assert themselves.

Reception procedures are of obvious importance. The first person that a visitor meets should be a designated member of the school staff who is able to ascertain the reason for the visit and judge whether the visitor should be allowed into the school. It is good practice for anyone in the school who is expecting a visitor to notify the receptionist of the visitor's name and expected time of arrival. Visitors who arrive without an appointment should not be allowed to pass the reception area without proper verification. Wherever possible, visitors entering the school should be required to sign in and, perhaps, wear visitor badges. Any car registration number should also be noted. Apart from any other consideration, this process will act as a check if there is a fire or other emergency that requires the building to be vacated.

Pupils should not be involved in any way in dealing with unwelcome visitors. If, as happens in many schools, there is a rota for pupils to welcome visitors, the pupils must have clear guidelines on what to do if they are faced with potential trouble. The arrangements should ensure that there is always a responsible adult within easy call, and there should be enough pupils working the rota at any one time to enable one of them to summon help quickly.

The school should review its physical security and take whatever steps it can within available resources to ensure that fences and gates are in good condition. If there are rights of way across school playgrounds and playing fields, the local authority should be asked to relocate or close such rights of way.

Out of school

Generally speaking, schools do not have responsibility for what happens off the school premises, although if there is a known or obvious danger at any particular time the school cannot ignore it. Thus, if there is potential trouble outside the school, children may need to be protected by being escorted by adults, or the police may need to be called. If incidents occur in the neighbourhood of the school, it may be relevant to warn parents and students of the need to be vigilant. That may be particularly true in relation to students who arrive late and do not, therefore, have the inbuilt protection of significant numbers en route for school. Staff are not, however, obliged to put themselves in a position of danger and cannot be required to do so. The school also has a duty to ensure that children cannot leave the school during the course of the day without proper reason, and (particularly for younger children) that there are clear arrangements for children to go home or for parents to collect them at the end of the school day. Again, it is a matter of degree just how far a school needs to go but, in general, the younger the child, the greater the responsibility. The duty owed to a five-year-old who wanders off site is quite different from that owed to a year 11 student who deliberately leaves without consent. Schools can usefully establish guidelines for dealing with external dangers. These will vary from school to school but the following points are relevant.

- The primary responsibility for maintaining order outside the school rests with the police, who should be called at the first sign of trouble.

- There should be a clear written procedure (with contact names and telephone numbers) available for immediate reference by anyone who might need to summon police assistance. Remember that it may be needed in a situation of great urgency and panic.

- If there is evident danger outside the school, pupils should be required to remain within the school boundaries until the police make conditions safe. Staff should be instructed not to intervene.

- Any rota for patrolling outside the school must be on a voluntary basis and no one should be disadvantaged in any way by declining to participate.

- Staff must be advised not to intervene in any physical disturbance. If their mere presence is not enough to prevent trouble, the police should be called immediately. It would clearly be an advantage if staff on patrol had mobile telephones. Indeed, with the universality of mobile telephones we may not be far from the time when it would be held negligent not to ensure that patrol staff were so equipped.

- In no circumstances should pupils be asked to patrol or otherwise get involved in external security duties.

- Schools, particularly primary schools where the pupils are more vulnerable, should make sure that parents know where the school's responsibility ends.

- Staff may also be vulnerable if they are working in school after school hours, and the school has a responsibility to take reasonable steps to make them safe. The threat can come from disaffected pupils as well as from those coming from outside. The school does, therefore, need to secure the premises from intruders and also ensure that pupils staying in school after hours are supervised – this ties in with the responsibility, mentioned earlier, to keep such pupils safe.

Discipline and Pupil Safety

It is now clearly accepted law that, when dealing with violence between pupils, the school (and any governor pupil discipline committee or appeal panel deciding whether or not to uphold an exclusion) needs to pay proper regard to the victim and to the school community. This shows that governing bodies have to be aware at all times of the overall implications of their actions. A school that fails to cover foreseeable problems may find itself fighting a negligence claim even though, for example, the particular incident took place off the school premises.

One aspect relates to the conduct of pupils outside school hours. The law is not specific on how far the school can exercise its disciplinary policy beyond the school gates, but there have been indications from the courts that some degree of control is acceptable and this is now reflected in the Guidance on exclusion covered in detail in Chapter 8. One case established that a school was entitled to exercise disciplinary powers over a pupil who acted violently towards another pupil of the school off school premises, and the probability is that any reasonable rules involving pupil behaviour will be upheld. Schools are entitled to protect themselves and their community and, with the potential expansion of areas in which negligence claims could arise, might in the future be held to have a responsibility to do so. Schools should, therefore, consider making rules relating to:

- behaviour in the immediate vicinity of the school;

- behaviour when travelling to and from school, particularly when in school uniform and therefore being identified with the school;

- behaviour between pupils at any time, at least where the school can be identified.

Bullying

Schools can be liable if they fail to prevent bullying and this has become a major area for litigation. The duty is to take such steps as are reasonable to ensure that pupils are not bullied. There is no absolute duty to prevent bullying – the law does not require schools to do the impossible – but the school is expected to be aware of professional thinking on the subject and to apply that in a proper manner. It is well known that bullying can have a serious adverse effect on a child and, if not dealt with in time, can lead to permanent damage. Circular 10/99 spelt it out:

> 'The emotional distress caused by bullying in whatever form – be it racial, or as a result of a child's appearance, behaviour or special educational needs, or related to sexual orientation – can prejudice school achievement, lead to lateness or truancy and, in extreme cases, end with suicide.'

That damage can be identified both in terms of causation and effect. If it leads to academic under-achievement, there can be a consequential impact on the child's potential in the labour market and, although it is difficult, it is not impossible to quantify that in terms of financial loss.

Much work has been done in relation to bullying and the DfES has published a very comprehensive tool pack called 'Bullying – Don't Suffer in Silence'. That is required reading for schools, failure to deal with bullying and bullying issues in line with the pack may be seized upon as evidence that the school has been negligent. It will not be conclusive evidence but the opportunity to challenge what the school has done on this basis puts the school on the back foot.

It is still unclear to what extent the school can be held responsible for out-of-school bullying. A recent case, confirmed by the Court of Appeal, absolved the school from liability for bullying that took place out of school. The Court of Appeal considered that the school had done all it could reasonably have been required to do in the circumstances but the view expressed by the judge who heard the evidence, namely restricting the school's obligation to taking reasonable care to prevent such bullying spilling over into school, in other words to taking suitable defensive measures in school, was considered by the Court of Appeal to be too restrictive. The question here is the same one that has to be answered in every negligence case, namely whether what the school did, or did not do, was reasonable taking all the facts into account. The Court of Appeal made it clear that it was up to the school to make a professional judgment based on accepted good practice and that there was a balance to be struck between the interests of the various children involved. It also acknowledged that an ineffective intervention, especially where the bullying takes place out of school, may actually make the situation worse. Doubts about the likely effectiveness of action could justify doing nothing. Conversely, because each case turns on its own facts, there may well be circumstances in which the school should take action. If there is clear evidence that the bullying is by other members of the school, then the school may be justified in applying, and indeed may be held to be under a duty to apply, the school's discipline policy and may apply such sanctions as are available. Clearly, however, the school cannot be held responsible for failing to prevent events that occur when the pupils are out of range of the school's supervisory net.

It is relatively easy for a claim for damages on behalf of a child who can be shown to have been bullied to succeed. Claims will be dealt with under the school's insurance policy but that is not a satisfactory answer, especially as the insurers will look at the financial equation of settling against fighting and will settle a claim when the cost of defending looks unattractive. Schools may find themselves tarnished with the stigma of a settled claim even though the evidence may be inconclusive. This can seriously damage morale.

The obvious answer is to make sure that the school cannot be criticised in what it has done in any given situation. To achieve this, the school needs to be able to show the following:

- compliance with formal legal requirements;
- awareness of responsibilities throughout the school;
- awareness amongst the pupils of the school's expectations and of what to do if they are bullied or know of others being bullied;
- proper responses to reports or indicators of bullying;
- records demonstrating compliance with the above – no matter how good the system, one must be able to show (possibly several years after the event) that it was properly applied in the particular case. Locating the records can be as much of a problem as creating them. A pupil can bring a claim at any time up to reaching the age of 21 and possibly

even later depending on circumstances – out of sight is by no means out of mind.

The first essential is a specific anti-bullying policy which anyway is a statutory requirement. The school will have behaviour and discipline policies which interrelate and these will be developed by the school to reflect the ethos, expectations and characteristics of the school. These policies may vary, in tone if not ultimately in content or expectations, from school to school, but the components of a bullying policy are likely to be similar in most schools. Separating it from other policies enhances its visibility and makes it less likely that it will be overlooked.

The governing body needs to be closely involved in the formulation of the policy and will need to ensure the following:

- awareness amongst all staff of the importance of detecting and dealing with bullying;

- Guidance, perhaps in the Staff Handbook, on the indicators of bullying in terms of both perpetrator and victim;

- Guidance on the steps to take if bullying is detected or suspected;

- a clear policy on how perpetrators will be dealt with. The sanctions need to be clear, made known to all pupils and be seen to be applied consistently and fairly. A 'zero tolerance' policy is often advocated, here and also in relation to substance abuse. This needs to be treated with some caution. 'Zero tolerance' implies that there will only be one outcome if the relevant rule is breached, usually permanent exclusion. That is attractive at first sight but it raises other issues. There may be instances where the headteacher feels that permanent exclusion is not justified notwithstanding the policy. Reinstatement by an appeal panel, or not excluding in the first place, may have serious consequences for the policy because it indicates that zero tolerance does not actually mean what it says. The message becomes confused. It is better to leave some leeway, so that whilst a certain outcome, say permanent exclusion, will be regarded as the norm in the overwhelming number of cases, it will not be automatic. There should be criteria against which the responses are assessed and the decision taken, rather than a policy that requires an automatic penalty. The facts may indicate one response but that feels wrong for the particular individual. Thus, for a given offence, permanent exclusion will 'normally' or 'save in the most exceptional circumstances' be the consequence. This does leave the child/parent with the opportunity to argue that their case should be an exception but if the criteria are laid out, the point can be met;

- a clear policy on how the victim will be dealt with. Lawyers dealing with parental complaints often find that measures have been taken (with the best of intentions to protect the child) that leave the victim feeling isolated from other children and feeling that the remedy is worse than the disease. Clearly if, as must be the case, a central part of the policy is to ensure that acts of bullying become known, action taken following the policy must not operate as a disincentive to report incidents of bullying.

The policy should be:

- short and explicit. It should be clearly distinguished from the procedure laid down for implementing the policy – often the two are combined in school policy documents, which leads to a lack of clarity and effectiveness;

- made widely known. The headteacher has a statutory duty to circulate the school's general discipline measures in writing to staff and parents each year, but that is the formal minimum. No reasonable opportunity should be lost to keep the policy in the front of people's minds. Possibilities are reproduction of the policy in pupils' homework or activity diaries, display in classrooms, and inclusion in the school prospectus and as an appendix to the home–school agreement;

- reinforced regularly for both pupils and staff in, for example, assemblies and classroom situations such as registration periods. There could well be whole-school in-service training on the subject from time to time, and schools should consider sending particular teachers on specialist external courses. The objective (apart from the obvious one of reducing the incidence of bullying) is to be able to demonstrate that the school has taken its responsibilities seriously and has devoted reasonable resources to them.

Most important of all is having a clear procedure for dealing with individual and repeated bullying. Once a member of staff becomes aware of bullying there must be a process which ensures that all those who deal with both the perpetrator and the victim know about it. That is not to say that everyone has to jump into action, but it is important that the school responds in a collective and consistent way. In particular, where the victim needs to be supported, everyone must know of the need and how to provide for it. Early awareness may in itself go a long way towards containing the problem. Each school will decide its mechanisms and they will vary depending on the size of the school. The common factors will be:

- definition of roles and responsibilities;

- focus on reporting – whether by a parent, an adult (not necessarily a teacher), the victim or another pupil. Bear in mind that a pupil will not necessarily go to the most obvious person, but to an adult that the child can trust;

- an investigation process. Since this could result in an exclusion, any investigation should be rigorous, bearing in mind the possible need to produce compelling evidence to the Pupil Discipline Committee and on any subsequent appeal.

One case demonstrated the value of good policies. In that case:

- there were policies in place which were consistent with DfES Guidance – in this case Circular 8/94 on bullying;

- there was a distinction drawn by the judge between episodes of bullying and one-off assaults;

- the school had taken note of the complaints of bullying and had acted;

- the school's systems and arrangements for discipline and for countering bullying were reasonable; and

- the school could not have taken action in advance to prevent the bullying and the response and sanctions were reasonable.

As a result, the school was held not to be liable for the incidents that had actually occurred.

In the light of the revised Guidance on exclusions which entitles a school to exclude permanently for bullying even for a first offence and which effectively reduces the likelihood of an appeal panel directing reinstatement in such cases, schools may need to be able to show good cause for not permanently excluding someone who can be shown to have bullied another pupil. Failure to exclude permanently without good reason may in itself be treated as evidence of negligence in dealing with the problem.

Out-of-school Activities

Out-of-school activities must be properly arranged and supervised. The DfES has produced comprehensive Guidance on all aspects of school visits, home and abroad, which includes lists of useful contracts and specimen forms that can be used in the organisation of trips and visits.

Responsibility falls clearly into two areas. The first is the preparation for the trip, ensuring that all concerned understand their functions and that foreseeable problems are planned for. Risk assessment is identified as a critical element in the planning process. The Guidance contains detailed advice on how to go about risk assessment and it particularly cautions against complacency when places such as a local swimming pool are visited frequently. The responsibility for risk assessment is placed on the person actually leading the group. This may involve co-operation with the centre or organisation that is to host the visit, and it is important to establish who will do what and that there is no danger that misunderstandings may lead to a vital task being overlooked. The burden during the trip is on the supervising member of staff and is quite high. There may, for example, be an increased risk to pupils because of the bad behaviour of a few in the party, and the person in charge has to be vigilant and take any necessary precautions. Even so, the test will never be other than what is reasonable in all the circumstances. The problem is that children are endlessly inventive, and the ways in which an accident can arise are limitless. Whilst accident prevention is the first priority, making sure that there is proper insurance cover comes very close behind.

The LEA should have its own general Guidance in place and should provide training, insurance (at least for community schools) and emergency arrangements.

The DfES Guidance seeks to place specific responsibilities on the school governing body. Even though that might not now represent the strict legal position in the light of the new division of responsibilities between the governing body and the headteacher, most governing bodies will have a special concern about safety of pupils on school trips and would be well advised to follow it. The Guidance urges the governing body to ensure that:

- the visit has a specific and stated objective;
- the headteacher or group leader shows how the plans for the trip comply with regulations and guidelines with particular

emphasis on the school's health and safety policy, indicating that external visits need to be covered by the policy;

- the headteacher or group leader reports back after the visit;

- the governing body is informed of 'less routine' visits well in advance. Clearly the governing body needs to be satisfied that any special planning required is in place;

- proposals for visits involving an overnight stay or travel outside the UK are assessed. If necessary, the governing body should refer such proposals to the LEA for approval.

Governing bodies can quite properly delegate these responsibilities to a committee and could possibly designate a single governor as having special responsibility. Clearly, it would defeat the object of the Guidance if that single governor were to be the headteacher. The headteacher has quite separate responsibilities which the Guidance sets out in detail. These may overlap with those of the group leader and the Guidance makes clear that if the headteacher pays a visit to a group which is under the control of another person, that other person stays in control (and with responsibility) and the headteacher should follow instructions.

There are particular responsibilities in leading activities that are inherently or potentially dangerous. Any school organising, for example, a Duke of Edinburgh Award trip involving camping and initiative exercises by the students must make sure that those in charge have appropriate qualifications and/or experience and have contingency plans to cope with emergencies. The students must be properly equipped for the conditions they may encounter and must be fully briefed on what they should and should not do. They must have clear written instructions to cover emergencies and should be required always to be in groups of at least two. Systems must be in place to maintain proper contact with the groups, and parents must know what arrangements have been made and how they may contact the school if the need arises. Similar considerations arise, to a greater or lesser degree depending on the element of risk, to all activities outside school. Even a trip to the theatre requires a briefing to the students on what to do if the group gets fragmented.

Where the visit is to a recognised activity centre, the school needs to check whether it is licensed for the activity in question. If it is, then responsibility can safely be left with the centre, but the organiser needs to establish how far the licence extends. There may be elements, such as catering and accommodation, that are outside the scope of the licensing scheme and the school needs to check these elements for itself. Where the centre is not licensed, the school will need written assurances on a range of matters. The Guidance goes into considerable detail on this. It is difficult to avoid the conclusion that, at least for UK-based activities, it is essential for a responsible person from the school to visit the centre during the planning stage and certainly before the school becomes contractually bound.

Frequently, parents are asked to sign indemnities purporting to release the school from liability in the case of accident. These may be effective where damage to property arises: they will rarely, if ever, be effective to exclude liability for injuries resulting from negligence on the part of the school. Note, however, that the school can exclude its own liability if the activity is organised by a third party rather than by the school and the third party confirms direct to the parents that it accepts responsibility. The position needs to be made very clear to parents, and the school should check that the third party has all necessary insurances. In any event, parents must be given full information about the proposed trip so that they can make an informed decision as to whether their child is to participate. They must also be given an opportunity to advise the school on any special medical aspects, and the school must take these into account in the planning. Finally, parents must be given clear information about cost – any charging must comply with the general law about charging for such activities – and must be given reasonable time to find the money.

Teachers are required to act as they would as the responsible parent. They must help with discipline and control and must stop the visit or a particular activity if they think the risk to the health and safety of the pupils is unacceptable. Adult volunteers have similar obligations although they must not be left in sole charge and cannot discontinue a visit or activity: they should make any concerns known to the group leader.

Pupils have their own responsibility. They must be briefed on how to avoid risk and instructed on how they should behave, including advice on being sensitive to local codes and customs when abroad. The Guidance makes it clear that pupils whose behaviour may be considered to be a danger to themselves or others on the trip should not be allowed to go. Where possible, the curricular aims of the visit should be achieved by other means. The school must take account of any special educational needs of individual pupils in order to make sure that the visit is accessible in educational terms and that such pupils are safe.

Travelling

The journey poses its own problems if the school uses its own transport. The school has an obvious duty to ensure that its minibus is properly equipped, in roadworthy condition, serviced and maintained to a high level, taxed and insured, and driven only by competent and qualified people holding a full driving licence. Drivers must be over 21 and must pass an additional test qualifying them to drive small passenger-carrying vehicles, i.e. vehicles which can carry nine to 16 passengers. The qualification also requires meeting higher medical standards than required by the ordinary driving licence. Certain drivers, who held full licences prior to 1 January 1997 and whose licence does not require renewal and shows an entitlement to drive vehicles in categories A, B or D1 may drive minibuses with a maximum of 16 passenger seats without passing the additional test or meeting the higher medical requirements provided the driving is not for hire and reward. Furthermore, a person who is over 21 and has held a car licence for at least two years may drive a minibus for a non-commercial body for social purposes provided this is done on a voluntary basis and is not for hire and reward. This obviously will not apply to school staff but may cover parents who volunteer to drive. There are, though, different views as to what constitutes hire and reward. The DVLA web-site at www.dvla.gov.uk/drivers/drvmbus indicates that hire or reward 'encompasses any payment in cash or in kind by (or on behalf of) passengers which gives them a right to be carried'. Thus, a school that makes a charge to pupils for a school trip involving a minibus almost certainly is providing the journey for hire or reward. By contrast, taking a body of pupils by minibus to, for example, a sports fixture where the pupils (or parents) pay nothing would not be hire or reward and the driver may be able to take advantage of one of the exemptions. DVLA have, though, been quoted anecdotally as saying that a member of staff would automatically be driving for hire or reward by virtue of being a paid employee. That is a difficult construction to accept and the best test is probably to check with insurers as to the circumstances in which they would regard a driver as driving for hire or reward. They should then check that the school's policy is written sufficiently widely to ensure that anyone who drives is covered. The consequences of driving while uninsured need not be spelt out.

The school will need a special permit so that it does not have to comply with the licensing requirements that apply to public service vehicles, and it is important to see that this is obtained and renewed. Apart from anything else, failure to do so could lead to the school inadvertently being uninsured. Usually, the driver will also have the responsibility of supervising the passengers, and journeys need to be planned so that the burden on the driver is not excessive. The dangers of an over-tired driver with a party of schoolchildren do not need to be stated. The Guidance indicates that responsibility for the minibus will normally rest with the chair of governors or the headteacher. Whilst recognising that compassion may lead governing bodies to wish to share responsibilities with hard-pressed headteachers, it is felt that this is an obligation that the chair of governors should resist accepting.

The Defensive Driver Training Centre has made a series of recommendations relating to school minibus journeys. These include:

- the presence, where possible, of a second member of staff to supervise the pupils and assist in navigation;
- all passengers to have and to wear seat-belts. It is illegal to allow three children to occupy two seats;
- a rest period of at least 20 minutes if the journey is of two to three hours' duration;
- keeping windows closed to reduce road noise;
- banning cans of drinks so as to avoid sudden sharp noises and the possibility of a can rolling under foot pedals;
- carrying a mobile telephone, first-aid kit, fire extinguisher and warning triangle.

Care must also be taken to ensure that the vehicle is not overloaded. Logic suggests that a minibus should be able to take a full complement of passengers, plus luggage on the roof-rack. However, this could lead to the vehicle being above the maximum design weight and therefore overloaded. Apart from it being illegal to drive an overloaded vehicle, the insurance policy may be invalidated, as it also could be if the vehicle has not been properly maintained. It may, therefore, be necessary to take luggage in a trailer but here again care needs to be taken to ensure that the vehicle still complies with regulations relating to emergency escape – a rear door will not be regarded as a suitable emergency exit when a trailer is being towed.

If the journey is by public transport, the responsibility of the school is one of supervision only, but is still a heavy one. Care is needed to ensure that there are enough staff to attend fully to the pupils, especially if the group is not self-contained and is in contact with members of the public.

As always, the critical test is one of reasonableness. The school is not required to ensure safety in all circumstances; accidents do happen and the courts accept that 100 per cent supervision is not feasible. Nevertheless, shortage of resources will not in itself be a defence to a claim if the available resources have not been appropriately deployed.

Where teachers or volunteers (who should be carefully selected) use their own cars to take pupils on visits, they must be sure that their insurance covers such use (and that it is not use for hire or reward which normally is not permitted under individual private car insurance policies) and that their cars are roadworthy. The Guidance suggests that the headteacher should seek assurances on this. That is a surprisingly limited responsibility. It would be good practice for the headteacher to insist on seeing insurance documentation and, where appropriate, MOT test certificates as a minimum.

Schools will carry insurance cover against claims for physical injury and it may be that cover can also be obtained against claims for negligent provision of education. If the school wants its insurers to deal with a claim, it must not get involved in correspondence or discussions with the claimant, but must immediately refer the claim to the insurance company which will normally then handle it entirely.

Particular issues arise with overseas trips. To what extent does a school need to investigate the locale? Where the trip is an exchange visit, and the host school is taking on overall responsibility, what is the duty of the visiting school? Where pupils will be staying with families, what checks should the school make?

The broad principle is that the usual risk assessment needs to be conducted in the same way as for any other trip. Where the trip is organised by an agency or, for example, a charity specialising in such ventures, the school needs to be satisfied that the agency has carried out risk assessments and that it applies the same standards as the school itself would apply. Certainly, the school need not make its own physical inspection, tempting though a foreign trip may be for the relevant school staff.

Where the trip is effectively under the aegis of an overseas school, the school needs to know that the receiving school has procedures and standards that broadly equate to those that would be applied at home. If they do, and the school is satisfied that suitable risk assessments have been carried out for the activities that are contemplated, then there is no reason why the trip should not go ahead even if representatives of the school have not made an inspection. However, there does need to be a degree of close contact with the host school and (especially if it is contemplated that the event may become a regular one) a preliminary reconnaissance would be sensible.

Frequently, the school party will be supervised by the school, even though the host school takes on responsibility for organising the activities. If those leading the school party feel that the standards being applied by the host do not conform with those that would be applied at home, they have no option, embarrassing and professionally difficult though it may be, but to insist that the higher standards are applied. They should withdraw the pupils from the activity if the host will not comply.

Exchange visits present real difficulties. Where a school in the UK acts as a host, it takes on a responsibility to the visiting children. A council of perfection requires that all host families be subjected to Criminal Records Bureau (CRB) enhanced checks and that should be done if it is at all practicable. Parents who object immediately place themselves under suspicion, even though there may be no other evidential basis for that suspicion, and they should not be allowed to act as hosts. However, many schools will be diffident about doing this, as it can be seen as an implied slight on the integrity of the parents. If schools decide not to run checks, they must be sure that they know the families well enough to be confident that there is no measurable risk. Where it is the foreign school that is the host, the school needs to know what precautions the host school takes and a judgment made. Parents should be given as much information, in general terms, of the risk assessments carried out so that they can make an informed decision as to whether their children should participate. It would also be sensible, if the trip is one of some magnitude or if it is intended to be the first of a series, to see whether the school's insurers have any comments or recommendations to make.

NUTRITIONAL STANDARDS

Schools are now obliged to comply with regulations as to the nutritional standards that are to be met when providing school lunches. This is done first by creating five categories of food, namely (to quote the regulations):

'A *Fruit and vegetables.* These include fruit and vegetables in all forms (whether fresh, frozen, canned, dried or in the form of juice);

B *Starchy foods.* These include bread, chapattis, pasta, noodles, rice, potatoes, sweet potatoes, yams, millet and cornmeal;

C *Meat, fish and other non-dairy sources of protein.* These include meat and fish in all forms (whether fresh, frozen, canned or dried), including meat or fish products, eggs, nuts, pulses and beans, other than green beans;

D *Milk and dairy foods.* These include milk, cheese, yoghurt (including frozen yoghurt and drinking yoghurt), fromage frais, milkshakes and custard, but not butter or cream;

E *Foods containing fat and foods containing sugar.* These include margarine, butter, other spreading fats, cooking oils and fats, oil-based salad dressings, mayonnaise, salad cream, cream, chocolate, crisps, biscuits, pastries, cakes, puddings, ice-cream, rich sauces, gravies, jam, sugary soft drinks, sweets, sugar and jelly, but not any foods falling within any other group.'

Schools are then required to make provision within those groups according to whether they are primary or secondary schools. Thus, primary schools must ensure that, on each day, food from each of the groups A, B, C and D is available so that (again, quoting the regulations):

'(a) within group A:

(i) fresh fruit, fruit tinned in juice, or fruit salad shall be available every day;

(ii) a fruit-based dessert shall be available at least twice in any week;

(iii) a type of vegetable (which does not fall within group B) shall be available every day;

(b) within group B, fat or oil shall not be used in the cooking process on more than three days in any week;

(c) within group C:

(i) fish shall be available at least one day in any week;

(ii) red meat shall be available on at least two days in any week.'

Sources of protein in group C can include dairy sources of protein.

The secondary school requirement is different and gives much greater flexibility, no doubt reflecting the wider range of choice and style of provision in secondary schools. Here the regulations provide that on each day two types of food from each of groups A, B, C and D shall be available so that:

'(a) within group A, both a fruit and a vegetable shall be available;

(b) within group B, on every day that a food cooked in oil or fat is available, a food not cooked in fat or oil shall also be available;

(c) within group C, fish shall be available on at least two days in any week and red meat shall be available on at least three days in any week.'

Special schools may adopt either framework.

The eagle-eyed will note the absence of any reference to group E in either the primary or secondary requirements. This reflects the regulations.

WELFARE

The Children Act 1989 was a milestone in the development of child welfare law, but its impact on mainstream day schools is somewhat marginal. It widened the categories of those who are to be treated as parents by including not only natural parents but also those who have parental responsibility by agreement or by court order. This has important implications for schools. Clearly, they have to deal with those who fall within the category; equally clearly, they have no responsibility to those who fall outside it. It is a complete answer to such people that if they feel that they should be allowed to exercise rights, they should obtain a court order. This is particularly relevant in the case of the natural unmarried father who has no inherent rights. Local authorities holding care orders come within the category of parent, as do those in whose favour a residence order has been made. The wide definition does not only apply in relation to child welfare: it will also apply, for example, in determining who is entitled to vote in a ballot on the election of parent governors.

In Loco Parentis and the Right to Punish

Received wisdom (doubted by one writer who thinks that the school's powers derive entirely from legislation and that the *in loco parentis* doctrine no longer applies) is that schools are *in loco parentis* while the child is in their care and can do anything that a reasonable parent would do, provided consent has not been refused. This has always been the justification for the imposition of sanctions and generally regulating the behaviour of children in school. It covers the giving of detentions, but the school needs to tread carefully here. There is no express absolute right to detain a child, and if the detention were unreasonable, or not in accordance with procedures, it could constitute false imprisonment. Because of this, schools have express rights to detain without parental consent provided certain conditions are met. They are that:

- the headteacher has established a detention policy and procedure, has made this known generally within the school and has taken steps to bring it to the attention of all parents. This could be in the school prospectus and/or the annual report to parents, as well as being included in the published school rules and behaviour policy;

- the detention is imposed either by the headteacher or by a member of staff who is specifically or generally authorised to give detentions;

- the detention is reasonable. In determining reasonableness, the following will be taken into account:

  - the detention must be a proportionate punishment for the offence. This will raise the issue of whether whole-class detentions, where the particular offender cannot be identified, will be regarded as reasonable. This may also raise human rights issues dealt with in Chapter 14;

  - whether there are particular circumstances about the pupil being detained that the school knows, or ought to know, about. This may include the pupil's age, any special educational needs, any religious requirements (as, for example, a need to be home on a particular day or by a particular time) and travel arrangements that may need to be made;

- the parents are given 24 hours' notice. Any reasonable means of giving notice is permitted; by implication, this would include pupil post.

Children Act Rights

One very helpful aspect of the Children Act 1989 is that it gives explicit powers to those who, without having parental responsibility, have the care of the child. This is wide enough to include teachers, at least while the child is in school or under the care of the school as, for example, on a school trip. The person with care of the child may do whatever is reasonable to safeguard or promote the welfare of the child: schools should rely on this as justification for taking decisions in an emergency when a parent cannot be contacted. It is, however, limited in its scope: it cannot be used as a justification for acting contrary to parental wishes where those wishes are known or there is an opportunity to discover them before the action has to be taken.

Child Protection Procedures

Child protection is a key issue that schools have to address. It arises in two distinct ways.

(1) Protection of Children from Abuse or Violence Occurring Away from the School

Schools need to look out for victims and draw them to the attention of the welfare authorities. There needs to be cogent evidence that the child may be suffering significant harm, and it is not something that will be taken lightly. Conversely, the authorities should notify the school when a child is put on the 'at risk' register, and the school must then monitor the child's progress with particular care. Any causes for concern should be reported.

(2) Incidents of Abuse Within the School by a Pupil or a Member of Staff

Cases of suspected abuse by staff are particularly sensitive and are difficult to deal with. The child's interest is paramount, but the member of staff also has rights which should not be infringed. A set of guidelines has been established by the teachers' professional associations, and these have been approved by the DfES. Some LEAs have different procedures, but each school must be sure that it has a procedure in place that will ensure the following:

- protection of the child against possible further incidents. This may involve suspension of the member of staff, but suspension should not be automatic;

- an investigation, if necessary by the police, in which the evidence is properly preserved and the outcome is not prejudiced. This, fundamentally, requires that the child is not interviewed in an inappropriate manner;

- protection for the member of staff, who may be innocent and whose right to a proper hearing in the event of eventual disciplinary action should not be prejudiced. A particularly delicate area is the extent to which the member of staff is informed of the allegations: at least one LEA procedure denies this right where there are allegations of serious sexual abuse, and this can place the employee in an impossible position;

- keeping the number of governors involved in the case to a minimum so that disciplinary action and appeal processes are not compromised. This is not a special rule relating to abuse cases but applies to all staff disciplinary processes. It is particularly important because of the serious nature of this type of allegation and its implications for the career of the member of staff involved;

- that any possible prosecution is not compromised. This will normally mean that any internal action (other than suspension where this is the right course) will not take place until after a decision has been made whether or not to prosecute. If there is a prosecution, any disciplinary action would normally be deferred until the case has been heard, although this can have serious budgetary implications, bearing in mind that suspension would be on full pay;

- that confidentiality is maintained in respect of any records that are kept in relation to the pupil. Such records fall into a category which is protected from disclosure and the school is under a duty not to disclose them.

WHEN SCHOOL IS NOT THE ANSWER

Pupil Referral Units

One aspect of pupil welfare is the intractable problem of the child who, for one reason or another, cannot cope within a school. The child may be a persistent non-attender or may have behavioural problems that have led to successive permanent exclusions to the point where there is no school able (or in some cases willing) to offer him – the great majority of such pupils are boys – a place. The answer, partial and not self-evidently satisfactory, is admission to a PRU. Technically and legally, a PRU is a school established by the LEA for pupils of compulsory school age who might otherwise not receive suitable education. Children can be referred to a PRU either on an exclusive basis, so that the PRU is the only education provider, or alongside the mainstream or special school so that the child remains on the roll of both and can return to the school at an appropriate time. Indeed, DfES Guidance states explicitly that the aim of a PRU is to return the child to mainstream education, recognising implicitly that the very nature of a PRU is not conducive to assisting the child to become an integrated member of society. The administration of PRUs is outside the scope of this book, but a number of points are worth noting.

- Part of the funding of a PRU will come from the money that follows the pupil. Where a child is permanently excluded from school, the school loses a proportionate part of its budget for that financial year, and the LEA can use that money as part of the PRU funding.

- Although a PRU is required to offer a balanced and broadly based curriculum it is not bound to follow the full National Curriculum, nor to conduct assessments at the end of the relevant Key Stages. PRUs do not, therefore, have to follow the disapplication procedures if they feel that particular aspects of the National Curriculum are not appropriate for individual pupils.

- A PRU can be named in a school attendance order.

- A pupil may be excluded from a PRU, although permanent exclusion will not remove the obligation on the LEA to provide education for the child in school or otherwise. Parents have the right to make representations to the LEA against exclusions, but there is no formal appeal right to an independent appeal committee if the LEA declines to reinstate a permanently excluded child.

On-site Special Units

In some instances, schools will have their own on-site special units designed to provide for children with special educational needs. These units may be specially funded or may be established from within the school's Local Management of Schools (LMS) budget, supplemented by the resources flowing from the individual statements. In either case, the unit forms part of the school and is in all respects subject to the control of the governing body. A pupil who is dealt with exclusively within the unit will nevertheless be on the roll of the school and be entitled to equal treatment with all other pupils. Similarly, staff employed to work in the unit will have the same rights and status as other staff.

RELEVANT GUIDANCE

Activity Centres

Circular 22/94, 'Safety in Outdoor Activity Centres: Guidance'.

School Visits

'Health and Safety of Pupils on Educational Visits' – a good practice guide.

Child Protection

Circular 9/93, 'Protection of Children: Disclosure of Criminal Background of those with Access to Children'.

Circular 11/95, 'Misconduct of Teachers and Workers with Children and Young Persons'.

DfES Guidance DfES/0027/2004 'Safeguarding Children in Education', September 2004

School Discipline

Circular 10/99, 'Social Inclusion – Pupil Support'.

Circular 9/94, 'The Education of Children with Emotional and Behavioural Difficulties'.

Security Report of the Working Group on School Security.

Bullying

'Bullying – Don't Suffer in Silence – An Anti-Bullying Pack for Schools' (DfES Non-Statutory Guidance 64/2000).

Administering Medicine

'Supporting Pupils with Medical Needs' – a good practice guide.

Circular 14/96, 'Supporting Pupils with Medical Needs in School'.

Chapter 13

PARENTAL RIGHTS AND DUTIES

*The obligation to educate children – LEA powers relating to school admissions –
Information for parents – Holidays and the length of the school day – Other rights
and responsibilities – Relevant guidance*

THE OBLIGATION TO EDUCATE CHILDREN

Parents do not have to send their children to school. Their obligation iis to ensure that their children receive efficient full-time education suitable to their ability, aptitude and SEN. This can be in school or otherwise, although in view of the requirements of the National Curriculum the burden of providing efficient education outside school is substantial.

If a child is not at school full time, the LEA can require the parent to show that the legal requirements are being met. If the parent cannot do this and the LEA thinks that the child should be in school, it must serve a school attendance order, which will name the school that the child is to attend. The parent has the right to nominate the school to be named, and this is dealt with below.

Failure to comply with a school attendance order without reasonable excuse is a criminal offence and can be prosecuted in the magistrates' court. Similarly, a parent whose child fails to attend the school where he or she is a registered pupil can be prosecuted. The only reasons accepted for not sending a child to school are:

- the child's illness;

- absence on days set aside for religious observance for that child's faith;

- unavoidable cause relating to the child. This is not defined more closely, so it is open to the court hearing the case to form its own view on the circumstances and decide whether the particular facts constitute unavoidable cause. Those facts must, however, relate to the child: it would not, for example, be a valid reason for not sending a child to school if the parent had other commitments that made it difficult or impossible to get the child to school;

- that permission has been given by the school. It is, therefore, unlawful for parents to take children on holiday during term time unless the school agrees. There is a widespread belief that parents are entitled to take a child out of school for a holiday of up to two weeks during term time but that is not correct. The school is not obliged to give permission. If parents do take the child away without prior consent, the school is placed in an invidious position. It must either bow to the pressure and approve the absence, or maintain its position and then record the absence as unauthorised, thereby adversely affecting its unauthorised absence statistics;

- that the school is not within walking distance and the LEA has not made suitable transport arrangements or offered a place at a suitable school within walking distance. Walking distance means two miles for under-eights or three miles for older children and is measured by the nearest available route.

The last ground raises the issue of free transport. In simplistic terms (and this is not an area of law that can be readily summarised), LEAs have to pay for school transport only if there is no suitable school within walking distance. What constitutes 'suitable' depends on circumstances, and LEAs must take account of parental choice, any SEN and also, where a denominational school is preferred, the religion of the parents. Parental choice is not, however, conclusive, and each LEA will have its own policy. Guidance from the DfES indicates that it regards the nearest 'suitable' school for a child aged between five and 16 as the maintained school closest to the home by the nearest available route that offers an efficient full-time education suitable to the child's age, aptitude and any special educational needs. This may, in some cases, be rather too narrow a test and it may sometimes be necessary for the LEA to consider other issues such as the racial mix of the available schools, in Wales at least the language in which the school teaches, and issues relating to bullying or potential bullying. Those will, however, be the exception rather than the rule and in the great majority of cases any mainstream non-denominational school within walking distance that has a place available will be considered 'suitable'. Where there is no suitable school within walking distance, parents are entitled to have free transport to the nearest school, even if the LEA has no specific transport arranged to that school and does have transport available to another school equally 'suitable' that is further away.

LEA POWERS RELATING TO SCHOOL ADMISSIONS

The 'normal' admissions process is dealt with in Chapter 7. Over and above this, LEAs have significant powers to direct that a school admit a pupil. These powers, and how they are exercised, vary according to whether the pupil has or does not have a statement of SEN.

Pupils with Statements of Special Educational Needs

The governing body is obliged to admit a child where the school is named in a statement of SEN. This obligation, however, does not affect any power of a school to exclude a pupil who is already a registered pupil there.

A parent may specify the school to be named in a statement of SEN. The LEA must comply, unless it considers that:

- the school is unsuitable; or

- attendance is not compatible with the provision of efficient education for the children with whom the child would be educated (note the difference from the test applied to non-statemented applicants which is a general test of prejudice to efficient education and is not limited to a consideration of the impact of admission on other children); or

- attendance is not compatible with the efficient use of resources.

One consequence of this duty to comply with parental preference is that the LEA may be forced to name a school even though the child does not meet entry requirements (for example, a religious qualification) that would apply to non-statemented children unless it can, and is prepared to, argue that the school is unsuitable on those grounds.

The LEA has a duty to consult the governing body, but the governing body has no right of appeal to the SEN and Disability Tribunal and no right to refer the matter to the Secretary of State unless the LEA has acted unreasonably, in the sense that it has made or is proposing to make a decision that is irrational rather than just one with which the school disagrees. The parent has no right of appeal to the admissions appeal panel (this avenue is not open to parents of children with SEN statements) but does have a right of appeal to the Tribunal against a refusal by the LEA to name a particular school. There is no restriction on the power of the Tribunal, and LEAs must be strongly tempted to meet parental preference in virtually all cases so as to avoid the time and cost of defending an appeal.

The statementing process, of which this is part, is dealt with in Chapter 5.

Other Pupils

Where a non-statemented child in the area of an LEA has either been refused admission to, or has been permanently excluded from, every school which is a reasonable distance from his home and provides suitable education, the LEA may give a direction specifying a school which is a reasonable distance from the home and from which the child is not permanently excluded, even though the school may previously have refused admission to the child. The governing body is obliged to admit that child. This applies only in respect of schools for which the LEA is not the admissions authority – patently an LEA has no need to give a direction to itself to admit a child to a school whose admissions it controls.

Before making a direction, the LEA must consult with the parents and with the governing body of the school proposed to be specified. It must give notice of its intention to make the direction, and the governing body may within 15 days refer the matter to the Secretary of State for determination. The direction may not be made until the time for reference has expired or, if appropriate, the Secretary of State has made a determination.

These provisions extend to all maintained schools other than maintained special schools. They are intended to ease the problem of the parent who cannot find a school place, often because the child has been permanently excluded from one or more schools in the area. Whether they will do so may depend on how literally the provisions are interpreted, particularly bearing in mind that admission authorities and LEAs do not have to accede to parental preference for two years following a second exclusion. On the exact wording, the power for the LEA to act does not arise until the parent has made a positive application for a place to all the local schools (other than any from which the child has been permanently excluded). It will, therefore, only be effective where there is significant parental co-operation with the LEA, and the parent wants the child to be found a school place. Parents are not always so motivated, and the LEA does, therefore, have the alternative power to make an attendance order as mentioned earlier. The order will name a school, but the parent must first be given the opportunity to express a preference. The LEA must comply with that preference after consulting in a similar way with the governing body, which again has the right to refer the matter to the Secretary of State for determination.

In each case, the LEA may not specify a school other than one for which it is responsible for admission arrangements if admitting the child in question would lead to the infant class size limit being exceeded.

A school that is the subject of a direction must be within the LEA's area unless a determination has been made by the Secretary of State.

No school may be specified in an attendance order if the child concerned has been permanently excluded from that school. However, in this context and in calculating whether a child has been permanently excluded twice, no account is taken of an exclusion that was overturned on appeal, even if the appeal panel exercised its right not to direct reinstatement to the school.

INFORMATION FOR PARENTS

In addition to the prospectus (dealt with in connection with admissions in Chapter 7) information is made available to parents through the governors' annual report and annual meeting and in reports on pupils.

Governors' Annual Report to Parents

Each school year, the governing body of every maintained school must produce a report on the activities of the school. It must send a copy to every parent and it must, except in the circumstances outlined below, hold a meeting which all parents may attend. The report must be sent to parents at least 14 days before the date of the meeting.

The report is required to contain a great deal of specific information:

- the date, time, place, agenda and purpose of the annual parents' meeting;

- details of any action on any resolutions taken at the last annual meeting;
- the way in which the governing body has discharged its function in the previous year;
- progress in implementing the post-OFSTED action plan;
- a report on the school's SEN provision covering:
  - a statement about the school's policy indicating its success during the year and any significant changes made to it;
  - details of any consultation on SEN with the LEA;
  - how SEN resources have been applied;
- National Curriculum assessment results and, in secondary schools, examination results and the destination of school-leavers. As with the prospectus, the requirements as to how these results are published can change from year to year and care must be taken to report in the current format;
- a report on the governing body's targets (set in accordance with Circular 11/98 and dealt with in Chapter 3) in relation to the National Curriculum. The targets themselves have to be specified, together with information about the number of eligible pupils, how they performed and national comparative data;
- attendance and unauthorised absence statistics;
- a financial statement showing how LEA funding has been applied and giving details of gifts and governors' travelling and subsistence expenses, if any;
- information about professional development undertaken by teaching staff. This will comprise a summary of the nature, amount and purpose of such training, both inside and outside school. The report should summarise the number of non-contact days used for training, the training undertaken, the subject areas involved, other training courses funded by the school and other professional development activities. Guidance suggests that this information could also include a note of the school's total budget for professional development and comments on the impact it has had on improving standards and quality of teaching and learning;
- information about school security. It is up to each school to decide what it will include, but the report should not include

any negative information that may draw attention to weaknesses or otherwise increase risk to the school;

- information on how the school provides for pupils with disabilities including:

  - arrangements for the admission of disabled pupils;
  - the steps being taken to prevent disabled students being treated less favourably than other pupils;
  - the facilities provided to assist access to the school by disabled pupils;
  - information about the accessibility plan which the governing body is required to prepare and implement. This is dealt with in detail in Chapter 6;

- the names, status and period of appointment of governors, with information on how governors may be contacted, including the name and address of the chair of governors and the clerk to the governors (which can be the school address);

- a report on the consideration of any resolutions passed at the previous annual meeting of parents.

In addition, DfES Guidance (Circular 7/99 for primary schools and 8/99 for secondary schools) suggests that schools consider including information that prior to 1999 was mandatory such as:

- school term and holiday dates;

- a description of steps taken by the school to develop or strengthen links with the community;

- information on whether the school's sporting aims have been met, and sporting achievements during the year;

- details of any changes to the school's prospectus during the year.

The Circulars suggest that governing bodies consider whether this information is included in the annual report or given to parents by other means during the course of the school year.

The Secretary of State can, after consultation, add to these requirements and it is, therefore, essential to check each year as to the current requirements. The Secretary of State consulted in Summer 2001 on a proposal that the annual report be combined with the school prospectus but, perhaps surprisingly, given the work required to produce a good annual report, governors were opposed to the idea, on the grounds that the two documents had different purposes and addressed different audiences. Nevertheless, government is likely to take further steps to simplify the amount of information that has to be published and the way it is disseminated. Proposals intended to come into effect in September 2005 for a school profile may well replace elements of the prospectus and annual report. To quote from the DfES consultation document DfES 03352004 launched in March 2004:

'3 The Proposals

3.1 The Profile would bring together the key information about a school's performance and the school's view of its future in a short, accessible document.

3.2 We envisage that a school Profile would:

- Be for use by parents and carers of pupils at the school, parents and carers of prospective pupils and others interested in the performance of the school;

- Give a comprehensive view of the breadth and depth of the school's work;

- Be short and easy to understand and use;

- Reduce the work for Head Teachers, Governors and others in schools, by providing in one place a range of information about the school;

- Encourage an inclusive approach, by showing how schools serve the full range of their pupils;

- Be a standardised document in a common, comparative format, with much statistical data derived automatically from existing national databases. It would be compiled and accessed electronically; and

- Replace the statutory annual report to parents and increase the flexibility around elements of the school prospectus.

3.3 We propose that the Profile should contain the following information:

- Data on pupils' attainment and progress, set against benchmarks for schools in similar contexts;

- How the school serves all its pupils;

- The most recent assessment by OFSTED, set against the school's own self-assessment;

- What the school offers, in terms of the broader curriculum, including extra-curricular activities;

- The school's priorities for future improvement;

- What the school offers to the wider community; and

- Other information, including contextual information about the school.

3.4 We envisage that the Profile should be in a standardised format for all schools. It should be relatively short – perhaps between two to four sides of A4 – and it should allow for easy comparisons between schools. However, there would be nothing to prevent schools from publishing more information than the Profile contains.

3.5 We see the Profile being compiled and accessed as an electronic document, which could be printed. Much of the basic statistical data could be provided automatically and derived from information already supplied by schools to the DfES or supplied by OFSTED. This would be combined with information provided direct by the Head Teacher and Governing Body of the school. We would also want parents, governors and teachers to have access to the Profile via links with government websites.

3.6 We intend to develop and test the fine detail of the school Profile in local trials and in the light of responses to this consultation document.'

Governing bodies are required to consider whether the report should be produced in languages other than English. The LEA can direct schools to produce the report in other languages and in a particular form.

Annual Meeting of Parents

The governing body must hold an annual parents' meeting every year which is open to parents, the headteacher and anyone the governors decide to invite. It is not, unless the governing body so decides, an open public meeting, and the press has no right to attend. Teachers other than the headteacher have no right to attend, although most governing bodies would be happy to see them at the meeting.

The content and procedure of the annual parents' meeting used to be closely regulated. Those requirements have now been relaxed, and provided the meeting does achieve its purpose, it can be conducted as the governing body sees fit. The purpose of the meeting is both to provide an opportunity for discussion of the manner in which the school has been and will be conducted, and to deal with issues raised by parents.

The circumstances in which the annual parents' meeting need not be held have been extended too, which will come as something of a relief to some governing bodies since the attendance at these meetings (even in active and well-supported schools) is usually small. The meeting need not be held if:

- subsequent to an OFSTED inspection, the governing body had held a parents' meeting within the preceding year specifically to discuss the inspector's report before drawing up its action plan;

- in any school year the governing body holds at least one meeting with parents, at least two governors attend (at least one of whom must not be a staff governor) and the parents are given the opportunity to discuss the school's performance and the way in which its has been and will be conducted;

- notice is given by the governing body with the governors' report asking parents to state in writing within a specified period of at least seven days whether they require the meeting to be held, and the parents of fewer than 15 pupils respond.

As previously, the meeting need not be held at all if the school is a community or foundation special school based in a hospital or a school (other than a community or foundation special school based in a hospital) and at least half its pupils are boarders and the governing body decides that it is impracticable to hold the meeting that year.

In practical terms, this means that schools that feel that the annual meeting is unproductive and that time and resources could be better used elsewhere do have an opportunity to avoid having to hold it. In practice, though, it only requires the parents of 15 pupils to say that they want the meeting to be held, so the chances of avoiding the meeting are slim, especially in larger schools where, ironically, the turn-out is probably less representative of the parental body than in small schools. The governing body needs to be pro-active to avoid having to hold the meeting, it does not, though, need to indicate the consequence of failure to respond.

Annual Reports on Pupils

Schools are required to report annually on each pupil. The report goes to parents of pupils under 18, and to the pupil if over that age. Parents of pupils over 18 can also be provided with the report if special circumstances warrant it. It can be sent by post or by pupil post. The report must give information showing the pupil's educational achievements in relation to the relevant Key Stage, dealt with in detail in Chapter 3. Although the general pattern is not likely to change, the detailed requirements change with some frequency and it is always necessary to check the current regulations by reference to the latest DfES Guidance (for Key Stage 4 and beyond) or booklets issued by the QCA and DfES jointly for the earlier Key Stages. The current reporting requirements are given below.

All Pupils

The following information has to be included in all pupils' reports:

- brief particulars of progress in the subjects studied and activities in which the student participated as part of the school curriculum. The DfES advises that there should be a short commentary which highlights strengths, particular achievements, and weaknesses. Weaknesses may possibly (to be more positive) be expressed as targets for development;

- results of public examinations and vocational qualifications or credits towards such qualifications;

- details of general progress. The DfES suggests that this may include an overall view of progress including comment on behaviour, contribution to the life of the school and special achievements during the year;

- details of the arrangements for discussing the report with teachers.

All Pupils of Compulsory School Age

In addition, the following information has to be given for all pupils of compulsory school age:

- brief particulars for each National Curriculum foundation subject studied, including religious education. If the information includes particulars of levels achieved there must also be an indication of whether or not those levels have been determined in accordance with statutory arrangements;

- a summary of the student's attendance record. This should show the number of sessions (in half-days) since the student entered the school or since the last report, whichever was the later, and the percentage of unauthorised absences;

- at the end of each statutory Key Stage, the report must state what levels have been arrived at by statutory assessment and must indicate where a student has been excepted from any attainment target as a result of a disapplication of the provisions of the National Curriculum. It must also contain a brief commentary setting out what the results show about the pupil's progress in the subject. The commentary should draw attention to particular strengths and weaknesses and explain any significant differences between the teacher assessment and the test or task result;

- there are detailed reporting requirements at the end of each Key Stage, which include the requirement to report not only on the particular student, but also on how the student compares with other students in the school. Additionally, at the end of Key Stage 3, the school must also supply the latest available information on national performance. Inevitably, these statistics will be at least a year out of date.

The report must be sent during the school year. The timing is at the discretion of the headteacher, and the reporting requirements can be spread over more than one report during the year. Where the information depends on external examination or assessments, the reporting of that information (but not the rest of the report) may be delayed until 30 September.

School-leavers

Different arrangements apply at Key Stage 4 and beyond, although the essential principles of reporting to parents remain the same. Headteachers are required, as a bare minimum, to provide the following information to all pupils aged 16+, who are designated as 'leavers', on their school achievements:

- the results of any public examinations, qualifications achieved and credits towards them, including vocational qualifications or credits towards vocational qualifications;

- brief particulars of achievements in other subjects and activities studied as part of the school curriculum.

Schools have a statutory obligation to report under the heading 'Achievement in Education' and to use the format prescribed by regulations or in a format to the same effect when reporting on school-leavers. They must:

- include information about the examinations taken by the pupil, and qualifications and credits towards qualifications achieved;

- ensure that the form is signed by a teacher or tutor familiar with the pupil and also by the pupil;

- include brief particulars of achievements, subject by subject.

Where a pupil is aged 18 or over, the headteacher must report directly to the student and provide the same information, but not necessarily in the same format, as to 16+ pupils. Reports must be issued by the end of the school year for both age groups at the very latest (one report per annum is a statutory minimum) except where examination results are involved, when the end date becomes 30 September. The extra month is, of course, to allow time for the examination results to become available.

Reports to New Schools

As mentioned in Chapter 16, when a child moves schools, the headteacher of the old school must send the pupil's educational records together with a report (in the Common Transfer Form format) to the receiving school (whether State-maintained or independent). The report must contain, in summary:

- the statutory assessment results in English, mathematics and science (by subject and by attainment target where appropriate), and the school year in which the assessments were made;

- the teachers' latest assessments against the attainment targets in the core subjects since the last statutory assessment, or since the pupil arrived in the school if that is more recent;

- any public examination results including vocational qualifications or credits.

The report must be sent within 15 school days of the request being received from the new school or the pupil ceasing to be registered on the roll of the old school. The reporting requirement does not apply to a pupil who has been at the old school for less than four weeks, or when the headteacher cannot reasonably find out which school the pupil has gone to.

HOLIDAYS AND THE LENGTH OF THE SCHOOL DAY

For all schools, the academic year has to contain 390 half days, of which 10 (usually five full days) will be allocated to staff in-service training and pupils will not attend. Every full day has to be divided into two sessions with a break between them, unless there are exceptional circumstances which make this impracticable. It is no longer mandatory for the annual report to parents to give details of term dates and the times of the school day but this is a convenient opportunity to do so. These in the main are decided by the governing body but the detail varies between the different types of schools. Enough time has to be allowed for delivery of the curriculum, and the advised minimum teaching time per week is 21 hours for pupils aged five to seven, 23 hours for eight- to 11-year-olds, and 24 hours for those who are 12 and over. The DfES suggests that 14- to 16-year-olds should be taught for 25 hours per week. In addition, the day has to allow time for collective worship, registration and between-lesson breaks. OFSTED will comment on the length of the school day when reporting following an inspection.

The current division of the school year into three terms is not laid down by legislation and has been supplanted in a significant number of LEAs by a division into six shorter terms with, in effect, extended holidays replacing the current half-term break and with a shorter summer holiday. Some doubt has been expressed as to the educational benefits of the six-term year and plainly such a change has massive implications nationally, particularly affecting the tourist industry. It also raises issues regarding the timing of public examinations and university entrance and the adoption of the six-term year may itself be influenced by changes in university admission procedures. The decisions on this will be made by schools and LEAs locally in accordance with the following procedures.

Community and Controlled Schools

The LEA sets the dates on which the school year begins and ends. Some LEAs will also set the beginning and end of school terms; others leave that to individual schools. The governing body of each school sets the times of the day and the time of the mid-day break. As a result of new regulations applying to England, before a change can be made the governing body must do the following:

- consult the LEA, the headteacher and all employees;

- prepare a statement setting out the proposed changes. The statement must include any written comments from the LEA and must give details of when a meeting is to be held to discuss the changes. The statement is to be published in English (and/or Welsh in Wales) and such other languages as the governing body thinks fit or the LEA may direct. The meeting is open to parents, the headteacher, and such others as the governing body invite;

- send the statement to all registered parents at least two weeks before the date of the meeting;

- consider comments made at the meeting before making a decision;

- advise the LEA and parents of the decision and when it is to take effect. At least six weeks' notice must be given unless the proposed change relates to either the beginning or the end of the school day, in which case at least three months' notice must be given. A change to the start or finish of the school day can only be implemented at the beginning of a school year, which means that the decision must be taken no later than 1 June. Any other change can only take place at the start of a school term.

VA and Foundation Schools

All dates and times are determined by the governing body which must consult with the LEA on the timing of the school day, but only in relation to matters that may directly involve the LEA, such as transport provision. All must consider how parents and pupils will be affected, but no other formality is required and changes can be made at any time.

OTHER RIGHTS AND RESPONSIBILITIES

Parental Rights Relating to Religious Education, Collective Worship and Sex Education

Parents have the right to withdraw children from participation in these areas subject to certain conditions. This is dealt with in detail in Chapter 3.

The Home–School Agreement

Parents will be supplied with a copy of the school's home–school agreement and will be expected to meet the school's expectations specified in the agreement. Although the agreement does not create legal duties or rights, conduct that does not comply with the agreement may be relevant to the relationship between the parent and the school. Home–school agreements are dealt with in detail in Chapter 8.

The Right to Complain

Schools are now required to establish and publicise formal complaints procedures although very many schools have done so for some time. The DfES has issued a 'toolkit' about the form and content of a complaints procedure. This, oddly, does not have the status of formal statutory Guidance which means that schools are not specifically required to have regard to it. That, perhaps, is just as well because although much of what it does say is practical and schools may well find it useful, it does need to be looked at carefully and critically before adopting all of its suggestions.

One advantage of a clear complaints procedure is that individuals to whom a complaint is addressed can direct complainants to the procedure rather than having to deal on an *ad hoc* basis. This offers protection to the headteacher and to governors who may be approached by people that they know well (parent governors of primary schools are particularly vulnerable to the playground equivalent of 'doorstepping') and it helps to give uniformity and consistency to the process. Governing bodies should require individual governors to refer all complaints to the headteacher or to a complaints co-ordinator and for those complaints to be dealt with inside the procedure. Otherwise, governors can compromise the process and cause significant problems for the headteacher and school staff. The handling of complaints is essentially part of the overall management and direction of a school and is not something for governors to deal with personally. It is good practice for a governor who refers a complaint to be advised of the outcome but in any event that governor should not play any part in the subsequent procedure and should certainly not sit on any governor panel or committee that eventually may deal with the complaint.

Complaints procedures should be simple and manageable, with as little formality as is consistent with ensuring fairness. Any complaints procedure should require a preliminary attempt to resolve matters informally. The first formal stage should be dealt with by the headteacher (or, in larger schools, the toolkit suggests that a member of staff should be given this initial role, with the headteacher reconsidering the matter if necessary), with a right to require the matter to be referred either to the chair of governors or, as recommended by the toolkit, to a governor committee if the complaint is not resolved. Typically (unless the procedure provides for further stages of appeal, perhaps to the LEA or diocese) the governor stage of the complaints procedure will draw the complaints process to an end. A complaint involving the headteacher can best be dealt with initially by the chair of governors, with a right to refer it to a governor committee.

The toolkit refers to the governor stage as an appeal in front of a clerked governor panel that is independent. Whilst the toolkit does emphasise the need for the hearing to be as informal as possible and non-adversarial, the procedure it endorses is quite formal, similar in many ways to Discipline Committee proceedings. It requires written material to be seen by all parties. It suggests that the complainant's case is heard first with the headteacher being given the opportunity to cross examine the complainant and any witnesses called. The headteacher then presents the case on behalf of the school, with the complainant having the right to cross examine the headteacher and any witnesses. The complainant then summarises the complaint followed by the headteacher summarising on behalf of the school and finally the panel will determine the appeal in private and communicate its decision to the parties in the manner and within the timetable established by the procedure.

Employees who are the subject of a complaint will often be advised by their professional association not to attend or give statements in connection with a formal complaints hearing, because to do so may leave them exposed to subsequent disciplinary action, and the toolkit does not deal with the consequences of decisions of this sort. It is worth noting as a parallel that the revised Guidance on exclusion appeals gives any member of staff who gives evidence to the appeal panel the right to be accompanied by a representative or friend. The same should apply to any requirement or request to a member of staff to attend an internal complaints hearing.

There are other complaint mechanisms. LEAs must have a procedure whereby complaints in relation to the curriculum can be dealt with. Because this is a prescribed complaints procedure, the school-based procedure cannot be used. This procedure is dealt with in detail in Chapter 3. Aside from this, the mechanisms for complaint (short of going to court) are:

- representations to the Secretary for State that a school or an LEA is acting unreasonably or unlawfully; or

- referral to the Local Commissioner for Administration (better known as the Local Government Ombudsman) on the grounds of maladministration that has led to injustice.

The Secretary of State route can be slow and, by the time the decision is known, the problem may have gone away or may have become incapable of solution. Furthermore, the Secretary of State will approach the matter in the same way as the courts on judicial review so that a finding of unreasonableness is very difficult to obtain: the actions complained of need to be irrational rather than simply actions with which the Secretary of State disagrees. The Secretary of State has the power to give directions but cannot specifically award compensation. The Ombudsman has the power to recommend remedial action, which can include the payment of compensation. The Ombudsman's recommendations are not, however, binding and it has been known for such recommendations not to be accepted nor acted upon. In either case, the complainant must have been through 'any available process' first, which means using the curriculum complaints procedure or any school-based procedure.

School Uniform

This can be a contentious area but the right of a school to have uniform and to require pupils to abide by it is quite clear. There are, though, constraints imposed by human rights and non-discrimination legislation and these were demonstrated by the High Court case involving uniform for Muslim girls that is referred to in Chapter 14 and Chapter 8. In June 2004, at about the same time as this case was decided, DfES issued Guidance. The Guidance was not based on the case but is consistent with it.

The Guidance makes it clear that governing bodies are responsible for deciding whether their school should have a uniform policy, and if so, what it should consist of. It is the responsibility of the headteacher to enforce it. The Guidance says that parents should raise complaints with the governing body, saying that governors should be receptive to any reasonable complaint (rather begging the question as to what is reasonable and in what context) but this seems to ignore the formalities of the advised complaints process which would normally require a parent first to seek an internal resolution before the matter goes to governors.

It deals with a number of specific points:

- **Cost** This should be given high priority to avoid pupils or their families feeling socially excluded. This applies both to existing and prospective pupils – parents of prospective pupils should not be deterred from applying to a school because of the cost of its school uniform. In this context, the Guidance urges the avoidance of what it describes as 'designer items' such as blazers that are only available from one supplier. The policy should incorporate items that are readily available off the peg from different shops.

- **Consultation** Governing bodies should behave reasonably and should consult parents for their views and concerns before deciding on the introduction of a new uniform policy/dress code, or amending an existing one.

- **Physical education** Where the uniform policy includes clothing required for PE the Guidance says that schools should adopt a sensitive, flexible approach. There are issues of comfort, expense and discrimination to consider, especially for girls. Modesty will often be relevant but there are also questions relating to health and safety and to how effectively the curriculum can be delivered if inappropriate clothes are worn.

- **Non-compliance with the policy** The Guidance repeats the essence of what is said in the Guidance relating to exclusions, namely that headteachers can discipline pupils for breach of uniform policy but that exclusion is not an appropriate response to breaches of school uniform policy, except where it is part of a pattern of defiant behaviour generally. The Guidance suggests that schools should be considerate and discreetly try to establish why a pupil is not adhering to their uniform policy. If it is on financial grounds, it may be right to give parents time to purchase what is needed. Pupils should not be made to feel uncomfortable or discriminated against because parents cannot provide them with the uniform.

- **Equality issues** The Guidance reminds schools of responsibilities under the Sex Discrimination Act 1975, the Human Rights Act 1998 and the Race Relations Act 1976 and of the need to have a race equality policy which requires them to assess the impact of all their policies, including uniform or dress codes, on children.

- **Cultural, race and religious requirements** Anticipating the case mentioned above and in fact reflecting the approach taken by the judge, the Guidance says that whilst pupils must adhere to a school's uniform policy, schools must be sensitive to the needs of different cultures, races and religions. DfES expects schools to accommodate these needs, within a general uniform policy, and gives as examples allowing Muslim girls to wear appropriate dress and Sikh boys to wear traditional headdress. It goes on to say that DfES does not consider it appropriate that any pupil should be disciplined for non-compliance with a school uniform policy, which results from them having to adhere to a particular cultural, race or religious dress code. However, the question of the extent of such obligation was addressed in the case mentioned and the approach of the court was that, at least in a non-denominational school, a uniform that complied with a generally accepted view of a particular religious requirement was enforceable even against a pupil who considered that requirement to be insufficient to secure proper religious observance.

- **Sex discrimination issues** The Guidance makes it clear that schools should ensure that their uniform policy does not discriminate on the grounds of gender; for example, girls should normally be allowed to wear trousers. Uniform rules should not disadvantage one gender compared with the other. However, in a denominational school it may be lawful to discriminate to ensure compliance with religious observance. It may, for example, be proper for an orthodox Jewish school to prohibit girls from wearing trousers and to require them to wear long skirts because that reflects orthodox Jewish religious requirements.

- **Home to school travel** The Guidance refers to the need to encourage children to walk and cycle to school and schools should consider this when deciding on the form of uniform. The Guidance encourages schools to include light colours and reflective materials as part of the uniform for road safety reasons in winter months.

RELEVANT GUIDANCE

Transport

Circular Letter 21/11/1994, 'School Transport'.

Admissions

Code of Practice on Admissions and Code of Practice on Admission Appeals.

Information

Circular 7/99, 'School Prospectuses and Governors' Annual Reports in Primary Schools'.

Circular 8/99, 'School Prospectuses and Governors' Annual Reports in Secondary Schools'.

Targets

Circular 11/98 'Target Setting in Schools'.

Reports on Pupils

Current Circular, 'Reports on Pupils' Achievements in Primary Schools' (issued annually).

Current Circular, 'Reports on Pupils' Achievements in Secondary Schools' (issued annually).

Records of Achievement

Circular 8/90, 'Records of Achievement'.

Complaints

'School Complaints Procedure' reference LEA/0180/2003 published by DfES May 2003.

Chapter 14

HUMAN RIGHTS

Introduction – Human rights in the context of schools – Conclusion – Relevant guidance

INTRODUCTION

The direct effect of the Human Rights Act 1998 coming into force in October 2000 was twofold. First, it incorporated the European Convention for the Protection of Human Rights and Fundamental Freedoms 1950 (European Convention) into English law and required that English law be compatible with the Convention. Secondly, it required that all public bodies complied with the Convention in carrying out their functions. State-maintained schools are public bodies for this purpose and thus the Act, and the Convention, have direct relevance to their day-to-day activities. The Act has also had an indirect effect, in that it created a new awareness (and, dare it be said, a new area for lawyers) in the community at large, so that people generally now expect that their 'human rights' (however, and however wrongly, they may perceive them) will be respected. Whether the increase in volume and intensity of parental complaints that many schools perceive stems from this is unproven and probably incapable of proof, but undoubtedly the Human Rights Act 1998 has given a significant boost to the culture of consumerism in education and probably other public services.

The compatibility of English law with the Convention is not a matter that concerns schools, and schools do not need to worry over many of the grey areas, where there may be doubt as to whether existing law or existing laid-down procedures meet Convention requirements. The incompatibility of such law or procedures are matters for the courts and the Government: schools can only comply with the law as it stands. Even the courts cannot change incompatible laws, but can only make a declaration of incompatibility and then leave it to the Government to decide whether and how to legislate. Schools need to concentrate on the way they function, working to the general rule of thumb that if what they do is transparent and fair, they are unlikely to have a problem.

HUMAN RIGHTS IN THE CONTEXT OF SCHOOLS

The human rights enshrined in the Convention which will be relevant to schools are:

- the right to education, respecting the right of parents to ensure such education and teaching is in conformity with their own religious and philosophical convictions – *but* this duty is limited so far as is compatible with the provision of efficient instruction and training and the avoidance of unreasonable public expenditure;

- the right not to be subjected to inhuman and degrading treatment or punishment;

- the right to a fair and public hearing within a reasonable time by an independent and impartial tribunal established by law;

- the right to respect for private and family life;

- the right of freedom of thought, conscience and religion;

- the right of freedom of expression; and

- the right *to enjoy the freedoms set out in the Convention* without discrimination on any ground such as sex, race, colour, language, religion, political or other opinion, national or social origin, association with a national minority, property, birth or other status.

Rather than consider these in terms of each right, it is probably more useful to look at how the Convention may impact on particular areas of school activity.

Admission to Schools

It is clearly established that the Convention does not go so far as to entitle parents to insist on a place in a particular school. The obligation (which is an obligation on the State) is to provide an education system which gives all citizens access to schools which are suitable. Provided that there is a range of schools available covering at least the major religious and philosophical teachings, the right under the Convention is met. The proviso relating to efficiency and public expenditure is connected to the religious and philosophical convictions element and not to the issue of providing an education system and enables the State not to provide specifically for minority religions or philosophical doctrines. Thus, the current mix of denominational and non-denominational schools probably meets the criteria, although this has not yet been tested in court. Even if it did not, individual schools are not concerned with this issue because they are powerless to change the situation.

A challenge may be made to the current law entitling denominational schools to restrict entry or give preference to those adhering to the particular faith. The argument that this is contrary to the Convention right to education would presumably be met by the entitlement for parents to ensure education in conformity with their own religious and philosophical convictions. If you do not allow denominational schools, arguably you do not allow this opportunity. Thus, those who feel strongly that their children should only be educated with those of the same religious background may claim that their human rights would be infringed if there were no denominational schools or if the denominational schools were obliged to take a mix of pupils. Until this issue is taken through the courts, denominational schools must clearly continue to apply the existing law in relation to admissions.

It follows from this that refusing a place is not a breach of the right to education although parents and their advisors frequently try to argue the point on admissions appeals.

Curriculum

The European Court of Human Rights in Strasbourg has laid down that:

> 'the State, in fulfilling the functions assumed by it in regard to education and teaching must take care that information or knowledge included in the curriculum is conveyed in an objective, critical and pluralistic manner. The State is forbidden to pursue an aim of indoctrination that might be considered as not respecting parents' religious and philosophical convictions.'

This quite clearly gives aggrieved parents and others the peg on which to hang claims that the degree or nature of the religious education is not balanced. Denominational schools will need to be aware of this, although the likelihood is that the courts will be slow to interfere, particularly as parents have the right to withdraw their child from religious education and collective worship even in denominational schools and even if they are members of the faith or denomination that the school adheres to. Further, the fact that the Strasbourg judgment places the responsibility on the State rather than on individual schools suggests that it is the overall structure of religious education that will be scrutinised. On that footing, the existing basis for determining 'the agreed syllabus' which must, in the words of the legislation, 'reflect the fact that the religious traditions in Great Britain are in the main Christian, whilst taking account of the teaching and practices of the other principal religions represented in Great Britain' should at least meet the 'objective' and 'pluralistic' tests so far as content is concerned. The manner of delivery is a matter for each school and here some denominational schools may have a theoretical problem if they feel that the teaching of religions other than their own, or teaching them in a comparative or pluralistic way, is inappropriate. However, the risk of challenge by a parent (and it is difficult to see who other than a parent or student could bring such a challenge) will presumably be unlikely since the parents will, almost by definition, have a similar view to that held by the school.

Discipline and Punishment

The discipline process must not involve punishment that may be regarded as inhuman or degrading. Fortunately, the legislation on school discipline, including detention, and the related Circular 10/98 on restraint of pupils and Circular 10/99 on social inclusion and particularly exclusion, have clearly been framed with the Convention in mind. Subsequent Guidance has explicitly recognised human rights issues. Schools must keep the Convention requirements in mind when formulating and applying their discipline procedures. They must, in particular, recognise and apply the doctrine of proportionality, which means that punishment must be proportionate to the offence. Furthermore, punishment must relate to the individual. It is likely that the mass punishment of a group, particularly if this is because the individual offenders or perpetrators cannot be identified, would be a breach of the Convention, although the chance of a particular case actually being taken to court must be remote.

Bullying is certainly an area of concern. As well as allegations of negligence, parents may well claim that bullying that is not properly dealt with is an infringement of the right not to be subjected to inhuman and degrading treatment. The probability is that a case which fell within this category would also give rise to a negligence claim, so the introduction of the Convention right does not add to schools' obligations in this area. However, these obligations will have heightened prominence and more claims are likely to be brought. As ever, schools need to be sure that they have good procedures and, most importantly, that these are known and acted upon.

The Convention right to fair trial is of importance in relation to permanent exclusion. The Courts have decided that the current process of internal determination followed by an appeal to an independent appeal panel complies with Convention requirements. This was not, though, an entirely straightforward decision. There is a clear tension between the role of the LEA as the body of ultimate responsibility for the future education of the excluded child and its role in establishing the independent appeal panel. This tension is added to by the fact that the legislation and the Secretary of State Guidance relating to permanent exclusion gives the LEA a role in the process prior to and at appeal that may influence the eventual decision. How 'independent' does that leave the appeal panel? The answer lay in redefining and limiting the role of the LEA in what it can and should do in relation to the governing body review of the headteacher's decision and the appeal panel. The LEA is no longer entitled to express a view on the appropriateness of the decision. It must confine itself to factual statements about the effect of the exclusion on the child's future education and about the way other schools in the LEA have dealt with comparable situations.

Is a permanent exclusion, particularly where there is good reason to think that the effect will be to take the child out of the education system, a breach of the right to education? Might it be an inhuman or degrading punishment? The precedents from the European Court of Human Rights suggest not, in each case, although an LEA that fails to provide education for a permanently excluded child may well be in breach of the Convention. That, perhaps, was one underlying consideration in the framing of Circular 11/99 which imposes obligations on the LEA to provide for such children.

Statutory Guidance

A necessary part of the same case relating to exclusion was an examination of the role of the Secretary of State in issuing Guidance. Much Guidance, and that on exclusion is no exception, is written in quite peremptory terms. Headteachers, governing bodies, LEAs, appeal panels (and indeed everyone with any involvement in decision-making processes) are statutorily required to 'have regard to' Guidance issued by the Secretary of State under his statutory powers. Guidance will normally make it clear whether or not it is issued under statutory provisions. For example, the Complaints Toolkit is explicitly stated not to be statutory Guidance even though the legislation relating to complaints procedures requires all concerned to have regard to Guidance issued by the Secretary of State. When the Guidance is specifically statutory Guidance, to what extent is it binding on those required to have regard to it?

The issue raises a key human rights challenge. If Guidance is to all intents and purposes mandatory, the Secretary of State is pre-empting decisions that are the responsibility of others to make. In the case of permanent exclusion, that raises an evident conflict with the roles of governors and appeal panels. How can the appeal right be described as an independent one and how can it be said to be compliant with the human rights legislation? The answer is that 'have regard to' means no more than the plain words require. The independence of the appeal panel is secured by its entitlement to deviate from the Guidance that is given provided it does so in a rational manner. The limitation on the power of the Secretary of State that is implicit in this decision is a real one. Guidance is frequently perceived as virtual legislation: it is not, and those who treat it in that way may themselves risk acting in a way that breaches one or more of the Convention rights. It is important that decision-makers treat Guidance as just one, albeit important, element in their decision-making processes and do not treat it as determinative.

Special Educational Needs

It has been suggested that the Convention right not to be discriminated against by reason of status could have a significance in relation to pupils with SEN, whether statemented or not. Disadvantaging a pupil with such needs might be considered unlawful discrimination in the exercise of the right to education, so schools do need to be alert to the issue. The extension of the disability discrimination legislation to the general field of education is, perhaps, in part a response to this and if that legislation is complied with no human rights issues should arise. In the meantime, schools need to be sensitive to possible claims of discrimination. One step that they should take is to ensure that they can show that any funds allocated in the budget for SEN are in fact used for that purpose.

Personal Rights

The three rights relating to individual freedoms, respect for private and family life, freedom of thought, conscience and religion, and freedom of expression, clearly have implications for how schools behave towards pupils, parents and staff.

Pupils may try to, and in one case did, argue that rules relating to, for example, school uniform, haircuts, jewellery, body piercing and the use of mobile phones infringe privacy and/or freedom of expression. It is now clear that the courts will uphold rules relating to school uniform where they are non-discriminatory and may relate to health and safety or be rooted in the ethos of the school or the standards that the school seeks to maintain. In particular, it was decided that a requirement that a Muslim pupil wore a particular version of the school uniform that had been developed in consultation with the local Muslim community did not breach the pupil's human rights when she was denied the right to wear a different form of dress to meet her religious requirements. The court held that the school uniform policy and its enforcement had a legitimate aim and was proportionate. The legitimate aim was the proper running of a multi-cultural, multi-faith, secular school. The limitation, i.e. the restriction on what might be worn, was also proportionate to the legitimate aim pursued. This case has to be seen in its context, namely of a community school with an ethnically mixed pupil base including a substantial number of Muslim pupils, none of whom had raised any objection to the policy. It should also be noted that the school's policy was very clear and was articulated to parents at Open Evenings and in the school's prospectus before they applied. The particular pupil had applied to the school from outside its normal catchment area and the judge clearly felt that this element of positive choice of the school with knowledge of the uniform requirements, coupled with the fact (perhaps of dubious relevance given that an individual's religious views may develop and change during the education process) that the pupil had been in the school for two years wearing the permitted version of the uniform before raising any objection, had a bearing on the proportionality issue.

Although this case does support the proposition that a school may be entitled to impose a uniform policy on pupils even against their religious beliefs, that entitlement must depend on the school being able to show a reasoned and proportionate case. It would be sensible for schools to review uniform policy to see that what is required can be justified and does not involve unnecessary restriction or, for that matter, unreasonable cost.

Any school rule that has a restrictive effect should also be considered against the Convention rights, and schools should be able to demonstrate the rationale for it, including the proportionality of the rule to the situation that the rule seeks to avoid or redress. It should go without saying that this rationale should be recorded in writing, preferably in the minutes of the relevant governing body or committee meeting that approved the rules, so that the school cannot be accused of *ex post facto* rationalisation.

It is less likely that the Convention rights of parents will be infringed, although this may not deter many from saying otherwise. Schools will need to be sensitive when making enquiries about home background or personal family circumstances. Again, proportionality is important and the existence of Convention rights should not unduly deter schools from making enquiries where this is felt to be clearly in the interests of the child.

Generally, the Convention rights do not add significantly to the rights of employees because the existing employment protection and anti-discrimination legislation probably goes further than the strict Convention requirements. However, the Convention does protect staff in the way that they are treated as individuals. Whether Convention rights add to what is in any event regarded as good practice is debatable. A good employer will respect the Convention rights of his employees as a matter of course, although the right of freedom of expression may prove to be an area of some potential conflict in terms of a teacher's right to express views in the classroom. This will need to be read and interpreted in the light of teachers' professional duties. One might also, not entirely tongue in cheek, ask who will be the first teacher to argue that excessive workloads breach the Convention right to respect for private and family life.

CONCLUSION

Where does this leave governors and headteachers in the day-to-day running of their schools? Recent legislation and DfES Guidance has quite clearly had the Convention in mind and it is difficult to think of any areas of school life where following accepted good practice will lead to a human rights problem. There was much publicity and speculation as to how far the advent of the Act would affect school functions. Four days after the Human Rights Act 1998 came into effect, the *Times Educational Supplement* carried stories raising human rights issues relating to:

- refusal of admission of a non-Catholic child to a Roman Catholic school;

- the right of denominational schools to appoint same-faith staff;

- the right to detain a pupil;

- suspension of staff as 'inhuman or degrading punishment'; and

- exclusion as a denial of the right to education.

None of these 'challenges' materialised and such court decisions as there have been have been made in favour of schools and of the existing legislation. That is likely to continue and the courts will interpret the Act in a sensible and conservative manner. However, public expectations will be high and parents (and perhaps staff) will not be slow to claim human rights violations when things they do not like happen in schools. Despite this, schools that have procedures in place that comply with what is generally regarded as good practice and which are applied in a proper manner have nothing to fear.

The key is fairness in all dealings. Pupils and parents may be quick to complain about unfair treatment and some teachers may need to consider their teaching and pupil management style so as not to put themselves at risk of such complaints. The real issues over human rights in education are likely to relate to actions over which schools have little control. The challenges may come in relation to a particular school in a particular case, but they will be challenges to the structure of the education system and there is nothing that individual schools can do to prevent or anticipate this. Certainly, schools should not change their ethos, standards or policies unless these do not give an entitlement to fair dealing for all involved.

RELEVANT GUIDANCE

DfES Guidance 0194/2000, 'The Human Rights Act and Your School'.

Chapter 15

FUND-RAISING

Charitable status – Trustee responsibility – Lettings – Other fund-raising activities – VAT – Business Activities – Relevant guidance

It is now an accepted feature of school management that schools have to look beyond their official funding if they want more than what may be regarded as basic necessities. Despite increases in funding (at least in some LEA areas) it is still necessary for fund-raising organisations such as PTAs to raise money for books and other elements of daily school life. Voluntary fund-raising has, therefore, become a necessary part of school life and brings its own pitfalls. Charity law and tax law become essential tools.

CHARITABLE STATUS

All schools that are not run for profit are, in one sense, by definition charitable. Indeed, foundation and voluntary (both aided and controlled) schools are statutory charities which, unlike most voluntary bodies, are exempt from the obligation to register with the Charity Commission or file accounts. However, community schools are, by statute, not themselves charities. It is not entirely easy to see the logic for this: it presumably stems from the concept of the community school as an emanation of the LEA, although one would have thought that since the governing body is incorporated, there was sufficient separate identity to warrant those schools being treated as charities in the same way as voluntary and foundation schools. The effect of this difference is that, as will be described below, community schools have to set up a separate charitable trust to take the benefits of charitable fund-raising.

Any fund-raising organisation whose object is to raise money for schools will probably be a charity without necessarily realising it. Any organisation with a turnover in excess of £1,000 per annum to be applied at the discretion of that organisation for education or other charitable purposes is a charity and is legally required to register with the Charity Commission. Any person who takes part in the running of such a body will be a charity trustee even if not named as such, and will be bound by the trusteeship rules. Probably the only exception is a body that has no discretion how it applies its funds but has to hand them over to trustees of a charity for the purposes of that charity. Thus, a PTA that is willing to give up all control over the money it raises and leave it entirely to the school to use as it sees fit may avoid the need to register. In practice, few PTAs will wish completely to deny themselves the right to spend on behalf of the school or the right to decide how their money is to be used. Most of them will establish themselves within an umbrella body such as the National Confederation of Parent Teacher Associations and will be able to obtain charitable status and Charity Commission registration easily by using standard constitutional documentation already approved by the Charity Commission. An alternative to setting up the PTA as a charity, and thereby reducing the need for volunteer parents to take on trustee responsibility, is for the school to set up its own independent trust and for the PTA to be represented among the trustees. All funds raised by the PTA will be passed to the trust. Because the PTA has no discretion as to what it does with those funds, it is not required to register as a charity, but it can still exercise its discretion as to how funds are to be raised and then have a voice in deciding what to do with them.

It is, in any event, good practice for a school that has a significant income from voluntary sources to set up its own charitable trust. It enables a clear distinction to be drawn between LEA and informal funds, although it is good practice to bring details of any informal or voluntary funding that comes under the control of the governing body into the school's financial statements. It is now a requirement that all private income be reported globally in the financial information that all schools are statutorily required to deliver to the LEA and funds from voluntary sources would come within this category. However, schools that wish to demonstrate transparency and accountability will produce information in much greater detail than the basic legal requirement.

Charities should have a written constitution and school fund-raising bodies are no exception. To avoid delay and difficulty with the Charity Commission, it is highly desirable to use a standard form of deed and to ensure that the Charity Commission knows that it is based on a specified model. There is an appropriate form published by the Secondary Heads Association for use by schools, and as mentioned, the National Confederation of Parent Teacher Associations have a model for PTAs to use. Trusts of this kind set up by the governing bodies of foundation and voluntary schools, provided that the trust is under the control of the governing body and exists for the sole purpose of supporting the school, do not need to be registered with the Charity Commission: all other schools must register their trusts and any trust set up for a voluntary or foundation school that is not controlled by the governing body must also register.

TRUSTEE RESPONSIBILITY

Charitable status brings with it responsibility and accountability. It also raises the issue of personal liability for trustees. It is not only those who are formally appointed as trustees who have charitable trustee responsibility. This extends to anyone involved in the management of a charity. Members of a management committee will be treated as charitable trustees. Sometimes a charity is set up as a company limited by guarantee, which has many administrative advantages. The directors of such a company, as well as others directly involved in its management, will have charity responsibility.

Trustee Obligations

Trustees have a variety of obligations. School PTAs will not normally own property or have employees so their relevant obligations are:

- to act together in the interests of the charity and only according to its constitution;
- not to go outside the scope of the charity;
- to act prudently, taking professional advice where necessary;
- not to take any personal gain from being a trustee;
- to keep full and clear accounts to be filed each year with the Charity Commission (unless the charity is one of those mentioned earlier that is not required to register with the Charity Commission).

Personal Liability

Trustees who act in good faith and take proper care will not be personally liable for the obligations of the charity. Personal liability can arise only if:

- the charity suffers a loss as a result of trustees acting unlawfully, imprudently or outside the scope of the charity's objects; or

- if the trustees commit the charity to debts that exceed the charity's assets.

Tax Advantages

There are substantial advantages in fund-raising under a charitable umbrella:

- charities are exempt from income and corporation tax except on investment income;

- charities can take advantage of tax-efficient ways of fund-raising.

There are two possible tax relief schemes.

(1)   Gift Aid

Lump sum payments of any amount made by individuals out of taxed income – which means that the donor must be an income tax payer for the school to benefit – can be made under the Gift Aid scheme. The effect of this is that, in addition to the amount received from the donor, the school can reclaim basic rate income tax. This increases the value of the gift to the school by about one-quarter. The donor may also gain a benefit because the gift qualifies for relief against higher rate tax: the effective cost of the gift to a higher rate taxpayer is then only about 80 per cent of the amount given. The exact values depend on the rate of basic and higher rate income tax. The lower the basic rate of tax, the less the tax benefit to the school. Conversely, the bigger the gap between basic rate and higher rate, the cheaper it is for higher rate taxpayers to give any particular gross amount.

The process is very simple. Donors are required to complete a simple form stating the wish of the donor that the donation (referring either to the specific donation or declaring the wish in relation to all donations made since 6 April 2000) be treated as a Gift Aid donation. The Gift Aid form can be completed after the gift has been made, so schools should ensure that they have a stock of forms and should send them to any substantial personal donor even if the donor does not suggest it. It is even possible to deal with the Gift Aid formalities over the telephone, but whoever does this needs to be confident about the identity of the donor and must in any event confirm the details to the donor in writing in a prescribed way.

Voluntary and foundation schools that wish to utilise Gift Aid to the full may want to consider asking all parents to sign a general Gift Aid form on joining the school. This will enable the school to make income tax repayment claims on all payments (including voluntary contributions to school or class activities) that it considers qualify for relief without the need to obtain further signatures to Gift Aid forms while the relevant children are registered as pupils at the school. This must be done with caution. The school must be sure that the parent in question is a taxpayer and that can give rise to difficulties, especially if a parent's situation changes and the school is not aware of this. Perhaps the best rule of thumb is that no tax reclaims should be made in respect of parents whose children are in receipt of free school meals or who are known to be in receipt of state benefits of any kind. That may mean that some opportunities for tax claims will be missed, but this is preferable to making a claim that is not justified.

Tax relief is not available to either the school or the donor if the donor gains any benefit directly referable to the gift. This will not usually be a problem. The law that specifies that schools cannot charge for education provision has the side effect that a donor's generosity has to be for the general good rather than for that donor's child. It would not be lawful under the general provisions relating to charging in State schools to give something to donors or their children that others in the school do not have. Indeed, it is unlawful for schools to seek to raise funds from parents by way of voluntary contributions unless the terms of the request or invitation made by or on behalf of the school for contributions for the benefit of a school or school activities make it clear:

- that there is no obligation to make any contribution; and

- that pupils will not be treated differently according to whether or not their parents have made any contribution in response to the request or invitation.

The DfES interprets this as meaning that every letter or other document relating to voluntary contributions constitutes a 'request or invitation' and must, therefore, contain such a statement. This means that those schools which ask for regular contributions and send out reminders or 'invoices' – a practice which is fraught with danger – must include the statement on each document sent to parents.

In theory, there is no reason why Gift Aid payments from parents should not be used to provide direct classroom teaching that would otherwise not be available, so long as the teaching is open to all pupils and not merely to those whose parents pay. The Charity Commission has issued Guidance to the effect that it is a legitimate use of charitable funds to add to mandatory or discretionary provision. Funds raised from parents can, therefore, quite properly be used to enhance classroom teaching.

It ought, again in theory, to make no difference how the funds are applied by the school in considering whether Gift Aid tax relief is available, but the point has not been settled by the courts and schools should be cautious. The Inland Revenue will scrutinise any such arrangements very closely before agreeing that tax relief is available, and professional advice should be sought before implementing such a scheme. The governing body should, in any case, consider very carefully the issues involved in committing teaching resources that are to be paid out of voluntary funds because the employer liabilities will continue even if the flow of money dries up. It is far better to avoid the issue and a potential challenge by making it clear that funds are being raised for the general purposes of the school, and ensuring that the funds are not directly used to provide facilities that a school would be expected to provide out of public funds.

Gift Aid cannot be used to pay for those facilities, such as instrumental tuition and certain school visits, for which charges can lawfully be made. This reflects the restriction, mentioned above, that no benefit may be obtained in return for a Gift Aid payment.

Gift Aid has replaced the old fund-raising method using Deeds of Covenant. Anyone who is still making regular payments under old covenant deeds should be asked to sign a Gift Aid declaration. Tax repayment claims cannot now be made for payments received under Deeds of Covenant.

(2)   Charity Vouchers

There are organisations such as the Charities Aid Foundation (CAF), themselves registered charities, that act effectively as charitable bankers. Individuals pay lump sums to them under Gift Aid. The charity claims the tax refund and credits the individual's account. The individual then writes vouchers in favour of other charities using the full value of the original payment plus the tax relief. The recipient charity presents the voucher for payment as though it were a cheque. The recipient charity cannot reclaim tax, so any donor using this method should be pressed to give an amount that includes the tax refund.

The attraction of vouchers is that donors can set themselves a charitable budget with one payment and then make their individual contributions with a minimum of formality. Indeed, CAF operates a card system, issuing a card like a credit card, under which donations can be made simply by giving the recipient charity the relevant account number. The voucher organisation will need to be satisfied that the money is destined for a charity. This presents no problem for registered charities because it will be enough to quote the registered number. Indeed, donors giving via CAF can make donations to registered charities via the Internet. If foundation or voluntary schools wish to accept charity vouchers, they will need to demonstrate to the organisation that they are exempt charities: this is most easily done by referring to section 23 of the School Standards and Framework Act 1998, which is the section that establishes such schools as exempt charities.

LETTINGS

Schools can derive significant income from the letting of school premises out of school time. This is dealt with in detail in Chapter 11. In summary, the agreement for any letting should cover:

- the date and timing of the letting;
- the price to be paid;
- who will pay;
- the area and facilities to be used;
- whether the agreement is for a single occasion or for a period, and how it will be terminated;
- insurance;
- responsibility for any damage caused.

An underlying objective in the negotiation of lettings should be that all cost is covered by the user. Schools may not use their delegated budget to support use of premises other than for education, so, at worst, lettings have to be self-supporting. Clearly, if they are to play a significant role in enhancing the funds available to the school they need to be carefully costed and properly run. There is no point in making £50 from a letting and having to pay the caretaker £60 in overtime for the extra hours the school was kept open.

Many of these considerations will apply also to fund-raising events held at the school, for example dances held by the PTA. Whilst the school may not be looking directly for income from the letting, insurance and health and safety issues are still relevant.

OTHER FUND-RAISING ACTIVITIES

There are any number of different methods of fund-raising used by schools. Many of them contain traps for the unwary: whilst the vast majority of people who participate do so out of goodwill and would not think for a moment of holding the school legally liable, the possibility should not be ruled out and advice should be sought. Schools should draw up guidelines for any fund-raising event held so that there are precedents available for subsequent generations of fund-raisers. It is not sensible to have to reinvent the wheel with each cohort of parental volunteers, and the school needs protection from well-meaning, but possibly not very well-informed, helpers. For example:

- lotteries or draws have special rules relating to their promotion and the printing of tickets;

- car-boot sales may need planning permission, particularly if they are held in school playgrounds on a regular or frequent basis. It may be possible to hold sales in playing fields that do not form part of the school premises more frequently and without planning permission, but this is a complex and specialised area where competent professional advice should always be sought;

- dances and other social functions may require a liquor licence and may also raise issues of copyright and performing rights for the music being played. Even the school play may run into problems in this area. Modern plays, i.e. those written by a living author or one whose death has occurred within the last 70 years, will be in copyright, and the copyright owner may impose restrictions on when and where performances can take place as well as requiring royalty payments;

- sponsored runs or similar sponsored events will need parental consent not only for pupils to take part in the event itself, but also for the collection of sponsorship. Clear ground rules need to be established if pupils are to be allowed to canvass the neighbourhood for contributions;

- even the ubiquitous jumble sale can produce legal problems, at least in theory. If goods are sold that are not of saleable quality, the school could have a liability to the buyer. This is not very likely where the item is clearly old, but it is not difficult to foresee this arising if new goods are being sold or if the school holds an auction and the lots are not described accurately in a catalogue or by the auctioneer. Some schools hold auctions of 'promises' where, instead of goods being sold, the buyers are invited to bid for services such as will-writing or a guided walk around a local beauty spot. It is impossible for the school to monitor what is being offered and even less to control the eventual performance. There should, therefore, be a clear disclaimer by the school of any responsibility in relation to the services sold;

- the school fête produces problems in abundance, many of which are touched on above. There may be raffles, the sale of alcohol, sales of goods and, particularly, health and safety issues arising from the various attractions. Anyone hiring a 'bouncy castle', for example, should check that the operator has current insurance. It is worth considering taking up references for operators or suppliers who are unknown. Food preparation and sales may involve issues of hygiene which can be particularly sensitive where the work is being done by parents. Even the cake stall poses problems in this area, but they are largely insoluble, and the best the school can do is to check its own insurance (which should be done as a matter of course).

VAT

VAT only becomes a serious concern for schools that seek to raise substantial money by activities that might loosely be described as 'of a business nature'. Activities such as car-boot sales, auctions, tuck shop and selling advertising space for a functions brochure all might fall into this category, and if the turnover exceeds the VAT threshold the school will have to register for VAT. This, in turn, will mean that the school will have to account for VAT out of its income or raise charges so as to include VAT. VAT is never chargeable on voluntary donations, and the ordinary educational activities of the school are exempt. VAT implications generally are covered in more detail in Chapter 10.

BUSINESS ACTIVITIES

Increasingly, schools look to different forms of business activities to raise additional funds. This is a controversial area, because of the potential conflicts between educational and commercial aspirations. A paper, 'Commercial Activities in Schools – Best Practice Principles' produced jointly by the DfES, the Consumers' Association and the Incorporated Society of British Advertisers (ISBA) grappled with these issues and produced a generic guide setting out principles to be applied in three areas, sponsored resources such as teaching packs and materials, sponsored activities such as competitions and projects and collector schemes. The overall objective is that the 'educational benefits should outweigh the potential disbenefits'. The more important aspects of the advice can be summarised as follows:

- The school should have a single policy developed in consultation with the whole school community. This will provide a framework for making decisions in relation to new commercial activities.

- Activities should add educational value.

- Materials should not encourage unhealthy, unsafe or unlawful activities.

- Information supplied should be accurate and current.

- Expressions of opinion should be distinguished from statements of facts.

- Explicit sales messages should be avoided where possible.

- The level of branding should be appropriate to the activity.

- Restrictions should not be imposed on schools in return for benefits that the school gains.

The paper contains checklists for both schools and businesses to enable the school to assess whether the benefits outweigh the disbenefits and the business to assess whether the proposal meets the best practice principles.

RELEVANT GUIDANCE

School Charity Law

Debra Morris, *Schools: an Education in Charity Law* (Dartmouth Publishing Company).

Charities

The Charity Commission publishes a range of leaflets (obtainable free from St Alban's House, 57–60 Haymarket, London SW1Y 4QX) on relevant topics including 'Responsibilities of Charity Trustees' and 'Charities and Fund-raising'.

Tax Relief and Tax Schemes

The Inland Revenue issues leaflets (obtainable free from FICO (Trusts and Charities), St John's House, Merton Road, Bootle, Merseyside L69 9BB) on Gift Aid, deeds of covenant and tax relief for charities.

Chapter 16

RECORDS

Access to records – Disclosure of examination results to the media – Disclosure of records in court proceedings – Information to be held by schools – The Freedom of Information Act 2000 – Record maintenance – Relevant guidance

ACCESS TO RECORDS

Schools are required to maintain certain information about pupils and to make that information available to parents and certain other entitled people in accordance with the Data Protection Act 1998 (DPA 1998) for confidential information about individuals and under the freedom of information legislation for more general information.

The information that has to be kept comprises two categories. One is the curricular record which is defined as 'a formal record of a pupil's academic achievements, his other skills and abilities and his progress in the school'. It is the duty of the headteacher to keep this record and to update it each year. The second category is described as the educational record, which by reason of its width of definition will include the curricular record but which is much wider. The expression 'educational record' means any record of information (other than records made by a teacher for that teacher's own personal use) which is processed by or on behalf of the governing body of, or a teacher at, any maintained school or non-maintained special school and which relates to any person who is, or has been, a pupil at the school and which originated from, or was supplied by or on behalf of, a defined range of people namely:

- an employee of the maintaining LEA (which will include all staff employed at a community school);

- in the case of a VA, foundation or foundation special school or a non-maintained special school, any teacher or other employee at the school (including an educational psychologist engaged by the governing body under a contract for services);

- the pupil to whom the record relates; and
- a parent of that pupil.

It is important to note the limited extent of educational records. In particular, they do not include information that comes from third parties who are not employees either of the maintaining LEA or the school, no matter how relevant that information may be in relation to the particular child.

Educational records must be disclosed to all entitled persons, i.e. to any parent (which includes any person having formal parental responsibilities) if the pupil is under 16, to both the pupil and parent if the pupil is 16 or 17, and to the pupil (to the exclusion of the parent) if 18 or over. Pupils also now have a general right to see their records (this is the substantive change from the old regime) unless it is obvious that they do not understand what they are asking for. All requests for disclosure must be in writing and the school may charge the cost of supplying copies. It is considered that in assessing the cost of supplying copies, the time reasonably taken by a member of the school staff in collating and making the copies may be charged for, although there has been no decided case establishing the point beyond doubt.

The curricular record must also be disclosed on request to any school (including an independent school) or other educational institution (including institutions of further or higher education) to which a pupil applies or is being considered for transfer. If the pupil is transferring to another school, certain prescribed information (depending on the Key Stage that the pupil has reached but including information regarding strengths and weaknesses) has to be supplied, together with all other educational records, to the new school using a form, known as the Common Transfer Form, which has been prescribed for the purpose. The Common Transfer Form can be downloaded from the DfES web-site and schools are encouraged to transfer the information electronically if the receiving school agrees. There is a core requirement for basic information, including information on ethnicity, English as a second language, position on the SEN Code of Practice scale and attendance.

Certain material or information, even though it falls within the definition of an educational record, should not be disclosed, namely material that, if disclosed, would be likely to cause serious harm to the physical or mental health or emotional condition of the pupil concerned or to any other person. It is up to the person who holds the record to decide whether any material comes within this category. This will include material that may be relevant to the question of whether the pupil concerned is or has been the subject of or at risk of child abuse.

In addition to the duty to disclose educational records, schools must also provide examination information, as follows:

- parents of students in the last year of Key Stages 1, 2 or 3 can request written information about the student's level of attainment in the core National Curriculum subjects (if such information exists – it does not have to be compiled especially to meet the request) if this has not been provided under the statutory requirements;

- secondary schools must have available for inspection the latest comparative information, at both school and national level, about GCSE, GCE A and AS level, and diploma and vocational qualifications. Parents who want copies of this information can either be given the material or be told where they can obtain it.

Schools are also required to report each year to parents. This is dealt with in Chapter 13.

DISCLOSURE OF EXAMINATION RESULTS TO THE MEDIA

Schools may wish to disclose students' examination results for publication. There is no objection to publishing generalised information and the statutory league tables and similar data fall within this category. If, though, schools wish to publicise individuals and their results their ability within the confines of the Act to do so will be dependant on the nature of its 'notification' to the Information Commissioner. Schools will have notified the details of its processing using the Information Commissioner's notification templates. These detail the purposes for which schools process the data together with a description of the types of data held and details of any recipients to whom personal data may be disclosed – within this category falls the media.

Even though a school's notification may allow disclosure of results, it is still necessary to ensure that those students to whom the data relates are aware of the purposes of the disclosure. On the whole, parents and pupils will be conscious of this but it may also be necessary to explain the form in which examination results are to be published. Pupils may, for instance, object to publication of results where, say, they are to be published in grade order as opposed to alphabetically. Specific consent may not be deemed necessary, but pupils and parents should be made aware of their right to object to publication. Generally, although there may not be a legal obligation to do so, it would be good practice to obtain specific consent to information about an individual to be given to the press or other media – it is better to have such consent in writing but an oral consent, noted in writing, would suffice.

Who has the right to object? As the rights afforded to individuals under the Act are not affected by age, as long as the affected students are able to understand what is involved, it is they and not their parents who should be informed of the uses and disclosure of data and it is they who have the right to object to processing. In cases where students are not capable of understanding their rights, or the consequences of publication, the relevant information should be disclosed to the parents or guardians.

DISCLOSURE OF RECORDS IN COURT PROCEEDINGS

Schools are often asked to make their files available for the purpose of court proceedings. This can cause great concern, particularly when the pupil may be the subject matter of those proceedings and there is material on the file that the school feels ought not to be disclosed.

The first rule is that schools should comply strictly with the regulations regarding disclosure. No information should be disclosed unless the regulations authorise disclosure, and nothing should be disclosed to any party who is not within one of the categories entitled to receive information. The second rule is that the school must comply with any court order requiring disclosure even of material that would normally be protected or to people who would not normally be entitled. The school's response, therefore, to any request that is not authorised must be that the person requesting disclosure should obtain a court order. Schools should not be intimidated by threats or pressure: their duty is to refuse all unauthorised disclosure.

Quite apart from the regulations, there is a principle of public interest immunity that protects schools from disclosure of information where it is not in the public interest for that information to become known. The law recognises, however, that there may be a conflict between the legitimate interest of individuals and the needs of the community. The court will, therefore, in each case form a view as to whether the interests of justice make disclosure necessary. This is done by the party seeking disclosure serving a summons on the school requiring the school to produce the information to the judge or the magistrates, depending on the type of case. That summons must be obeyed, even though it may be time-consuming or unpalatable. Failure to do so is contempt of court and may be punished. The school will then produce the file to the court. None of the parties or their lawyers, or the jury in criminal cases, will be present or see the file. The judge or the magistrates will consider whether what is in the file is relevant to the case. If it is not relevant, that is the end of the story. If it is relevant, the court will then go on to consider whether the interest of preserving confidentiality is more important than making the information available to the person seeking it. Clearly, this will depend on what is in the file and what the case is about. If the court then orders disclosure, that, again, must be obeyed. The school has done its duty and has protected the interests of the pupil.

This procedure is straightforward and ought not to present the school with serious problems. The court will normally expect the headteacher or a deputy headteacher to attend with the file. The school may feel more comfortable being represented by a solicitor or a barrister, and that is permitted but, unfortunately, the school will have to bear the cost.

INFORMATION TO BE HELD BY SCHOOLS

In addition to the prospectus and the pupil-specific information that schools have to produce, schools have to keep a wide range of information available for inspection, including:

- statements of curriculum policy produced by the school and LEA;

- the school's Instrument of Government;

- agenda and minutes of governors' meetings, including committee meetings, together with copies of all documents referred to. Confidential minutes and other confidential documents must be kept but not disclosed;

- all regulations, DfES Circulars and Guidance and administrative memoranda relating to the National Curriculum;

- all school inspection records. The requirements for publication and distribution of OFSTED reports are dealt with in Chapter 4;

- detailed information relating to the school's SEN policy and its implementation (see Chapter 5);

- current schemes of work;

- syllabuses in use in the school, including the religious education syllabus or the arrangements for religious education in VA and foundation schools with a religious foundation;

- details of the arrangements for dealing with complaints in relation to the National Curriculum.

THE FREEDOM OF INFORMATION ACT 2000

The Freedom of Information Act 2000 (FOI Act 2000) was brought into force with the intention to promote openness and accountability amongst public authorities by giving individuals rights of access to information held by such authorities.

In order to achieve this, public authorities are required to adopt and maintain 'publication schemes'. The FOI Act 2000 has been gradually phased in. Schools were required to have schemes in place by 29 February 2004, with the exception of maintained nurseries who had until 30 June 2004. The Information Commissioner, responsible for both regulation of the FOI Act 2000 and DPA 1998, has developed model publication schemes which can be adopted by schools and nurseries and which have been approved for a period of four years. These model schemes can be accessed via the Information Commissioner's web-site at www.informationcommissioner.co.uk.

The model schemes are said by the Information Commissioner to have been produced in order to reduce the burden of bureaucracy on the schools. It is not easy immediately to see how this is achieved.

The scheme will set out what information the school holds and where and how the information can be accessed by an interested individual. Although they can adopt their own scheme, schools have been urged to adopt the appropriate model scheme. The school must then publicise the scheme (it is suggested through a newsletter, the annual report or on the school's web-site), and then publish information in accordance with it.

A publication scheme is a guide to the information which the school commits itself to make available on a routine basis, and must set out the categories of information the school publishes, the form in which it is published and whether or not charges apply. The model schemes suggest four categories – the school prospectus, governors' documents, pupils and curriculum (in the sense of information about policies that relate to pupils and the curriculum, rather than confidential information about any individual pupil) and school policies and other information relating to the school. In adopting or reviewing a publication scheme the school must have regard to the public interest in allowing access to the information it holds, and in the publication of reasons for its decisions. Governing bodies must review the scheme annually.

With effect from January 2005, schools will be required to comply with requests for information which have not already been made available through the schools publication scheme – known as the 'Right to Know'. Requests must be made in writing and schools, on the whole, will have 20 working, i.e. school, days in which to respond. In the event of a school being unable to provide the required information within the 20 working days, the applicant should be informed that the school will require the full 40 calendar-day period designated under the Data Protection Act 1998. That may be less than 20 working days where holiday periods are included.

Schools, amongst other public authorities, will not be required to release information where an exemption from disclosure applies; this will be where there is a duty of confidence, i.e. where sensitive information has been provided to the school on the understanding that it would not be disclosed. It will also apply to matters which in their nature are properly treated as confidential, most notably Governing Body 'Part II' or confidential business. The FOI scheme cannot be used as a back-door method of obtaining information that would otherwise be protected from disclosure.

Information may be made available in paper form or by publication on the schools web-site. However, even where information is made available on a web-site, schools will still be expected to make hard copies available upon request. Not everyone has access to the

Internet. The scheme will specify the charges to be made for the supply of copies.

For Guidance on records management in relation to the FOI Act 2000, information can be obtained from the National Archives web-site at www.nationalarchives.gov.uk.

RECORD MAINTENANCE

For How Long Should Records be Kept?

Schools are faced with a real problem in knowing for how long records should be kept. Clearly, pupil records must be kept for as long as the pupil is registered, and the responsibility to keep records ceases if the pupil transfers to another institution which is then entitled to receive the records. In other cases, the records should, in theory at least, be kept indefinitely: the school may at any time be asked to supply a reference and this in itself justifies keeping the records for a significant period after the child has left school. More importantly, it is now established that schools have a potential liability if they have been negligent in their education provision; very few cases are likely to be brought and even fewer are likely to succeed, but resisting such cases will be difficult if pupil records are not available.

A further consideration is the need to preserve records for audit purposes. One particular recent development since the establishment of the Learning and Skills Council (LSC) has been that the LSC auditors will ask to see attendance records for sixth formers. Some secondary schools do not keep those records once the students have left school. Failure to do so may cause them difficulties subsequently.

Many years ago, The Society of Archivists published an invaluable guide to the management and retention of school records, 'School Records, Their Management and Retention', available from the Society at Information House, 20–24 Old Street, London EC1V 9AB. Although it is old, and some of its terminology may have been overtaken by events, it remains the best (if not the only) authoritative guide. It is written from the perspective of the archivist and historian, which may send shudders through the spine of hard-pressed school administrators looking for space for current paperwork, but it is also an admirable survey of the legal position and it goes into great detail. It is very useful as an indicator of what records a school might be expected to have and, as a bonus, it is, in fact, eminently readable.

The guide envisages that records will be transferred to a local records office when they no longer need to be kept in school, and it covers the action to be taken by the records office in terms of what should be kept permanently and what should be reviewed periodically. It is sensitive to the difficulty of keeping records in schools and following its recommendations should, in fact, reduce the volume of retained material. It has detailed Guidance for record offices in deciding what to keep permanently once the records are transferred from the school, but this is beyond the scope of this book.

Records are divided into a number of different categories, with recommendations for retention in school for different periods. In each case, the recommended period starts only when the records cease to be current. The categories, with a broad survey of the advice, are as follows:

- *management records*: three years (six years for the personal records of heads and deputies);
- *governing body material*: generally for the current period only, except minutes, staff-produced papers, curriculum complaints records, correspondence and trust endowment papers which should be kept for six years, and annual parents' meeting proceedings, OFSTED action plans and proposals relating to acquiring grant-maintained status which should be kept for three years;
- *school organisation records*: 10 years for administrative and general files, six years for staff meeting minutes and the school logbook (where kept), five years for the visitors' book and a range of shorter periods for other documents such as the prospectus, staff circulars and newsletters to parents;
- *school council records (where the school has one)*: three years for minutes and correspondence;
- *liaison with the LEA, the DfES and (for formerly grant-maintained schools) the Funding Agency for Schools*: six years for returns to the DfES and one year for records such as secondary transfer sheets and attendance returns;
- *inspection records*: six years generally;
- *health and safety records*: such records require very long retention periods. The guide advises 30 years for health

surveillance records, 20 years for safety incident reports and 10 years for most other records. Shorter periods are advised for health and safety reports and fire precautions logbooks (six years), COSHH records (five years), accident books (if kept in addition to safety incident reports) (three years from the date of the last entry) and one year for health and safety policy statements;

- *pupil records*: other than records that transfer with the pupil, such as primary school pupil records, most records should be kept for six years. Exceptions are attendance registers (three years) and absence letters (two years);

- *staff records*: the guide suggests that salary cards be kept for 85 years. This is to ensure that records are available throughout the lifetime of anyone who works in a school. They may be needed for pension reference purposes. Files relating to teachers and to administrative and technical staff should be kept for 12 years, and statutory sick pay notifications for six years;

- *material relating to teaching and the curriculum*: most records need not be kept when they are no longer current. Exceptions are examination results and curriculum development papers (six years), aggregated assessment results (five years) and curriculum returns (three years);

- *finance records*: for this category, the recommended periods may be shortened if the appropriate auditors consent. Generally, records should be kept for six years, but the headteacher's budget report need be kept only for one year on the grounds that a copy will be with governors' papers anyway;

- *property records*: records relating to loans and capital grants should be kept for 12 years; other records should mostly be kept for six years, but inventories of furniture and equipment, records of insurances and title deeds need not be kept when they are no longer current. Obsolete title deeds may, however, be of significant archival interest;

- *careers records*: correspondence files should be kept for six years but other material need not be kept when it ceases to be current;

- *records of extracurricular and miscellaneous activities*: school magazines and any school history should be kept permanently in school, and it is suggested that speech day reports and prize lists be kept for six years. Other material need only be kept for short periods but there may be records, such as programmes of events and photographs, that should be kept for historical reasons, and schools might prefer to keep them on the premises rather than at the records office;

- *old pupils' associations and parent–teacher associations*: generally, the guide suggests that this material be kept for six years.

Record-keeping Systems

Any system for keeping records becomes pointless if a record cannot be found or cannot be read when it is needed. Schools need to have a proper system in place for holding and tracking everything. If records are kept on computer or microfilm, there must be a guarantee that in years to come the necessary hardware and software will still be available. The retrieval system and procedure must also take account of the fact that much of the information may be confidential and should be disclosed only in limited circumstances. Furthermore, the Data Protection Act 1998 imposed limitations on the use and disclosure of computerised material. The Act extends to manual records relating to individuals created after 23 October 1998. Manual records existing before that date will also be subject to the revised and extended provisions of the Act from 2007 and schools that have not done so should at least look at how their old records are filed and managed. One principle of the data protection legislation is that records should not be kept longer than is necessary for the purposes for which they were created, although it is permissible to keep material for historical reasons. Schools should have a system in place for the scheduled destruction of obsolete material: this is especially relevant to old (pre-23 October 1998) manual records and it may be worthwhile trying to weed these out before 2007 so they never come within the ambit of the 1998 Act.

RELEVANT GUIDANCE

DfES Guidance 15/2000, 'Pupil Records and Reports'.

DfES Circular 17/89, 'The Education (School Records) Regulations 1989'.

INDEX

References are to page numbers.